Frontiers of Consciousness

Edited by John White

Frontiers of

THE MEETING GROUND

Consciousness

BETWEEN INNER AND OUTER REALITY

Julian Press

Published by The Julian Press, Inc., a member of The Crown Publishing
Group, One Park Avenue, New York, New York 10016, and simultaneously in
Canada by General Publishing Company Limited

JULIAN PRESS and colophon are trademarks of The Julian Press, Inc.

Manufactured in the United States of America

Library of Congress Cataloging in Publication Data
Frontiers of consciousness.
    1. Consciousness—Addresses, essays, lectures.
I. White, John Warren, 1939–
BF311.F76   1985   150   84-27864
ISBN 0-517-52774-X
ISBN 0-517-55704-5 (pbk.)

10   9   8   7   6   5   4   3   2   1

1985 Edition

Contents

Frontiers of Consciousness

Introduction

What is consciousness? What is this remarkable capacity you have for awareness?

Consciousness is something greater than all the contents of your mind. Stop and notice what is going on in your mind now—how many different things are happening. You are processing visual information as you look at this page. You may also be listening to conversation or the noise of passing traffic. At the same time you are aware of your body position and its relation to other objects in space, and of the tension you have placed on various muscles. You may also be aware of an itch or some kind of ache. Perhaps you have a line from a song running through your mind over and over. Tastes and smells are also coming into your awareness while all this is happening. And you might even in your imagination be roaming through time and space back to the days of the pharaohs or out to some other planet.

But none of this is equal to consciousness. They are the contents of consciousness—not consciousness itself. Thoughts are not consciousness because you can be aware of your thoughts. Likewise you can experience awareness without thoughts. Therefore awareness—consciousness—is distinct from thought. The stream of consciousness may carry many things: thoughts, dreams, emotions, images, sensations of all sorts. And different factors may affect the stream: poor nutrition, lack of sleep, ionizing radiation—just as wind, landslides, and freezing weather do with running water. But the stream itself goes on while the contents change and vary.

Then again: What is consciousness? It appears the question cannot be answered. If mind is its own greatest mystery, consciousness is the enigma behind mind. All you think and hope and imagine and fear and desire—all is mediated through consciousness. And since a mental act precedes physical action and behavior, consciousness is primary here too.

No matter what aspect of life you choose to examine, the deeper you analyze it, the more it becomes clear that finally you must come to a consideration of consciousness. If consciousness is the means whereby we know what we know and do what we do, then it is the fundamental ground of all experience and cannot be described in terms of anything else.

As science probes ever deeper into the nature of man and the universe in search of omniscience, a paradox emerges. The paradox is this: At the subtlest levels on which "objective" science operates, objectivity becomes impossible. The very act of observing changes the situation. It is like a physicist trying to measure the absolute temperature of water or an anthropologist trying to describe the behavior of a small, primitive tribe. In both cases, the presence of the observer or observing instrument alters the situation beyond ability to account for it. Subjectivity intrudes. The observer and the observed merge; man and environment become united. And since there are no limits to what constitutes your environment (other than arbitrary ones), it turns out—just as sages and mystics have said for ages—that you and the universe are one, bound by consciousness.

The study of consciousness has been called noetics, from the Greek word nous, meaning "mind." Apollo 14 astronaut Edgar D. Mitchell, in his book Psychic Exploration, proposes the Greek letter omega, Ω, be used as a symbol for noetics and consciousness. Noetics, he says, is the field in which outer space research converges with the investigation of inner space. The knowledge gained by modern experimental science using its rational/objective/empirical approach is fitting hand in glove with the knowledge given to us by ancient experiential religion using an intuitive/subjective/privately perceived mode. Consciousness is the meeting ground between inner and outer reality.

An example of that meeting can be seen in this fact: The earth's magnetic field, which intensifies and decreases with a frequency of about 10 cycles per second, can in some circumstances actually entrance a person by inducing a 10 c.p.s. brain wave in him. That brain wave is called the alpha rhythm. It is characterized by subjective feelings of pleasant relaxation and inner-directed awareness Such a state is experienced in meditation. But it is totally inappropriate for someone engaged in an activity such as, say, flying an airplane, where outer-directed alertness is necessary for monitoring instruments and scanning the sky. Yet it appears that some airplane crashes may have been due to the pilot's brain becoming entrained by the earth's magnetic field oscillation, resulting in a light trance. Quite possibly we all experience such moments of entrancement —times when we daydream or just sit quietly thinking of almost nothing. But for a pilot who must be responsible for the lives of his passengers, such moments can be fatal.

There are positive aspects to this meeting of outer and inner, however. Consciousness research can do more than just point out dangers to life. It can apply knowledge beneficially, as in negative ion generators that promote rapid healing of burns and the relief of asthma, and that enhance reflexes and perception. Moreover, noetics can help answer some very basic questions about life—questions that have traditionally been the province of religion and philosophy. The following chapters demonstrate this vividly. Thus the list of gains from this emerging science of consciousness is large and promises to provide much more.

A final word to the reader: The "frontiers" identified here are in a sense illusory. Consciousness is holistic and there is a basic unity to all knowledge. For example: The overlap among biofeedback, meditation research, and psychic research is such that a clear distinction is difficult to make. There are areas of mutual concern to scientists in each of these disciplines. This is apparent in the fact that some parapsychologists have employed biofeedback devices in their studies, some biofeedback researchers have used meditators as their subjects, and some meditators have developed psychic abilities concomitant with their experience in meditation. For another example, meditation is showing itself to be a form of self-administered therapy for physical and psychological ailments. In view of such research and activity, it is not surprising that the American Psychiatric Association recently formed a task force on meditation research that will include the examination of psychic phenomena.

But you do not have to wait for institutions to begin the important work of examining the mind-body relationship and the nature of consciousness. The following sections and introductory notes can provide instruction, guidance, and resource information to start you on your own program of research. The tools and techniques for the advancement of knowledge and spiritual growth are largely within your reach already. Therefore this book is an invitation to you—an invitation to enter the laboratory of yourself. The more you know about yourself, the more you know about the world. Thus wisdom grows. And perhaps as noeticists explore the frontiers of consciousness, an answer to our initial question will emerge.

Now, open the door to the workshop of your mind/body, and step in . . .

J.W.

I
Transpersonal
Psychology

Transpersonal psychology is the fourth major psychological approach to the study of man. The first three—behaviorism, psychoanalysis, and humanistic psychology—were too limited in their view of human capacities and potentialities for the people who formally declared transpersonal psychology as a "fourth force" in 1968. Chief among them were Dr. Abraham Maslow (who had been instrumental in the emergence of humanistic psychology as a "third force" in the early 1950s) and Anthony J. Sutich (who launched and edits the Journal of Transpersonal Psychology).

Fourth force psychology covers a wide range of human affairs. All of them, however, are aimed at man's ultimate development—not simply a return from unhealthiness to normality—as individuals and as a species. Cosmic consciousness, transcendence of the self, ecstasy, peak experiences, self-actualization, universal values, maximal sensory awareness and interpersonal encounter, spiritual disciplines, the sacralization of everyday life—these are some of the concerns of transpersonal psychology. It assumes that a capacity for these experiences is present in everyone, although they are unfortunately realized by too few. It further assumes they are biologically rooted and positive experiences—that is, healthy and good. The last assumption is that they can be empirically studied and enhanced in people.

Studies in transpersonal psychology point toward development of a science of consciousness. In 1969 the first conference on voluntary control of internal states was organized by Dr. Elmer Green of The Menninger Clinic in Topeka, Kansas, and held at nearby facilities in Council Grove. The conference has since become an annual event there. Con-

ferees include scientists, psychologists, theologians, yogis, psychics, mystics, and others whose work centers on human growth.

Like all evolutionary ideas, transpersonal psychology (as the term implies) transcends the people and organizations constituting it. Its chief spokesperson, however, is the Association for Transpersonal Psychology, which publishes the Journal of Transpersonal Psychology. *The* Journal *is located at Box 3049, Stanford, California 94305. Another transpersonally oriented organization is the International Cooperation Council, an umbrella for more than a hundred organizations around the world. ICC, which publishes* The Cooperator, *is located at 17819 Roscoe Boulevard, Northridge, California 91324. A third organization, the American Metapsychiatric Association, considers the relation between psychiatry and mystic/psychic experiences. Dr. Stanley R. Dean, 2121 North Bayshore Road, Miami, Florida 33137, is the founder and head of AMPA.*

Recently it has become possible to earn a Ph.D. in transpersonal psychology. For details contact the Humanistic Psychology Institute (HPI), an organ of the Association for Humanistic Psychology, at 325 Ninth Street, San Francisco, California 94301, or the California Institute of Asian Studies, 3494 21st Street, San Francisco, California 94110.

Other useful guides to transpersonal experience include Abraham Maslow's Toward a Psychology of Being *(Van Nostrand, 1968), Aldous Huxley's* The Perennial Philosophy *(Harper & Row, 1945), Teilhard de Chardin's* The Phenomenon of Man *(Harper & Row, 1961), Kazimerez Dabrowski's* Mental Growth Through Positive Disintegration *(Gryf Publications, 1970), Gopi Krishna's* The Secret of Yoga *(Harper & Row, 1972), Dane Rudhyar's* The Planetarization of Consciousness *and my own* The Highest State of Consciousness *(Doubleday-Anchor, 1972).*

J.W.

1 The
Ultraconscious Mind

Stanley R. Dean

---

*Never throw away hastily any old faith, tradition or
convention. They may require modification, but they
are the result of the experience of many generations.*
Sir Oliver Lodge

One fortunate result of the current interest in psychedelic phenomena
has been to focus psychiatric attention upon a subject that was hitherto
preempted by religion, philosophy, and mysticism. That is as it should
be, for psychiatry should rightfully play a leading role in man's unceasing
quest for expanded forms of consciousness—with or without drugs.

The term "expanded consciousness," as used here, refers to a suprarational, suprasensory level of mentation whose existence, especially in
the Orient, has been known since antiquity under a variety of regional
and ritual terms: *nirvana* of Buddhism; *satori* of Zen; *samadhi* of yoga;
unio mystica of Catholicism; *shema* of cabbalism; Bucke's *cosmic consciousness*; and existentialism's *kairos*—to name a few.

Miraculous powers have been attributed to it, and from it has sprung
the highest creativity and genius known to man. Yet it has received surprisingly little attention from modern science, and still remains one of
the greatest enigmas of the mind.

For the sake of uniformity I have referred to it as "Ultraconsciousness" [1], and I hope that in an age in which man has embarked upon a
systematic exploration of the outer reaches of space, he shall at long last
embark upon an equally systematic exploration of the outer reaches of
the mind, even though it takes him far beyond the unconscious that
Freud's intrepid pioneering established as a relay station.

There is a facetious saying that psychiatry has developed so amazingly in recent years that it is now almost impossible to find a normal person.

Yet the secret of mental health still remains a secret!

Is it not possible that in our headlong quest for new answers, we may be overlooking some old ones? As science annihilates space and accelerates communication between the modern culture of the West and the ancient culture of the East, that possibility recurs with increasing frequency. That is as it should be. Today East and West enjoy a transcultural relationship unique in world history, and full of promise for a vast expansion of our knowledge of human behavior.

It provides us with an unequaled opportunity to rediscover ideas that, if too long hidden, might be lost.

Let us examine some of them. In so doing, my purpose is to epitomize, dramatize, and perchance catalyze what others have stated much better than I can do.

To begin with, Western psychiatry has concerned itself chiefly with psychology and physiology, but scarcely at all with Eastern spirituality. Yet the latter is trying desperately to catch up with and integrate with the scientific-material-objective progress of the West. The two should not remain mutually exclusive. The time is ripe for large-scale integration and we should meet it halfway, if for no other reason than the very practical one that healing factors are intrinsic in Eastern spirituality that might well enrich our current psychotherapeutic armamentarium. As practitioners of the healing arts, we simply cannot afford to dismiss any therapeutic procedure that holds potential promise.

No psychiatrist should look down on what he is not up on!

Man has always been fascinated with the world of the spirit. There is a natural tendency for the uncluttered mind to drift toward the abstract, and we need not fear that science will be compromised by it, for many scientific facts began as abstract theories. It is even intriguing to speculate that as computer machines take over more and more of the chores of calculation and conceputalization, man's liberated mind may again resume its age-old contemplation of the enigma of the spirit.

Mysticism, according to Aldous Huxley, is the only one effective method that has yet been known for the radical and permanent transformation of personality. A modern philosopher, George Plochman, cautions that the "mystical is neither an asylum of ignorance nor a place where for some reason logic leaves off so that we have to keep quiet" [2]; and Freud himself, in Vol. IV of his collected papers, said, ". . . psychoanalysts must discover secret and concealed things from unconsidered and unnoticed details, from the rubbish-heap, as it were, of our observations" [3]. In order to do that, David Bakan points out, "Freud had to let himself descend into chaotic depths . . . to absorb and appreciate them . . . and to re-enact imaginatively the syncretism involved in their generation in order to apprehend their nature rationally . . even at the risk of temporarily violating logic and so-called common sense" [4]. Furthermore, as Harold Kelman has pointed out, Freud, through his concepts of free association and the unconscious, dared to challenge the supremacy of pure reason, and intentionally or unintentionally set in motion a reunion of pragmatic West with mystical East [5,6]. Kelman maintains that free association could be a step toward the ultraconscious or what he terms "*kairos*," if used as pure catharsis rather than for the purpose of object interpretation. He asserts that in freer and freer association it is not enough for the forms, the objects, the phenomena to emerge—they must continue until they are reabsorbed, attachment to them diminishes, and they entirely disappear—until there is complete formlessness, intuitive insight, suprasensory lucidity, and ultimately *nirvana* or, to use my term, Ultraconsciousness [5, 6].

In his presidential address to the APA Convention, Chicago, May 1957, Francis J. Braceland said: "In the light of history this new (Freudian) psychology heralded the end of a purely mechanistic concept of man . . . no one approach to psychiatric disorder can claim a monopoly upon wisdom, understanding and therapeutic efficiency . . . we espouse a comprehensive form of psychiatry and . . . *integration* is the watchword in our emphasis . . . the net result of the evidence (from *all* branches of study) underscores the need to approach psychological problems from the humanistic point of view which affirms man's spiritual nature" [7].

My own interest in the Ultraconscious is that of an eclectically oriented psychiatrist. I am assuredly not a mystic nor do I want to convey any notion of academic pretentiousness—far from it. My role is simply that of an observer and reporter who had an opportunity to see at first hand some of the attendant phenomena and to make a film of the Zen-Buddhist ritual during my visits to the Orient.

This discussion is not an endorsement but merely a plea that science should at long last seek a rational explanation and a common denominator for what has so far been regarded as inexplicable. In coining the working term "Ultraconscious," I am fully mindful of Konrad Lorenz's admonition that ". . . we should not imagine that the invention of a term provided the explanation of the process in question." That explanation must still be sought [8].

Of course each cult firmly believes—and on occasion has defended that conviction to the death—that *its* method, *its* ritual, *its* ceremonies, *its* liturgical *potpourri* is the *only* path to salvation; but to the objective observer it must be obvious that a common denominator underlies all of them and that science provides the most reasonable hope of finding that denominator. What a fertile field for research—and how sadly it has been neglected. The realm of the mind is one of the last great uncharted areas in modern medicine. But although some of it may be difficult to convey, perhaps it can be *divined* without yet being clearly conscious or *defined*.

Says Alan Watts in *Psychotherapy East and West*: "Present psychotherapy is concerned with the relation between man and society. But that is not enough. Society is a group phenomenon creating separate cultures. But beyond that are universal phenomena transcending *all* cultures. Therefore, psychotherapy should not restrict itself to the mere sociality of man, but should uncover his universality. Put another way, it should concern itself with the relation between man and cosmos, not merely between man and society" [9].

In closing my introduction, I make no apology for my relative ignorance of the subject, for I am reassured by the wisdom of Sir George Pickering, past president of the British Medical Association, who candidly stated, "The older I have become, the more sure I am that an awareness of ignorance is the *sine qua non* for a good scientist. One begins scientific work by asking a question, and one proceeds to gather material to try to answer it . . . Becoming familiar with a set of phenomena is a necessary preliminary to understanding them: the next step is the realization of how ignorant we all are as to how and why the events happen . . . and then the collection of information and the formulation and testing of hypotheses. You will see then that I am contrasting ignorance and indifference" [10].

Description

I shall use Zen as an example of the attainment of Ultraconsciousness merely because I have had an opportunity to observe it personally and not because it is exclusive or better or worse than the various other disciplines.

"Zen" is a Japanese word (derived from the Chinese *ch'an* and the Sanskrit *dhyana*) that refers to a high state of consciousness in which man finds union with the "Ultimate Reality" of the universe. This state is called *satori*; the closest English equivalent is the word, "enlightenment," but even so, Zen and satori are not only enlightenment but also the way to its attainment.

Suzuki describes it as a "throwing oneself down the precipice . . . a letting go the hold." "At last," he states, "all psychic faculties become charged with a new energy hitherto undreamed of. A penetrating insight is born of the inner depths of consciousness as the new source of life is tapped and with it Zen yields up to its secret. This realization is called 'satori' " [11].

As to how that is accomplished, Suzuki says, "So long as there are conscious strivings to accomplish a task, the very consciousness works against it and no task is accomplished. It is only when all traces of consciousness are wiped out that Buddhahood is attained . . . the idea is that when every effort is put forward to achieve a task and you are finally exhausted and have come to the end of energy, you give yourself up so far as your consciousness is concerned. As a matter of fact, however, your unconscious mind is still intensely bent on the work and before you realize it you find the work accomplished. This is what is meant by 'to accomplish the task by No-mind'. . . . Philosophically speaking, therefore, no special conscious strivings are necessary; in fact, they are a hindrance to the attainment of enlightenment" [12].

This concept of No-mind is basic to Zen. It literally means an immobilization of mental faculties wherein the mind ceases to think. It is achieved by intense concentration, controlled breathing, fixation of gaze, the disciplined environment of a Zen institute, and the inspiration of a Zen master. It may require years to achieve. However, the late Zen Master, Horyu Ishiguro, whose institute I was privileged to visit and film in Tokyo, had developed a method of streamlining the training period to a matter of several days. He discarded the traditional, the time-consuming methods that were concerned more with precision of manner and ceremonial exactitude than with inner problems, but retained the essential principles of Zen, i.e., the teaching of students to achieve a state of no-thought, no-feeling, to be completely in "nothing," to sit quietly and to be absorbed in *koanzammai* (Zen questions). His objective was clearly stated in his manual:

"Everyone wishes to become free from inner pains. These pains arise because he feels them or thinks of them. Therefore, it stands to reason that if he neither feels nor thinks anything at all, he will get no pains. From morning till night everyone lets his mind wander from one thing to another and keeps feeling different sensations. Thus, he presumes that the mind *has* to be used in the wandering state. Buddha succeeded in finding a method of using the mind in the immobile state, which is the essence of Zen, and by thus freeing the mind, arrived at *satori* (Ultra-consciousness)" [13].

The important thing in all this is that when the mind stops thinking, it does not stop *being*, for then the mind becomes automatically inundated with a flood of awareness, intuition, cosmic identification, and rapture that transcends description and transforms the entire personality at its ultimate peak. Although in some, only partial attainment may occur.

Dr. Richard Bucke in his book, *Cosmic Consciousness*, [14] lists the following phenomena at the ultimate peak of cosmic consciousness, as he called it. Similar experiences have been reported with LSD [15].

1. An awareness of intense light. The individual has a sense of being immersed in a dazzling flame or rose-colored cloud or perhaps rather a sense that the mind is itself filled with such a light. In the East it is called the "Brahmic Splendor." Walt Whitman speaks of it as "ineffable light—light rare, untellable, lighting the very light—beyond all signs, descriptions, languages." Dante states that it is capable of "transhumanizing a man into a god" and gives a moving description of it in these lines of mystical incandescence from *Il Paradiso* of the *Divine Comedy* [16]:

> The light I saw was like a blazing river
> A streaming radiance between two banks
> Enameled with wonders of the Spring
> And from that streaming issued living sparks
> That fell on every side as little flowers
> And glowed like rubies in a field of gold.
>
> Fixing my gaze upon the Eternal Light
> I saw enclosed within its depths,
> Bound up with love together in one volume,
> The scattered leaves of all universe:

> Substance and accidents, and their relations
>> Together fused in such a way
>> That what I speak of is one single flame.
>
> Within the luminous profound subsistence
>> Of that Exalted Light saw I three circles
>> Of three colors yet of one dimension
>
> And by the second seemed the first reflected
>> As rainbow is by rainbow, and the third
>> Seemed fire that equally from both is breathed.

2. With the sensation of light the individual seems bathed in emotions of supreme joy, rapture, ecstasy, triumph, assurance—an ecstasy far beyond any that belongs to the merely conscious self.

3. In addition to these sensory and emotional experiences there comes to the person an intellectual illumination quite impossible to describe. In an intuitive flash he has an awareness of the meaning and drift of the universe, an identification and merging with creation, the infinite, the immortal. He obtains a conception of *the whole* that dwarfs all learning, speculation, and imagination, and that makes the old attempts to understand the universe petty and even ridiculous.

4. A feeling of transcendental love and compassion.

5. Fear of death falls off like an old cloak; *physical and mental suffering vanishes*. This property alone should be of particular interest to the physician and psychiatrist and should give us an incentive to understand and utilize it in the treatment of the physically and mentally ill.

6. A reappraisal of the material things in life and a realization of the total unimportance of riches and abundance compared to the treasure of the Ultraconscious. This, however, does not lead to indolence and idle dreaming, for it is accompanied by . . .

7. An extraordinary quickening of the intellect, an uncovering of latent genius, an enhancement of mental and physical vigor and activity.

8. A sense of mission. The revelation is so moving and profound that the person cannot contain it within himself, but is moved to transmit the great secret to all fellow men.

9. Finally, a charismatic change in personality—an inner and outer radiance, as though charged with some divinely inspired power, a magnetic force that attracts and inspires others, a veritable transfiguration of being.

What significance does all this have for the scientist, the physician, the psychiatrist? It may mean that if systematic investigation corroborates the validity and importance of the Ultraconscious, the psychiatrist may have to relearn the difficult role of philosopher-physician as well as scientist-physician.

Such investigation is already well under way in Japan. Sato of Kyoto University has done much to define and analyze the psychological aspects [17]. Kasamatsu of Tokyo University has conducted careful tests on subjects in the ultraconscious state and has listed the following findings [18]:

1. *Visual tests.* A slight but definite increase in vision.
2. *Respiration.* A decrease in the respiratory rate to 4 per minute; an increase in tidal volume; a decrease in oxygen consumption to a level 20–30 percent below normal oxygen consumption.
3. *Metabolism.* A decrease in metabolic rate that could not be explained merely by the decreased respiratory rate, but which might also be due to the decrease of energy metabolism in the brain.
4. *Electroencephalogram.* Decreased alpha frequency but with increased amplitude; periodic, but inconstant appearance of theta waves. Significantly enough, Kasamatsu found that these results differed considerably from similar tests in hypnotized subjects.

Discussion

This paper is a plea for the scientific investigation of the Ultraconscious—a suprarational, suprasensory state of mentation whose existence has been known since antiquity, to which miraculous powers have been attributed, and from which have sprung profound sociological and religious events.

Today's technological progress in space and communication provides us with unequaled transcultural opportunities to rediscover ideas that if too long hidden might be lost.

Systematic research on the Ultraconscious may provide an important addition to our psychotherapeutic armamentarium, not only because its attainment exerts an ennobling influence on the mind, but because of its extraordinary ability to bring about freedom from mental and physical suffering.

Freud may well have been an unwitting pioneer in that direction in the sense that he dared, through his concepts of free association and the unconscious, to challenge the supremacy of pure reason and paved the way for the release of psychology and psychiatry from the grip of an "exact science," thereby greatly broadening their scope.

Although most people have never experienced the summit of the Ultraconscious, simple questioning might well elicit the information that many have had flashes and *formes frustes*. It is probably latent in all of us, and like the unconscious, could be revealed by appropriate disciplines and techniques. These might even conceivably become more or less standardized and available for general study and therapy instead of being confined to religious or regional areas.

Despite my paucity of personal experience, repeated contact with its charismatic qualities in others has given me an intense awareness of its scope, and similar exposure would probably produce a like awareness in other psychiatrists. Once their interest was aroused, the use of LSD and other psychedelic drugs for research will undoubtedly enhance our understanding of the ultraconscious.

However, clinical practice also provides ample scope for observation and awareness. Kelman believes that major and minor degrees of illumination could be helped to happen in patients, could be recognized when they did happen, and could be used by informed psychiatrists to augment present psychotherapy. A simple first step would be merely to ask patients if they had any Ultraconscious experience and then encourage them to talk about it. I venture to say that my colleagues might be amazed at the abundant material that would be elicited. And if the resulting pharmacological and clinical material were collected, pooled, and collated, the resulting data might well represent the initial breakthrough to a practical understanding of this hitherto inscrutable subject.

References

1. Dean, S. R. "Beyond the Unconscious: The Ultraconscious." *American Journal of Psychiatry*, Vol. 122, No. 4, October 1965.
2. Plochman, G. K. "A Note on Harrison's Notes on *Das Mystiche*." *Southern Journal of Philosophy*, Vol. 2, No. 3, Fall 1964.
3. Freud, S. *Collected Papers*, Vol. 4. Hogarth Press: London, 1964.
4. Bakan, D. *Sigmund Freud and the Jewish Mystical Tradition*. Van Nostrand: New York, 1958.
5. Kelman, H. "Free Association: Its Phenomenology and Inherent Para-

doxes." *American Journal of Psychoanalysis*, Vol. 22, No. 2, 1961.

6. ———. " 'Kairos' and the Therapeutic Process." *Journal of Existential Psychiatry*, Vol. 1, No. 2, Summer 1960.

7. Braceland, F. J. "Psychiatry and the Science of Man." Presidential address delivered at the 113th Annual Convention of the American Psychiatric Association, May 13–17, 1957, Chicago, Ill.

8. Lorenz, K. *On Aggression*. Bantam Books: New York, 1967.

9. Watts, A. *Psychotherapy East and West*. New American Library: New York, 1960.

10. Pickering, Sir George. "The Great Value of Ignorance." *Medical World News*, 11 June 1965.

11. Suzuki, D. T. *Selected Writings on Zen Buddhism*. William Barrett, ed. Doubleday-Anchor: New York, 1965.

12. ———. *The Zen Doctrine of No-Mind*. Rider and Co.: London, 1949.

13. Ishiguro, H. *The Scientific Truth of Zen*. Zenrigaku Society: Tokyo, 1964.

14. Bucke, R. M. *Cosmic Consciousness*. Dutton: New York, 1964.

15. Pahnke, W. and Richards, W. "Implications of LSD and Experimental Mysticism." *Journal of Religion and Health*, Vol. 5, No. 3, July 1966.

16. Dante, A. *The Divine Comedy*.

17. Sato, Koji. "The Concept of 'On' in Ruth Benedict and D. T. Suzuki." *Psychologia* (Dept of Psychology, Kyoto University, Japan), Vol. 2, 1958.

18. Kasamatsu, Akira. *Science of Zazen*. Koishigawa Tokyo University, Department of Neuropsychiatry: Tokyo, 1963.

2 Final Integration
in the Adult Personality
A. Reza Arasteh

All your anxiety is because of your desire for harmony.
Seek disharmony; then you will gain peace. Rumi[1]

Contrary to most psychologists who study children, animals, or the mentally ill in order to find principles that will contribute to the understanding of maturity or final integration, I believe that insight into the nature of fully integrated individuals can greatly increase our knowledge of the mature man who exists potentially within the child. It can make psychotherapy a more effective and meaningful technique and can guide the socially adjusted person to his state of individuation [2].

This paper is an attempt to formulate a psychological theory for the study of final integration in the adult personality. It is not a report of an experimental study. Rather, it is based on personal visionary experience, objectivization of that experience, clinical study of cases of two cultures, and an analysis of final integration in autonomous individuals.

Several visionary experiences and a few experimental studies almost a decade ago convinced me of the significance of final integration in the adult personality. After seeking an understanding of it for the last few years, I have been able to formulate its psychological theory, its laws and mechanisms and to propose it as a measure for man's progress, health, and security, as well as a guide in training analysts, psychologists, leaders, and educators.

The first psychical vision occurred in 1955 when I wrote a book (in Persian) entitled *The Process of Human Growth* [3]. At that time I was deeply influenced by the works of Piaget, Erik Erikson, and those in the Committee on Human Development at the University of Chicago. In a conscious way my book sought to interpret the stages of human growth according to these Western concepts. Yet, when I came to discuss maturity, my thinking unconsciously led me away from Western thought; nor did I feel any sympathy for the pleasure principle and pragmatism, both of which seemed to me inadequate for interpreting human behavior in the state of maturity, even though they might be considered the foundation of growth. Moreover, I felt that not even social realism was sufficiently explanatory. Finally, I concluded my book with a poem from Rumi, the fully integrated man of thirteenth-century Persia:

> I have resolved conflict within myself;
> I feel only as an identity;
> I seek unity, I speak unity,
> I know oneness and I see oneness [1].

Motivated by this feeling I studied the life history of certain great men from Eastern and Western cultures. I developed insight into the wisdom of the Far East and also into the concepts of Western psychoanalysts, especially Erich Fromm. Then I systematically analyzed the lives of Al-Ghazzali (died 1111 A.D.) [4, 5] and Rumi (died 1273 A.D.) [1, 6, 7], representatives of Islamic culture, and Goethe, the universal man of the West [8, 9, 10]. As a result, I came to believe that there exist certain universal characteristics, psychological laws and mechanisms that all individuals share regardless of time, place, and the degree of culture. This paper is an attempt to introduce this subject.

I shall take up the following questions: 1) What are the characteristics of final integration? 2) What kind of individuals are psychologically ready for it? 3) What are its psychological laws, and what mechanisms have been used in various cultures to attain it? 4) What contributions can it make to the state of developmental psychology?

Some Characteristics of Fully Integrated Persons

My understanding of final integration is that it is an experience of inner evolution that begins with a state that I have named "existential moratorium"; it leads to anxiety, detachment from social realities, the attainment of a state of "void," and rebirth in totality, where one in the process of living externally creates "forms" and internally attains happiness. It is a universal state regardless of time, place, and the degree of culture. It is characterized by certainty, and the search for truth and satisfaction, which are the final manifestations of the drives for preservation, activity, and sex, respectively. Thus, it is related to an *unterbau* (infrastructure) of growth but it accepts cultural and existential states as transcending structures added to the natural state [11, 12, 13].

In Zen Buddhism, final integration is the state of deciphering *koan* (the state of enlightenment), *koan* referring to what everyone brings into this world at his birth and tries to decipher before he dies [14]. In Near Eastern thought, Sufism (the art of rebirth) can be stated as "individuality in non-individuality," that is, becoming a creative truth by passing from "I-ness" to "he-ness" to "one-ness" (universality) [15]. In Khayyám's description it is an overflowing of the state of being born without attributes [16]. In classical Chinese philosophy this state is called *tao* and is compared to the water current that resistlessly moves toward its goal. "*Tao* is the fulfillment, wholeness or vocation performed, beginning and end, and complete realization of the meaning of existence in innate things" [2]. It is also expressed in literature and art. Shakespeare (or whoever wrote the works attributed to him) portrayed the individual who has solved the contradictions between day-to-day roles and the single role of life; so too, perhaps, with Leonardo da Vinci and his Mona Lisa. In our age Tagore's universal man, related to humanity, is characterized by benevolence and grace [17]. In Goethe it is an insight into *entelechy*, which requires that the individual strive for its unfolding [9].

In recent Western thought the problem of final integration is becoming more recognized in our age of increasing anxiety. It has been noted under such names as "spontaneous expression without reservation" [18, 19, 20], "peak experience" [21], "becoming one's self" [22], "intensive visionary experience" [23], "dynamic insight" [24], "autonomy" [25], as well as other phrases.

In short, the state of final integration is the end of the vertical growth of the adult personality and the beginning of the horizontal expansion into creativity. It exceeds the objectivization of the ego and is concerned with the liberation of the ego. This state is further marked by intense awareness of various spheres of reality: the existential reality of essence versus the natural reality of appearance, the reality of meaning versus the reality of oneness. In a similar way there exist subspheres of reality within the cultural reality that appear in physical, spiritual and social patterns. It is significant that all Western and Eastern modes of attaining maturity in the adult personality have recognized as an essential quality the ability to become aware of multiple realities [26].

The fully integrated person also becomes aware of the duality of thinking: that which is made by the mind and that which is achieved by sudden awareness, insight, and intuition. He discovers different laws of behavior as related to different states, and through insight he recognizes that in the natural state behavior is immediate and the function of drives. At the highest level of the rational and cultural state, other factors such as values and interest come between subject and object, thereby creating the following trends [12, 27, 28]:

Perception of value $= f$ (natural drive)
Interest $= f$ (perception of value)
Conscious act $= f$ (interest).

Finally, in the transcultural state the distance between subject and object once more disappears. Values, interest, and action all submerge into one and behavior becomes spontaneous; the function of insight—sudden awareness—is rooted in the creative force that man's essence shares with the cosmic essence [20]. In this state everything in the world comes anew, like the swift current of the sea. Like flashes of lightning a succession of insights illuminates one's mind and increases one's vision. In such a state universal trust appears; imagination, perplexity, fantasy, and suspicion disappear entirely. There comes a time when the illuminist feels that the current has become too rapid; no care of any kind then lingers in his mind and words have no use for him. He seems unconscious, although he experiences a dream-like awareness [6, 7, 29].

Even so a hundred thousand "states" came and went back to the unseen, O trusted one.

Every day's "state" is not like [that of] the day before: [they are passing] as a river that has no obstacle in its course.

Each day's joy is a different kind, each day's thought makes a different impression [7].

It is through these intuitive flashes that separation of subject and object ceases to exist. When this union takes place, when man and woman become one, the fully integrated man is that one; when the units are eliminated, he is that unity. When unity is attained one can claim that he is whom he loves and whom he loves is he, as it was experienced by Abi Sa'id Abi Al-khay'r [30]. These creative moments differ from sublimation: in sublimation a half-integrated man utilizes a medium to reduce his inner conflict, and that is why he fails to create in his relatively relaxed state. Furthermore, the results of sublimation do not at all compare in terms of quality with the creative products of integrated persons. In the life of integrated persons creativity is a process, an end in itself; in the half-born, sublimated person it is a means. The truly creative phenomenon is the most basic manifestation of man's final integration [20, 31, 32]. Creativity in integrated persons is highly related to their anxiety-free expression, their positive feelings, and their spontaneous expression. This dual image of creativity in sublimated and in healthy persons has also been observed by Guirdham, who differentiates between them: "No one would deny that a great deal of modern art is neurotic in origin and highly subjective. This being so we accept that such creative activity arises within the personality (social self) and that its completion is dictated by it. When, however, we come to the higher flights of art we seek for other explanations. All great art is a possession from without, in which the mind of the artist acts as a reflective screen and in which his personality serves as an instrument" [33].

In sublimation the unrestful, crying, social self dominates; the self's intellect is subdued. In real creation the restful "I," the real self within us, manifests itself. As early as 1937 Gordon Allport wrote that the creative person becomes a process whose act cannot be regarded as serving instinctual or other motives; such an individual creates even without reward. His creation becomes his life [34]. In the same vein H. H. Hart says: "Creation results from a synthesis that occurs in the unconscious ego and is fostered by the freedom from repression" [31]. Goldstein considers culture an expression of man's creative power and a way of realizing his nature [35]. I might also add that regardless of the time and place, man, since his separation from nature, has tried numerous ways, destructive and creative, social and otherwise, to regain his "lost paradise," his state of certainty and unity. The process of creativity has best served as a means of developmentally expanding man's awareness in order to attain a new harmony. It is not surprising that the best cultural products of the East, and often of the West, have been developed by fully integrated people. Nor is it difficult to understand that in creativity as a process man deciphers himself and arrives at final integration [20, 34].

In the process of rebirth one creates in terms of physical objects and new ideas. In the final state one becomes a constant creative attitude. It is in the state of creative attitude that one finds joy in deeds that benefit others regardless of hoped-for rewards. It is also in the state of creative attitude that one functions naturally and spontaneously without having a desire to record, to write, or to create in terms of physical objects. His creative attitude comforts and produces joy as he experiences life in its entirety [20].

Fromm's concept of "spontaneous experience without reservation" is comparable to Maslow's "peak experience" [21]. However, Fromm believes that the concept of creativity is not limited to creating something new, something physical in terms of an art object, but that this concept must be extended to the human reality that exists beneath, thus bringing about something new, namely a creative attitude [37]. According to Fromm the best general quality of creativity is an ability to see (or to be aware) and to respond. The experience "to see" and respond in this sense occurs in a situation ". . . of complete relatedness, in which the seer and seen, observer and observed, become one, although at the same time they remain two" [37]. The condition for such a creative attitude is summarized in the phrase: ". . . creativeness means to be born before one dies" [37].

Furthermore, final integration gives integrated persons an insight into human lives, and their own life histories. Indeed, they can write the detailed history of their own lives. They possess enormous energy and ability to carry the pains of others without burden. Their insight into human evolution, history, and nature contributes to their "subjectively objective" state of mind. They have great ability to endure, and they can also stand solitude without boredom; they can truly live in any community. Finally, they are not only related to their fellowmen, to history, but also to the nonhuman environment. Natural phenomena become symbolic of a universal communication. They see natural objects as units resembling life. This relatedness is expressed by Rumi:

> All the atoms of the universe, in secret
> Are communicating day and night that
> We are hearing, we are aware, we are joyful.
> We aren't in communication with nonconfidants [20].

In his excellent study, *The Non-Human Environment*, Searles cites numerous examples to indicate the significance of relatedness to the non-human environment in health, creativity, and normalcy [38]. Buber sees it as an "I-it" relationship [39]; similar is Fromm's concept of "unity" [37]. Under the condition that one can also retain his own sense of identity: "The productive orientation involves a creative relatedness not only with one's fellowman but also with the non-human environment" [38].

In an active sense the transcultural state is characterized by the sudden intuitive experience of "I am." This "I" is neither the "I" that acts under the pressure of drives in the natural state, nor the "I" that is recognized by some Westerners as the "I" that thinks, or as Transcendental Ego (Husserl), or as objectivization of the Ego (Katz). It is that "I" that is the result of union of subject and object and an experience of illumination, thus related to all [40].

Various Ways of Attaining Final Integration

A number of factors may motivate and provide a shock, which then instigates existential awareness. For example, these factors may be a critical ego; an achieved superego; acculturation; awareness of the partiality of the social self; purity and sensitivity; early intellectual growth; accidentally finding oneself in a quest situation; being in a situation in which power, wealth, and fame may lose their security value; a traumatic experience such as the loss of a loved object; and continuous struggle against social and mental obstacles. In other words, the attainment of final integration in the succession of identities is open to those who have: 1) experienced the social self as a fragmented self (Rousseau); 2) become aware that reason alone does not provide trust and certainty (Al-Ghazzali); 3) doubted their own hierarchy of values by coming in contact with another set of values, for example, through contact with two cultures, minorities in one culture or via social-class mobility (Nietzsche); 4) found religion and culture as a means of further self-realization (Rumi); 5) received a genuine avocation and examined their inner selves (Socrates); 6) attained final integration through constant struggle, resistance, and directed effort ('Attar, a Persian of the eleventh century); 7) progressed slowly, perhaps due to their scientific accomplishments, after which they found the time to give meaning to their final integration through artistic media (Khayyám, C. P. Snow); 8) found that they were sensitive enough to apprehend man's situation in a few tragic signs (Buddha); 9) grew in a creative environment (Goethe); 10) tasted life in companionship and were awakened by the death of the beloved (Gilgamesh) [41].

It does not matter how one arrives at the stage of final integration, but rather whether one adopts a suitable mechanism of rebirth.

Mechanisms and General Psychological Laws

At this point I wish clearly to state that, in my view, the biological birth of the individual, his self-growth within the family, and social patterning, are all means of attaining a "final rebirth." All of us are born in a family; we all possess certain healthy or unhealthy attitudes toward our parents and we all become social beings. However, both these processes (the familial and the social), as well as the biological endowments upon which they are based, provide the means for final rebirth—for becoming a man, a "mankind."

Therefore, the general assumption in the theory of final integration is that there are infinitely simple and complex stages of rebirth between one's biological birth and one's birth in totality. However, there exists a general law of identity and rebirth that governs all stages of growth. This general law begins with separatedness and ends with the state of relatedness to an object of desire. Separation from former objects of desire produces a crisis resulting in a crisis of unrelatedness through search and ultimately attachment to a new object of desire. After the individual perceives his object of desire, his hope flowers, his longing for attachment and his anxiety about the search grow. He makes further progress by developing sympathy, resistance to vicissitudes, patience, and a sense of orientation. These principles govern the succession of identities, some of which all individuals must face. Specifically, identification also has its general laws, which begin with the perception of the value of an object and the growth of interest in it, thereby building up will in the subject to actualize the perceived value—to become one with it. Thus, from the very early years of childhood, affection, interest, and volition accompany sensory perception, conceptualization, and intellectualization. The motive of perception of values in early childhood comes from unconscious drives; later consciousness and intellect may play a part in the evaluation and process of identification.

The most intense periods of rebirth are at about the age of two, adolescence, and especially in adulthood during the process of final integration. All these periods are closely related to value orientation. In the period prior to final integration one's awareness of man's existential dilemma grows. He faces the nature of life and death, joy and pain, creativity, and being busy doing nothing. In short, one's awareness of many "I's" and no "I" comes to his state of awareness and constantly compels him to give an account to himself [42]. Perhaps Kamal, a young adult of two cultures, described it properly: "Which of these two 'I's' was 'I'? Was the real 'I' that familiar ego who belonged to the shopkeeper's class, or was it the 'I' which conquered every obstacle in going to college? Perhaps my real 'I' was the professional salesman or the innovator of a new business? The kind benevolent son or the crafty entrepreneur? Was it the proud heroic Turk of bygone days or the imitative man of today; the Muslim-oriented or the Western national; the adventurer who beckoned me to leave my life of comfort or the reticent one who held me back? Which one of these was the real 'I'? The 'I' which criticized me or that which made mistakes?" [11].

If a man faces his existential dilemma, then the task becomes not one of giving three hours a week to a psychiatrist, but entering the state of anxious search that requires complete concentration and entrance into an "existential moratorium." "Existential" as an adjective is used here to differentiate this state of anxious search from the sociopsychological moratorium that Erikson views as a prerequisite for adolescents to become adults in the social sense [43]. However, the processes of existential and sociopsychological moratoria are both instruments of rebirth. The sociopsychological moratorium provides a means of rebirth as a social man, and in the transcultural state the existential moratorium provides a means of rebirth in totality. In brief, the transcultural state of human growth is a universal state regardless of time, place, and the degree of culture and is characterized by satisfaction, certainty, and the search for truth, which are the manifestations of the drives in relation to sex, preservation, and action, respectively.

Moreover, not only is this state universal, and not only is it in this state that men are equal, but equally important, the mechanisms and psychological laws that give birth to this state are universal regardless of the names and titles that are given them. I have used the term "existential moratorium" to designate the mechanism of rebirth in totality. My knowledge of integrated persons in both East and West has led me to confirm the universality of the existential moratorium. Experientially, those who sought rebirth in the transcultural state adopted an existential mechanism that began with detachment from their previous state, followed by quest, anxiety, a vague awareness of the new state, an increase of anxiety, and love for that state, as well as effort, devotion, trust, and hope in identifying with it. There then occurs rebirth in a universal state, directly and indirectly, leading to insight into an inner evolution of life and finally union with this inner process.

However, the form that the mechanism of rebirth takes in final integration is influenced by the culture, place, and time in which the individual has lived. European culture, which approached the state of final integration through the development of rationality and external measures of security, has given birth to psychoanalysis, namely, the Freudian, Jungian, and Frommian schools, and more recently to logotherapy and existential therapy. Near Eastern culture, due to external insecurity, an insight into the inadequacy of faith per se and rationalism in securing certainty, developed the art of rebirth known historically in Sufism as *tariqat* (path), in contrast to *shar'iat*, which stressed religious law [30, 44, 45]. In a more direct way, the Far East, perhaps due to overpopulation and closeness to nature, developed the "ways of liberation." In actuality, these three approaches are similar to one another, if not identical, and can be summarized in the phrase "mechanisms of rebirth."

In the Near Eastern culture the mechanism of rebirth in final integration takes place in two major psychological steps, both of which are interrelated. In brief, the Sufis assert that a seeker faces two major tasks: to dissolve his present status (*fana*), then reintegrate again. "Unless you are first disintegrated, how can I reintegrate you again?" [1, 46, 47]. Disintegration here refers to the passing away of the conventional self; reintegration means rebirth in the cosmic self. *Fana* is the removal of the "i"; *baqa* is the process of becoming "I." Instead of being related to the partial self-intellect, reintegration means bringing to light the secrets of the total personality. In a practical sense it means cleansing one's consciousness of what Rumi calls fictions, idols, and untruths and purifying the heart of greed, envy, jealousy, grief, and anger so that it regains its original quality of becoming mirrorlike to reflect the reality within it [6, 7]. *Fana* means, in fact, a liberation from self-intellect, and *baqa* is affirmation of truth and love [46]. In going through the process of rebirth the principle of individual differences is recognized. In other words, rebirth in integration requires: 1) detachment from such external values as fame and wealth; 2) the selection of a guide; 3) detachment from inner veils; 4) intentional isolation; 5) traveling and arriving at the state of nothingness and 6) integration into "everythingness" [48].

Unlike the modern Western and Islamic cultures that forced man to arrive at psychotherapy and the "art of rebirth" through intellectual and religious development, respectively, Far Eastern culture arrived at the art of liberation as formulated in Taoism, Vednata, Yoga, and especially Buddhism through the development of a rigid social order. Conventionality formed the individual's false self, which challenged man's true nature and finally became synthesized in the real self by going through the process of the "art of liberation."

In India, historical events gave way to a caste system that set the limit of personal growth for every individual from his birth to his death. Each caste set up the pattern of behavior, developed filters of communication, particular variations of language, phrases, and attitudes, and acquired a sense of interrelatedness [49]. The reaction to this social system, which was predetermined and inevitable, was a kind of cosmology that from the emergence of *Bhagavad-Gita* to Buddhism has served as a progressive path of liberation from conventionality—that is, a process of relating man to his own destiny rather than to the limited caste system.

Similarly, Chinese culture developed a social order that made the individual's existence subject to his family, community, and social system as a whole. As a reaction to Confucianism, Taoism developed as an effort to bring man back to his original reality.

The Far Eastern art of liberation shares certain characteristics with both modern psychotherapy and the "art of rebirth" of the Near East. In all these systems there is no doctrine, as they do not advocate a school of philosophy. All are individualistic and are chiefly concerned with man's rebirth. If even God's image comes into the picture, His image is for man as a transfer, not man for His glory. These processes all act as a midwife for the detachment from one's state and rebirth in a new one.

In traditional Hindu philosophy, the art of liberation was one stage of man's personality growth known as "forest life." After man had played his social role as a member of his community, after he had achieved the honor of being a husband and parent and had fulfilled the social duty of educating his children for society, he would then, if awakened, concern himself with his existential dilemma. He would take the courageous step of "isolation from comradeship," separation from dear ones, in order to contemplate, adopt some way of personal analysis and try to find his true self [49]. This process is essential when we remind ourselves that in the beginning of the state of final integration one finds conventional life a hindrance as well as a means of attaining the birth of the true self. Without living in society life is not possible, and yet one cannot attain final integration without leaving it. In other words, without becoming first a Confucianist, that is, living strictly according to a social norm, one can have no foundation for becoming a Taoist, a liberated whole.

In Zen Buddhism, liberation from *maya*, that is, from social institutions, from the veil of language and logic, from conventionality, and from the way the *maya* forms our character, furthers enlightenment (*satori*) [14]. This process of liberation, in fact, begins within life in society and can be expressed in terms of a progression from one stage of life to the next; from mother- and environment-fixation to relatedness to objects and possession in childhood to the world of utilization in adolescence, and to action and provision in society. In this continuous reincarnation (a symbolic term for continuous rebirth), from stage to stage, one finds that *maya* is not reality. One becomes aware of this illusion and tries to liberate oneself. This sense of awareness produces a great anxiety and demands further search for enlightenment. In this state one begins his existential moratorium; it is his own task to find the truth about himself and for himself. But the guide (*guru*) is necessary. He puts the student in a situation in which he can liberate himself and become aware of that situation; that is, the guide creates contradictory situations that the individual student must resolve. For example, the student finds it both a necessity and a hindrance to think of *maya* itself. The student must practice in specific situations and resolve the contradiction, perhaps by insight, into an object of love.

In this way, insight into the role of *maya* and its artificiality gradually grows. Once the *guru* has resolved the conflict he can lead the way to liberation. In fact, in both Zen and Near Eastern Sufism the relationship between the guide and the seeker seems, culturally speaking, authoritarian, but in reality this is not so. Two souls are constantly communicating. They share meanings; one gives, directs, and stimulates, the other receives and unfolds knots of psychical structure. It is not that the novice is obedient to an order but that he is receptive to evolutionary changes. The more the seeker transcends, the less guidance he needs from the guide. This guidance promotes a rebirth and the guide serves only as a transfer in this path. Through his guidance the student loses *maya*; he becomes empty and feels no boredom while doing nothing; at the same time he is receptive to everything. To become fully aware and fully responsible signifies unity, integration, and enlightenment [50, 51].

In the words of Suzuki the mechanism of liberation involves five steps: the first and second steps are that "many" are generated from "one" and "one is many" (*sho chu hen, hen chu sho*). They are interrelated and it is in the thinking process that they stand opposite one another. It is noteworthy that Rumi also advocated the release from this contradiction and illustrates the unity of one and many by comparing discrete grapes (resembling the reality of many) to the grape juice (the world of oneness). The interrelatedness of these steps supports the fact that it is the principle of oppositions that makes each reality meaningful. The third step is a transitory one and concerns the life of the student. The first two steps transform themselves into the conative, and the student becomes a living, feeling, willing personality. In this process of going from one to many, then from many to one (*sho chu sho*), the student not only perceives his coming from *sho* but he realizes that duality is *maya* and in the mind. The fourth step, *ken chu shi*, is a station in which the student guards himself from returning to the world of duality. This step is life itself and exists apart from intellectual paradoxes. One's real life starts here, and here all actuality begins. The fifth stage, *ken chu to*, is the actualization and the assurance of the fourth, which compares with the state of *reza* (satisfaction) in Near-Eastern Sufism [52].

Similar mechanisms of individual rebirth undoubtedly existed in the history of the West. A vivid example of this rebirth in creativity is Goethe. Neither literary critics nor such Freudian psychoanalysts as Eissler have succeeded in unfolding Goethe's genius, for both a proper theoretical foundation and a method have been lacking. However, an understanding of Goethe's personality and rebirth will serve to enrich the foundation of Western psychoanalysis and transcend it toward Eastern wisdom [8].

Goethe attained a state of being that, if understood at the time, could have saved the West a century of searching for an answer to man's dilemma. Yet the West had to follow its cultural course and arrive at an understanding of unconscious forces by a further explanation of consciousness, subsequently leading to the development of psychoanalysis.

The discovery of psychoanalysis as a technique in the West can become a means of delivering both the East and West. However, this task is not possible without modifying somewhat the theoretical assumptions of psychoanalysis. Specifically, it must be related to an integrated theory of man and to a universal theory of culture which will encompass the great variability in human growth—from psychoses to a state of final integration in the adult personality. As an example, the interpretation of the transcultural state, without an improvement upon the theoretical assumptions of psychoanalysis, will suffer defeat, as is evident in Wheelis's *The Quest for Identity* [53] and Fingarette's *The Self in Transformation* [54].

It is quite apparent that both authors wrote their books from personal experience, their awareness of their existential dilemmas, and their insight into the problem of identity in our time. Each of them, after being awakened—that is, detaching himself from his traditional values and his former social self—fell into the predicament of the existential dilemma of life where he raised the crucial questions: "Who am I?" and "Where am I going?" His previous identity faced his potential rebirth: being versus becoming. He became fully aware of the state of this existential dilemma and reflected: "As man becomes aware of himself as apart from his environment and as separate from his fellowmen, the original oneness of life with its matrix is lost. . . . The manhood of man depends upon his alienation and his awareness of mortality" [53].

This existential alienation is the dawn of rebirth in final integration in the adult personality. Yet neither Wheelis nor Fingarette perceive that with the realization of the existential dilemma man clings to the edge of the transcultural state while being pulled down by cultural forces. Thus, he cannot gain total help from cultural mechanisms. Rather, he must discover a new mechanism in order to facilitate the process of rebirth in final integration of the adult personality. Instead of finding the concept of "existential moratoria" to solve his dilemma, Wheelis adopted a "sociocultural moratorium," similar to that of Erikson [43], to deal with the problem of helping man enter the third stage of human growth. In short, the subject matter of these two books relates to the transcultural state, but the suggested solutions stem from the cultural state and a limited theory of man.

However, a few psychoanalysts and therapists, among them Harry Stack Sullivan [55], Karen Horney [56], Erich Fromm [57], Viktor Frankl [58], Arthur Guirdham [33], and Harold Kelman [59, 60], have discovered that Freud's limited ideas of man's nature were basically due to the time in which he lived. It is quite likely that if Freud were living today he would not be an orthodox Freudian. Erich Fromm has contributed greatly to a critical appraisal of Freud's basis of thinking and to a redefining of his concepts in terms of man's relatedness to nature and to his fellowmen [57]. Frankl, in establishing a school of logotherapy, has extended the Freudian concept of reality and introduced the importance of values and goals in therapy [58]. Thus Frankl has related the technique of psychoanalysis to the second level of human growth, that is, the cultural stage. Whereas men like Suzuki [52] and Watts [50] have introduced Eastern wisdom to the West, Kelman has analyzed deeply the way in which the West is approaching the core of Eastern wisdom and has clarified the Eastern state of final integration [11]. In the same way, Karen Horney transcended psychoanalysis by identifying new unconscious forces in man and society [56]. These contemporary developments in psychoanalysis along with man's progress in physics will, I believe, gradually unfold the deepest of man's potentialities.

However, what is required is a more universal technique, based on the East-West heritage, which will give insight into man's situation in history and in the cosmos. Furthermore, such a new technique must be suitable for guiding all types of individuals from a disturbed state to one of full development. It must be flexible. This universal quality requires that a new mechanism of human development be related to an integrated theory of man and a comprehensive theory of culture encompassing the natural, cultural, and existential states.

In a forthcoming article [12] I have proposed such a new technique, namely, psychocultural analysis, as a way of discovering the principles of behavior (the origin of action) in man, society, place, and time. Psychocultural analysis as a technique seeks to discover contradictions that exist between these principles and finally suggests how they can be resolved in such a way that the successions of rebirth end in final integration, where man, instead of claiming "I think; therefore I am," can say, "I live; therefore I am."

Application to the Therapy of Young Adults

The question now arises: How can this treacherous road toward rebirth become a possibility for present-day man? How can we benefit from it? It is my belief that in the past this "soul-searching" task was open to only a few but now the strong egos of young adults who are experiencing great anxiety make them ready for final integration. If educational facilities do not waste their opportunities, and if society allows them to experience their social role and responsibility, which they are ready to accept at an earlier age, then their awareness can be guided toward final rebirth. Furthermore, it can contribute to the rebirth of young scientists who are fragmented due to overspecialization; religious and educational leaders who are seeking a new frame of reference; and political and social leaders who are interested in a permanent peace, or even the nonintellectual with a pure heart who longs for truth. Although this process of rebirth is open to all, it is a prerequisite for psychotherapists and counselors. As a measure it contributes to the clarification of concepts of health and relates it to the developmental stages of man. Thus in the natural state health becomes the satisfaction of drives; in the cultural state it becomes a dynamic concept that requires some degree of tension for transcending one's state; and it is only in the transcultural state that health becomes a constant and is submerged in the creative process. In terms of progress, the qualities of the state of final integration serve as a guidepost directing all cultural forces toward man's final drama of rebirth.

Conclusion

Regardless of language, cultural and temporal differences, certain individuals of various Eastern and Western cultures have adopted the same goal in experiencing final integration; moreover, the reality behind the ways they have adopted is similar in all. The name makes no difference; it is the experience that is the same. The common denominator, the process of breakthrough, comes with the inner experience of life. This is essential for its result, not its process. It results in certainty, in positivity and a mature attitude. It is also synthesized in a state of receptivity known as "no-knowledge" in Taoism, "emptiness" in Zen Buddhism, "nothingness" and "poverty" in Sufism, and "the void" in the writings of Al-Ghazzali and Guirdham.

As a result of this inner experience of evolution—biological and social —one realizes that Aristotelian logic is an art of true thinking and does not have much voice in the art of living. On the other hand, one finds that the logic of living, growth, and rebirth are dialectic. It is essential to understand that this realization of perception of reality through dialectic logic is what Taoism, Zen Buddhism, Sufism, Freudian psychoanalysis, and Marxist "socioanalysis" all share. Rebirth in a new psychical state arises from an awareness of existing conflict and its resolution. Thus, when a novice falls into an existential dilemma, which happens when he senses socioindividual conflict or man-nature conflict, he is ready for rebirth. This state of awareness is common to all, and without a need for betterment or psychotherapy, neither the Zen master nor the analyst can contribute to anyone's life. These mechanisms for stimulating personality change thereby produce anxiety, which in turn is an essential source of psychical energy for the search for final rebirth. The nature of this anxiety differs from neurotic longing. It is the ratio between what one is aware of as an object of love and his own state of inadequacy. It is the hope and fear of this visionary experience that makes his anxiety different from that of the mentally ill. He is aware of his anxiety and does not flee from it, for to escape from it means a lack of worth in seeking the goal. This concept of anxiety focuses on another common element evident in all schools of psychotherapy: specifically, the roads to the inner voice (Jung) [2], the good life (Rogers) [22], *satori* (Zen Buddhism [14], rebirth in totality (Sufism) [48] and the fully born man (Fromm) [37].

References

1. Rumi, M. J. M. B. *Diwan-e-Shams e Tabriz*. Amir Kabir Press: Tehran, 1959.
2. Jung, C. G. *The Development of Personality*. Bollingen: New York, 1954.
3. Arasteh, A. Reza *Cheguneggi e Rushd e Adami*. Atash-Kadeh: Tehran, 1955.
4. Al-Ghazzali, H. M. *The Alchemy of Happiness*. C. Field, trans. Ashraf Press: Lahore, no date.
5. ———. *The Confessions of Al-Ghazzali*. C. Field, trans. Ashraf Press: Lahore, no date.
6. Rumi, M. J. M. B. *Fihi ma Fihi.*
   Fruzanfar, ed. University of Tehran Press: Tehran, 1959.
7. ———. *The Mathnawi*. R. A. Nicholson, ed. and trans. (six volumes). Luzac & Co.: London, 1960.
8. Eissler, R. K. *Goethe: A Psychoanalytic Study*. Wayne University Press: Detroit, 1963.
9. Husemann, F. *The Art of Healing*. Trans. R. K. Mackaye and A. Goodschall. Rudolf Steiner Publishing Company: London, 1938.
10. Schweitzer, A. *Goethe: Four Studies*. C. R. Joy, trans. Beacon Press: Boston, 1949.
11. Arasteh, A. *The Succession of Iden-*

tities: Outer and Inner Metamorphoses, unpublished. Presented as a lecture at George Washington University School of Medicine, Department of Psychiatry, November 1962.

12. ———. "Normative Psychoanalysis: A Theory and Technique for the Development of Healthy Individuals." *Journal of General Psychology,* Vol. 73, July 1965.

13. Huxley, J. *Knowledge, Morality and Destiny.* Mentor: New York, 1957.

14. Fromm, E., Suzuki, D. T., et al. *Psychoanalysis and Zen Buddhism.* Harper & Brothers: New York, 1960.

15. Al-Gillani, A. K. *Al-Ansan'el Kamel Fi Ma'rifti-e Awakhir wa'lawail.* Summarized in Nicholson, R. A. *Studies in Islamic Mysticism.* Cambridge University Press: Cambridge, 1925.

16. Khayyám, O. *Rubbayyat.* M. Frughi and M. Ghani, eds. Sami Publishing Company: Tehran, 1941.

17. Tagore, R. *A Tagore Reader.* A. Chakravarty, ed. Macmillan: New York, 1961.

18. Fromm, E. *Man for Himself.* Rinehart: New York, 1947.

19. ———. *The Sane Society.* Rinehart: New York, 1958.

20. Kelman, H. "Oriental Psychological Processes and Creativity." *American Journal of Psychoanalysis,* Vol. 23, No. 1, 1963.

21. Maslow, A. "Lessons from the Peak Experience." *Journal of Humanistic Psychology,* Vol. 2, 1962.

22. Rogers, C. *On Becoming a Person.* University of Wisconsin Press: Madison, 1961.

23. Huxley, A. "Visionary Experiences." Address delivered to the Fourteenth International Congress of Applied Psychology, Copenhagen, 1962. Reprinted from the Proceedings in *The Highest State of Consciousness.* J. White, ed. Doubleday-Anchor: New York, 1972.

24. Fromm-Reichman, F. *Principles of Intensive Psychotherapy.* University of Chicago Press: Chicago, 1950.

25. Reisman, D. *The Lonely Crowd.* Yale University Press: New Haven, 1950.

26. Stein, M., Aidich, A. J., et al. "Identity and History: An Overview" in *Identity and Anxiety.* M. Stein and A. J. Vidich, eds. The Free Press of Glencoe: Chicago, 1960.

27. 'Attar, F. *Musibat Namdeh.* Tehran University Press: Tehran, 1961.

28. Winter, N. J. *The Life and Thought of Avicenna.* Indian Institute of Culture: London, 1952.

29. Jami, Nur-ud-din. *Flashes of Light: A Treatise on Sufism.* E. H. Whinfield and M. Kazvini, trans. Royal Asiatic Society: London, 1928.

30. Abi Sa'id Abi Al-Khay'r. *Asrar Mana.* Ministry of Education Press: Tehran, 1948.

31. Hart, H. H. "The Integrative Function in Creativity." *Psychiatric Quarterly,* Vol. 24, 1950.

32. Anderson, H. H., ed. *Creativity and Its Cultivation.* Harper & Brothers: New York, 1959.

33. Guirdham, A. *Cosmic Factors in Disease.* Gerald Buckworth: London, 1963.

34. Allport, G. *Personality: A Psychological Interpretation.* Henry Holt: New York, 1937.

35. Goldstein, K. *The Organism.* American Book Company: New York, 1939.

36. Fromm, E., *The Art of Loving.* Harper & Brothers: New York, 1956.

37. ———. "The Creative Attitude," in *Creativity and Its Cultivation.* H. H. Anderson, ed. Harper & Brothers: New York, 1959.

38. Searles, H. *The Non-Human Environment.* International University Press: New York, 1960.

39. Buber, M. *The Life of Dialogue.* University of Chicago Press: Chicago, 1955.

40. Koestenbaum, P. "The Sense of Subjectivity." *Review of Existential Psychology and Psychiatry,* Vol. 2, No. 1, 1962.

41. Sanders, N. K., ed. *The Epic of Gilgamesh.* Penguin Books: London, 1960.

42. Schachtel, E. G. *Metamorphosis: On the Development of Affect, Percep-*

tion, *Attention and Memory*. Basic Books: New York, 1959.

43. Erikson, E. *Identity and the Life Cycle*. International University Press: New York, 1959.

44. Arasteh, A. *Man and Society in Iran*. E. J. Brill: Leiden, 1964.

45. Arberry, A. J. *Sufism: An Account of the Mystics of Islam*. George Allen & Unwin: London, 1950.

46. Nicholson, R. A. *Studies in Islamic Mysticism*. Cambridge University Press: Cambridge, 1921.

47. Al-Hujwiri. *Kashf al Mahjub*. R. A. Nicholson, trans. Luzac & Co.: London, 1936.

48. Arasteh, A. Reza, *Rumi: Rebirth in Creativity and Love*. Ashraf: Pakistan, 1965.

49. Sharma, C. *Indian Philosophy: A Critical Survey*. Barnes and Noble: New York, 1962.

50. Watts, A. *The Way of Zen*. New American Library: New York, 1957.

51. Watts, A. *Psychotherapy East and West*. Pantheon: New York, 1961.

52. Suzuki, D. T. *Introduction to Zen Buddhism*. Rider & Co: London, 1949.

53. Wheelis, A. *The Quest for Identity*. Norton: New York, 1958.

54. Fingarette, H. *The Self in Transformation*. Basic Books: New York, 1963.

55. Mullahy, P. *Oedipus Myth and Complex*. Hermitage Press: New York, 1948.

56. Horney, K. *New Ways in Psychoanalysis*. W. W. Norton: New York, 1939.

57. Fromm, E. *Sigmund Freud's Mission*. Harper & Brothers: New York, 1959.

58. Frankl, V. *Man's Search for Meaning*. Ilse Lasch, trans. Beacon Press: Boston, 1962.

59. Kelman, H. "Perspectives on Psychoanalysis." *Journal of Existential Psychiatry*, Vol. 3, No. 9, 1962.

60. Kelman, H. "Self-Realization and Masochism" in *Science and Psychoanalysis*, J. H. Masserman, ed. Grune & Stratton: New York, 1959.

II
The Nature of
Madness

Folk wisdom and philosophy have long maintained that divinity is next to madness. In English literature the theme runs from Lear *and* Hamlet *through* Moby Dick *to modern novels and poetry. This insight into the borderline relationship between some deranged states and mystical enlightenment is receiving confirmation from modern psychology and psychopharmacology. It began in medical experimentation with what used to be called "psychotomimetic" drugs—that is, drugs that were thought temporarily to induce or mimic symptoms of psychosis as a clinical means of studying the nature of madness. Later it became clear that psychoactive drugs or psychedelics (as they are now called) could with careful attention to a patient's expectations ("set") and surroundings ("setting") be used for beneficial trips through one's psyche. Jean Houston and Robert E. L. Masters'* Varieties of Psychedelic Experiences *(Holt, Rinehart, 1966) is the best survey of journeys through the chemistry of consciousness.*

From another quarter—psychoanalysis—has come a powerful and supporting statement about what is sane and what is not. Norman O. Brown's Life Against Death *(Wesleyan University Press, 1959) and* Love's Body *(Random House, 1966) examine the affinity between madness (both demonic and divine) and normality. He concludes that "the disease called man" is sick because of his ego, and that only by breaking through the illusion of personality can humanity find happiness and fulfillment. J. R. Salamanca's novel* Lilith *(Bantam, 1961) is a modern classic that beautifully portrays the theoretical examination Brown and others such as R. D. Laing in* The Politics of Experience *(Ballantine,*

1967) and Wilson Van Dusen in The Natural Depth in Man *(Harper &
Row, 1972) have made. Less cosmic in scale but equally enlightening is
Hanna Green's fictional (but autobiographical)* I Never Promised You a
Rose Garden *(Signet, 1964). An excellent conceptualization of the rela-
tionship among psychotic, ecstatic, artistic-creative, and meditative states
is found in Roland Fischer's "A Cartography of Ecstatic and Meditative
States," published in* Science *(Vol. 174, No. 4012, 26 November 1971).*

*In this section Elsa First describes the "alternate realities" of four
modern scientists who have uttered "Non serviam" to the social pressures
that usually force individuals to perceive the world along certain lines to
which the group conforms. (The article was written as an introduction
to two interviews—one with John Lilly and one with Phyllis Chesler—in*
Changes *magazine.) And Wilson Van Dusen, formerly chief psychologist at a mental hospital, relates his experience with patients who claimed
they were under the influence of ontologically independent nonhuman
entities—i.e., "spirits." It is a thoughtful and especially significant article
because of burgeoning interest in the occult and paranormal dimensions
of life.*

J.W.

3 Visions, Voyages
and New Interpretations of
Madness
Elsa First

John Lilly's work is almost a perfect test case for anyone who wants to start rethinking the relationship between creativity and "madness." To understand Lilly, you have to see him in the context of the history of religion: as a man who has had certain "religious" experiences in a post-religious society.

You also have to look at him in terms of the history of science: as a scientist who, in good scientific tradition, has felt it necessary to question some of the fundamental assumptions of science itself. One assumption he questions is that science can or should deal only with nonunique, and therefore repeatable, "external" events. If that sounds mind-blowing, hold on. You will also have to look at him in terms of the history of psychiatry.

Psychiatry tends to say that a person who has certain experiences that no one else can understand or share or perceive (hallucinatory experiences, for example)—and who then insists on valuing them as "real" and will not accept reducing them merely to the projected contents of his mind—is "mad." John Lilly has taken up this awkward position, and in doing so, has joined the many who are raising interesting questions about the conventional psychiatric definition of "madness."

What if a person has certain unique experiences and manages to get society to accept his version of them? What if—as with some far-out theory-making in science—it will be a long time before it is clear whether or not *anyone* will be able to accept it? What if you live in a society—like many American Indian societies, for example—that believes that dreams have as much reality as everyday life, and that you can get important information in your dreams about how to conduct your life as well as how to deal with the spirit world?

How did John Lilly get into his extraordinarily difficult-to-hold position? A motif that runs through Lilly's thought, from the dolphin days through his many later changes, is his willingness to *entertain* ideas. In *Mind of the Dolphin,* he wrote:

> This peculiar concept of "entertaining" ideas frees us up from being "serious" about these ideas. Thus we can look at them, savor them, even experience possible realities postulated by them, and come away unscathed . . .

This idea comes out, transformed, and much harder to grasp, in *The Center of the Cyclone,* as:

> Within the province of the mind, what I believe to be true is true or becomes true within the limits to be found experimentally and experientially.

In between these two formulations, John Lilly was "entertaining" many curious ideas in his LSD experiments: for example, the idea that there are suprahuman beings who affect our lives. He found that entertaining such an idea—or as he put it, programming himself to believe in the possibility—enabled him to meet such beings on his trip and to experience them as extraordinarily real. (With training, people can also produce such experiences in trance states: that is, you can have a visual experience of a "mythical" being whom you have temporarily assumed to exist.) People who stumble on such visionary experiences, either with or without drugs, often become frightened and feel they are "going mad," particularly if the images seem out of their control, and with intense anxiety bring themselves "back to reality" as soon as possible. Lilly decided that such experiences were not per se evidence of madness.

John Lilly, like Tim Leary, has always been fiercely aware that the establishment thinks he has risked blowing his mind by exploring altered states of consciousness, and that many would say he has freaked out. But if Lilly has blown his mind, he has done it in a way that calls into question the whole ordinary notion of "sanity" and "madness." This is exactly the point of what he is doing, as he would readily say.

What is sanity? Is sanity just being in touch with ordinary everyday reality? What if there is a higher form of sanity which consists of being accessible to all possible experiences of the human mind, and *accepting all kinds* of "meaningfulness" in those experiences (even if what is meaningful in one state of consciousness doesn't make sense in another state of consciousness, and vice versa) and *then* trying to integrate them in a new way? Because this is exactly what John Lilly says he is doing. He is trying to integrate alternate experiences of reality. As he puts it:

> Construct a model that includes the consensus reality and the new one in a more inclusive, succinct way. No matter how painful such revisions of the model are, be sure they include both realities.

"Consensus" reality? Can you look at solid, tangible, ordinary reality as an option? This is what the consciousness explorers are telling us: What we call "reality" is merely "consensual reality," one of many possible descriptions of the world, all of which depend on the state of consciousness of the describer. And much that is conventionally considered "madness" is simply characteristic of the human organism operating in a different way from that required by everyday life.

One vivid and sympathetic way into all this is through Carlos Castaneda. The central drama in Castaneda's apprenticeship, from his first encounter with Mescalito, is Castaneda's struggle with accepting his hallucinatory, visionary, and other "nonordinary" experiences as "real." He keeps trying to reduce these experiences to explanations in terms of ordinary reality, often experiencing acute anxiety and disorientation when he can find no way to do so. Don Juan keeps trying to show him that this is not the issue: there are simply different kinds of "reality."

At the climax of Castaneda's apprenticeship, near the end of the third book, *Journey to Ixtlan*, Castaneda enters the world of sorcery so completely that, alone on a mesa, he meets a coyote who soundlessly talks to him.

The next day Don Juan explains:

> "What stopped inside you yesterday was what people have been telling you the world is like. You see, people tell us from the time we are born that the world is such and such . . . and naturally we have no choice but to see the world the way people have been telling us it is . . . Yesterday the world became as sorcerers tell you it is. In that world coyotes talk, and so do deer . . . and all other living beings. But

what I want you to learn is *seeing*. Perhaps you know now that *seeing* happens only when one sneaks between the two worlds, the world of ordinary people and the world of sorcerers. Yesterday you believed the coyote talked to you . . . but . . . to believe that is to be pinned down in the world of the sorcerers. . . not to believe that coyotes talk is to be pinned down in the realm of ordinary men."

Soon after, Castaneda asks Don Juan if he couldn't have taught him to *see* without bringing him into the situations of extreme danger that sorcery entails. Don Juan replies:

"No. In order to *see*, one must learn to look at the world in some other fashion, and the only fashion I know is the way of a sorcerer."

At this point we realize what Don Juan was leading Castaneda toward during the whole ten years of his apprenticeship. He was not simply teaching him sorcery. He was giving him an alternate description of reality so vivid that he can never again take our ordinary reality as the only one.

Reality? In some circumstances, the fabric of everyday reality wears awfully thin. Getting close to your own death can do it. As Lilly mentions, this is part of Don Juan's teaching, too: being always aware of the nearness of death.

Lilly now says that it is since his near-death encounter with his "guardians" that he took his experiences in other "spaces" as real. In *Cyclone*, his "transformation" appears more gradual, subtle, and shifting: "There were times when I denied these experiences . . . . any validity other than my own imagination. There were other times when I felt they had a very secure reality, and I had a feeling of certitude about their validity . . . One thing that does stick with me is the feeling of reality that was there during the experiences . . ."

"Transformation" would mean that his disparate experiences of entering the "guardian spaces" with or without LSD cohered and were fully accepted as evidence of a loving divine consciousness in the cosmos. The "far-out spaces" could only fully become outer rather than inner spaces in a religious framework. This conversion crystallized—as conversion experiences are said to—around the resolution of an anguishing personal conflict. There was an LSD therapy session set up to work on the problem of his being a "coldly logical" unloving computer. In the ses-

sion he went through the "dark night of the soul" by being a meaningless program in a meaningless cosmic computer. Then his guardians
"disguised" as robot programmers tried "to get some love back into" the
Lilly-robot. He recovered early feelings of love for his mother.

"During the next few days I was to experience and feel love of the
intensity that I had felt earlier in my childhood. I went through all sorts
of emotions that I had been blocking off . . . because of my 'scientific
knowledge.' For the first time I began to consider that God really existed
in me . . . The experiences I'd had in the tank experiments with . . .
entities . . . with the two (guardians)—were a shared organized aspect
of the universe, the Network."

Recovering love, breaking through detachment and shattering the
scientific framework, came about together. Lilly had started by entertaining belief in the entities in order to re-experience them. He was now
free to see ordinary "consensual reality" as merely a "model" constructed
by the mind. And to say that our experiences of reality depend on the
given "belief system."

(Our consensual model depends on the clear distinction between subject and object of ordinary waking consciousness—a distinction which
we are socialized into making in childhood. This distinction disappears
in the mystical states. This is where G. Spencer Brown's new post-Aris-
totelian logic—mentioned (by Lilly) as the latest thing for mathematical heads—comes in: Aristotelian logic is also based on the self/object
distinction. Does our sense of what is real depend on our being a distinct
"I" in a world of objects we can touch? Or can we take mystical states
as an intuition of real unity between ourselves and the cosmos?)

In *Cyclone* Lilly says that reading R. D. Laing helped him resolve
intellectually how he could take his spaces as real without considering
himself mad. People are considered mad if they cannot emerge from
altered states at will, or if they talk about their visions in a way that dis-
turbs their associates, he concludes. But is the "psychotic" solution of
conflict identical with the religious-conversion solution? Or are there
psychological differences—apart from the question of whether the solution gains acceptance? Or proves adaptive by bringing the person "back"
to ordinary reality in a new way? . . .

The explorers of altered states of consciousness all announce that
man has a vast potential for other ways of experiencing reality that west-

ern rationality has shut out and made taboo by calling them primitive or childish or mad or extrasensory. Don Juan berates Castaneda for continually moving between only two "points"—"feeling" and "understanding." He says there are altogether eight possible "points" or positions for the human mind. How we would like to know what those other six possibilities are! But even if we knew, could we turn them to use in late-twentieth-century America? Which brings us, by a commodious vicus, to the societal view of madness, and R. D. Laing. . . .

"I don't take schizophrenia as a *fact*," Laing said at Hunter College on his recent visit to New York. "I don't object, however, to people taking it as a *hypothesis* and investigating it . . . In my approach to a person who has been diagnosed as a 'schizophrenic,' I just don't let this come between us . . ."

What is Laing up to? Part of his effort is simply to make us genuinely feel that we owe the "mad" person the same human respect we owe the "sane." He is trying to do away, once and for all, with treating the schizophrenic as a pariah, an attitude that seems always to creep back in whenever we look at schizophrenia as just a well-known syndrome of mental disorder. That is one reason Laing keeps trying to look at schizophrenia as a breakdown in the social process, instead of as an individual problem. The more we can look at madness—as people did in Shakespeare's time—as a sign that something is wrong in the state of Denmark, the more we will be able to respect the mad.

Here are some things Laing said to a seminar of staff psychiatrists at a teaching hospital recently when asked his definition of madness:

> In *The Divided Self* I said that psychosis is gauged by the degree of disjunction between people. This is not a definition of madness, but of the social circumstances out of which the attributions of madness are made. . . . Some people feel that they're always out of it . . . that meaning and reality is being in, and that they're out of touch and outsiders . . . Some people feel that they're "in" in a way that they don't want to be. . . . What they're "in" may be other people, the family, society . . . The textbook "fear of engulfment and persecution" prior to a psychotic break must be considered as this. . . . Some people are happy about what they're in, but are afraid it's starting to crumble . . . Some people are neither in nor out. They're always in transition, always discovering new things, always being sur-

prised. It's painful . . . never getting in or out, really . . . like being stuck in a manhole . . . you never know if your death is coming the next minute . . . they feel futility, hopelessness, impotence . . . everything fails . . . it's tedium and despair.

There are an infinite number of worlds the mind can construct . . . some are scary, some little understood, some might actually be incomprehensible. Some of them are certainly maladaptive and dysfunctional in our society. . . . The cluster of acceptable forms [of symbolization, meaning-assignment] varies through history, in different social circumstances. What is outside the acceptable cluster may, under special conditions of role allocation, be accepted as genius.

"Madness is gauged by the degree of disjunction between people . . ." This is beautiful and cunning. What Laing has done is to widen the traditional psychiatric view that a person is "mad" insofar as he is out of touch with other people's feelings. He extends it to: a person is "mad" insofar as he out of touch with the body of accepted meanings of his own culture. Laing has always been a gifted translator of the schizophrenic and schizoid anxieties about being "in" and "out"—what in conventional psychiatric terms would be referred to as fear of loss of ego boundaries or of merging with the object (being too in) or feelings of de-personalization and unreality (being too out). Here he makes them a metaphor—and more than a metaphor—an expression of the person's relation to his own culture.

Laing's obstinate elusiveness about "madness," his refusal to define it, comes down to this: We should not look at any mental expression as "sick" in itself. We can only say that person has had certain experiences, valid for himself, that he was unable to interpret and make coherent in a way that communicated itself acceptably to his fellows. . . .

We could try to place Don Juan, Castaneda, and Lilly in Laing's framework. Don Juan—with the culture in which sorcery played an integral part already in ruins around him—is regarded by the younger, town Indians as a doddering eccentric. Lilly is trying to put things together that were long ago sundered in Western culture (and many will feel we are not yet ready for a new synthesis). And Castaneda felt he was risking madness in attempting to enter an alien way of thinking that his own culture could not support. He hints that he broke off with Don Juan the first time because he felt he was becoming paranoid from thinking like a sorcerer.

Phyllis Chesler, author of *Women and Madness*, writes out of a tradition that could be called the politicizers of madness. Very loosely, this is the party of Wilhelm Reich, Thomas Szasz, Michel Foucault, and also R. D. Laing. They undermine the medical notion of madness by showing us that madness is a matter of social definition. They point out that madness is defined by the power structure to exclude the socially undesirable. They carefully demonstrate that all psychiatry, however humane, that treats madness as a disease is inherently judgmental and authoritarian—because the psychiatrist is trying to bring the patient back to the fold of that society's prevailing notion of reason. The politicizers share a sense that madness may be the impotent rebellion of the oppressed. The mad have something to tell us about how society has made their lives intolerable, about what we have excluded from our definition of the human.

Foucault concludes *Madness and Civilization*—in which he traces how the concept of madness and attitudes to the insane changed in Europe with the rise of the bourgeois idea of Reason—by writing: "The world that thought to measure and justify madness through psychology must justify itself before madness."

Phyllis Chesler in *Women and Madness* takes all the politicizer's arguments one step further. They showed that psychiatry represents the social order; she adds that it represents a *paternalistic* social order, with all its hidden assumptions about women: women are expected to be dependent, self-sacrificing, and nonaggressive. If they are not, they are liable to be labelled as sick or to view themselves as neurotic. . . .

"The mad are always eloquent," Phyllis Chesler says. On this point the politicizers and the consciousness explorers come together. With Reason suffering from the worst Credibility Gap in its history, the mad begin to look like visionaries—as well as victims.

So what about Saint Theresa? Or Saint Francis talking to the animals? Brother Fox. Brother Coyote. Brother Dolphin. All those vegetarian kids whispering to their plants nowadays, as if they were Indian sorcerers.

Can our "mad" perceptions really tell us something more about the world? Could there be a new form of sorcery that did not end in paranoia? Is there a way to take alternate realities seriously in the absence of a coherent religious framework without risking psychosis?

Castaneda has given many of us our first real insight into something we knew about theoretically from anthropology, but couldn't enter before: how American Indian societies used the capacity for controlled hallucination, trance, and deliberate dreaming to serve centrally useful social functions. One wonders who, if anyone, was considered "mad" in aboriginal societies.* We have a new admiration and romantic nostalgia for the Indian's sense of the aliveness and brotherhood of all nature—of which humankind is only a part. Yet we find a Lilly's intuition of cosmic brotherhood hard to make use of. With our clear-cut distinctions between "reality" and "fantasy," have we cut ourselves off too much from the wellsprings of human meaning?

A last word from the viewpoint of everyday experience: Some people enter altered states of consciousness more easily than others. They may be what the psychopharmacologist R. Fischer calls the "perceivers" rather than the "judgers" (those whose perceptions vary more readily and widely under LSD or psilocybin). This facility may also be linked with the traits we loosely group together as "schizoid." The tendency to have different selves has two sides to it: on the one hand "schizoid" people seem to have a hard time staying close to other people in a steadily averagely warm way. Sometimes they're remote, "detached," "withdrawn," super-cool; at other times a sudden wave of intense feeling floods through. (They're people who take off suddenly, preferably without actually saying goodbye, as if the time they could bear to be with others had suddenly run out . . .) On the other hand, not having a relatively firm identity means you can get out of yourself more easily. You're suggestible, can adopt other people's point of view. You can look at things from odd, "inhuman," Martian angles—which evidently links with certain kinds of creative originality. These are often the people who as little kids stayed longer than other kids did in a world where things were alive and animals talked; who perhaps preferred to play that they were things, or machines, or animals . . .

There are risks in cultivating altered states of consciousness. One of these risks comes poignantly home in the sorcerer Don Gennaro's parable at the end of *Ixtlan*: After his encounter with his "ally," which com-

---

* According to anthropologist Roger W. Wescott, psychosis (paranoid or catatonic schizophrenia) is everywhere regarded as a grave illness, although some peoples believe that the misfortune of the sufferer may bring good fortune to others, since psychotics are sometimes temporary mediums, transmitting messages from "other worlds" not otherwise accessible under normal circumstances. *Editor.*

pleted his initiation into sorcery, Don Gennaro tries to find his way home, but realizes that he cannot ask for help from the Indians he meets on the way, " 'because they were not real.' " " 'They were like apparitions,' Don Juan explained. 'Like phantoms.' " At first the reader thinks this means they were hallucinations. Gradually you realize that these people *are* what we would call real people, only for Don Gennaro they will never be fully real again. It sounds, then, as if the price to be paid for becoming a sorcerer may be a permanent alienation from ordinary human attachments. Though the sorcerers would say they have simply learned to *see.*

4 Hallucinations as the World of Spirits

Wilson Van Dusen

Introduction

I will compare the detailed accounts of patients' hallucinations to Emanuel Swedenborg's descriptions of the world of spirits. So few know of Swedenborg's work that he needs some introduction. Emanuel Swedenborg, who lived from 1688 to 1772, was one of the last men to have encompassed practically all human knowledge. Just as a sample, he was fluent in nine languages, wrote 150 works in seventeen sciences, was expert in at least seven crafts, was a musician, member of parliament, and a mining engineer. Among many scientific accomplishments he first propounded the nebular hypothesis, did the first exhaustive works on metallurgy, wrote on algebra and calculus, found the function of several areas of the brain and ductless glands, suggested the particle structure of magnets, designed a glider and an undersea boat, engineered the world's largest drydock, etc., etc. In a way he outdid himself. Had he stopped with these little accomplishments he would have been remembered. But having mastered all the physical sciences he then took on psychology and religion. His findings here were so rich and incredible that it cast a shadow over his name. He probably explored the hypnogogic state* more than any other man has ever done before or since. In this region he broke through into the spiritual world. While living a productive and successful life in the world, he had daily intercourse with spirits, which he candidly described in one of his thirty-two religious volumes titled

---

* The state between waking and sleeping. *Editor.*

Heaven and Hell (Swedenborg Foundation, 139 East 23 St., NYC). There were a number of miracles, such as the time he reported in detail a fire in Stockholm when he was hundreds of miles away, or when he would talk to departed relatives and friends and bring back accurate information that shocked the living. He delved into the symbolic language of the Bible and, for instance, wrote twelve volumes on the psychological meanings buried in Genesis and Exodus. This later work is so rich I've reserved my later years for understanding it. He had gone too far. He estranged the religious by not supporting any one religion while talking of the root values that underlie all religions. He was tried as a heretic and his works banned in his native Sweden. He was criticized for not going to church regularly. He didn't because he found church shallow and boring. He gradually became relatively unknown except for a small group of followers in many countries who continue to study his works.

One amusing anecdote occurred when Swedenborg wrote John Wesley, the founder of Methodism, that he had learned in the world of spirits that Wesley strongly wanted to see him. Wesley, surprised, acknowledged this and set an appointment months in the future because he was to go on a journey. Swedenborg wrote back he was sorry but he could not then see Wesley for he was due to die on a given date, which, of course, he did!

Spirits and Madness

By an extraordinary series of circumstances a confirmation appears to have been found for one of Emanuel Swedenborg's most unusual doctrines—that man's life depends on his relationship to a hierarchy of spirits. Out of my professional role as a clinical psychologist in a state mental hospital and my own personal interest, I set out to describe as faithfully as possible mental patients' experiences of hallucinations. A discovery four years ago helped me to get a relatively rich and consistent picture of the patients' experiences. Though I noticed similarities with Swedenborg's description of the relationships of man to spirits, it was only three years after all the major findings on hallucinations had been made that the striking similarity between what twentieth-century patients describe and Swedenborg's eighteenth-century accounts became apparent to me. I then collected as many details as possible of his description. I found that Swedenborg's system not only is an almost perfect fit with patients' experiences, but even more impressively, accounts for otherwise quite puzzling aspects of hallucinations. I will first describe how I worked and my findings, and then relate this to Swedenborg's work.

All the people involved hallucinated. They included chronic schizophrenics, alcoholics, brain-damaged and senile persons. The subjects of this study came to the attention of friends of the public because of unusual behavior. The average layman's picture of the mentally ill as raving lunatics is far from reality. Most of these people have become entangled in inner processes and simply fail to manage their lives well. In the hospital most have freedom of the grounds and the average visitor is impressed that, aside from occasional odd bits of behavior, the patients have most of their powers and appear like almost everyone else. Many return home in a month or two never to need mental hospitalization again. Some become so enmeshed in inner processes that they slip to lower levels of mental disorder. The most severe disorder is usually that of a person who sits all day involved in inner processes, who obediently obeys the request of hospital staff to dress, eat, bathe, and sleep in the hospital routine.

The people described here range from a few months in the hospital to twenty years. Most would be like the patients on the hospital grounds who strike the visitor as not unlike themselves. A conversation with one of these patients might indicate to the visitor that the patient has an unusual set of beliefs—for instance, that he is kept in the hospital by a gang of thieves or that ordinary clouds are radiation pollution. In many, even unusual beliefs would not be apparent. Most conceal that they hear and see things because they are wise enough to know the visitor doesn't and wouldn't understand. Their adjustment within the hospital is relatively good. Many do productive work ten to thirty hours a week. It is when they return to the relatively complex and demanding outside world that their adjustment often worsens. None of the patients at the most severe level of mental disorders could be included in this study because they couldn't describe their hallucinations well enough.

After dealing with hundreds of such patients, I discovered about four years ago that it was possible to speak to their hallucinations. To do so I looked for patients who could distinguish between their own thoughts and the things they heard and saw in the world of hallucinations. The patient was told that I simply wanted to get as accurate a description of their experiences as possible. I held out no hope for recovery or special reward. It soon became apparent that many were embarrassed by what they saw and heard and hence they concealed it from others. Also they knew their experiences were not shared by others, and some were even concerned that their reputations would suffer if they revealed the obscene nature of their voices. It took some care to make the patients comfortable enough to reveal their experience honestly. A further complication was that the voices were sometimes frightened of me and themselves needed reassurance. I struck up a relationship with both the patient and the persons he saw and heard. I would question these other persons directly, and instructed the patient to give a word-for-word account of what the voices answered or what was seen. In this way I could hold long dialogues with a patient's hallucinations and record both my questions and their answers. My method is that of phenomenology. My only purpose was to come to as accurate a description as possible of the patient's experiences. The reader may notice I treat the hallucinations as realities because that is what they are to the patient. I would work with a patient for as little as one hour or up to several months of inquiry where the hallucinated world was complex enough.

Some may wonder why one should believe what these patients report. The patients cooperated with me only because I was honestly trying to learn of their experiences. They were not paid or even promised recovery or release from the hospital. Most of my subjects seemed fairly sensible except for the fact of hallucinations that invaded and interfered with their lives. On several occasions I held conversations with hallucinations that the patient himself did not really understand. This was especially true when I dealt with what will be described as the higher order hallucinations, which can be symbolically rich beyond the patient's own understanding. There was great consistency in what was reported independently by different patients. I have no reason to doubt they were reporting real experiences. They seemed to be honest people as puzzled as I was to explain what was happening to them. The differences among the experiences of schizophrenics, alcoholics, the brain-damaged, and senile were not as striking as the similarities; so I will describe these hallucinated worlds in general.

One consistent finding was that patients felt they had contact with another world or order of beings. Most thought these other persons were living persons. All objected to the term hallucination. Each coined his own term such as The Other Order, the Eavesdroppers, etc.

For most individuals the hallucinations came on suddenly. One woman was working in a garden when an unseen man addressed her. Another man described sudden loud noises and voices he heard while riding in a bus. Most were frightened and adjusted with difficulty to this new experience. All patients describe voices as having the quality of a real voice sometimes louder, sometimes softer, than normal voices. The experience they describe is quite unlike thoughts or fantasies. When things are seen they appear fully real. For instance, a patient described being awakened one night by Air Force officers calling him to the service of his country. He got up and was dressing when he noticed their insignia wasn't quite right; then their faces altered. With this he knew they were of The Other Order and struck one hard in the face. He hit the wall and injured his hand. He could not distinguish them from reality until he noticed the insignia. Most patients soon realize that they are having experiences that others do not share, and for this reason learn to keep quiet about them. Many suffer insults, threats, and attacks for years from voices with no one around them aware of it. Women have reported hearing such vile things they felt it would reflect on them should they even be mentioned.

In my dialogues with patients I learned of two orders of experience, borrowing from the voices themselves, called the higher and the lower order. Lower-order voices are as though one is dealing with drunken bums at a bar who like to tease and torment just for the fun of it. They will suggest lewd acts and then scold the patient for considering them. They find a weak point of conscience and work on it interminably. For instance, one man heard voices teasing him for three years over a ten-cent debt he had already paid. They call the patient every conceivable name, suggest every lewd act, steal memories or ideas right out of consciousness, threaten death, and work on the patient's credibility in every way. For instance, they will brag that they will produce some disaster on the morrow and then claim honor for one in the daily paper. They suggest foolish acts (such as: Raise your right hand in the air and stay that way) and tease if he does it and threaten him if he doesn't. The lower order can work for a long time to possess some part of the patient's body. Several worked on the ear and the patient seemed to grow deafer. One voice worked two years to capture a patient's eye, which visibly went out of alignment. Many patients have heard loud and clear voices plotting their death for weeks on end, an apparently nerve-racking experience. One patient saw a noose around his neck which tied to "I don't know what," while voices plotted his death by hanging. They threaten pain and can cause felt pain as a way of enforcing their power. The most devastating experience of all is to be shouted at constantly by dozens of voices. When this occurred the patient had to be sedated. The vocabulary and range of ideas of the lower order is limited, but they have a persistent will to destroy. They invade every nook and cranny of privacy, work on every weakness and credibility, claim awesome powers, lie, make promises, and then undermine the patient's will. They never have a personal identity though they accept most names or identities given them. They either conceal or have no awareness of personal memories. Though they claim to be separate identities they will reveal no detail that might help to trace them as separate individuals. Their voice quality can change or shift, leaving the patient quite confused as to who might be speaking. When identified as some friend known to the patient they can assume this voice quality perfectly. For convenience many patients call them by nicknames, such as "Fred," "The Doctor," or "The Old Timer." I've heard it said by the higher order that the purpose of the lower order is to illuminate all the person's weaknesses. They do that admirably and with infinite patience. To make matters worse they hold out promises to patients and even give helpful-sounding advice only to catch the patient in some weakness. Even with the patient's help I found the lower order difficult to relate to because of their disdain for me as well as for the patient.

The limited vocabulary and range of ideas of the lower order is striking. A few ideas can be repeated endlessly. One voice just said "hey" for months while the patient tried to figure out what "hey" or "hay" was meant. Even when I was supposedly speaking to an engineer that a woman heard, the engineer was unable to do any more arithmetic than simple sums and multiplication the woman had memorized. The lower order seems incapable of sequential reasoning. Though they often claim to be in some distant city they cannot report more than the patient sees, hears, or remembers. They seem imprisoned in the lowest level of the patient's mind, giving no real evidence of a personal world or any higher-order thinking or experiencing.

All of the lower order are irreligious or antireligious. Some actively interfered with the patients' religious practices. Most considered them to be ordinary living people, though once they appeared as conventional devils and referred to themselves as demons. In a few instances they referred to themselves as from hell. Occasionally they would speak through the patient so that the patient's voice and speech would be directly those of the voices. Sometimes they acted through the patient. One of my female patients was found going out the hospital gate arguing loudly with her male voice that she didn't want to leave, but he was insisting. Like many, this particular hallucination claimed to be Jesus Christ, but his bragging and argumentativeness rather gave him away as of the lower order. Sometimes the lower order is embedded in physical concerns, such as a lady who was tormented by "experimenters" painfully treating her joints to prevent arthritis. She held out hope they were helping her, though it was apparent to any onlooker they had all but destroyed her life as a free and intelligent person.

In direct contrast stands the rarer higher-order hallucinations. In quantity they make up perhaps a fifth or less of the patient's experiences. The contrast may be illustrated by the experience of one man. He had heard the lower order arguing a long while how they would murder him. He also had a light come to him at night like the sun. He knew it was a different order because the light respected his freedom and would withdraw if it frightened him. In contrast, the lower order worked against his will and would attack if it could see fear in him. This rarer higher order seldom speaks, whereas the lower order can talk endlessly. The higher order is much more likely to be symbolic, religious, supportive, genuinely instructive and communicate directly with the inner feelings of the patient. I've learned to help the patient approach the higher order because of its great power to broaden the individual's values. When the man was encouraged to approach his friendly sun, he entered a world of powerful numinous experiences in some ways more frightening than the murderers who plotted his death. In one scene he found himself at the bottom of a long corridor with doors at the end behind which raged the powers of hell. He was about to let out these powers when a very powerful and impressive Christlike figure appeared and by direct mind-to-mind communication counseled him to leave the doors closed and follow him into other experiences which were therapeutic to him. In another instance the higher order appeared to a man as a lovely woman who entertained him while showing him thousands of symbols. Though the patient was

a high school-educated gaspipe fitter, his female vision showed a knowledge of religion and myth far beyond the patient's comprehension. At
the end of a very rich dialogue with her (the patient reporting her symbols and responses) the patient asked for just a clue as to what she and
I were talking about. Another example is that of a Negro who gave up
being useful and lived as a drunken thief. In his weeks of hallucinations
the higher order carefully instructed him on the trials of all minority
groups and left him with the feeling he would like to do something for
minorities.

In general the higher order is richer than the patient's normal experience, respectful of his freedom, helpful, instructive, supportive, highly
symbolic, and religious. It looks most like Carl Jung's archetypes, whereas
the lower order looks like Freud's id. In contrast to the lower order it
thinks in something like universal ideas in ways that are richer and more
complex than the patient's own mode of thought. It can be very powerful emotionally and carry with it an almost inexpressible ring of truth.
The higher order tends to enlarge a patient's values, something like a
very wise and considerate instructor. Some patients experience both the
higher and lower orders at various times and feel caught between a private heaven and hell. Many only know the attacks of the lower order.
The higher order claims power over the lower order and indeed shows it
at times, but not enough to give peace of mind to most patients. The
higher order itself had indicated that the usefulness of the lower order is
to illustrate and make conscious the patients' weaknesses and faults.

Though I could say much more on what the patients reported, and
quote extensively from dialogues with hallucinations, this is the substance of my findings. I was very early impressed by the overall similarities of what patients reported even though they had no contact with
each other. After twenty patients, there wasn't much more to be learned.
I was also impressed by the similarity to the relatively little shown in the
biblical accounts of possession. These patients might well be going
through experiences quite similar to what others experienced centuries
ago.

Several things stood out as curious and puzzling. The lower order
seemed strangely prevalent and limited. In the face of their claim of
separate identity, their concealing or not knowing any fact (birthplace,
schooling, name, personal history) that would set them apart was unusual. Their malevolence and persistence in undermining the patient was

striking. And why would they consistently be unreligious or antireligious? Just the mention of religion provokes anger or derision from them. In contrast, the higher order appeared strangely gifted, sensitive, wise, and religious. They did not conceal identity but rather would have an identity above the human. For instance, a lady of the higher order was described as "an emanation of the feminine aspect of the Divine." When I implied she was divine she took offense. She herself was not divine but she was an emanation of the divine. I couldn't help but begin to feel I was dealing with some kind of contrasting polarity of good and evil. The patients' accounts of voices trying to seize for their own some part of the body such as eye, ear, or tongue had a strangely ancient ring to it. Some people might suspect that my manner of questioning fed back to the patients what I wanted to hear, but after I addressed on hallucinations an audience including patients, many warmly commended me for capturing their own experiences too. As incredible as it may seem, I'm inclined to believe the above is a roughly accurate account of many patients' hallucinatory experiences.

I read and admired Swedenborg's work for some while, primarily because his religious experiences fit with my own and partly because of his immense knowledge of the hypnogogic state and the inner structure of the psyche. His doctrine regarding spirits I could neither affirm nor deny from my own experience, though it seemed a little incredible. As I describe Swedenborg's doctrine in this matter, the similarity with my own findings will become apparent.

Swedenborg describes all of life as a hierarchy of beings representing essentially different orders and yet acting in correspondence with each other. The Lord acts through celestial angels, who in turn correspond on a lower level to spiritual angels, who in turn correspond to a third lower heaven—all of which corresponds to and acts into man. On the opposite side there are three levels of hell acting out of direct contact into man. Man is the free space and meeting ground of these great hierarchies. In effect, good and its opposite, evil, rule through this hierarchy of beings down to man who stands in the free space between them. Out of his experiences and choices he identifies with either or both sides. These influences coming from both sides are the very life of man. The man who takes pride in his own powers tends toward the evil side. The man who acknowledges that he is the receptacle of all that is good, even the power to think and to feel, tends toward the good side. In the extreme of evil, spirits claim power over all things and seek to subjugate others. In the extreme of good, angels feel themselves free in that the good of the Lord acts freely through them. Swedenborg's doctrine of the effect of spirits with man is simply the lower aspect of a whole cosmology of the structure of existence.

Such is the equilibrium of all in the universal heaven that one is moved by another, thinks from another, as if in a chain; so that not the least thing can [occur from itself]: thus the universe is ruled by the Lord, and, indeed, with no trouble (SD 2466). From this order of creation it may appear, that such is the binding chain of connection from firsts to lasts that all things together make one, in which the prior cannot be separated from the posterior (just as a cause cannot be separated from its effect); and that thus the spiritual world cannot be separated from the natural, nor the natural world from the spiritual; thence neither the angelic heaven from the human race, nor the human race from the angelic heaven. Wherefore it is so provided by the Lord, that each shall afford a mutual assistance to the other. . . . Hence it is, that the angelic mansions are indeed in heaven, and to appearance separate from the mansions where men are; and yet they are with man in his affections of good and truth (LJ 9).

Each, man or spirit, is given to feel he is free and rules. Yet all are ruled (SD 3633). Even the world of matter is created and sustained by the Lord through the spiritual world (DP 3). It is normal that man does not feel himself to be the subject of a spiritual world. Swedenborg repeatedly enjoins that one is not even to attempt to become aware of the world of spirits, because it is dangerous (HH 249, AC, 5863). In the normal man spirits are adjoined to the man's spirit (AC 5862) or, what is the same, to more unconscious levels of his mind so that man is not aware of them. They flow into his feelings or into the matrix of thought (AE 1182). Spirits think spiritually and man naturally so that the two correspond to each other. In modern terms one would say spirits are in the unconscious and there live out their desires in what is to man the origin of his thoughts and feelings. In the normal situation man is not aware of their action, taking it to be his own thought and feeling. They, too, do not feel themselves to be in the life of a man. To all of man's experiences they have corresponding spiritual experiences. They do not see or hear the man's world. The spirits adjoined to man have dispositions similar to the man's. As Swedenborg says, with a bit of humor, enthusiastic spirits are with the enthusiastic (AE 1182). Thus they act together. Man is free to act, but by this relation to a hierarchy of spirits his tendencies are conditioned (AC 5850). His identification with good or evil tendencies, by his acts, furthers the conditioning in one direction or another. Good spirits or angels dwell in the most interior aspects of man's mind—in his loves, affections, or ends (AC 5851). They think by generals or universals (AC 2472), or as modern psychology would put it, they think more abstractly. One of their thoughts would cover thousands of a natural man's thoughts. The soul, spirit or interior man are the same thing (AC 6059).

> ... being thus supereminent, spiritual ideas or thoughts, relatively to natural, are ideas of ideas, thoughts of thoughts; that by them, therefore, are expressed qualities of qualities and affections of affections; and, consequently, that spiritual thoughts are the beginnings and origins of natural thoughts (CL 326:7).

Evil spirits reside in a lower but still unconscious area of mind, the personal memory. Those like the man are joined to him and they take on the memory of the man and neither the man nor they know that they are separate. They are in what Swedenborg calls his scientifics, or the facts and tendencies stored in the memory.

To some this whole conception of Swedenborg's sounds strange and even highly improbable. Scientifically it appears beyond any real test. If man cannot know these spirits, nor do they even know they are with man, the matter is like the worst speculation and not open to examination. In Swedenborg's personal diary and other works he tells how he felt gifted by the Lord with the experience both of heaven and hell and could examine over a period of many years their exact relationship to man. To learn of the powers and tendencies of evil spirits he was attacked by them as though he were a man possessed, yet it was not permitted that he be injured by them. In this respect his account sounds very much like madness with hallucinations and delusions. Yet the many documents that have been gathered* testify to his normal and even

---

* Tafel, R. L., *Documents Concerning Swedenborg,* 3 Vols. Swedenborg Society: London, 1890.

Action, A. *Letters and Memorials of Emanuel Swedenborg,* 2 Vols. Swedenborg Scientific Association: Bryn Athyn, Pa., 1948.

Trobridge, G., *Swedenborg, Life and Teaching.* Swedenborg Society: London, 1945.

prosperous life as a nobleman, respected scientist, and man of the world. Apparently he was a gifted man who was allowed to explore experiences that other less gifted persons are caught within.

The diagnosis of schizophrenia did not exist in his day, it having been first clearly delineated in 1911 by Eugen Bleuler. He did speculate on the nature of madness, sometimes describing it as being too involved in one's own fantasies (SD 172), and sometimes ascribing it to pride in one's own powers (spiritual madness) (AC 10227:3). He gave much description of possession by spirits and what they did. Present day psychosis always involves some degree of self-pride (spiritual madness) but the hallucinated aspect looks most like what Swedenborg described under the general headings of obsessions (to be caught in false ideas) and possession (to have alien spirits acting into one's thought, feelings, or even into one's bodily acts) (HH 257). He indicates that normally there is a barrier between these spiritual entities and man's own consciousness. He also makes quite clear that if this barrier of awareness were penetrated, the man would be in grave danger for his mental health and even for his life (HH 249).

If evil spirits knew they were with man they would do all sorts of things to torment him and destroy his life. What he describes looks remarkably like my own findings on the lower-order hallucinations. Let us consider lower-order hallucinations and possession by evil spirits together. You will recall that I said lower-order hallucinations act against the patient's will, and are extremely verbal, persistent, attacking, and malevolent. They use trickery to deceive the patient as to their own powers, threaten, cajole, entreat, and undermine in every conceivable way. These are all characteristic of possession by evil spirits that takes place when the spirits are no longer unconscious, but have some awareness of themselves as separate entities and act into consciousness.

It is not clear how the awareness barrier between spirits and man is broken. In Swedenborg's case he had a way of minimal breathing and concentrating inwardly for most of his life—a practice that resembles the yogic pranayama and pratyahara, which is calculated to awaken inner awareness. In the context of his whole system of thought one would surmise this inner barrier of awareness is penetrated when the person habitually withdraws from social usefulness into inner fantasy and pride. This would conform to contemporary social withdrawal, which is the earliest aspect of schizophrenia. I am relatively certain that religious faith alone doesn't prevent hallucinations because many patients try to save them-

selves by their faith. Observation would suggest useful social acts (char-
ity) would come closer to preventing schizophrenia.

All of Swedenborg's observations on the effect of evil spirits entering
man's consciousness conform to my findings. The most fundamental is
that they attempt to destroy him (AC 6192, 4227). They can cause anxiety or pain (AC 6202). They speak in man's own native tongue (CL
326, DP 135). (The only instances I could find where hallucinations
seemed to know a language other than the patient's were from the
higher order.) They seek to destroy conscience (AC 1983) and seem to
be against every higher value. For instance, they interfere with reading
or religious practices. They suggest acts against the patient's conscience
and if refused, threaten, make them seem plausible, or do anything to
overcome the patient's resistance. Swedenborg says these spirits can impersonate and deceive (SD 2687). This accounts for one puzzling aspect. Patients say voices can shift and identify as they speak, making it
impossible to identify them. Or if a patient treats them as some known
individual they will act like them. They lie (SD 1622). Most patients
who have experienced voices for any length of time come to recognize
this. They tell a patient he will die tomorrow and yet he lives. They
claim to be anyone including the Holy Spirit (HH 249). It took some
while for a woman patient to come to realize the male voice in her probably was not Jesus Christ as he claimed. She considered him sick and
proceeded to counsel this voice, which improved and left her! He claimed
he could read my mind, but I showed her by a simple experiment that
he couldn't.

> When spirits begin to speak with man, he must beware lest he
> believe them in anything; for they say almost anything; things are
> fabricated by them, and they lie; for if they were permitted to relate
> what heaven is, and how things are in the heavens, they would tell so
> many lies, and indeed with a solemn affirmation, that man would be
> astonished; . . . They are extremely fond of fabricating: and when-
> ever any subject of discourse is proposed, they think that they know
> it, and give their opinions one after another, one in one way, and
> another in another, altogether as if they knew; and if a man listens
> and believes, they press on, and deceive, and seduce in divers ways
> (SD 1622).

Though most patients tend to recognize this, most still put faith in
their voices and remain caught by them. For instance, one lady felt a

group of scientists including a physician and engineer were doing important but painful experiments on the ends of her bones. Even though I couldn't find a trace of medical knowledge in the physician or any mathematical ability above simple sums in the engineer, she continued to believe in them.

Many voices have indicated they will take over the world, or have already done so, which bit of bragging Swedenborg noticed too (SD 4476). They can suggest and try to enforce strange acts in the patient and then condemn him for compliance (AC 761). They draw attention to things sexual or simply filthy (SD 2852) and then proceed to condemn the person for noticing them. They often refer to the person as just an automaton or machine (SD 3633), a common delusional idea that many schizophrenics adopt. In the normal condition these spirits cannot see and hear the world of man (AC 1880), but in mental illness they can (SD 3963). For instance I was able to give the Rorschach Ink Blot Test to a patient's voices separately from the patient's own responses. Since I could talk with them through the patient's hearing, they could hear what the patient heard. Though they seem to have the same sensory experience as the patient, I could find no evidence they could see or hear things remote from the patient's senses as they often claimed.

There are a number of peculiar traits of the lower-order hallucinations on which Swedenborg throws light. If voices are merely the patient's unconscious coming forth I would have no reason to expect them to be particularly for or against religion. Yet the lower order can be counted on to give its most scurrilous comments to any suggestion of religion. They either totally deny any afterlife or oppose God and all religious practices (AC 6197). Once I asked if they were spirits and they answered, "The only spirits around here are in bottles" (followed by raucous laughter). To Swedenborg it is their opposition to God, religion, and all that it implies that makes them what they are.

Another peculiar finding is that the lower-order hallucinations were somehow bound to and limited within the patient's own experiences (AC 7961). The lower order could not reason sequentially or think abstractly as could the higher order. Also it seemed limited within the patient's own memory. For instance, one group of voices could attack the patient only for things he had recalled since they invaded him; and they were most anxious to get any dirt to use against the patient. Swedenborg throws light on this when he indicates evil spirits invade man's memory and scientific (the facts he has learned). This accounts for their memory limitation, their lack of sequential and abstract reasoning, and their extreme repentiveness. As I indicated earlier, it is not uncommon for voices to attack a person for years over a single past guilt. It also accounts for the very verbal quality of the lower order as against the higher order's frequent inability to speak at all (AC 5977).

Swedenborg indicates the possibility of spirits acting through the subject (AC 5990), which is to possess him. This I have occasionally seen. For instance, the man who thought he was Christ within a woman sometimes spoke through her, at which times her voice was unnaturally rough and deep. She also had trouble with him dressing at the same time she was because she would be caught in the incongruities of doing two different acts at once.

Another peculiar finding which Swedenborg unintentionally explained is my consistent experience that lower-order hallucinations act as though they are separate individuals and yet they can in no way reveal even a trace of personal identity, nor even a name. Nor can they produce anything more than was in the patient's memory. Most patients have the impression they are other beings. They will take on any identity suggested but they seem to have none of their own. This strange but consistent finding is clarified by Swedenborg's account. These lower-order spirits enter the man's memory and lose all personal memory. The personal memory was taken off at their death, leaving their more interior aspects. That they discover they are other than the man allows obsession and possession to take place and accounts for their claiming separate identity and convincing the patient of this. But their actual lack of personal memory comes from their taking on the patient's memory.

It may be that in the deeper degree of schizophrenia the spirits have taken on more of their own memory. Swedenborg says this would lead man to believe he had done what he had not done (AC 2478, HH 256). For instance, delusional ideas are a belief in what has not occurred. Some patients speak of themselves as dead and buried and their present identity as of another person. "For were spirits to retain their corporeal memory, they would so far obsess man that he would have no more self-control or be in the enjoyment of his life than one actually obsessed" (SD 3783). I am just guessing at this point that the most serious of the mental disorders, where a person is totally out of contact and jabbers to himself and gesticulates strangely, are instances where these spirits have more memory and act more thoroughly through the person. It is then symbolically accurate that they are dead and someone else lives.

I deliberately looked for some discrepancy between my patients' present experiences and what Swedenborg described. It appeared I had found it in the number of spirits who were with one patient. They may have three or four most frequent voices but they can experience a number of different people. Swedenborg says there usually are only two good and two evil spirits with a person (AC 904, 5470, 6189). He also gives instances where spirits come in clouds of people at a time (SD 4546). I later learned that where there is a split between the internal and external experience of a person, as in schizophrenia, there can be many spirits with a person (SD 160). Also as patients' voices themselves have described the situation, one spirit can be the subject or voice of many (HH 601). This was the case with the lady who had a team of researchers working on her bones. They themselves were in a kind of hierarchy and represented many. Only the lowest few members of the hierarchy became known to the patient and myself. Swedenborg refers to such spirits as the subjects of many.

Both Swedenborg and the medieval literature speak of the aim of spirits to possess and control some part of a patient's body (SD 1751, 2656, 4910, 5569). Parts involved in my observations have been the ear, eye, tongue, and genitals. The medieval literature speaks of intercourse between a person and his or her possessing spirit, giving these spirits the names of incubi and succubi depending on their sex.† One female patient described her sexual relations with her male spirit as both more pleasurable and more inward than normal intercourse. Swedenborg makes clear that those who enter the affections or emotions enter thereby into all things of the body. These more subtle possessions are more powerful than simply having voices talking to one, and can easily account for affective psychoses where there is a serious mood change (AC 6212, SD 5981). One older German woman was depressed by tiny devils who tormented her in the genital region and made her feel the horror of hell. There are many impressive similarities between the patients' experiences of lower-order hallucinations and Swedenborg's obsession and possession by evil spirits.

† See *Demoniality; or, Incubi and Succubi* (17th Century), London, 1927.

The higher-order hallucinations are quite a bit rarer, do not oppose the patient's will, but rather are helpful guides and are far more abstract, symbolic, and creative than lower-order hallucinations. In Swedenborg's terms the higher order would be angels who come to assist the person. As Swedenborg describes it, they reside in the interior mind, which does not think in words but in universals that comprise many particulars (AC 5614). The higher order in one patient visually showed him hundreds of universal symbols in the space of one hour. Though he found them entertaining, he couldn't understand their meaning. Many of the higher order are purely visual and use no words at all, while the lower order talk endlessly. One patient described a higher-order spirit who appeared all in white, radiant, very powerful in his presence and communicated directly with the spirit of the patient to guide him out of his hell. Swedenborg describes how the influx of angels gently leads to good and leaves the person in freedom (AC 6205). I've described the incident where the patient recognized good forces first as a sun that withdrew from him when he was frightened, whereas all his experiences of the lower order had been attacking. It was this simple respect for his freedom that led the patient to believe this was another order.

Swedenborg indicates that good spirits have some degree of control over the evil ones (AC 592, 6308; SD 3525). Higher-order hallucinations have made the same comment—that they can control lower-order ones but it is seldom to the degree the patient would desire. In some respects they overcome the evil insofar as the patient identifies with them. In one case I encouraged the patient to become acquainted with these helpful forces that tended to frighten him. When he did so their values merged into him and the evil plotters, who had been saying for months they would kill him, disappeared. I seem to see some kind of control of the higher order over the lower, though the nature and conditions of this control are not yet clear. Again, precisely in agreement with Swedenborg. I found evil spirits cannot see the good but the good can see the evil (HH 583). The lower order may know of the presence of the higher order but they cannot see them.

It remained a considerable puzzle to me for over a year why the higher-order hallucinations were rarer since they were far more interesting to the patient and myself and potentially more therapeutic. Again, Swedenborg has an explanation that fits beautifully with my findings. I have noticed the higher order tends to be nonverbal and highly symbolic. He indicates angels possess the very interior of man. Their influx is tacit. It does not stir up material ideals or memories but is directed to man's ends or inner motives (AC 5854, 6193, 6209). It is for this reason not so apparent and hence rarer in the patients' reports.

Conclusion

There are a number of points that make the similarity of Swedenborg's accounts and my own findings impressive. My patients acted independently of each other and yet gave similar accounts. They also agree on every particular I could find with Swedenborg's account. My own findings were established years before I really examined Swedenborg's position in this matter. I'm inclined to believe Swedenborg and I are dealing with the same matter. It seems remarkable to me that, over two centuries of time, men of very different cultures working under entirely different circumstances on quite different people could come to such similar findings. Normally such a separation in time, cultures, and persons should have led to greater differences. Because of this I am inclined to speculate that we are looking at a process that transcends cultures and remains stable over time.

Then I wonder whether hallucinations, often thought of as detached pieces of the unconscious, and hallucinations as spiritual possession might not simply be two ways of describing the same process. Are they really spirits or pieces of one's own unconscious? If the hallucinations came up with confirmably separate histories it would tend to confirm the spiritual hypothesis. We have already touched on their singular absence of a personal history and how this fits into the spirit model. In a way there are too many aspects of the matter that do not explain as well by the unconscious model as by the spiritual—consider for instance the gifts of the higher-order spirits. The difference between the unconscious and spirit models grows darker when one considers that lower-order spirits can only get in if they have tendencies like the person's own unconscious. Conversely, I think higher-order spirits act only in the direction of the individual's own higher, unconscious, unused potentialities. If this is so, it makes it difficult to separate them out as other than the person's own. One way of checking this occurs if the hypothesis of spirits leads to successful treatments fundamentally unlike what would occur from the hypothesis of a personal unconscious. I would hope that further work might settle the matter for spirits or for a personal unconscious. But it might be that it is not either/or. If these two views should be the same thing, then my brothers may be my keeper and I theirs simultaneously.

There are many unsettled matters beyond that of spirit possession. For instance the experiences Swedenborg described can be awakened in normal individuals by a study of the hypnogogic state. With the experience of alien forces in this state one comes to recognize their operation on impulsive thoughts in normal consciousness. One could also ask how possessing spirits might be removed. The several ways this can be accomplished is another study in itself.

It is curious to reflect that, as Swedenborg has indicated, our lives may be the little free space at the confluence of giant higher and lower spiritual hierarchies. It may well be this confluence is normal and only seems abnormal, as in hallucinations, when we become aware of being met by these forces. There is some kind of lesson in this—man freely poised between good and evil, under the influence of cosmic forces he usually doesn't know exist. Man, thinking he chooses, may be the resultant of other forces.

References

AC—*Arcana Celestia*, 12 volumes
AE—*Apocalypse Explained*, 6 volumes
CL—*Conjugal Love*
DP—*Divine Providence*
HH—*Heaven and Hell*
LJ—*Last Judgment*
SD—*Spiritual Diary*, 5 volumes

These works are inexpensively available from:

The Swedenborg Foundation
139 East 23rd Street
New York, New York 10010

III
Biofeedback

Biofeedback: the word induces near-religious reverence among some people. They see it as a space age panacea for all illness and a means of instant enlightenment. Electronic yoga, it's been called.

But it is no such thing—not yet, at least. The potential of biofeedback is great in many fields—medicine, psychiatry, business, education, athletics, space travel, and psychic research, to name some. But the misinformation about it in the popular press and the misuse of biofeedback terminology by some groups advertising "mind development" have caused deep discomfort to biofeedback researchers who took great care to point out the tentative nature of their findings.

The word biofeedback is too recent to be found in dictionaries, but it can be defined as "an instrumental technique for human self-monitoring and control of physiological processes and psychological states, using scientific technology to present information to a subject externally about what is proceeding internally." In a more general sense, biofeedback includes operant conditioning of animals, although there is no self-monitoring involved in this aspect. (Still to be debated is the question of whether use of a polygraph to demonstrate primary perception in plants constitutes biofeedback. For more on this, see Section VI, Paraphysics.) The term was coined in 1969 at the first meeting of the Biofeedback Research Society by compressing the phrase "biological feedback."

Although biofeedback studies go back as far as 1922, it was not until the 1950s that electronic technology and psychophysiology became solidly linked in the study of somatic processes and human potential. In the 1960s biofeedback came into its own, and by 1969 there was such a large body of researchers and interested parties that some formal organization was needed. Thus the Biofeedback Research Society was born.

The Society is the best source of information on the subject. Its Feedback Bibliography *has about eight hundred titles. For information, write to: Francine Butler, Psychiatry Department #202, University of Colorado Medical Center, Denver 80220. The Aldine-Atherton annual* Biofeedback and Self-Control, *begun in 1970, is the definitive set of texts. A useful but somewhat sensationalized general introduction for the layman is* Biofeedback *by Marvin Karlins and Lewis M. Andrews (Lippincott, 1972). Jodi Lawrence's* Alpha Brain Waves *(Nash, 1972) is also valuable.*

5 The Yogi
in the Lab
John White

So Kipling was wrong. These days East *is* meeting West—and ever more the twain shall meet—especially in the laboratory.* Science is reexamining the nature of man and the findings weigh heavily on the side of the ancient wisdom of the East. The mind-body dualism characteristic of Western thought since Plato's time is being discarded as illusory, false. Instead, a unitive or holistic view of man—as held by Buddhism, Hinduism and Taoism—is developing.

Behind this is the work of Freud, Pavlov, and W. B. Cannon, the Harvard physiologist. These and other pioneers in psychosomatic medicine have demonstrated that mind and body are one, that many physical disabilities have a psychological basis, "for as a man thinketh in his heart, so is he." Man can and does become what he thinks. The "thinking" is unconscious and negative, of course, but the shell-shocked soldier, the businessman with ulcers, and the housewife with migraine all have one thing in common: a psychologically caused physical condition.

But what if the thinking were conscious, voluntary, and oriented toward hope and pleasure? Instead of reacting to vaguely defined fears and pressures, what if we began to act on the basis of clearly understood

* The world's first conference on scientific yoga was held in New Delhi, India, in December 1970. Its purpose: "To foster the evolution of Supra-Mental Man through the discovery of new techniques for developing cosmic awareness." Sponsored by Centre House in London and the International Yoga Institute in Bangalore, the four-day meeting brought scientist and yogi together "to employ this awesome pool of organized thinking for research into those divine vistas once contemplated by the ancient sages."

thought processes? Would we develop new abilities instead of disabilities? These questions have led to some strange but important research now going on.

In the past such men as Emile Coué ("Every day in every way I'm getting better and better") and Norman Vincent Peale (*The Power of Positive Thinking*) approached the problem in a rudimentary way dealing with simple attitudes and mental "sets." Now scientists are investigating altered states of consciousness and their accompanying physiological states to discover how man may gain voluntary control of his brain and other internal organs.

Western science has scoffed at the idea that a person simply could think himself into control of body functions, which by definition are involuntary. The autonomic nervous system keeps the heart, blood pressure, respiration, temperature, and digestion working even during sleep. Since these functions do not depend on volition or conscious control they traditionally have been considered involuntary—beyond deliberate intervention and regulation.

In the East, however, the opposite notion is commonly accepted. Yogis have practiced autoregulation of the body as a means of changing consciousness and ultimately attaining divine union. (*Yoga* means "yoke" or "union.") There are medically documented cases of yogis who could suspend their heartbeat for up to eighteen seconds, reverse peristalsis, even reduce metabolism and respiration so that breathing seems to cease completely and the pulse is indiscernible. In this condition some yogis have shown no ill effects when dug up after having been buried alive for days.

A yogi named Hamid Bey performed amazing feats here in America in the 1920s. In one instance three doctors using stethoscopes counted his heartbeat, one listening at each wrist and the heart. Their findings: the left wrist pulsed 96 beats a minute, the right 64, and the heart 84—all at the same time [1]. Such results have made clear the need for a reexamination of "involuntary" body functions.

Through Western technology many Eastern religious practices that seemed to verge on trickery are being validated and explained by hard data. Using such scientific equipment as the electrocardiograph (EKG) for measuring heart activity, the electroencephalograph (EEG) for measuring brain activity, the electromyograph (EMG) for measuring muscle activity, the electrooculograph (EOG) for measuring eye muscle activity, audio oscillators, digital frequency discriminators and omnidirectional tilt detectors, scientists can study what is going on inside the human organism. The technique is called physiological feedback—or biofeedback.

Norbert Weiner made the term "feedback" popular in his 1948 classic *Cybernetics*. ("Cybernetics" comes from the Greek and means "steersman" or "he who watches where he goes to control where he goes.") But the term "feedback" had been used first in an AT&T publication soon after World War II. In the next few years feedback studies mushroomed in electrical engineering literature, and biologists soon adopted the term for their own purposes.

Today the word has wide application. A shriek from a public address loudspeaker may indicate too much feedback. Applause from an audience is feedback for actors. Votes represent (or should represent) feedback to politicians. Through increased or decreased sales, dollars are a form of economic feedback for businessmen. In the body politic as in the body, feedback is essential for healthy functioning. However, these forms of feedback have been either unconscious (in the body) or imprecise (in social situations).

Now through the new technique for self-monitoring, called biofeedback, both those persons serving as experimental subjects and patients in therapy have a means of rather precise internal scanning which can open the door to learning (or in the case of neurosis, unlearning) physiological and psychological data previously beyond the range of their awareness. The theta and alpha brain waves (electrical rhythms of 5 to 7 and 9 to 12 cycles per second respectively, as measured by an EEG), heartbeat, blood pressure, body temperature, and gastrointestinal activity are subject to conscious control, just as Oriental practitioners have claimed for centuries.

Obviously, all this stands conventional medicine on its head. New ways—drugless ways—of dealing with chronic headaches, insomnia, and epilepsy and simple preventive techniques for high blood pressure and heart diseases are being developed. Biofeedback also can deal with character disorders and neurosis (although this is the least developed aspect of the field so far).

The thrust of Western medicine has been on cure but now must be oriented toward prevention, a much more efficient approach to maintaining good health. Moreover, once the preventive process becomes internalized and an adequate degree of voluntary control is achieved, the electromechanical devices become unnecessary. This work is so new that no studies are available to show how long the learning will last. Periodic retraining sessions may be necessary. But preliminary information indicates that when awareness of the relationship between biological activity and a "feeling state" has been achieved, the learning may last for months and even years.

The results of biofeedback experimentation so far indicate a hitherto overlooked human potential that can be released to improve physical and mental health, and promote creativity. Beyond that, the work seems to lead toward a marvelous convergence of science and religion.

That is still to come, however. Right now, in the laboratories . . .

Meditation and Biofeedback

Director of the awesome-sounding Psychophysiology of Consciousness Project at the Langley Porter Neuropsychiatric Institute in San Francisco is Dr. Joe Kamiya. His research concerns physiological feedback training and the psychophysiology of meditation.

"It is the possibility of correlating the electrical activity of the brain with the subjects' reports of their experience and their behavior which has intrigued me as a psychologist," Kamiya says, "for I feel it is a more solid approach than building hypothetical mental mechanisms on the basis of verbal reports alone" [2].

In the laboratory Kamiya helps persons learn to control their brain states, especially the alpha brain waves. Alpha indicates a state of relaxed, serene, yet alert wakefulness in which floating images—but no deliberate thought—occasionally are reported. EEG electrodes are attached to the scalp to detect alpha waves and a loudspeaker sounds a tone when they occur, spontaneously or not. This biofeedback technique helps subjects become aware of what is going on inside them and to control it.

In 1958 Kamiya began by having volunteers simply discriminate between the presence or absence of spontaneous alpha waves. He monitored the EEG and controlled the signal tone, sounding it randomly and asking the subject whether he thought he was in alpha. His subjects usually became 75 to 80 percent correct in their discrimination within three hours. They were not able to describe how they did it but obviously they had succeeded in internally perceiving that which they could not describe because English and most languages lack the vocabulary. (By contrast, Sanskrit has dozens of words for describing different states of consciousness, and Indian Buddhists, according to Lama Anagarika Govinda, have classified 121 mind states.)

As his work developed Kamiya wondered if persons could be trained to control brain waves as well as to discriminate between states. The answer was clearly affirmative. He found his subjects could turn on or suppress the alpha rhythm at will, although the extent to which they could enhance it in amplitude and duration remains in question. All agreed that turning on alpha was preferable to suppressing it. (Incidentally, word of a new kind of "turn-on" spread, and Kamiya reports he now is besieged by volunteers!)

Kamiya will not speak publicly about the meaning of his work except to say, "The significance is essentially unknown. That's what we're trying to find out."

Despite his professional caution the parallel between the alpha state and Zen meditation is striking. The word "Zen" came into the Japanese language about the eighth century A.D. from China where the corresponding term was *ch'an*, the meditative or dhyana school of Mahayana Buddhism using modified yoga practices. Alpha waves have proved to be the predominant brain rhythm during early and middle stages of Zen meditation, and theta wave activity predominates at the end. Zen meditation produces a relaxation of bodily and mental tension and when fully developed brings a mental condition called *satori*, deep peace and clear ecstatic consciousness and oneness with all creation. This highest state of consciousness is the goal of Zen.

Visceral Learning

While Kamiya works with brain waves in San Francisco, Dr. Neal E. Miller of Rockefeller University in New York is studying how people can learn to control their internal organs. A pioneer in the field of visceral learning, Miller is a former colleague of Dr. José Delgado, at the Yale School of Medicine, who is exploring physical control of the brain. Miller is demonstrating the possibility that men can acquire mental control of the involuntary centers of the brain that regulate internal functions.

Miller began his most important work in 1965* with the help of graduate student Jay Trowill who now teaches at the University of Massachusetts. Miller began trying to produce a change in the heart rate of rats that had been paralyzed by curare, the substance used by South American Indians for poison arrows. Curare paralyzes skeletal muscles but not internal organs. Thus the rats couldn't "cheat" by using muscular exertion to speed up or slow down their heartbeats.

After three difficult years of exploring animals, methods, and equipment, work largely done by Trowill, by 1965 all preliminary problems had been solved. Electrodes were implanted in the brains of rats so that their "pleasure centers" (in the hypothalamus near the base of the brain) could be stimulated. Every time a rat spontaneously increased his heart rate, an electronic monitoring device flashed signals to his brain. Intense pleasure presumably rewarded the rat and he thereby was conditioned to learn that he could get more of the pleasant stimulation by increasing his heart rate.

In the very first experiment Miller and Trowill found that rats with only an hour's training could increase and decrease their heart rates by some 20 beats a minute over the normal 400, about a 5 percent variance. In subsequent experiments Miller changed the machine's response to require higher degrees of control. After attaining one level of control the rats had to do even better to be rewarded. Coaxed in this manner the rats attained an average of 20 percent change—from a slow 320 beats a minute to a fast 480—and some averaged even higher.

Other experiments based on the technique of increased rewards produced equally amazing results. The rats learned to control the activity of their intestines, kidneys, stomachs, blood pressure, and brain waves. Even Miller was surprised and "greatly delighted" when the rats showed such selective control they could dilate blood vessels in one ear while the other ear remained normal.

This work has vast implications for man. Tongue-in-cheek, Miller

* Prior to this Miller had challenged the Pavlovian hypothesis of conditioned response by teaching thirsty dogs both to increase and decrease salivation, using water as a reward. According to classical conditioning theory either one or the other response was possible but not both because salivation is "involuntary."

says, "I believe that people are at least as smart as rats. The question is whether they can be trained as well."

He has begun to teach cardiac patients to control their heart rates. Electrodes in the brain to stimulate "pleasure centers" are unnecessary for human beings. Their desire for improvement is incentive enough. Wires taped to chest and leg tell a monitoring device whenever a slight heart rate deceleration occurs spontaneously and the patient hears a beeping tone that provides feedback on his condition. One man's abnormally fast rate of 95 to 100 beats a minute had dropped to about 65 after three weeks.

But Miller warns that he is not announcing a miracle cure for anything. "It could be due to placebo effect," he cautions. "Although these results are promising, a good many more tests will have to be made before we can be sure it is an effective method of treatment."

Other scientists now are investigating the regulation of blood pressure, digestive disorders, and epilepsy; the latter signals an impending seizure through recognizable brain wave activity. In Miller's report on his work, "Learning of Visceral and Glandular Responses," published in *Science*, January 31, 1969, he said that he and three others had "some success in using the method . . . to train epileptic patients in the laboratory to suppress . . . the abnormal paroxysmal spikes in their electroencephalograms."

At Harvard Medical School Drs. David Shapiro and Bernard Tursky have spent seven years teaching both healthy and ailing persons how to change blood pressure. An associate, Dr. Gary Schwartz, has four groups of students at work on a related problem: one group to raise blood pressure and heart rate simultaneously, a second to lower them simultaneously, a third to raise blood pressure while lowering heart rate and the last to increase heart rate while lowering blood pressure. And in Maryland Dr. Bernard Engel of Baltimore City Hospital is training elderly heart patients to slow their heart rates and his results show that some retain this ability for more than a year.

Is all this new? Not to some Orientals. Aldous Huxley in *Tomorrow and Tomorrow and Tomorrow* wrote about an Eastern friend, a yogi, to whom "pain is merely an opinion." The yogi proved it by sticking skewers through his flesh. He also could slow his heart to 40 beats a minute and increase it to 150 merely by thinking of it. Huxley comments, "It would be extremely convenient to be able to treat neuralgia or lumbago as opinions, to calm the heart, to take the cramps out of one's viscera in moments of emotional stress, to plunge at will into profound and restorative sleep."

It may be that science is about to provide this convenience.

Training for Creativity

In a small room of the Menninger Foundation research building in Topeka, Kansas, Dr. Elmer E. Green and his wife Alyce use biofeedback to teach subjects self-regulation of internal states. Their subject wears a special jacket equipped with a built-in respiration gauge that gives a readout to one of the pens on their 24-channel polygraph. Other channels record the raw EEG on left and right sides of the brain; frequency of theta, alpha, delta, and beta brain waves; muscle tension; blood volume and flow in the subject's hand; galvanic skin potential and response; and heart rate. Brain waves, temperature changes, and arm muscle tension also register as vertical bars of light on a screen in front of the subject. These light bars give him an easily understood indication of his internal physiological activity.

First the man in the jacket tries to relax his arm completely. Monitored by an electromyograph, his muscle relaxation records graphically as the bar of light lengthens, rising five inches from bottom to top—100 percent success. Next he wills the temperature in his hand to rise. Thermistors on his skin detect the heat change and in a few minutes a second bar of light reaches its maximum height, equal to the first. The hand temperature has risen 10° Fahrenheit.

Both muscle tension and temperature are functions of the peripheral nervous system. Thus, the subject has performed exercises preliminary to the conscious production of sustained alpha waves, for which voluntary control of the central nervous system is a requisite. Now the subject begins to turn on alpha and soon a third bar of light rises to its maximum height. He has achieved 100 percent continuous alpha for ten seconds. The bar continues to rise or fall as it computes an average percentage of sustained alpha over ten-second periods.

Even if their work stopped here, the Greens have obtained many worthwhile results. One of their subjects has eliminated her chronic headaches for almost a year, using techniques learned at the Menninger

Lab. She also has alleviated her long-lasting insomnia by increasing the temperature of her feet at night.

The matter of temperature control has direct relation to the phenomenon called *tumo*, which is the yogi's term for the power to regulate body heat voluntarily. In Tibet, lamas have been photographed standing naked in the snows for up to twenty-four hours as an act of worship or endurance. The College of Magic Ritual (which existed there before the Red Chinese took over) once offered courses in telepathy, clairvoyance, and tumo. The final tumo exam required a student to sit naked on a frozen lake and to use the heat of his body to dry one by one a pile of wet sheets. This ability has been recorded and documented but never adequately explained.

However, the Greens are interested primarily in experimenting with lowering alpha frequency and increasing the percentage of theta rhythm. For this research two more bars of light have been added to the feedback screen in the lab to indicate lowering alpha and continuous ten-second theta.

This research—voluntary control of alpha and theta brain rhythms—in Elmer Green's words, is specifically to explore "the general processes, conditions and contents of consciousness during a state of deep reverie." Reverie, he says, is a state of inward-turned abstract attention or internal scanning akin to some dreamlike states. This condition is associated with the low-frequency alpha and theta waves. In reverie has been detected the hypnagogiclike imagery that is "the *sine qua non* of creativity for many outstanding people."

The hypnagogic state of consciousness occurs in the transition from wakefulness to sleep and from sleep to wakefulness (in the latter case called "hypnopompic"). In these states dreamlike images appear behind the closed eyelids, coming into awareness fully developed rather than having been logically or discursively developed by the intellect.

Green notes many instances in which unconscious processes reveal themselves to the waking self through hypnagogiclike imagery in words, symbols, and gestalts that result in brilliantly creative solutions to perplexing problems. German chemist Kekule's theory of molecular construction arose from a series of reveries in which he saw atoms gamboling before his eyes. "I saw how the larger ones formed a chain," he wrote. "I spent part of the night putting on paper at least sketches of these dream forms."

Jules Henri Poincaré (1854–1912), the outstanding mathematician of his age, arrived at some of his most important discoveries in a similar fashion, and Robert Louis Stevenson envisioned full-blown publishable plots.

"There are literally hundreds of other anecdotes which show beyond doubt that in some way not yet perfectly understood, reverie, hypnagogic imagery . . . and creativity are associated," the Greens now declare.

Apparently reverie is a naturally occurring condition that may be used for problem-solving and other creative activity. Through biofeedback these dreamlike states may be brought into waking life—not as the hallucinations of a sleep-deprived person or a "speed freak," but in a healthy and constructive manner.

Biofeedback and ESP

Today we accept the idea that the human species has psychic ability (called "psi") through which paranormal phenomena can manifest. Whether everyone has the ability is moot. J. B. Rhine in *The Reach of the Mind* hypothesizes that psi is an ancient faculty, one that man used in prehistory but that was isolated and made dormant when the cortex "exploded" into growth and overlaid the older parts of the brain about a hundred thousand years ago. In Rhine's view everyone possesses some degree of psi and developing it is mainly a matter of recovering it.

On the other hand, some authorities—Arthur Clarke, for example, in *Childhood's End*—think that psi is a new human faculty. He sees its emergence as due to an ongoing evolutionary process by which more and more individuals are using a latent talent.

The question of whether psi is old or new remains unresolved. What is apparent and important, however, is that psi ability is real. In the training of a yogi, for example, there comes a point in his development when he may discover enormous mental powers called *siddhis*. Not only extrasensory phenomena (telepathy, clairvoyance, precognition, and retrocognition) but also psychokinetic phenomena (levitation, teleportation, astral projection) may appear. The trainee's guru traditionally directs him away from exploration of these powers because they represent mere byways along the path toward the goal of yoga: divine union.

Now science is using biofeedback to investigate the nature of the psi ability associated with yogic training. In 1961 three Indian researchers— Anand, Chhina and Singh—established the presence of alpha rhythms in yogis practicing meditation. Following their lead other researchers are assessing possible electroencephalograph correlates of ESP, especially alpha rhythms.

At the Dream Laboratory of Maimonides Medical Center in Brooklyn, research associate Charles Honorton is exploring the effects of feedback-augmented alpha activity on his subjects' ability to guess the order of symbols in a standard deck of ESP cards. The hypothesis is: "Subjects showing significant increments in EEG-alpha activity following a series of operant training sessions would also show significant gains in clairvoyant card-guessing performance" [3].

Results of Mr. Honorton's EEG feedback studies so far have not made it possible to assess the hypothesis. The trouble, he reports, is that only one of the ten subjects showed a significant increase in alpha during the EEG feedback condition (as opposed to a nonfeedback run in which alpha was also measured). Therefore the study must be regarded as insufficient. Several variables could have affected the study, however, so a series of alpha-training studies are in progress to test the hypothesis further. The near-complete second study, Honorton says, has had good results in alpha training, and lab personnel are in the process of analyzing the ESP results.

ESP investigation is not new in the Dream Laboratory. Since 1962 Stanley Krippner, its director, and Montague Ullman, head of the department of psychiatry at the Center, have been using sleeping subjects to show that telepathy exists and can occur in the dream state. They have interpreted their findings as "supporting the idea that extrasensory effects can be made to appear in dreams on a greater-than-chance basis" [4].

Elsewhere and meanwhile things are humming along electric-well. The Biofeedback Research Society's first meeting in October 1969 in Santa Monica, Calif., had 142 members participating in three full days of intensive discussion and information exchange. Reports on ten subjects included measurement of subjective space and its changes, feedback and ESP, condition and control of autonomic functions and methodologies of feedback and their clinical applications.

By March 1970 membership was nearing 300. The Society's director, Dr. Barbara Brown of the Veterans' Hospital in Sepulveda, Calif., issued a summary listing 136 projects in progress among members. Typical descriptions ran:

Attempt to train old and young subjects to vary the frequency of the alpha rhythm and to observe the effect on ESP scoring.

Development of a theory of consciousness.

Use of feedback of heart rate and electromyograph feedback with psychotherapy patients.

A taxonomy of altered states of consciousness.

Alpha rhythm and psi-effects.

Investigating EEG and other variables as predictors of epileptic seizure.

By word of mouth, through conferences, personal correspondence and professional publications, news of biofeedback research was disseminated. Established periodicals such as *Journal of the American Society for Psychical Research, Psychophysiology*, and Montreal's *R. M. Bucke Newsletter* have helped to spread the word. Two new journals, only a few years old, are widely read among biofeedback researchers and others concerned with states of awareness. *The Journal for the Study of Consciousness* originates with Dr. C. A. Musès in Santa Barbara, Calif., while farther up the coast in Stanford, Anthony J. Sutich edits the *Journal of Transpersonal Psychology*. Prestigious names stud their editorial advisory boards: Alan Watts, Arthur Koestler, Gardner Murphy, Montague Ullman, Ralph Metzner (former editor of the now-defunct *Psychedelic Review*), and until his recent death, Abraham Maslow. Books such as Rasa Gustaitis' *Turning On*, a popularized survey of many nondrug methods of sensory enhancement and behavior change, and Charles T. Tart's solidly professional *Altered States of Consciousness* have had important impact.

Where is all this likely to lead?

Joe Kamiya says that his work will be aimed at making objective maps of subjective space as a means of describing experiences more accurately. Ecstasy, for example, might be described in electrical, biochemical, and physiological terms as so much alpha, so much theta, etc. This is not to say that achieving a particular frequency and amplitude on the EEG chart means one has attained *samadhi* (the readings might indicate only a superficial state of relaxation) but undoubtedly they are a part of such a state of awareness.

Kamiya notes that four primary qualities—sweet, sour, salt, and bitter —account for our sense of taste. He wonders about the primary dimensions of consciousness. Is it possible to say there are x number of states or moods such as calm, agitated, sleepy, infatuated, infuriated? What are the physiological characteristics of each state and is there any correlation between them and psychiatric disorders?

Better techniques for discrimination and control must be developed, Kamiya says. "I feel that the rather simple kind of electronic analysis that has been done so far doesn't do justice to the EEG, and more complex analyses using computers will be required." Present gross measurements will be replaced by more sophisticated ones through on-line computer analysis, for there are many variables to be measured. For example, alpha can occur in greater amounts on one side of the brain than the other at the same time. What, if anything, does this indicate?

Actually the matter of brain waves is somewhat confusing because scientists have not yet decided whether there are clear divisions indicating distinct phenomena and separate brain functions or whether brain waves form a continuous spectrum. Arbitrarily, delta waves are defined as ranging from 0.5 to 4 cycles per second, theta from 5 to 8 cps, alpha from 9 to 12 (some say 9 to 12, others 8 to 13) and beta from 13 to 30 cps.

"They're divided like that for convenience's sake," says Barbara Brown. A reading of 8.5 cps might be high theta or low alpha, depending on the interpretation of the operator, since the EEG reading is merely a statistical summary of noise activity of synapses (where nerve impulses are transmitted from one to the other) and this goes on at the top of the head, not deep within the brain. Are qualitatively different processes going on in delta, theta, alpha, and beta? Is there a difference between the theta that sometimes occurs in sleep and the theta of Zen meditation? Does low amplitude alpha relate to a set of feelings and mental states different from high amplitude alpha? Answers to these and other questions are not yet agreed on.

As a further complication, there is now some question as to whether the alpha rhythm is a brain wave at all. In New Scientist (March 1970) Olof Lippold of University College in London published his findings, which indicate that alpha rhythms are artifacts of eye movements, not brain activity. In his opinion, the background tremor of the external eye muscles, a constant condition due to tension, is the source of alpha rhythms. Perhaps "brain waves" do not mirror brain processes at all.*

Whatever the case, Elmer Green thinks it may be possible to develop a "science of consciousness." Working definitions could be derived using biofeedback tools and techniques for investigating the physiological and psychological dimensions of states of internal awareness. In addition, Dr. Green's work points up the obvious benefits of psychosomatic self-regulation to avoid moodiness and tension, to help nature keep the body healthy, and to enhance creativity.

A science of consciousness assumes a theory of consciousness—on which there are widely variant points of view. Roger Wescott, head of the anthropology department at Drew University, speculates (in *The Divine Animal*) that the stuff of consciousness may be bioluminescence, a form of internal radiation generated and perceived by the brain. But Gunther Stent, a molecular biologist at Berkeley, writes in *The Coming of the Golden Age* that the brain is not capable of explaining itself. That is, the relationship between brain mechanisms and mind, while accounting for the contents of consciousness, will not fully explain the *fact* of consciousness itself.

Stent's argument is a powerful one. A listing of the electrophysiological concomitants to various altered states of consciousness does not equal an explanation of those states.

The determinants of consciousness, according to ancient oriental traditions, are far more than simple body processes. In those traditions, consciousness in people is a reflection or a localization of Universal Consciousness, of the intelligence pervading the cosmos, residing everywhere, even to a low degree in the crudest forms of matter. All creation is interconnected in a great chain of being. The deepest center of man is the deepest center of the universe and the person who is truly self-knowing is universally aware, cosmically conscious. Therefore he can say, "I am the universe; I am Universal Mind."

Scientists in the West, except for a few mavericks, have long disregarded the problem of consciousness, having no operational definition of it. The late Sir Russell Brain considered the problem and insisted that "consciousness is a primary element in experience and cannot be defined in terms of anything else" [5]. However, through scientific study

* That this is not the case was proven by obtaining alpha waves from people who had lost their eyes, including the extraocular muscles. *Editor.*

of creativity in recent years, the way is opening for a recognition, a re-knowing, of high truths in Eastern religions and myths about the nature of consciousness.

In the act of creation men come closest to realizing their divine nature. Saints and seers who have achieved enlightened states frequently resort to images and metaphors based on sexual union to describe their experiences. The mystical meaning of sex is one path to understanding the mystery of divine creation.

Then there is the intriguing connection between dreams and creativity—the revelation, Ira Progoff says in *Myths, Dreams and Religion* that dreams "are a primary medium for intuitive insights into the ultimate nature of human existence."

Art gives us another key to unlocking the riddle of the universe. In the artist's act of creation he comes closest to self-transcendence. James Joyce recognized this and used it in *A Portrait of the Artist as a Young Man*. Toward the end, when Stephen Dedalus is expounding his theory of art, Joyce has him say, "The mystery of esthetic like that of material creation is accomplished. The artist, like the God of the creation, remains within or behind or beyond or above his handiwork, invisible."

If we take at face value the description of creative acts given by artists and scientists alike, our conclusion must be that the true creator is an outside force or principle acting through the medium of a human being. "A thought occurred to me . . . " "An idea came into my mind . . ." "I was struck by the notion that . . ." Conscious individual action becomes important only when the conception is complete. In the meantime, creativity involves a passive waiting until, in those deep collective layers of the psyche, something has happened to the individual that then rises to awareness.

John Dewey, less recognized in psychology than in education but highly respected in both, noted that the concept of mind as a private psychic consciousness identifiable with the self is fairly modern. "In both the Greek and medieval periods," he wrote in *Democracy and Education*, "the rule was to regard the individual as a channel through which a universal and divine intelligence operated. The individual was in no true sense the knower; the knower was the 'Reason' which operated through him."

Aldous Huxley wrote in "The Education of an Amphibian" (*Tomorrow and Tomorrow and Tomorrow*, 1964): "My existence does not

depend on the fact that I am thinking (*Cogito ergo sum.*—Descartes),*
it depends on the fact that, whether I know it or not, I am being thought
—being thought by a mind much greater than the consciousness which
I ordinarily identify with myself."

In the act of creation men can recover—with new awareness—the
primal unity with the Creator called God, Buddha, Allah, Brahma, Tao,
etc., from which they came. Science seems to be approaching this most
fundamental insight through the study of states of consciousness—especially the higher creative states—and the nature of the brain-mind
relationship.

Arthur Koestler, following Dr. Paul B. MacLane's theory, suggests in
The Ghost in the Machine (1968) that man's predicament is the result of
an incomplete or aberrant evolutionary experiment. Man, Koestler says,
really has three brains, not one. He has a reptilian brain (the medulla ob-
longata, evolutionarily the oldest part), a lower mammalian brain, and
the neocortex. The neocortex performs logical thinking, while emotions
and human irrationality are the province of the other parts that have not
been properly integrated and brought under control. The result: a schizoid
brain, a schizoid society.

Biofeedback apparently offers an approach to integration of our
schizoid brains—the same integration achieved in the past by mystics,
meditators, and yogis who spent years in disciplined preparation for the
enlightenment. It appears possible that science now has the opportunity
to turn feedback into feedforward and thereby to help achieve what
José Delgado calls a "psychocivilized society." Such a prospect seems
remote, but the need for achieving it never has been greater. It is abundantly clear that unless there is a general expansion of consciousness the
evolutionary experiment called man will cancel itself.

This change of consciousness can come through a new appreciation
of ancient wisdom. In the process of relearning this wisdom, modern
science may attain omniscience. But this will not elevate science above
religion. Rather, it presages a synthesis on a higher level, a fusion of
insight and instinct, a development of informed intuition and emotional
understanding.

We started with Plato and the mind-body dualism characteristic of
Western thought since his time. It is fitting that we end with him. In

* "I think; therefore I am."

the utopian state which now seems possible through technology, information will become transformation and with it will come general agreement with Plato's definition of science: "the clear intellectual perception of fundamental moral truth."

References

1. Luce, Gay Gaer. *Current Research on Sleep and Dreams*. United States Department of Health, Education, and Welfare Publication No. 1389, 1967.
2. Kamiya, Joe. "Operant Control of EEG Alpha Rhythm," in *Altered States of Consciousness*, Charles T. Tart, ed. John Wiley: New York, 1969.
3. "An Exploratory Study of Feedback-Augmented EEG-Alpha Activity and ESP Card-Guessing Performance," prepared by The William C. Menninger Dream Laboratory of Maimonides Medical Center, January 1970.
4. Ullman, Montague, and Krippner, Stanley. "An Experimental Approach to Dreams and Telepathy." *American Journal of Psychiatry*, March 1970.
5. Brain, Russell. *Diseases of the Nervous System*. Oxford University Press: London, 1955.

6 EEG Alpha Feedback and

Subjective States of Consciousness:

A Subject's Introspective Overview

Durand Kiefer

Editor's Preface

This report is a "subject's introspective overview"* of "the first feedback *sesshin*" conducted as a psychophysiological experiment at the research department of the Veterans Administration Hospital in Bedford, Massachusetts, in February of 1970. It was originally prepared at the request of Dr. Thomas B. Mulholland, director of the Perception Laboratory at the hospital, who gave the report its title.

Dr. Mulholland, a past president of the Biofeedback Research Society and a leading authority in this field, in a paper published in the spring 1972 issue of *The R. M. Bucke Memorial Society Newsletter-Review*, says "when alpha is occurring abundantly, most people report that they are not paying attention, are not looking or seeing actively, yet are not drowsy. This state is one of being awake but relaxed. . . . If one

* The first Feedback Sesshin, February 2–18, 1970, held at the Perception Laboratory, Veterans Administration Hospital, Bedford, Mass. The meanings of the Zen terms, *sesshin, kinhin, dokusan*, etc., are more fully developed in the writer's papers, "Meditation and Biofeedback" in *The Highest State of Consciousness*, John White, ed., Doubleday-Anchor: Garden City, N.Y., 1972; and "What Is Mu?" in *Psychologia*, 1971, Vol. XIV, No. 2. The terms alpha and feedback as used in this account always refer to occipital-parietal EEG-alpha-wave audio-monotone binary feedback as used in this experiment, unless otherwise noted.

stays in a state of relaxed wakefulness for a long time without going to sleep, what happens? . . ."

It was largely to answer this question that "the first feedback *sesshin*" experiment was conducted in Dr. Mulholland's laboratory, in a sort of sixteen-day meditation marathon, from February 2 to 18, with Durand Kiefer as the subject. At that time Mr. Kiefer had had about ten years of daily Zen Buddhist meditation practice, which trains one to stay alert while relaxed, and this practice had included about fifteen "group intensive" Zen training sessions of four to seven days each. The style of these *sesshin*, as they are called in Zen, is described more fully in Mr. Kiefer's two earlier papers written in preparation for the Bedford laboratory *sesshin*, "Meditation and Biofeedback" published in *The Highest State of Consciousness*, John White, ed. (Doubleday-Anchor, 1972) and "What Is Mu?" published in *Psychologia*, Vol. XIV, No. 2, 1971 and condensed in *Mental Health Digest*, Vol. 4, No. 4, 1972. The Bedford laboratory *sesshin* differed from the Zen Buddhist format in important respects dictated mainly by exigencies of the scientific setting and personnel availability. But throughout, meditation was conducted daily from 5 A.M. to 9 P.M. with two-hour breaks for meals at 7, 12, and 5, as commonly done in Zen practice, but with experimenter-monitored EEG alpha feedback operating for three 45-minute periods between 9 and noon, and two between 2 and 4 P.M. In addition, corollary EEG-EOG sleep studies were conducted every third night. Mr. Kiefer usually wore some seven head electrodes, including EOG leads, at the corners of his eyes throughout each day, having had a special "holey" haircut for the purpose. But after one notable experience in the corridors of the hospital in this harness, while on his way to eat in the staff dining room, he was moved to take the remainder of his meals in his room in the research building. Bedford is a psychiatric hospital. The type of feedback used is described as "occipital-parietal EEG-alpha-wave audio-monotone binary feedback." Cdr. Kiefer's report follows.

Report

No mystical experience of the nature described by Pahnke and Richards in *Altered States of Consciousness* (C. T. Tart, ed.) resulted from the sixteen-day feedback sesshin as subject had hoped from previous separate Zen sesshin and EEG feedback experiences. Furthermore, the subject is convinced that achievement of this type of experience through meditation with occipital-parietal alpha feedback alone is very improbable, if not impossible. This conviction is based on the conclusion from feedback experience that alpha is simply a "steady state" phenomenon of the neural system interlocking brain and musculature, especially the oculomotor subsystem.*

This seemed apparent on the one hand from the ease with which very long alpha bursts could be maintained, almost continuously, for several minutes to over an hour if the cortex-motor-muscle complex became essentially static or inactive in a propioceptive mode that felt like a general paralysis or a conscious general anesthesia.† And on the other hand, by the ease with which alpha was interrupted by the slightest conscious change of either mental, neural, or muscular tension, such as by merely swallowing, for instance.‡

Thus the amount or distribution of tension in the brain-nerve-muscle complex seemed to have little or no effect upon alpha, while the slightest conscious change in the amount or distribution of tension blocked alpha instantly, but only for the duration of the change or transition, if it was brief. Hence it was possible to slowly shift body attitude from cross-legged on the floor to semireclining in a chair, for instance, after an hour of almost continuous alpha without interrupting the alpha-on time except for the few seconds necessary to orient the movement visually. Painful tension in the scalp, neck, or shoulders could continue for a half-hour (in the floor-sitting position) with almost continuous alpha and with the gradual diminution of the pain to a pleasantly neutral sensation in the same site, which could continue for another hour of very high alpha occurrence.

The most consistent and instantaneous alpha-blocker proved to be drowsiness, which often occurred after a few minutes of very high alpha ("steady state") incidence. It was noted several times, after longer con-

---

* Recent evidence indicates that EEG alpha is a sinusoidal pulse resonance in idle motor neurons in the brain, most notably the oculomotor neurons, but not necessarily confined to them.

† Giving rise to curiosity about the EEG of paralytics, and anesthesized and blind persons.

‡ Swallowing became quite difficult, although imperative, after ten or fifteen minutes of the "anesthesic" experience.

tinuous alpha periods, that a mere flicker of the order of 1/10 second in alertness would cause a corresponding flicker in the alpha feedback tone. On the other hand, if the essentially contentless alertness became active interest in any task, like alpha-enhancement for instance, this would also block alpha, most probably because of the covert corresponding motor-nerve and muscle tension which, according to Edmund Jacobson, invariably accompanies all active (self-conscious) "mental activity."

Thus continuous alpha-on in feedback, like dhyana or samadhi in Zen meditation, requires a very delicate regulation of the nervous system to maintain an exquisite balance between the degree of relaxation that produces drowsiness or sleep on the one hand, and the degree of active interest, or conscious effort (arousal or orientation in psychology—"attachment" or "clinging" in Zen) that produces alpha-blocking and ego-consciousness on the other hand.§

There seem to be two devices that can be used to achieve this balance, one "active" and one "passive," the latter much more effective and comfortable than the former, and usually developing from it, when not achieved initially.

§ When asked how to defeat drowsiness in *zazen* (sitting meditation) the Zen master Yasutani usually replies, "Increase your interest in zazen. If you fall asleep you are clearly not interested enough in what you are doing." However, if interest is sufficient only to prolong one's practice of zazen for several hours in any of the prescribed Zen postures, physical pain soon solves the drowsiness problem. But of course immensely increases the difficulty of maintaining the requisite passivity of mind, body and spirit! ("Blessed are the poor in spirit for theirs is the Kingdom of Heaven.")

The subject hoped, in volunteering for the experiment, that alpha feedback tone, from previous experience, would sufficiently promote the Zen master's interest-requirement to eliminate the pain substitute, without reaching the critical arousal level, but this did not occur after the first few days, so it was necessary to abandon the comfortable lounging chair that is usually provided feedback subjects and take up the painful zazen posture on the floor cushions simply to defeat drowsiness. Thus establishing that pain may be as much a necessary element of the feedback sesshin as of the Zen sesshin. It leaves open the question, however, of how the subject stayed awake for seven consecutive hours while meditating in a totally comfortable "womb-tank" in an entirely light-and-sound-proof sensory limitation laboratory several years before, after falling asleep in the same setting three hours out of four the day before that. An interesting answer may lie in the absence of any feedback, as well as any other stimulus in the sensory deprivation setting. Instrumentation was essentially the same in both experiments.

The passive style is marked by an alert but neutral, or indifferent, mental and emotional attitude or mood—a disinterested attention or un-self-conscious observation or alertness that William James calls dispersed attention, Krishnamurti calls passive awareness or alert passivity, and E. E. Green paradoxically labels passive volition. It is probably the condition ultimately produced by Jacobson's Progressive Relaxation, Schultz's Autogenic Training, Charlotte Selver's Sensory Awareness, and Bates's Seeing Without Looking, as described by Aldous Huxley in his book, *The Art of Seeing*.

If this general passivity could be permitted to happen at the outset of one of the five or six 45-minute feedback sessions each day without the permissiveness inducing drowsiness, with 5 to 15 minutes alpha would usually become almost continuous, and a comfortable "locked-on" propioception would occur in which it was felt that one's general passivity was indefinitely and effortlessly secure from any kind of interruption. This was the subjective state that usually produced the anesthesia that was finally interrupted after an hour or two only by something as fundamental as bladder pressure, thirst, hunger, or compassion for the attendant in the control room.

If the passive mode could not be allowed for 5 or 10 consecutive minutes at the start of a feedback (meditation) period because of wandering attention, hyperattention, or drowsiness, sometimes it could be painfully developed by taking up the unsupported, straight-backed, cross-legged Zen sitting posture on floor cushions, spreading a white towel across the knees, lowering the eyes and eyelids until the eyes were relaxed but a narrow gleam of white was just barely visible in the bottom of the otherwise dark field of vision, and then keeping this white screen blank of images or shadows by vigorously, but silently, chanting the Nembutsu in a rapid rhythm for 5 to 10 minutes without a break. If the chant could be maintained for 10 minutes with nothing moving on either the white screen or the dark screen of the eyelids, the brain rhythm was usually firmly interlocked with either the heartbeat or the breathing, and would continue automatically until dissolved by the general anesthesia that usually developed.

This "active" method, suggested by the blank-screen, or white paper, metaphor of some meditation teachers, is also reminiscent of Hubert Benoit's highly entertaining cinema-screen model of consciousness, with superimposed simultaneous exterior (real) and interior (imaginary) motion picture films, which may be slowed and finally stopped and dissolved, one at a time, by first closing the eyes and then meditating for long periods, as described in his psychological study of zazen called *The Supreme Doctrine*. Of course, meditation (dhyana, samadhi) is not complete until the static image of the blank screen itself, and then of its viewer, have also dissolved from consciousness. According to the literature, this is the last stage before satori, or enlightenment.

In the early stages of the "locked-on passive" or anesthetic condition, it was found that quite clear thinking could occur without interrupting continuous alpha. The nature of such thoughts varied greatly from a brief speculation on the physiology of the experience at hand to the casual visual recall of emotionally various memories.* So long as these brief word or picture sequences were not pursued (or "grasped" in the

* It is remarkable how creative, or at least imaginative, these "passive" thoughts could be expanded later between meditations. The vitality of the speculations thus recorded elsewhere could have sprung from the rigor with which any speculation was usually suppressed during the sesshin, or from the rest thus afforded the creative faculties during 10 hours of courting subjective passivity every day. In any case, creativity is often observed to accompany mind-quieting practices; like Krishnamurti's walking, Einstein's fiddling, and Mulholland's harmonicating.

In his famous *Platform Sutra* the Sixth Patriarch of Zen, Hui-neng, taught that it is not thinking that blocks our realization of the original (divine) nature that we are all born with—it is our love of thinking, our addiction and our loyalty (clinging) to it. As it is this automated thinking, according to Buddhist doctrine, that *is* the self that we experience as separate from our total field of consciousness (*cogito ergo sum*), the experience of a sort of hopeless slavery to the thinking habit sheds much light on both the Christian and Hindu mystics' meaning in contrasting love of self with love of God, God being their word for the undifferentiated, nonconceptual, or thoughtless consciousness we have all experienced occasionally, at least in early childhood.

Inasmuch as this undifferentiated consciousness most probably resides or originates in the diencephalon, we can say that God, or at least heaven (the kingdom of God) is the diencephalon, probably the seat of every "absolute" sense in all animals including man. If so, the dictum "Seek ye first the Kingdom of God and His Absolute Rightness (infallibility) and all (else) will be given you" takes on new meaning.

This may be a very novel view in both science and religion, but it may also be the elusive common denominator between them. Another is the general interchangeability of the concepts of energy and spirit as used by the two disciplines, including their respective "laws" or doctrines of conversion and conservation of energy or spirit.

Zen terminology) they went their placid way "like the reflection of geese that fly over the pond without disturbing it," and promptly disappeared from consciousness. The instant that they became "considerations," however, for elaboration or action of any sort, it was the alpha feedback tone that disappeared, and abruptly. The subject could then choose where his "heart"—his deepest interest—lay: in daydreaming, creative or otherwise, or in meditation, as signalled in this instance by a pleasant musical tone. By a very simple equation this choice could be seen as self-interest versus universal, or transcendent, interest and readily invited more speculation on the difference, if any, between "underlying interest," or motive that appears to direct our attention, and attention itself, in the neurophysiological sense.†

The anesthetic effect of continuous alpha incidence for periods of ¼ to 1¾ hours for several consecutive days failed to accumulate in the expected trancelike profound passivity that had previously been experienced on three occasions after six days of sesshin without feedback. Although some trancelike detachment was noted following the longest continuous alpha-on runs, it fell far short of the almost total rapture that appears to be a precondition of a veritable satori. This is quite unaccountable at this writing, in view of the promise of previous lengthy alpha feedback sessions of deeper entrancement with a little more duration. Perhaps an explanation lies in those reports of feedback experiments, both EEG and EMG, in which it is noted that naivete appears to be a distinct asset in learning control of subjective states. Especially since the same phenomenon has been observed of Zen sesshin initiates.

On one occasion what felt like a deep hypnotic trance (to this subject who had never previously experienced one), that occurred with feedback turned off for 10 or 15 minutes following a long continuous maintenance of the tone, very readily dissolved when it was interrupted by talk, and the experimenter reported that there was little or no alpha on the polygraph during this interlude.

At times, upon completion of several feedback sessions of an hour or more that generally displayed a highly satisfactory alpha occurrence, the

† This question of underlying self or transcendent interest, or motivation, seems particularly germane to the training of attention capabilities in school-children, who can probably be conditioned to pay attention to stimuli, in their self-interest, which a deeper interest transcends, possibly from infancy inasmuch as self-consciousness and therefore self-interest seem to be generally absent in infants.

phenomenon of an almost overwhelming affection for the experimenter (always the first person encountered) that had been first noted some years ago after sensory isolation experiments was noted again. In each case it was part of a general euphoria—very possibly of a simple egoistic nature, not surprising after several hours of almost continuous psychological "reinforcement."

At other times, when egoistic arousal by the tone, in a self-conscious effort to keep it on, promptly turned it off (probably because of the unconscious motor-nerve response noted by Jacobson), so that it was impossible for whole periods of 45 minutes to boost alpha percent-time much beyond 50, subject wondered dismally why the expected physiological conditioning action of feedback was obviously *kaput*, if it had ever existed. It was supposed that the greatest promise of feedback was its operant conditioning properties acting directly upon neural channels to alter an autonomic behavior (like visualizing) thus freeing self-will (the ego) from the nearly impossible psychological task of destroying itself when necessary to sanity.‡

‡ Of sanity the British psychiatrist R. D. Laing says in *The Politics of Experience* (Ballentine, 1966, pp. 144–145): "True sanity entails in one way or another the dissolution of the normal ego, that false self competently adjusted to our alienated social reality; the emergence of the "inner" archetypal mediators of divine power, and through this death a rebirth, and the eventual reestablishment of a new kind of ego functioning, the ego now being the servant of the divine, no longer its betrayer."

On February 18, 1970, in reply to a question of procedure from Erik Peper, who was conducting the experiment reported here, T. B. Mulholland replied, "A human subject is not a rat in a maze." Dr. Mulholland was, of course, simply expressing a generous point of view. But in physiological conditioning of saintly behavior lies the only hope of the race for tolerable survival in this century. There is no social solution to the problem of "evil"—of individual interior conflict, and it is always reflected, collectively, in society. Because individuals constitute society, "psychological" conflict constitutes social conflict. We will not have a better society until we have better people. And people-improvement is necessarily an individual, private project for each person.

But science (and technology) can help, even as religion (or rather mysticism) has helped, very occasionally, and still helps. The crucial question for science is finally: Do enough people want to be better, assuming better means more saintly, more loving and joyous, more selfless and less self-conscious? There is only one way to find out: offer them a reasonable chance at a price they can afford to pay, both psychologically and substantially. Meanwhile, the psychologist's definition of euphoria, according to Webster's, is "an abnormal feeling of buoyant vigor and health." *Regarde la condition humaine!!*

If by operant conditioning is meant a physiological conditioning that does have the capacity unconsciously to alter neural habit patterns through feedback, then it seemed clear to subject that EEG occipital-parietal alpha feedback is not operant conditioning. This provided further ground for his conclusion that a so-called mystical experience was probably not within the capacity of the type of feedback used in this experiment, if of any.

Another notable experience occurring during meditation (feedback) sessions was difficulty in distinguishing between drowsing and waking dreams, or fantasies, when consciousness was weaving in and out of the hypnagogic state. A waking fantasy seemed to carry over into a drowse, and vice versa. This confusion emphasized the fantastic nature of some daydreaming that is commonly regarded as cognition, and the cognitive nature of some hypnagogic dreaming that is usually regarded as fantastic!§

Possibly the most significant result of the experiment, at least for the subject of it, was an unscheduled and unexpected sudden change, on the fifth day, of the meditation method employed to enhance alpha. After extensive training for almost eight years in zazen, the sitting meditation of the Zen Buddhists, and after writing a paper "What Is Mu?" explaining one method of zazen taught by a Zen master in sesshin, and after proposing this meditation for this feedback sesshin, the subject shifted abruptly, in the middle of a feedback meditation session, from the Zen Buddhist meditation on the koan *mu*, to the Shin Buddhist meditation on the Nembutsu, which he adhered to rigidly, with the exception of one brief return of a few minutes to *mu*, for the remaining eleven days of the sesshin, although he had had no previous training in the use of the Nembutsu.

The shift was made in desperation when Zen koan practice for ten hours a day for four and a half days had failed completely to produce any appreciable subjective de-automatization, in Deikman's term (Deikman,

§ It is believed in some meditation circles that when one learns to stop daydreaming at will, his night dreaming ceases also and he enjoys always an uncommon, deep, and dreamless sleep that is much more refreshing than a restless sleep beset with dreams, whether good or bad. It was the great contemporary mystic, Krishnamurti, who replied, when asked the significance of dreaming, "If we pay enough attention to our subconscious when we are awake, it doesn't have so much to say when we are asleep."

A. "De-automatization and the Mystic Experience," *Psychiat.* 1966, 29, 329–343). Or any other noticeable effect, including consistent alpha. And the new method was embraced enthusiastically and permanently when it produced, within 10 or 15 minutes, all the desired effects, both subjectively and objectively, including notably improved alpha reinforcement, as described earlier for the "active" mode of meditation.

Although the experimenters, when informed of this change, seemed to attach no particular significance to it, both its immediate and continuous consequences were, and have been, crucial. Technically, the experiment ceased, at the point of this change, to be a sesshin, which is a term usually applied only to a certain Zen Buddhist practice. But there was always some doubt of the term's accuracy in this instance, mainly because of the absence of a qualified meditation coach, or Roshi, but also because of the absence of a group of subjects or students. It was because of these shortcomings of the experiment as a sesshin that it was not too difficult for its subject to abandon all his previous sesshin training in favor of an experiment of his own in a meditation style new to him.

More significant, however, is that this shift in meditation introduced the anomaly of a vigorous rhythmical subjective behavior to the experiment, which in turn quite promptly improved the alpha percent time, and subsequently, provided a fairly reliable method of boosting alpha time to very high percentages whenever an initially passive mood was not present at the beginning of scheduled feedback periods, as noted earlier.

And finally, its greatest significance lies in its persistence into the postexperiment daily life of the subject, where it has already, within a week, notably changed his entire life style, at least subjectively. This is attributed to the well-reputed power of the Nembutsu to establish itself with great persistence, when encouraged, not only in the devotee's consciousness, but his unconscious, as well.

The Nembutsu is simply a Japanese six-syllable mantrum or chant, "Na-mu-ah-mee-dah-bu" or Namu Amida Bu(tsu), meaning, very freely, "glory be to God." When allowed to surface in consciousness in all idle moments or in times of stress or crisis, it provides a very welcome substitute (and therefore workable answer) to any worry or other undue consideration that may be depressing its user to whatever degree. This is partly because of the capacity of any automatized (or automated) mantrum, or rhythmic phrase, to displace and dispel unwanted mental and emotional patterns. The Nembutsu's greatest power, however, lies in the

simple, modest, but supreme *elation* which Shin Buddhism attaches to
its aimless use.*

And now we have evidence that it can also produce generous quantities of EEG alpha-waves in a laboratory setting that offers promise of
being comparably redemptive.

Summary of Daily Interviews

The sesshin schedule included two fifteen-minute-maximum interviews of the subject daily at 11:45 A.M. preceding the lunch break, and
at 3:45 P.M. or 4:45 upon completion of each day's five or six feedback
sessions. The purposes of the interviews were:

1. To observe the general attitude and mood of the subject, and
compare it with his report of his subjective condition.

2. To provide the subject with a substitute for the "confessional" aspects of dokusan, the private interview with the Zen master of the conventional Zen sesshin, including some relief from the general subject-
isolation of the sesshin setting.

* In the "Orate Gama" (*The Embossed Tea Kettle*, Geo. Allen & Unwin,
Ltd., London, 1963. R. D. M. Shaw, Transl.), Hakuin Zenji (1685–1768),
founder of modern Zen, says of Shin, "Do not think that the Shingon or the
Jodo (Shin) teachings are worse or lower. People who belong to the Shin sect,
by merit of calling wholeheartedly upon the sacred name of Amida, are quite
assured that they will at some time see the pure land of the one and only Mind,
in the wonderful form of Amida Buddha." D. T. Suzuki devoted the entire
second section of his *Mysticism, Christian and Buddhist,* to Shin, and in his
Living by Zen (p. 166) Dr. Suzuki says, "The fact is undeniable that there
are more genuine and practically working cases of satori among lay devotees of
Shin than in Zen circles."

Of the Nembutsu, the father of koan Zen in Japan says in the *Orate Gama*:
"With regard to the efficacy of the sacred formula, there is no difference between repetition of the phrase and the use of a model subject for meditation
[a koan] which we use in the Zen system. . . . The great founders of the various
[Buddhist] sects all had plenty of capital-wisdom, yet they did not despise nor
reject this good medicine of The Six Syllables. . . . An ordinary mortal can
become a Buddha! This is like a tile or a stone becoming pure gold. . . . So with
all respect I urge everybody of all ranks to make use of this tablet-medicine of
The Six Syllables morning and night. . . ."

At first, the only morning interview question was "What are you feeling now?" The afternoon questions at first were:

"1. What are you feeling now?
2. How did you respond to the light?
3. How did you respond to the tone? (feedback)
4. Describe what happened in the session.
5. Did anything new happen in the meditation?"

On the seventh day these questions were all shortened to the same one for each interview, as noted. Morning and afternoon answers are:

DAY 1   11:45 A.M. Bad. Dissatisfied with learning progress, equipment failures, tone-off for alpha-on-and-beta-off feedback reinforcement, and reinforcement of one 2-minute sample score per 45-minute feedback session.

3:45 P.M. All right. (Feel better.) A familiar sesshin-induced indifference to unscheduled stimuli is very welcome.

DAY 2   11:45 A.M. Anesthesized (numb). Dissatisfied with learning progress, negative (silence) feedback reinforcement. Encouraged only by deepening indifference, inasmuch as "meditation is an exercise in acceptance."

3:45 P.M. Pain in the neck and effort to relax it takes too much attention. Fifty percent time tone-on is very irritating when it signals alpha-off, and cannot be reduced. EMG feedback to relax muscle tension would be helpful. If it was from voice-box muscle it might also relax thinking, if Jacobson's findings are correct. If so, it might also reduce amount of beta in the EEG. Light-on for alpha-on was a pleasant relief from tone-on for alpha-off.

DAY 3   11:45 A.M. All right. No comment.

4:00 P.M. Feel like an astronaut; pleasant at first, but tiring. Anesthetic or paralytic effect started about 2:30, resumed after 2:45 break and continued to end. Tone-on for alpha-on is very welcome change in procedure.

DAY 4   11:45 A.M. Feel numb (anesthesized). Difficult to talk. An internal-pressure sensation in top of head, not an ache. When a muscle quivered in left knee it seemed to interrupt alpha for quite a spell, which was followed by an unusually long alpha (tone-on) train.

3:45 P.M. Feel nothing. What is there to report that record doesn't show? Nothing unusual subjectively; except more conceptualization today than yesterday. There's a subjective state in which tone-signal seems directly connected to a mental state in an autonomous manner. This didn't occur today, like yesterday, so today's sessions were more effortful.

DAY 5   11:45 A.M. Shifted meditation from Zen koan, *mu*, to Shin chant, Nembutsu, because *mu* wouldn't stay in mind. Rhythmic chanting seems to greatly improve alpha time, and can be continued during "kinhin" breaks, to rhythmic dancing or running in place, or walking briskly in empty corridor.

3:45 P.M. Feel anesthesized again, like general anesthetic. After autonomous interminable bursts of alpha-tone finally stopped I would listen for footsteps, thinking the session had ended. The first time this occurred I saw unusual mirror-image of myself in my teens, against closed eyelids, very vivid and very pleasing. This started trains of thoughts which caused alpha-tone to be very intermittent, but only when it stopped altogether would I realize that I'd been thinking. Taking up the chanting again always restored the alpha-tone quite quickly. A small nerve inside right knee jittered autonomously quite a bit. Otherwise anesthesia toward end of afternoon was general except for slight pain immediately under shoulder electrodes during 2 P.M. session. After 3 P.M. shifted to reclining chair for remainder of session without interrupting chant, or general euphoria. Throat muscles continue to carry chant even with conscious effort to release it from mind. No need to keep eyes open to stay awake in this condition, as autonomous chanting seems to be also alerting. I feel great, wonderful, like hugging Erik, and everybody. Wonder whether a metronome would assist in automating this chanting?

DAY 6   11:45 A.M. Feel nothing. Very quiet and passive, without being drowsy, even with eyes closed. Don't feel like moving, especially for lunch. Just want to continue in this comfortable state. How about an all-day feedback marathon? It's like the mind is a computer that is reprogrammed by every new gestalt, like a change of scene. Now it seems to be set to idle indefinitely by programming this monotonous 6-syllable mantrum into it for indefinite repetition. Brain (computer) autonomously pulls in memory data to try to break the monotony which may be like an uninterrupted beat-frequency that is modulated by any change in input, including memory data, thoughts, muscle movement, feedback, etc. It's change in input, not input itself which modulates, as if Newton's second law were operating here also, possibly because brain has atomic structure also. The electron revolution may produce the fundamental sine wave of physics and electricity by oscillation in its plane of orbit, when projected on a time axis. As these insights are product of a reactivated brain-computer after hours of idling, possibly the computer works better after the kind of programming that is called "interior prayer," more common in the Orient than in the West where brain-computers are commonly overloaded and fatigued by a plethora of complex input data (stimuli).

3:45 P.M. Feel depressed because of necessity of interrupting feedback for lunch hour when it was going good and impossibility of getting alpha time up to high percentage again this afternoon. I wish we could just keep the setting undisturbed when alpha time is high and break only when it is low. If I could be alerted by outside stimuli when the polygraph shows drowsiness, it might help; drowsiness is the greatest obstacle to high alpha time, especially when first working into a feedback session. Then any new phenomenon also blocks alpha by alerting the nervous system until it can habituate. Thus it seems that alpha is a steady state phenomenon of the nervous system. When alpha is high I feel this steady state of the nerves as a kind of anesthesia, or total (physical, mental, emotional) quiet, which I call psychological comfort.

DAY 7   Note 1: To help try to reduce the tendency of the subject to oververbalize after long hours of meditation, the interview questions, from this morning to the end of the session, at his suggestion, were all dropped in favor of one commonly used by the Roshi when the student remains silent at interview time, "Do you have anything to say?"

11:45 A.M. Answer: "Why did you break it up?" (Meaning the feedback session, which subject felt was going well, with very high alpha time toward the end. The break occurred as scheduled for a two-hour lunch period.)

3:45 P.M. "No." To the additional question, "Was the light stimulus disturbing?" the answer was, "Un-huh."

Note 2: Evening feedback sessions were added this day at request of subject who wanted to continue to meditate, with feedback, for as much of each 24-hour day as he could. This evening he sat from 8:40 to 10:30, from 11:30 to 1:00 A.M. and started again at 1:15 A.M. but soon called it off to resume schedule at 5:00 A.M.

DAY 8   *Note:* No interview was taken this morning as subject wanted to continue meditation through noon-hour.

3:45 P.M. Nothing to say.

DAY 9   12:45 A.M. Lunch break: "It baffles me."

5:45 P.M. Kinhin break. *Interview question:* 'How do you move your muscles in such a way that massive alpha occurs?"

"The only move I recall is shifting from chair to zazen position on the floor about 3:30. Soon after that, until 4:30, it was a perfect zazen period, except for chanting the Nembutsu the entire period. General anesthesia set in, except for pain in skin of buttocks, and internal pressure sensation against top of head, both familiar Zen-sesshin sensations. It was a happy outcome of a puzzling, trying day. I feel very euphoric and affectionate. I'd like to continue meditating with feedback as long as I can."

6:15 P.M. (After quitting meditation for the day.) "It was a good afternoon; I learned a lot about meditation. From 2 to 3:30 I just sat on the chair and tried to let alpha build up autonomously, but it didn't. So I moved to the floor and did active zazen with Nembutsu, and that saved the day for me."

DAY 10   11:45 A.M. "It's very frustrating. When you try to increase alpha, it doesn't; when you give up and quit trying, it increases."

4:45 P.M. "No, I can't think of anything to say. I'm just puzzled, and that keeps the tone off. I can't keep it on because I worry about it, so it's been one long alternation between trying too hard and giving up. Finally I developed a painful tension in the back of my neck, in zazen posture. So I moved to chair to simply take a rest, and the tone came on quite steadily right away. But I was tired and comfortable and afraid of getting drowsy, so I overalerted to stay awake and defeated myself again."

6:45 P.M. In an extra interview, by request, with chief experimenter, Erik Peper, whom subject regards as a substitute Zen master for this sesshin, subject repeated his complaint of frustration with inability to remain defeated and indifferent to defeat, when this seems to be the only attitude that would now produce satisfactory alpha. In addition, he reported an autonomous jiggling of the eyeballs when he lay down with closed eyes to rest, and wondered if it was REM. Also, toward end of day some muscles twitch, especially in right leg, and his skin itches. At night his dreams, he says, are more active and vivid than usual. He wants to be able to request that feedback tone be switched off whenever he feels these symptoms coming on during a session. They only occur in the chair, not in the zazen (floor) posture, but latter is too painful to maintain more than an hour at a time unless a "high-alpha anesthesia" sets in. When this happens he gets the painless headache at the top of his head, and a general loss of body boundaries, except for pressure points (buttocks, etc.).

DAY 11   11:45 A.M. "Just before you came in there was a terrific general subjective tension buildup that called for a mighty all-out shout to release it. But I was afraid that that might panic somebody, and this hesitation seemed to dissipate the worst of the tension. Let's take an hour for lunch and start again at 1:00."

4:45 P.M. "It was a good day."

Note: After evening meal, there was an extra feedback session from 7:30–8:15 P.M. at subject's request.

DAY 12   10:00 A.M. Inter-session volunteered comment: "I have been noticing how any eye movement will block alpha. But I've noticed also that any visualizing or subvocal verbalizing also blocks alpha. It would be interesting to have a tiny springloaded signal-button on one finger of each hand, to signal whether an alpha blocking was caused by words or by pictures, inasmuch as eye movement is already being recorded by EOG electrodes."

11:45 A.M. Very frustrating morning; typical classical obstacle to meditation: swinging from daydreaming (busy-mind) to drowsing, both blocking alpha, with not enough pause between for reinforcement to get established.

5:00 P.M. (end of feedback day): "After I asked for no feedback tone because I felt I'd lost all control of it, I kept telling myself 'Let go, let go.' As a result I began to feel heavier and heavier, as if in a trance, and I wanted you to startle me out of it, as this has been known to produce *kensho*.* But I couldn't get this across to you without breaking the trance, so it was obviously too light, anyhow. I'd

* A synonym for *satori*, enlightenment. *Editor.*

like to be hypnotized into a deep trance sometime for feedback meditation."

DAY 13   11:45 A.M. *Question:* "What are you feeling now?"

Answer: "Indifference. No problem with drowsiness even with high alpha. There was a low hum in left side of head that was blocked by alpha tone. But it was also blocked with feedback turned off by stopping up ear with a finger, so it's purely an auditory thing. Right ear has a continuous high-pitched squeal that is familiar as a fatigue symptom. Also head feels light and swollen, like a balloon."

4:45 P.M. *Question:* "Anything to report?"

Answer: "Nothing. It's been a lousy afternoon just trying to stay alert and interested."

Note: At 9:45 P.M. feedback was resumed, but was discontinued at 10:15 P.M. in favor of scheduled EEG sleep-study.

DAY 14   *Note:* At 4:45 A.M., following sleep study, meditation with feedback was resumed until 6:45 breakfast break, then resumed again from 9:00 A.M. to 12:00 noon.

7:45 A.M. During breakfast break subject volunteered to chief experimenter (Peper): "I feel thoroughly discouraged. To maintain high alpha continuity is not impossible, but it seems right now to be more difficult than the reinforcement is worth. Perhaps the criteria for alpha feedback in this experiment is just too high for me. If so, I would greatly appreciate some relief from it in order to improve the reinforcing effect of the feedback."

12 noon. *Question:* "Anything to report?"

Answer: "I've made some important discoveries:

(1) Random thinking is possible without interrupting alpha, provided there is no emotional (interest) arousal, or excitement, induced. These observations that I am reporting now are examples of thoughts during feedback that didn't block it.

(2) On the contrary, a 1/10-second lapse of consciousness, as from drowsiness, breaks the feedback tone continuity sometimes for an instant, sometimes for quite a while, before recovery.

(3) A 1/10-second flicker of doubt, worry, or fear will break the tone continuity, which then always takes a while to recover.

(4) Some kind of tension, muscle or nerve, is necessary somewhere in the body in order to maintain consciousness, and this tension does not block alpha, although a conscious shift in mus-

cle or nerve tension does. As an example, when I first realized during a long continuous alpha burst that my scalp was very tense, I relaxed it, and this broke the tone, so I tensed scalp again to restore it. This occurred several times before I left scalp relaxed experimentally and discovered tone soon resumed in the relaxed state also.

(5) I always develop a pain in the back of my neck after more than a half-hour in the zazen posture on the floor after several days of zazen. This probably results from keeping the spine straight by 'reaching for heaven with the top of the head,' per zazen instructions which probably aim at insuring the necessary muscular tension to defeat drowsiness in this way. But this morning it was clear that long continuous alpha anesthesizes this neck pain, and any other pain in the body, converting it to a mere sensation of tolerable, localized tension or strain. This applies also to long overdue relief of bladder pressure, for instance, that without this anesthesia can become quite painful.

(6) This morning's long continuous alpha was coincident with continuous, aimless, and effortless subvocal chanting of the Nembutsu which had become quite an autonomous cycling of impulses in the speech muscles, almost, but not entirely, unconsciously. This automated muscular rhythm in the throat became more associated with the continuity of the feedback tone than with any wilful act of mine, in my anesthesized condition."

P.M. *Note:* The record in the control log for this entire afternoon is blank.

Evening. *Note:* Feedback was resumed at 7:05 P.M. and continued until 9:15 P.M.

DAY 15   *Note:* Two extra feedback sessions of 45 minutes each began at 5:15 and 6:15 A.M.

11:45 A.M. *Question:* "Anything to report?"

Answer: "No."

4:45 P.M. *Question:* "Anything to report?"

Answer: "I'm tired. My head feels heavy and solid. I still have random daydreams, fantasy and memories; but not too much. No trouble with drowsiness all day today. That's the whole picture."

6:00 P.M. Subject volunteered: "I feel punchy—very like I used to when I boxed in college and got punched in the head a lot. I'm also quite tired, fatigued, but it's a different kind of fatigue than I usually experience in 7-day Zen sesshins; it's not as complete, nor as welcome, but the punchiness—the head sensations—are worse. Alpha this afternoon seemed to be continuous for long stretches—10 to 20 minutes without a break—but it didn't seem to affect my mood or emotions; it was just tiring."

DAY 16   11:45 A.M. "Nothing to report. It's sad that I can still alternate between daydreaming and drowsing after two weeks of this."

LAST DAY   4:45 P.M. "Very good afternoon. The last hour was done as a standard zazen exercise, 'just sitting and breathing in and out,' as the Zen people say when zazen goes well. I note that you left the feedback on for this interview and the alpha-time continues quite high as we talk."

Editor's Postscript

This is one experimental subject's answer to Dr. Mulholland's question, "If one stays in a state of relaxed wakefulness for a long time without going to sleep, what happens?" In Dr. Mulholland's answer, he says, "By taking time out to be relaxed yet awake for an hour in a quiet place, people are finding out that they have thoughts. For some, this experience assumes the status of a major insight. Obviously after one 'discovers' thinking, he 'discovers' awareness and introspects on his thought flow."

It is editorially noteworthy, I think, that although Dr. Mulholland does not mention it, some other subjects, like Durand Kiefer, have discovered by this meditative practice of staying alert while relaxed for a long time that their thought flow is not only almost autonomic, like their breathing or heartbeat, but what is more insightful, it is not *entirely* continuous, but sometimes ceases momentarily, leaving them in a state of "pure" or empty awareness that is often quite elating. Such thoughtless or mindless awareness, however brief, tends greatly to increase conscious proprioception of bodily processes and conditions, especially the neural ones. As meditation training proceeds, these moments of effortless, fixed, noncognitive internal attention are reported to increase in both frequency and duration, ultimately leading, if training is continued long and seriously enough, to the more or less habitual state of relaxed generalized alertness of the so-called mystic. The relatively intuitive, innocent, and otherwise childlike behavior and attitudes that are usually evident as a result are also noteworthy from a psychophysiological investigation viewpoint.

If, on the other hand, as Dr. Mulholland observes, it is the subject's thoughts and their attendant emotions, rather than the occasional brief lapses in them, that most occupy the subject's attention, his report of his subjective observations is naturally reflective or emotional, or both, and of course reflects his mental and emotional habits of belief, expectation, and response.

Dr. Mulholland's observation that much of his subject's response to EEG alpha feedback tone is thus a conditioned value-system response appears to overlook the possibility that the EEG alpha feedback process is in itself conditioning, and hence that simple psychophysiological reinforcement, positive or negative, may account for much of the response behavior he cites as evidence for his psychological view of feedback. The example of the experiment reported here, as Dr. Mulholland cites it, would seem to be particularly one of direct muscle and visual relaxation response to positive reinforcement by feedback tone, which would be exactly the kind of conditioning aid to meditation that Cdr. Kiefer had hoped for in volunteering for the experiment.

IV
Meditation
Research

Meditation is perhaps man's oldest spiritual discipline. As a technique for helping people to find enlightenment—to know God or ultimate reality—it appears in some form in nearly every major religious tradition. The entranced yogi in a lotus posture, the Zen Buddhist sitting in zazen, the Sufi dervish whirling in an ecstasy-inducing dance, the Christian contemplative kneeling in adoration of Jesus: all can be properly described as practicing meditation. For meditation's core experience is an altered state of consciousness in which our ordinary language-based, culturally reinforced, and quite narrow sense of "I"—the ego—is diminished while a larger sense of self-existence-merged-with-the-cosmos comes into awareness.

Why should science examine a religious phenomenon? Because of the traditions associated with meditation: the development of incredible self-control over physiological functions, spontaneous and willed production of psychic phenomena, and the ability to enter unusual states of consciousness in a voluntary manner.

In the 1950s, researchers in India began to bring yogis into the laboratory to record their brain waves, heartbeat, and respiration. Likewise, in Japan, Zen monks were allowing themselves to be instrumentally monitored. As science and religion converged, a growing body of literature began to attract attention among physiological psychologists and biofeedback researchers.

In the 1960s, Maharishi Mahesh Yogi brought Transcendental Meditation to the West in a secular manner and encouraged scientific examination of his claims. A graduate student named R. Keith Wallace earned his doctorate in psychology in 1970 by studying the physiological effects of Transcendental Meditation and proposing that the meditative state was a fourth major state of consciousness—neither sleeping, dreaming, nor waking. Wallace's startling results were published in prestigious scientific journals, including Science (27 March 1970) and Scientific American (February 1972). Meditation research burst upon the scientific community. In 1973 the American Psychiatric Association began to establish a task force on meditation research.

What has the research established? Meditation works on many levels —physiological, psychological, social. It improves general health and stamina, decreases tension, anxiety, and aggressiveness, increases self-control and self-knowledge. Drug use and abuse are curbed, even stopped. Psychotherapy progresses faster than usual. Personal and family relations seem to improve. Meditators subjectively claim that it changes their lives. And except for borderline psychotics, meditation is safe, harmless, and easy to learn.

A fair sampling of the meditation research literature can be found in Charles Tart's Altered States of Consciousness (Doubleday-Anchor 1972), the Biofeedback and Self-Control annuals (Aldine-Atherton). My own What Is Meditation? (Doubleday-Anchor, 1974) also surveys the research. The Students International Meditation Society (SIMS), with more than two hundred centers around the United States, provides useful free material on Transcendental Meditation and other forms. Spiritual Community Guide (Box 1080, San Rafael, Calif.) and Year One Catalog (Harper and Row, 1972) can put you in touch with various meditative traditions and schools.

J.W.

7 Meditation Research:
Its Personal and Social Implications
Fred F. Griffith

A great many claims have been made in recent years for meditation as a panacea for personal and social problems. Various schools of meditation promise the meditator health, happiness, powers of concentration, and spiritual development. Scientific reports are often alluded to, but without the detail needed for a serious appraisal of their validity. It seems worthwhile to clarify the subject by gathering together the scientific data on the major forms of meditation and discussing it in relation to established psychological mechanisms and therapeutic techniques.

Trungpa [55], Goleman [24, 25], Naranjo [44], and others distinguish at least two general forms of meditation: a concentration form of meditation and a form that emphasizes detached awareness. Generally speaking the former is more characteristic of the yogic tradition and the latter of the Buddhist tradition. Yet as Goleman has pointed out, few of the traditional schools of meditation teach purely one form or the other; the exceptions are systems centering around a single technique, such as Transcendental Meditation. Since the differences between the forms of meditation are subjectively great and physiologically evident [19], it is of importance for meditation researchers whose subjects are not practicing a readily defined technique to indicate as fully as possible what technique of meditation has been studied. That this has often not been done represents a weakness in the scientific data available on meditation, and Goleman and Fischer [20] have done an important service in beginning to propose typologies for understanding different forms of meditation and their effects on the meditator.

Concentration meditative techniques involve a focusing of attention on a visual symbol, a sound or chant, or a bodily process such as breathing. Most frequently Sanskrit words or phrases known as *mantra* are used as a focus. These may be Hindu names for God such as *Rama* or *Hare Krishna* or they may be words symbolic of unity such as *Aum* or the Sufi *La ilāha illā 'llah* (There is no god but God). The meditator is taught to attend to the mantra, not as an effort of the will but rather in a passive way. When his attention wanders to fantasies or other thoughts, he is instructed to direct it back calmly to the mantra. In time, the meditator learns to attend effortlessly to the focus of meditation without being distracted by thoughts or external stimuli. This first quickening of concentration is what Goleman [24, p. 11] calls "access concentration," and presumably most of the studies of relatively inexperienced Western meditators have dealt with the physiological concomitants of this state of consciousnes.

The technique taught by Maharishi Mahesh Yogi, known as Transcendental Meditation (TM), is a form of yogic mantra meditation. Maharishi [42] speaks of meditation as "turning the attention inwards towards the subtle levels of thought until the mind transcends the experience of the subtlest state of thought at the source of thought." Emphasis is given to the idea that the technique does not involve forced concentration or contemplation or any form of physical or mental control; it is effortless and can be learned by anyone. Unlike most of the yogic schools of meditation, TM does not advocate any special diet or postures. The meditator is given a mantra by a teacher trained by Maharishi, and he is asked to meditate twice a day for about twenty minutes. A two-week abstention from drugs is asked of the meditator before his mantra initiation, and follow-up meetings and voluntary "checking" sessions verify the correctness of the individual's practice. With its stress on the ease and practical benefits of meditation and its lack of emphasis on Eastern philosophy and acts of renunciation, TM has been the most popular meditation technique in the United States. Since Maharishi's first visit to this country in 1959, over 250,000 people have learned TM [9].

Zen meditation, called zazen, is the best-known technique of what I have called the Buddhist form of awareness meditation. Krishnamurti, Gurdjieff, and Tibetan teachers such as Chogyam Trungpa have also taught techniques of awareness meditation. As Trungpa put it [55, pp. 52–53]:

In this kind of meditation practice the concept of *nowness* plays an important part. In fact, it is the essence of meditation. Whatever one does, whatever one tries to practice, is not aimed at achieving a higher state or at following some theory or ideal, but simply without any object or ambition, trying to see what is here and now. One has to become aware of the present moment through such means as concentrating on the breathing, a practice which has been developed in the Buddhist tradition. This is based on developing the knowledge of nowness, for each respiration is unique, it is an expression of *now*. Each breath is separate from the next and is fully seen and fully felt, not as a visualized form or simply as an aid to concentration, but it should be fully and properly dealt with.

The Buddhist meditator tries to remain aware of the present moment; he establishes a mental vantage point from which he observes the flux of his own mental states. Rather than concentrating on a given focus, the awareness meditator follows his own breathing and his own thoughts and sensations.

The Psychological Data: Yoga and Zen

The earliest physiological studies on yoga investigated claims that yogis acquire remarkable physical powers, such as the ability to suspend breathing or to stop the heart for some time; scientific study of meditation per se has been done only within the last two decades. Since much of the more recent and more thorough work has been done on TM, it will be discussed separately from studies done on less well defined yogic and Zen meditation techniques.

The physiological data on yogic meditation is rather confusing, taken as a whole. For instance, Das and Gastaut [14], who studied seven subjects, who were fully concentrated in meditation, report "definite acceleration" of cardiac and electroencephalographic (EEG) rhythms.*

* EEG is an electrical measurement of the activity of large numbers of brain cells. Fast beta rhythms are usually associated with arousal, slower alpha rhythms with relaxation, and even slower theta and delta rhythms with drowsiness and sleep.

On the other hand, other investigators [2, 4, 5] have recorded more alpha activity in subjects during yogic meditation than during control resting periods. Quite possibly, the subjects studied by Das and Gastaut were practicing a form of meditation qualitatively different from the other yoga meditators.

Other physiological changes that have been reported during yogic meditation include slower heart rate, slower respiration, and lower palmar conductance [3–5, 62]. All of these indicate that the subjects were more relaxed while meditating than while resting normally. In addition, the alpha blocking response is not observed in yoga meditators. In normal subjects, any startling stimulus will change a relaxed alpha EEG pattern into more aroused beta activity. However, a variety of stimuli failed to produce such a response in yoga meditators and they later reported no awareness of the stimuli presented, which included flashes of light, loud noises and the touch of a hot glass tube [2, 4, 5]. Further, there is some evidence that yoga meditators do not habituate to repeated stimuli when they are not meditating. Normal subjects quickly fail to notice repeated stimuli, such as the ticks of a clock.

The physiological data on Zen meditation is generally similar to that on yoga. EEG recordings of subjects doing zazen show the rapid appearance of alpha waves, which may slow into trains of theta waves [37]. Other physiological changes recorded in Zen meditators paralleling those in yoga meditators include slowed heart rate and respiration and decreased oxygen consumption [37, 53]. Unlike yoga meditators, who show no alpha blocking, practitioners of zazen showed consistent alpha blocking to stimuli presented twenty times; no habituation was observed.

As Victor Emerson [19] and others have pointed out, this difference is consistent with the essential differences in approach between concentration and awareness forms of meditation. Yogic meditators seek to attend to one focus until all inner and outer distractions fall away, while Zen meditators seek to remain aware of each here and now moment without getting carried away into discursive thought. Thus the experienced Zen meditator consistently shows alpha blocking for three to five seconds after a stimulus is presented and then returns to predominant alpha production while the yoga meditator shows no awareness of the stimulus at all.

In addition to the physiological testing, a few psychological studies have been done on Zen meditators. Kasamatsu and Hirai [36] noted no remarkable differences in Rorschach test scores between Zen practitioners and ordinary people. On the other hand, Maupin [43] reported interesting psychological effects on twenty-eight subjects who were taught a Zen breath-concentration technique; their subjective response to the exercise was compared with test results related to attention, tolerance for unrealistic experience, and capacity for "regression in the service of the ego." Capacity for regression and tolerance for unrealistic experience significantly predicted response to meditation, while attention measures did not [43]. A third study, done by Lesh [40], supported these results from Maupin's work and also showed that the practice of zazen helped counselors develop their empathic ability.

Transcendental Meditation

Since practitioners of TM are so much more readily available to Western researchers, and since TM is a well-defined technique, the physiological and psychological literature on TM is much more extensive than that on yoga or Zen. The first major study of TM was done by R. K. Wallace with twenty-seven adult subjects who had been practicing TM from one week to nine years, with an average of about two and a half years. Wallace summarized his results as follows [57, p. xiii]:

> During meditation oxygen consumption, carbon dioxide elimination, cardiac output, heart rate and respiration rate significantly decreased, and skin resistance significantly increased. . . . Base excess was calculated from the arterial blood gases and it significantly decreased during transcendental meditation. Arterial blood pressure, pH and pCO_2 increased insignificantly and arterial blood lactate decreased markedly during meditation and remained low after meditation.

Several other studies have confirmed these results [1, 7, 58–61]. Typical EEG changes during TM include predominant alpha production alternating with low voltage theta waves [6, 7, 12, 57, 58, 60]. In addition, Wallace noted that in most of his subjects, alpha blocking caused by repeated sound or light stimuli showed no habituation [58, p. 1752]. Surprisingly, this EEG pattern is more like that observed with Zen meditators than with yoga meditators, and if Wallace's observations are supported by others, they may call into question the simple concentration-awareness distinction between forms of meditation.

Several psychological studies have recently been carried out with practitioners of TM. Shaw and Kalb [see 34] found that twenty minutes of TM improved reaction times of meditators over their premeditation times; nonmeditators did worse after twenty minutes of rest. Similar findings have been reported in tests involving complex four-choice reactions and mirror star-tracing [12]. These findings suggest that the restful meditation state may improve alertness as well as some motor abilities, while ordinary rest may leave one unalert for some time.

Other investigators, studying long-term behavioral and personality changes in groups of meditators and control groups, have also indicated that TM seems to be beneficial. David Orme-Johnson [46] has found that regular practice of TM produces rapid galvanic skin response habituation and low levels of spontaneous GSR. These measurements are often found to be correlated with physiological and behavioral characteristics associated with good mental health, such as autonomic stability, outgoingness, field independence, and lessened susceptibility to a variety of stresses. Seeman, Nidich and Banta [51] gave Shostram's Personal Orientation Inventory, a test of "self-actualization," to a group of thirty-five subjects of similar background. Fifteen of the subjects were then taught TM, and two months later all thirty-five were retested. The meditators scored significantly higher in six of the twelve indices than they had previously, whereas the nonmeditators scored about the same as they had before. Changes between the two groups were especially notable on the subscales for spontaneity, self-regard, and acceptance of aggression. This study has been supported by another, conducted by Larry Hjelle [28]. Hjelle found that experienced meditators scored significantly higher than novice meditators on seven of the twelve subscales of the Personal Orientation Inventory; in addition, experienced meditators were significantly less anxious and showed more internal control. Further studies of this sort have been done with third-grade students by Linden [41] and with adult meditators by Pelletier [48]. Linden found that students who were taught meditation showed an increase in field independence and a decrease in test anxiety, with no change in reading grade level as compared with control groups. Pelletier demonstrated alteration of attention deployment between meditators and nonmeditators through the use of two measures of perceptual style.

Another investigation, done by Shelley [52], has indicated that TM practitioners are generally happier and more relaxed than nonmeditators. This finding is in line with other questionnaire data supplied by meditators about themselves. Meditators have reported that their physical and mental health has improved and that their use of drugs has lessened [8, 57], and the Students' International Meditation Society (SIMS) reports that further investigation of these claims is in progress. These reports thus far constitute only weak evidence, though, for a number of reasons. People who choose to learn TM are not a random sample of the population, and those who continue regular meditation may differ psychologically from other groups, such as drug users as a whole. Clearly, not all these differences can be attributed to the practice of TM. And subjects tend to answer questionnaires in a way that justifies their behavior, so that a person who has faithfully practiced TM would be likely to emphasize its merits. The recent work of Kanellakos and Lukas [7] promises to be better designed, but the full results have not yet been published.

All the physiological data on meditation indicates that meditation profoundly relaxes the body and mind, and the psychological studies that have been done show beneficial effects of meditation as well. Yet so far science has scarcely begun to test the claims for long-term meditation as taught in the East, where meditation is seen as a central technique in one's spiritual development toward enlightenment—the state of complete bliss, understanding, and union with reality. TM usually claims less, but its effects, too, are purported to be profound. Demetri Kanellakos [35, p. 300] summarized them as increased energy and efficiency at work; increased calmness; increased creativity and concentration; loss of desire for drugs, tobacco, and alcohol; improvement of posture, insomnia, and blood pressure; and better mobilization of body resources to combat strenuous circumstances. Several explanations for meditation's effectiveness have been proposed, and relevant theories to be discussed include unstressing, systematic desensitization, deautomization, and the bimodal model of consciousness based in part on data on hemispheric specialization in the human brain.

Unstressing

The theory most often invoked by TM teachers to explain the healthful effects of meditation speaks in terms of "unstressing." The idea underlying this approach was expressed by Green et al. as the "psycho-physiological principle" [26, p. 3]:

> Every change in the physiological state is accompanied by an appropriate change in the mental-emotional state, and conversely, every change in the mental-emotional state, conscious or unconscious, is accompanied by an appropriate change in the physiological state.

Therapeutic methods of Wilhelm Reich, Alexander Lowen, and Fritz Perls have made use of this principle; it has been confirmed in practice. "Unstressing" in meditation takes the form of completely involuntary and spontaneous muscular movements and proprioceptive sensations: momentary or repeated twitches, sighs, gasps, tingling, tics, jerking, swaying, pains, internal pressures, headaches, weeping, laughing, and so on. The experience covers the range from extreme pleasure to acute distress. Unstressing may be gradual during regular daily meditation, but during prolonged meditation sessions more extreme forms of unstressing may occur [23]. Maupin's [43] subjects who were taught zazen mentioned to him "hallucinoid feelings, muscle tension, sexual excitement, and intense sadness," and Deikman [15] and others have had similar reports from meditators.

The physical unstressing found in meditation is often paralleled by a subjective effect described by Charles Tart [54, p. 137]:

> Normally we carry out all sorts of activities with insufficient attention and/or insufficient awareness of our own reactions to them. This results in building up a tremendous backlog of partially processed experiences, unfinished business. The psychic-lubricant function of TM is to allow these things to come back into consciousness during meditation and, by virtue of now being conscious, to have the processing of them completed. Thus they no longer block other psychic processes. . . . Almost always when I find myself thinking about something else other than the mantra, it turns out to be something which I see (in retrospect) I did not pay sufficient attention to when it happened. It does seem to lose its "charge" or "potency" by now having become conscious, and then I go back to concentrating on the mantra.

During meditation, then, one's attention wanders from the mantra or other focus to other thoughts and sensations that seem to have awaited the opportunity for conscious mental expression. This mental catharsis, according to the psychophysiological principle, is always accompanied by a physiological change, but this may not be evident to the meditators. Autokinesthesia may be accompanied by thoughts or may seem to occur alone. Or one may notice only thoughts and no physical sensations, as in Herrigel's description of this process in zazen [27, p. 56]:

> This exquisite state of unconcerned immersion in oneself is, unfortunately, not of long duration. It is liable to be disturbed from inside. As though sprung from nowhere, moods, feelings, desires, worries, and even thoughts incontinently rise up, in a meaningless jumble ... It is as though they wanted to avenge themselves on consciousness for having, through concentration, touched upon realms it would otherwise never reach. The only successful way of rendering this disturbance inoperative is to keep on breathing, quietly and unconcernedly, to enter into friendly relations with whatever appears on the scene, to accustom oneself to it, to look at it equally and at last grow weary of looking.

Goleman [23] proposed that unstressing serves the same psychological function for the meditator as dreams do for the dreamer. Further, citing studies linking muscular stirrings with the appearance of dream REMs,* he proposed that "each movement in unstressing signals the release of a stored mental-emotional state, event, or impression, and each psychic event indicates the release of stress on the level of nerve-and-muscle."

The concept of physical and mental unstressing receives powerful support from Edmund Jacobson's lifelong study of relaxation. As early as 1925 he published a report on a technique called progressive relaxation [29]. This technique involved teaching subjects how to relax the principal muscle groups of the body to an extreme degree; subjects were also trained to be aware of the sensations of muscular tension and their location. Jacobson found that all sensory imagery disappeared with complete relaxation. Kinesthetic imagery, such as "inner speech," could likewise be relaxed away, and "with progressive muscular relaxation, not alone imagery, but also attention, recollection, thought-processes and emotion gradually diminish" [29, 31]. Like Wolpert [65], who found

---

* Rapid eye movements (REM) offer physical evidence that a person is dreaming.

slight muscular stirrings in subjects corresponding to the content of their dreams, Jacobson recorded action potentials and slight muscular contractions when a relaxed awake subject was asked to imagine a physical act [30, 31]. He later reported that "with progressive relaxation (a) the knee jerk and other reflexes dwindle and disappear along with (b) mental activities, including emotions, having generalized neurogenic deactivation effects on (c) the vegetative nervous system, in which the cardiovascular, the gastrointestinal, and other systems participate" [32, p. 549]. Jacobson's work offers supporting evidence for the theory that physical unstressing accompanies mental catharsis, and it has also served as the foundation for another approach toward an understanding of the effects of meditation, that of systematic desensitization.

Systematic Desensitization and Deautomization

The technique of systematic desensitization, as used by Wolpe [64], involves three operations: (a) Subjects are trained in muscle relaxation, following Jacobson's routine. (b) An anxiety hierarchy is constructed—i.e., a graded list of anxiety-eliciting stimuli. The patient is taught to visualize as vivid an image as possible for the items in the hierarchy. (c) The anxiety-eliciting stimuli are paired with deep relaxation. Starting with the least anxiety provoking item, each is presented and repeated until all anxiety is eliminated. Finally there is no anxiety elicited by any item.

Noting the physiological data that demonstrates meditation produces deep relaxation, Daniel Goleman has proposed that a psychological process much like that in systematic desensitization occurs during meditation [23, pp. 5–6]:

> With the inward turning of attention during meditation, the meditator becomes keenly aware of the random chaos of thoughts in the waking state . . . The meditator witnesses the flow of psychic events, plannings, paranoias, hopes, fantasies, memories, yearnings, decisions, indecisions, observations, fears, scheming, guilt, calculations, expectations, and on and on and on. The whole contents of the mind compose the meditator's "desensitization hierarchy" . . . As in the desensitization paradigm, the "hierarchy" is presented coupled with the deep relaxation of deep meditation. Unlike the therapy, de-

sensitization is not limited to those items which therapist and patients have identified as problematic, though those are certainly
included, but extends to all phases of experience . . . It is natural,
global self-desensitization.

Goleman lists a number of hypotheses that follow from his theory
and goes on to discuss the role of anxiety in psychological disorders.
Several investigators have linked the levels of lactate in the blood with
levels of chronic and acute anxiety [13, 18], and Pitts and McClure
[49] have shown that anxiety symptoms and attacks can be induced
by infusion of lactate. Paired with Wallace's [57-61] data on markedly
lowered blood lactate levels during and after meditation, these studies
have significant implications. Meditation would be a beneficial addition
not only in the lives of anxiety neurotics, but also for normals as well.
In the case of the former, anxiety attacks would abate as lactate levels
lowered. In the latter, perception of self and others should be improved.
Lesh's [40] findings that zazen practice helped counselors understand
and appreciate what their clients were expressing also support this theory.

Arthur Deikman, a psychiatrist, has suggested a similar but more
psychotherapeutically oriented interpretation of meditation phenomena
in terms of deautomization. Ordinarily, only a small part of our sensory
input reaches consciousness; the brain selects and modifies input. We
build models of the world based on our past experiences and present
needs and expectations. Further, our expectations and the limited nature
of our constructs limit awareness. "Offer a donkey a salad, and he will
ask what sort of thistle it is" [44, p. 191]. This conceptually mediated
selective awareness sharply contrasts with Fromm's psychological definition of enlightenment—the ultimate goal of most systems of meditation [21, pp. 115-116]:

> . . . a state in which the person is completely tuned in to the
> reality outside and inside of him, a state in which he is fully aware
> of it and fully grasps it. *He* is aware of it—that is, not his brain or
> any other part of his organism, but he, the whole man. He is aware
> of *it*, not as an object over there which he grasps with his thought,
> but *it*, the flower, the dog, the man in its or his full reality. He who
> awakes is open and responsive to the world, and he can be open and
> responsive because he has given up holding on to himself as a thing,
> and thus has become empty and ready to receive. To be enlightened
> means "full awakening of the total personality to reality."

Or as William Blake expressed it: "If the doors of perception were cleansed, everything would appear to man as it is, infinite."

Van Nuys [56] and others have pointed out that the essential element of all meditation techniques is that the meditator works to gain control over his attentional processes. Gaining mastery over one's attention is difficult work, for there seems to be a natural tendency for attention to shift constantly from one point of focus to another. In the *Bhagavad Gita*, Prince Arjuna says to Krishna, "The mind is restless, turbulent, powerful and obstinate. I deem it as difficult to control as the wind." The meditator learns to control his "obstinate" attention by focusing on one thing or thought as a preliminary to achieving the enlightened state of perception unmediated by wants or expectations. Deikman [15, 16] calls this process "deautomization," a process that permits

> the adult to attain a new, fresh perception of the world by freeing him from a stereotyped organization built up over the years and by allowing adult synthetic and associative functions access to fresh materials, to create with them in a new way that represents an advance in mental functioning. . . . The struggle for creative insight in all fields may be regarded as the effort to deautomize the psychic structures that organize cognition and perception. In this sense, deautomization is not a regression but rather an undoing of a pattern in order to permit a new and perhaps more advanced experience.

The experimental data seems to support Deikman's hypothesis that meditation serves a deautomizing function. Naranjo and Ornstein [44] summarize a number of studies on stabilized images and ganzfeld conditions that support the idea that concentration in meditation on a single input leads to a condition of blank awareness. And the studies conducted by Deikman himself [15] and by Lesh [40] with meditators argue that the meditation experience leads to new and heightened perceptions of reality.

In a more recent article, Deikman [17] has put his views on meditation into a different perspective. Meditation, he suggests, not only helps to break up habitual ways of perceiving, but also helps develop a receptive mode of functioning. He distinguishes two modes of being: an active mode and a receptive mode. The active mode emphasizes manipulation of the environment. It is characterized by striate muscle activity, sympathetic nervous system activity, beta brain waves, focal attention, object-based logic, and heightened boundary perception. The receptive mode, in contrast, is organized around intake of the environment. It is characterized by sensory-perceptual system dominance, parasympathetic nervous system activity, alpha brain waves, diffuse attention, paralogical thought processes, and decreased boundary perception. The meditator exemplifies the receptive mode, which should not be considered as regressive but rather as a different strategy for engaging the world in pursuit of a different goal. In normal activity, one exhibits a mixture of the modes; one may attack a problem unsuccessfully, only to have the solution manifest itself later, during a period of unfocused rest. Deikman suggests that the receptive mode is crucial to this kind of creative leap and that it may provide the experiential base for the values and world view of cooperation needed for the survival of our society as a whole.

The concept of active and receptive modes of functioning has received some support from neurological data on hemispheric specialization in the human brain. As Robert Ornstein [47] has pointed out, there is some evidence that the left side of the brain specializes in verbal, logical, and analytical tasks, while the right side specializes in spatial, intuitive, and synthetic functions. The left hemisphere is often referred to as the "dominant" hemisphere, reflecting our Western cultural bias, and Ornstein suggests that there may be practical value in developing the abilities of the other side of the brain through such techniques as meditation.

Another approach to fitting meditation into an overall theory of states of consciousness has been taken by Roland Fischer [20] and Ernst Gellhorn [22]. Both speak in terms of ergotropic and trophotropic systems, which loosely compare with Deikman's active and receptive modes. Ergotropic dominance consists of an increase in sympathetic discharges, in increased muscular tone, and in a diffuse cortical excitation. Trophotropic dominance is associated with increased parasympathetic discharges, muscular relaxation, and increased EEG synchrony [22]. Fischer suggests that meditative states lie along the trophotropic continuum, with yogic samadhi representing extreme trophotropic dominance; this recalls Wallace's [60] conclusion that TM results in a "wakeful hypometabolic state." Gellhorn, who deals more centrally with meditation, suggests that in most meditative states trophotropic discharges are mixed with ergotropic discharges. This combination of trophotropic and ergotropic activity prevents the meditator from falling asleep, and lesser ergotropic activity during yoga meditation would explain why yoga meditators, as opposed to Zen meditators, are uninfluenced by sensory stimuli. This ergotropic-trophotropic dimension is valuable for comparing the degree of arousal associated with various states of consciousness, but it cannot alone serve to clearly map the entire realm of consciousness. A great deal more work remains to be done before we shall have a clear idea of the psychological and physiological aspects of meditation states as compared with states induced by hypnosis, breathing exercises, psychoactive drugs, fasting, sensory deprivation, fatigue, sleep, dance, chanting, sex, biofeedback, and so on.

Meditation in Therapy and Education

Though the philosophy underlying meditation practice fits only awkwardly with the rather pessimistic Freudian theory [11], several writers have discussed the use of meditation for therapy and personal growth. Noyes [45, p. 35] has proposed that "the existential despair of so many in the Western world is directly traceable to the virtual absence of meditation in our way of life. Without meditation—that is, total attentiveness to the reality of at-one-ment—there can be no wholeness of self, no real spiritual life, no true relation." Other writings, too, indicate that meditative techniques may be of great value in psychotherapy. Kretschmer, in a review of meditative techniques used by Schultz, Happich, Desoille, and Frederking, offers an enthusiastic recommendation [39, pp. 82–83]:

Meditation helps the patient to an expanded consciousness and impersonal experience and knowledge. Meditation has an advantage in that it allows the transition to religious problems to consummate itself in a completely natural way. The course of therapy is shorter with meditation because one is not dependent upon the mood of dreams and comes more quickly, but diagnostically and therapeutically, to the psychic conflict. Finally, with meditation, the patient does not ordinarily transfer his problem onto the therapist and therefore the resolution of transference is usually unnecessary. . . . Meditation has a good chance of eventually becoming one of the leading therapeutic techniques.

This report of the role of meditation in therapy has been echoed by the Japanese psychoanalyst Kondo [38], who asked his patients to sit in zazen in addition to their interview sessions with him. He found that his patients became "charged with more psychic energy and vitality" and that their dreams began to show a more constructive pattern and their posture more stability. Kondo further made the point that his own practice of zazen had aided him as a therapist.

More recent studies of TM have underscored the possibility that meditation can aid other means of psychotherapy. Leonce Bondreau [10] has found meditation more effective than systematic desensitization in curing cases of claustrophobia and profuse perspiration. Harold Bloomfield, Michael Cain, Dennis Jaffe, and Al Rubottom have added to the praise for meditation as an adjunct to psychotherapy [9]:

> Preliminary reports suggest that meditation greatly speeds up the process of therapy, leads to deeper access into the psyche, and consistently gives better results than therapy without meditation. Its properties of relaxation certainly contribute to this, but in addition we suggest that some additional psychological properties of the experience of pure awareness affect the patients' ability to deal with highly frightening psychic material with a minimum of anxiety.

Bloomfield et al. go on to discuss research being conducted at the Institute of Living in Hartford, Connecticut. There Dr. Bernard Glueck is comparing groups of patients who have learned TM with others who have had biofeedback training and with control groups. The preliminary results show higher rates of improvement among patients who practice TM, and patients have responded favorably to being directly responsible for part of their therapy.

Though much of the discussion of meditation has centered on relating meditation techniques to better understood methods of personal growth, the possible benefits of teaching TM on a large scale have not gone unnoticed. For one thing, the possibility that TM may help curb drug abuse has attracted interest. Some of the early—and scientifically weak —questionnaire studies of TM practitioners demonstrated a remarkable decrease in the use of drugs, hard liquor, and cigarettes as subjects continued TM, and there have also been clinical reports of meditation alleviating drug abuse [8, 22, 33, 57]. Williams [63] reported that Benson and Wallace plan a careful study of drug use among ten thousand high school students, some of whom will be taught TM. This sort of careful investigation is certainly appropriate, since meditation promises to be beneficial in so many ways. Young drug users can accept TM as a way of personal development and the decrease in drug abuse among meditators seems to be a socially useful side effect.

The medical profession has shown interest in the possibility that meditation can help curb drug abuse and fight anxiety and hypertension, and educators have begun to explore the possibility that TM may be a valid addition to high school and college curricula. Linden's [41] study with third graders has indicated that meditation may help decrease test anxiety among students, and meditation more generally seems to be a way of helping students improve their functioning and well being. Accredited courses in the Science of Creative Intelligence developed by Maharishi have been offered at Stanford, Yale, and more than fifty other colleges in this country; these courses explore the philosophical and psychophysiological foundation of TM and other systems of exploring the human potential [50]. The Science of Creative Intelligence claims to help the student develop his learning potential and promises to give focus and meaning to other studies. As a technique of profound relaxation coupled with a direct approach to the Socratic "Know thyself," meditation seems to be an ideal addition to curricula.

To sum up, then, it seems well established that meditation techniques lead to a state of deep relaxation. This relaxation, along with self-observation of the mind's wanderings, seems to encourage physical unstressing coupled with mental catharsis; this process may facilitate personal psychological growth. Only weak evidence has thus far been published on the use of meditation as therapy for drug abuse and other psychological problems, and work is in progress in these areas. The relationships between meditation states and the many other altered states of consciousness remain unclear, and this is currently an area of interest for many psychologists.

References

1. Allison, J. "Respiratory Changes during Transcendental Meditation." The Lancet, 18 April 1970, Vol. 1.
2. Anand, B., Chhina, G., and Singh, B. "Some Aspects of Electroencephalographic Studies of Yogis." Electroencephalography and Clinical Neurophysiology, 1961, Vol. 13. Also in

Altered States of Consciousness. C. Tart, ed. Wiley: New York, 1969 and Doubleday-Anchor: New York, 1972.

3. _____. "Studies on Shri Ramanand Yogi during His Stay in an Air-tight Box." *Indian Journal of Medical Research*, January 1961, Vol. 49.

4. Bagchi, B. K. and Wenger, M. A. "Electrophysiological Correlates of Some Yoga Exercises." *Electroencephalography and Clinical Neurophysiology*, 1957, Suppl. 7.

5. _____. "Simultaneous EEG and Other Recordings during Some Yogic Practices." *Electroencephalography and Clinical Neurophysiology*, 1958, Vol. 10, Abst.

6. Banquet, J. P., "EEG and Meditation." *Electroencephalography and Clinical Neurophysiology*, 1972, Vol. 33.

7. *Behavior Today.* "Benefits of Meditation." 8 May 1972, Vol. 3, No. 19.

8. Benson, H. and Wallace, R. "Decreased Drug Abuse with Transcendental Meditation—A Survey of 1,862 Subjects." *Proceedings of the International Symposium on Drug Abuse.* C. Zarafonetis, ed. Lea and Febiger: Philadelphia, 1970.

9. Bloomfield, H., Cain, M., Jaffe, D., and Rubottom, A. "What Is Transcendental Meditation?" in *What Is Meditation?*. John White, ed. Doubleday-Anchor: New York, 1974.

10. Bondreau, L. "Transcendental Meditation and Yoga as Reciprocal Inhibitors." *Journal of Behavior Therapy and Experimental Psychiatry*, Vol. 3, No. 2.

11. Brar, H. S. "Yoga and Psychoanalysis." *British Journal of Psychiatry*, 1970, Vol. 116.

12. Brown, F., Stewart, W., and Blodjett, J. "EEG Kappa Rhythm during Transcendental Meditation and Possible Threshold Changes Following." Paper presented to the Kentucky Academy of Science, 13 November 1971. Available through Students' International Meditation Society, 1015 Gayley Ave., Suite 218A, Los Angeles, California 90024.

13. Cohen, M. E. and White, P. D. "Life Situations, Emotions, and Neurocirculatory Asthenia (Anxiety Neurosis, Neurasthenia, Effort Syndrome)." *Association for Research in Nervous and Mental Disease, Proceedings*, 1949, Vol. 29.

14. Das, N. N. and Gastaut, H. "Variation in the Electrical Activity of the Brain, the Heart and Skeletal Muscles during Yogic Meditation and Ecstasy." Fr., Eng. trans. by V. Emerson in *Electroencephalography and Clinical Neurophysiology.* 1957, Suppl. 6.

15. Deikman, A. "Experimental Meditation." *Journal of Nervous and Mental Disease*, 1963, Vol. 136. Also in *Altered States of Consciousness.* C. Tart, ed. Wiley: New York, 1969 and Doubleday-Anchor: New York, 1972.

16. _____. "De-automization and the Mystic Experience." *Psychiatry*, 1966, Vol. 29. Also in *Altered States of Consciousness.* C. Tart, ed. Wiley: New York, 1969 and Doubleday-Anchor: New York, 1972.

17. _____. "Bimodal Consciousness." *Archives of General Psychiatry*, 1971, Vol. 25, No. 6.

18. Demartini, F. E., Cannon, P. J., Stason, W. B., and Laragh, B. B. "Lactic Acid Metabolism in Hypertensive Patients." *Science*, 11 June 1965, Vol. 148.

19. Emerson, V. F. "Can Belief Systems Influence Neurophysiology? Some Implications of Research on Meditation." *R. M. Bucke Society Newsletter-Review*, 1972, Vol. 5, Nos. 1–2. Also in *What Is Meditation?* John White, ed. Doubleday-Anchor: New York, 1974.

20. Fischer, R. "A Cartography of the Ecstatic and Meditative States." *Science*, 26 November 1971, Vol. 174.

21. Fromm, E., Suzuki, D. and Martino, R. *Zen Buddhism and Psychoanalysis.* Grove: New York, 1960.

22. Gellhorn, E. and Kiely, W. F. "Mystical States of Consciousness: Neurophysiological and Clinical Aspects."

Journal of Nervous and Mental Disease, 1972, Vol. 154.

23. Goleman, D. "Meditation as Metatherapy: Hypotheses Toward a Proposed Fifth State of Consciousness." *Journal of Transpersonal Psychology*, 1971, Vol. 3, No. 1. See also his article in *What Is Meditation?* John White, ed. Doubleday-Anchor: New York, 1974.

24. ———. "The Buddha on Meditation and States of Consciousness, Part I: The Teachings." *Journal of Transpersonal Psychology*, 1972, Vol. 4, No. 1.

25. ———. "The Buddha on Meditation and States of Consciousness, Part II: A Typology of Meditation Techniques." *Journal of Transpersonal Psychology*, 1972, Vol. 4, No. 2.

26. Green, E., Green, A., and Walters, E. "Voluntary Control of Internal States: Psychological and Physiological." *Journal of Transpersonal Psychology*, 1970, Vol. 2, No. 1.

27. Herrigel, E. *Zen in the Art of Archery.* Pantheon: New York, 1953.

28. Hjelle, L. A. "Transcendental Meditation and Psychological Health." State University College at Brockport, N.Y., Dept. of Psychology. Paper submitted to the *Journal of Consulting and Clinical Psychology*.

29. Jacobson, E. "Progressive Relaxation." *American Journal of Physiology*, 1925. Vol. 36.

30. ———. "Electrophysiology of Mental Activities." *American Journal of Psychology*, 1932, Vol. 44.

31. ———. *Progressive Relaxation*, 2nd Ed. University of Chicago Press: Chicago, 1938.

32. ———. "Neuromuscular Controls in Man: Methods of Self-direction in Health and Disease." *American Journal of Psychology*, 1955, Vol. 68.

33. *Journal of the American Medical Association.* "Meditation May Find Use in Medical Practice," 1972, Vol. 219, No. 3.

34. Kanellakos, D. P. "Report on Some of the Current Scientific Studies of Transcendental Meditation." Students' International Meditation Society, 1972.

35. ———. "Transcendental Meditation," in *The Highest State of Consciousness.* John White, ed. Doubleday-Anchor: New York, 1972.

36. Kasamatsu, A. and Hirai, T. "The Science of Zazen." *Psychologia*, 1963, Vol. 6.

37. ———. "An Electroencephalographic Study on the Zen Meditation (Zazen)." *Folia Psychiatry and Neurophysiology of Japan*, 1966, Vol. 20. Also in *Altered States of Consciousness.* C. Tart, ed. Wiley: New York, 1969 and Doubleday-Anchor: New York, 1972.

38. Kondo, A. "Zen in Psychotherapy: The Virtue of Sitting." *Chicago Review*, 1958, Vol. 12.

39. Kretschmer, W. "Meditative Techniques in Psychotherapy." *Psychologia*, 1962, Vol. 5. Also in *Altered States of Consciousness.* C. Tart, ed. Wiley: New York, 1969 and Doubleday-Anchor: New York, 1972.

40. Lesh, T. "Zen Meditation and the Development of Empathy in Counselors." *Journal of Humanistic Psychology*, 1970, Vol. 10.

41. Linden, W. "The Relation between the Practicing of Meditation by School Children and Their Levels of Field Dependence-Independence, Test Anxiety and Reading Achievement." Ph.D. dissertation, New York University, 1972.

42. Maharishi Mahesh Yogi. *The Science of Being and the Art of Living.* SRM Publications: Los Angeles, 1966.

43. Maupin, E. "Individual Differences in Response to a Zen Meditation Exercise." *Journal of Consulting Psychology*, 1965, Vol. 29. Also in *Altered States of Consciousness.* C. Tart, ed. Wiley: New York, 1969 and Doubleday-Anchor: New York, 1972.

44. Naranjo, C. and Ornstein, R. *The Psychology of Meditation.* Viking: New York, 1971.

45. Noyes, H. "Meditation, the Doorway

to Wholeness." *Main Currents in Modern Thought*, 1965, Vol. 22, No. 2.

46. Orme-Johnson, D. "Autonomic Stability and Transcendental Meditation." Paper presented at the Stanford Research Institute, Menlo Park, Calif., 5 August 1971. Available through Students' International Meditation Society.

47. Ornstein, R. *The Psychology of Consciousness*. Viking: New York, 1972.

48. Pelletier, R. "Altered Attention Deployment in Meditation." Psychology Clinic, University of California, Berkeley, submitted for publication to *Psychiatry*.

49. Pitts, F. N., Jr. and McClure, J. N., Jr., "Lactate Metabolism in Anxiety Neurosis." *New England Journal of Medicine*, 21 December 1967, Vol. 277.

50. Rubottom, A. "Transcendental Meditation and Its Potential Uses for Schools." *Social Education*, December 1972, Vol. 36, No. 4.

51. Seeman, W., Nidich, S., and Banta, T. "Influence of Transcendental Meditation on a Measure of Self-actualization." *Journal of Counseling Psychology*, 1972, Vol. 19, No. 3.

52. Shelley, M. (summarized by G. Landrith). "A Theory of Happiness as it Relates to Transcendental Meditation," 1972. Students' International Meditation Society.

53. Shiomi, K. "Respiratory and EEG Changes by Cotention of Trigant Burrow." *Psychologia*, March 1969, Vol. 12.

54. Tart, C. "A Psychologist's Experience with Transcendental Meditation." *Journal of Transpersonal Psychology*, 1971, Vol. 3, No. 2.

55. Trungpa, C. *Meditation in Action*. Shambala: Berkeley, 1970.

56. Van Nuys, D. "A Novel Technique for Studying Attention During Meditation." *Journal of Transpersonal Psychology*, 1971, Vol. 3, No. 2.

57. Wallace, R. K. "The Physiological Effects of Transcendental Meditation." Ph.D. thesis, Dept. of Physiology, University of California at Los Angeles, 1970. Available through the Students' International Meditation Society.

58. _____. "Physiological Effects of Transcendental Meditation." *Science*, 27 March 1970, Vol. 167.

59. _____ and Benson, H. "The Physiology of Meditation." *Scientific American*, 1972, Vol. 226, No. 2.

60. _____, Benson, H. and Wilson, A. "A Wakeful Hypometabolic State." *American Journal of Physiology*, September 1971, Vol. 221.

61. _____, Benson, H., Wilson, A. and Garrett, M. "Decreased Blood Lactate during Transcendental Meditation." *Proceedings of the Federation of American Societies for Experimental Biology*, March-April 1971, Vol. 30, No. 2, Abst.

62. Wenger, M. and B. Bagchi. "Studies in Autonomic Functions of Practitioners of Yoga in India." *Behavioral Science*, 1961, Vol. 6.

63. Williams, G. "Transcendental Meditation: Can It Fight Drug Abuse?" *Science Digest*, February 1972.

64. Wolpe, J. "The Systematic Desensitization Treatment of Neurosis." *Journal of Nervous and Mental Disease*, 1961, Vol. 132.

65. Wolpert, E. "Studies in the Psychophysiology of Dreams: II." *Archives of General Psychiatry*, 1960, Vol. 2.

8 Intermeditation Notes: Reports from Inner Space

Durand Kiefer

On a Physiology of Unitary Consciousness

The training of attention on the physical act of breathing is almost universal at the technical level of meditation or contemplation practice throughout the various mystical disciplines. At length the specific focus of attention imperceptibly narrows to the conscious interoception of the muscle activity controlling the diaphragm. Control is not consciously exercised, but rather observed. It is a special form of interoceptive exercise that acts to divert self-conscious attention (self-consciousness) from mental constructions and images to simple physical or neural propioception.

Experiments have shown that self-consciousness tends to merge or identify with any focus of attention that is maintained for a sufficient period, depending upon temperament, training, and volition or motivation. Thus, if attention can be passively but firmly fixed upon simple interoception of an autonomic behavior of a voluntary muscle rhythm, such as diaphragmatic breathing, self-consciousness tends to identify with an organic, physiological, or real entity. In other words, the so-called mind and body are thus directly unified in consciousness; mental and physical consciousness merge in a single identity that is not perceived as either mind or body because it is both simultaneously. Hence, it is variously called God-consciousness, cosmic consciousness, original self-nature, and so forth. It conclusively dissolves the mind-body problem in the consciousness that there simply isn't any difference operationally. It is thus an incontrovertible experiential demonstration of the psychophysiological principle (which the Zen literature typically condenses to the expression "Not two!").

The sooner a physiological definition of this unitary state of consciousness can be firmly established, the sooner will medicine be able to authoritatively intervene to alleviate the general social miasma that arises from the progressive narrowing of our individual consciousness by our evolutionary overspecialization in self-conscious cerebration. If we may extend the concept of interoception to consciousness or sensation of specific sensory as well as motor responses in both the voluntary and autonomic nervous systems, opportunity arises to proceed directly toward a neurological definition of alteration in specific physical sensations. Furthermore, when such a specific sensation is willfully made the sole content of consciousness by an exquisite focus and control of attention (through extensive training of integral interoception and exteroception to the abnormal degree called superception) then opportunity is presented to define at first one state of consciousness and thence all states of consciousness in neurological terms.

From this viewpoint we may already extrapolate some of the neurological evidence to date to hypothesize that the sensation that we call active volition is probably an interoception of efferent impulses in the voluntary nervous system, while passive volition is equally conscious interoception of efferent impulses in the autonomic nervous system. It is the interoception of those motor impulses that can be either voluntary or autonomic, such as diaphragmatic breathing, that most readily furnishes opportunity for a merging of active volition with passive volition. This would account for the general use of diaphragmatic breathing, for instance, in the traditional interoceptive training exercises of most of the world's mystical disciplines. It could also account for the use almost as generally in such disciplines of some form of highly rhythmical nervous pattern behavior such as the persistent monotonous vocal or subvocal repetition of a mantram or japam, or the persistent jogging, dancing, or clapping, to the point of exhaustion, of the trance dance ritual. The common factor in this accounting is the voluntary-involuntary sensory channel overlap, or simultaneity, arising in the case of the rhythmical induction of trance, from the complete temporary habituation or conditioning of the rhythmic behavior in the entire nervous organization, thus converting the initial active voluntary nervous behavior to a final passive voluntary, or autonomic, nervous behavior. In the process, as in the prolonged fixation of attention on interoception of a simultaneously voluntary and autonomic biophysical cycle like breathing, active volition or self-consciousness is lost to a large or complete degree that is commonly called trance.

A highly sophisticated neurological examination of such mystically induced trance—either in the field or in the laboratory where chemical techniques, as well as physical ones like biofeedback and sensory isolation could be available to greatly amplify interoceptive consciousness— might bring medicine to the threshold, at least, of neurological understanding of that conscious dissolution of the mind-body alienation that the Zen Buddhists call enlightenment and the Vedantists and Sufis call liberation or realization. For a high degree of unself-conscious trance, either accidental or induced (when it is variously called *samai, dhyana, ch'an,* and even alpha- or theta-state), although not in itself a sufficient condition of that enduring realization of the absolute coidentity of body, mind, and sensory perception that is enlightenment, is a necessary precondition of such realization. Thus it is, or need be, the special skill of the teachers of so-called mystical disciplines to first induce, by an intense motivation to rigorous attention-training, the prerequisite unself-conscious trance, and then by psychological acumen to convert this trance to the traumatic realization of that total absence of center, or self, in the consequent timeless and limitless consciousness, that is kensho, or satori: "self-nature that is no-nature."

We live in the kind of world we do because we are the kind of creatures we are. If we want to change our world, to the same extent we must change ourselves. It isn't easy; innumerable attempts have been made since the dawn of history in the myth of Eden, but only a few, by such heroes as the Buddha, the Christ, and the Prophet, have clearly succeeded to any significant extent. General evidence of progress in the species as a whole has been insignificant.

Western psychologists of whatever *ism* still do not seem to appreciate how very difficult it is to change human nature; otherwise there would not be so much time, money, and energy spent in changing thought patterns and their attendant emotional displays. To change human nature, and therefore, the human condition to any appreciable degree, it is utterly futile to merely change cognitive responses, no matter how difficult or easy this may be. Human nature can change only when conscious cognition is entirely abated long enough for the individual to discover that conceptualization, however desirable, is simply not necessary to human consciousness. However fleeting this individual discovery may be, thereafter that individual is to some degree free of the unconscious soulless slavery to his own ever self-centered cognitive response that most clearly distinguishes his species. Thus it is only in the achievement of this freedom to some degree that human nature can be said to have changed. Ever since the acknowledged failure and abdication of this change function by all socialized religion, all human hope of self-improvement, and therefore of improvement of the world we live in, rests in a scattered handful of mystics and in the new universal religion of technology supported by its parent sciences, most particularly the science of medicine.

On a "State-specific" Base of Consciousness in VCIS Experiments

Charles Tart [14] suggests that a specified state of consciousness be used as a controlling criteria for experiments in altered states of consciousness (ASC). To the extent that voluntary control of internal states (VCIS) may be consideresd an ASC, two different states of consciousness (SoC) may be considered as specific to it, each with its special advantages as a base for the study of VCIS.

As suggested elsewhere in these notes, one of these basic SoCs may be called *passive volition*, following Elmer Green, but departing from his view of passive volition by defining it as the consciousness that occurs when directly controlling neuron behavior, as in EMG and EEG feedback control training in VCIS. Thus, the view is taken that in order to control neuron behavior, or neural response, it is necessary to be aware or conscious of neural response, and it is this awareness or consciousness that biofeedback provides and that may be called "passive volition." A possible physiological accounting for it as interoception of efferent impulses in the autonomic nervous system is proposed elsewhere in these notes. Here it is intended only to suggest that as it also occurs in meditation and contemplation, the meditative and the contemplative consciousness is also interoceptive; that is, a direct consciousness of neural condition, or relative tension level or activity in the central nervous system. To the extent that it is euphoric it may be seen as the homeostasis, or appropriate neural response, from which arises the single subjective phenomenon or SoC that we variously call health, joy, The Good, The True, and The Beautiful. To be technologically or medically useful, however, a quantitative index of this nervous condition, keyed to one or more physiological variables, would have to be constructed. If it is, it can be expected to lead to a psychoneurological definition of optimum consciousness that is basic to a physical definition of consciousness. This is simply a reminder that internal states (including those that we call subjective) must be identifiable directly and quantitatively on a neurological or other physical scale in order to define consciousness in the terms of a natural science. The key to achieving this suggested here is the consideration of conscious interoception of the sort practiced in some meditative and contemplative disciplines, and in some biofeedback training, to be in itself a specific subjective state, or state-specific SoC, in Charles Tart's term, which can be quantified in terms of bioelectrical correlates.

The SoC that Dr. Tart considers specific to common ordinary everyday moment-by-moment waking consciousness is, in the Buddhist view, simply self-consciousness or ego-consciousness. As an observed variable in meditation, contemplation, and VCIS (or Response Ability), it offers a second promising key to the direct correlation of consciousness with physiological phenomena that is necessary to a natural science of consciousness. In addition, an experimental program designed to establish voluntary control over self-consciousness would forward the voluntary control of the egocentricity that, according to most mystical doctrines, lies at the core of all psychological or mental discomfort and complaint and hence at the core of all psychosomatic disease and its attendant behavioral inadequacy. Conversely, a popular voluntary control of ego-consciousness or egocentricity could be expected to produce a gradual diminution of it generally with a consequent parallel improvement in general psychosomatic health on a grand scale. Since public health is collective private health, the implications for public health (and in its psychological dimension, sanity) of such a preventive psychosomatic medicine, or preventive psychiatry, are immense.

Much data in the voluntary control of ego-consciousness or egocentricity has already been generated, both from centuries of meditation and contemplation practice in several of the principal mystical disciplines, and more pointedly, in recent experiments in VCIS and in depth hypnosis. However, little if any of this data has been recognized or regarded as ego-consciousness control data. A thorough organization, analysis, and correlation of both existing and new data of this kind would be required for a clinical application of voluntary control of egocentricity, both as therapy and more important, as a preventive measure in the general social control of psychosomatic illness by the safeguarding of the public psychosomatic health.

Some of the data from recent experiments, referred to here, is classified as loss of ego-boundaries, loss of body-boundaries and loss of ego-identity (as in Tart's "Transpersonal Potentialities of Deep Hypnosis," [13] for instance). Most of the data, both recent and classical, upon which the extensive literature on "regression in the service of the ego," or adaptive regression, is based is also related to ego-consciousness control. There are a great many other areas in current psychophysiological and psychotherapeutic experimentation, such as "desensitization," "dysponesis," autogenic training, hypnotherapy and others, where the attenuation of self-consciousness is a great deal more significant and observable effect than any of the effects being reported.

The establishment of criteria for the identification of the so-called ordinary or everyday state of consciousness (SoC) as an essentially self-conscious, ego-conscious, or egocentric state, and the examination of changes in this state on a scale of degrees of augmentation or attenuation of this egocentric base would have the effect of establishing egocentricity or ego-consciousness as the most common (and most recalcitrant) of internal states on which to lay the broadest and firmest foundation for a science and technology of VCIS. While thus forming the foundation for a science of consciousness, a quantitative analysis of physical correlates of self-consciousness, with a view to establishing voluntary control of them, might also be expected to become the crown of natural science because of its potentiality for basically altering human nature, and hence the human condition, in its aspect of general psychosomatic health, through the development of a preventive psychiatry.

On Refinement of Taste Incidental to VCIS

As attention becomes progressively more present in time and space through persistent practice of attention control or memory suspension, as in meditation and VCIS training, preference for a harmonious substance of consciousness (which we call refined taste) characteristically becomes habituated because of the greatly heightened sensitivity to immediate sensory stimulation. As a result, persons who have succeeded to a considerable degree in thus regulating their attention are inclined to either seclude themselves in a kind of miniature world of their own simple design and decoration, like Zen monks and hermits, or to seek seclusion in a natural setting that is relatively simple, serene, and beautiful. For all sentient beings, quality of life is determined by quality of consciousness, but only those who have become fully aware, through some form of meditative exercise, of this equation of life with consciousness are likely to make any effort directly to control the quality of their own consciousness.

On the Engineering Attitude Toward Science and Art

It is as a trained mechanical engineer actively interested in psychosomatic health that I view the science and arts of medicine. The engineer's approach to either science or art is generally one of practical application. It has usually been an engineer's interest and vision that has translated scientific achievement into the technical achievement that has made our culture, and especially our politics, technological rather than scientific. This translation is usually a translation of scientific theory into engineering calculus or quantitative analysis and it now appears that the method is generally applicable, even to medical and psychological theory, for instance. A trite example is the familiar psychological application of Newton's Third Law of Mechanics: for every action there is an equal and opposite reaction. There are instances when his laws of inertia and of attraction seem to have equally evident psychological application. At the base of this translation is the essentially mathematical nature of grammatical logic, simple examples of which are the interchangeability of the verb, *is*, with the sign, $=$, and the religious axiom, God is All and Infinite, with the equation, $0 = 1 = \infty$.

On a Plausible Mechanics of Creativity or Intuition

These notes are indicative of the kind of verbalization that frequently floods consciousness after especially successful meditation sessions; that is, meditation in which all conscious discursive mentation is suspended for periods of five to thirty minutes without drowsiness or sleeping. Considerable browsing in the literature of mysticism and the life sciences between sessions can account for the vocabulary, but the syntax is sometimes so fresh that the following brief intermeditation note may have some bearing:

If creativity or intuition are seen as new associations or correlations of stored sense-data—that is, of recorded arrangements of groups of signs, symbols and images that constitute both memory and imagination*— then it could be expected that any mental exercise or practice that tends to dissolve or disrupt fixed associations would be conducive to creativity or intuition . In terms of engram theory this could mean that any stimulus or absence of it, such as abnormal EEG alpha or theta wave continuity, abnormal *dhyana* or *prajna* continuity, extensive sensory isolation in a fluid environment, ingestion of psychedelics, etc., that would tend to disrupt or erase existing synaptic configurations or mental† engrams without creating new ones should be conducive to immediately subsequent creativity or intuition.

On a Natural Science of Consciousness

If we take as our basic assumption or hypothesis that consciousness is a form of electrical energy in living cells discernible to humans through transient combinations of interoception and exteroception, with a capability of superception or total self-absorption, we avoid all the research problems posed by the various cartographical theories of consciousness recently advanced by Green and Green [6], Fischer [4] and Tart [14], while at the same time providing a useful framework for much contemporary psychophysiological research and for such helpful empirical and theoretical contributions as Baba Ram Dass [1, 2], Goleman [5], Tart [13, 14] and Green et al. [7].

* The boundary between the experiences designated by these two words is very broad and fuzzy; we often discover that we have imagined what we experienced as remembering, or remembered what we experienced as imagining. The latter accounts for much unconscious plagiarizing.

† A mental engram would be one formed principally by purely constructive, conceptual, semantic, or symbolic associations as distinct from a physical engram formed principally by purely sensory associations.

By examining consciousness experientially as an energy transfer process, we also direct research in consciousness away from semantic segmentation and classification of the perception continuum toward an interdisciplinary quantitative functional investigation of bioelectrical and biochemical correlates of sample perceptive behaviors, ultimately at the cell level, with some expectation that a science of consciousness will evolve from a combination of current sciences as a relatively exact science transmittable in a mathematical logic capable of generating technologies as dependable as those generated by Copernican, Newtonian and Einsteinian physics, and Darwinian and Pavlovian biology.

On a Medical Science of Consciousness

For a science of consciousness to be useful in medicine, and particularly in preventive medicine, it must be accurately and usefully, or technologically, related to neural hygiene or psychosomatic health, using these terms as composites, respectively, for the earlier unserviceable divisions of mental and physical hygiene, and of psychological and physiological or somatic health. Descriptions, identifications, and definitions offered in such a science must be scientific or predictive‡—i.e., reproducible in one's own experience by anyone who rigorously follows the procedures prescribed for developing the definitions. Furthermore, the definitions should include a behaviorally motivating or reinforcing element to provide an incentive for such replication.

Hence, the crucial necessity for medical and therapeutic science to confine the discrimination, classification, comparison, and evaluation of states of consciousness to those that can be identified and defined accurately in terms of quantitative physiological correlates and also referred to a quantitative scale on a desirability, well-being, or psychosomatic health axis that is consequently reinforcing to healthy or hygienic behavior.

Otherwise a science of consciousness will tend to become solely academic, with little or no behavioral application, providing another sad example of a human activity that is useless except for self-entertainment or gratification purposes, like most of our academic pursuits in these days.

‡ "Do as I did and you will observe what I observed, from which you may draw your own conclusions; mine are: . . ."

A good example is the treatise called "The Moon Illusion" [8] (Lloyd Kaufman and Irvin Rock, *Scientific American*, July 1962), in which a psychological explanation of the moon's apparent increase in diameter near the horizon is sought, when every celestial navigator knows that the illusion is a simple optical effect created by refraction of light rays through the increased thickness of the atmospheric lens when the moon (or setting sun) are near the observer's horizon. Another is the plethora of theoretical cartographies of conscious states that have recently appeared in some of the journals. They contribute little or nothing to a science of consciousness because they are not scientific; that is, they are not directly verifiable because they offer no behavioral prescription, no medicine, or no technique by which any of the states that they compare can be experienced. Nor do they provide any accurate or dependable criteria by which an experimenter can judge when or whether he has experienced any of these states. And finally, they do not directly motivate to the replication of any of the states compared, largely because they are not directly reinforcing to any particular behavior, but also partly because of their operational limitations noted.

On the Prospect of Psychotechnological Medication

As Arthur Koestler [10], Elmer Green [7], and I [9] have recognized, and Bernard Shaw [11], B. F. Skinner [12] and Kenneth Clark [3] have not, any form of psychotechnological intervention in social evolution that will be in any way acceptable to society must be based upon voluntary individual participation. This will require a new general motivation by efficient psychophysiological reinforcement that probably only a clinical application of some eclectic technique of cognition inhibition, such as a combination of temporarily induced amnesia, sensory isolation, and meditative or self-hypnotic interoception augmented by biofeedback, can be expected to provide.

The purpose of life is not moral behavior but enjoyment of life, which can be improved technologically only by identifying and removing some of the neural malfunctioning (nervous stress or dysponesis) that the civilization process has been imposing cumulatively on our species for millenia. Such technological medication is a physiological, especially a neurological, and not a social, task, and hence has been and probably will be forwarded much more effectively by the visionary physicists, biochemists, physiologists, and psychophysiologists like Elmer Green, Dean Wooldridge, Isaac Asimov, Robert De Ropp, Joe Kamiya, Thomas Mulholland, Johann Stoyva, and Thomas Budzynski, than by any of the so-called social scientists. The more physical or natural the attack upon the problem of human misery, the more effective will be a solution, as in all other historical scientific or technological endeavors, like medicine itself.

Only happy people can comprise a good society, and happiness at its physical base is neurological. Psychology *has* no physical base, the psyche being a concept or mental construct. A close comparison of the methodology of theoretical psychology and of classical theology discloses little essential difference. God and the psyche cannot be separated except for purposes of discussion; that is, for mental exercise or mentation. Mentation, like sensation, can provide much pleasure or entertainment, but since pleasure is necessarily cyclical, it contributes little or nothing to happiness, an essentially steady state of euphoric response of the nervous system that we variously call poise, presence, maturity, tranquility, serenity, satisfaction, fulfillment, realization, or contentment.

"Be happy," says the sage, "and you will be good." This is the only morality, for as we have noted, only happy people can constitute good society. But it is essential first to *realize*, individually, the experiential or neurological difference between *pleasure: pleasant stimulation* and *happiness: appropriate response*. Otherwise behavior instinctively or intuitively cycles from hedonistic to ascetic and back, as we may observe almost universally, touching happiness only momentarily at the points of equilibrium. And society, which is solely a collection of people (or behavior patterns in some views), pursues the same cycle, collectively.

On a Philosophy of Preventive Psychiatry

(VA Hospital, Bedford, Mass., December 3, 1969)
A great hospital in Detroit, Michigan, is named for Dr. Herman Kiefer, who was a pioneer in what became known throughout the United States as preventive medicine. In his time, about a hundred years ago, preventive medicine was a radical new philosophy of medicine that

has since provided great benefits to Western civilization, especially in the prevention of epidemics.

A notable exception is the statistical evidence from surveys of present United States medical practice that the general category of disease known as psychosomatic has reached unprecedented epidemic proportions in this country and abroad. It would appear, therefore, that there is a need for a radical new philosophy of preventive psychology. And to be as effective in the public interest as preventive medicine has been, a preventive psychology must have a medical, that is a physiological, foundation. Thus, it should be known as *preventive psychiatry*.

A philosophy of research for such a revolutionary science would necessarily extend the interest of classical psychiatry in depressive and anxiety states along the same axis through a new experiential scale to the equally significant states of elation and euphoria at its opposite end, in order to define psychosomatic health.

A physiological investigation on an elation-depression axis might employ various combinations of such approaches as:

1. EMG-measured residual tensions in the trapezius, frontalis, speech and eye muscles, replicating Edmund Jacobson, or the "dysponesis" of George Whatmore.
2. EEG, beta, alpha, theta, and delta correlates of 1.
3. Feedback control of steady potential (DC) electrical charge on elements of the nervous system.
4. Changes of ionization charge in the ambient atmosphere during 3.
5. Orientation or awareness index, as measured by spontaneity tests like reaction time, reaction type, startle reaction, etc.
6. Conventional attention index as measured by recall tests.
7. Electrodermal correlates of 5 and 6.
8. Chemical induction of euphoric states, as with hallucinogens, barbituates, amphetamines, diphenylhydantoin, morphine, etc., correlated with physiological variables.
9. Chemical or hypnotic induction of temporary total amnesia preparatory to meditation feedback training, to inhibit memory, or "wandering mind," interference.
10. Meditation feedback training in fluid-environment sensory isolation.

μ Index No.	I Index	II Main content of perception	III Extero-ception of en-vironment	IV Intero-ception of self (Self-Conscious-ness)	V Perception of target of atten-tion (Attention Control)
0	Busy mind	Thoughts and/or images (words and/or pictures)	Full	Full	None
1	Drowse	Sleepiness, dreaminess, indifference lapses of consciousness	Inter-mittent	Inter-mittent	None
01	Fant-asy	Brief, fleeting, vivid, realistic vig-nettes or words	Inter-mittent	Inter-mittent	None
001	Rev-erie	Sustained, elaborate, vivid, real-istic pictures or word sequences	Back-ground	Back-ground	None
2	Sleep	None. Loss of consciousness	None	None	None
02	Dream-ing	Images and/or thoughts (pictures and/or words)	None	Dream-self none	None
3	Pain	Muscular, or neural, pain	Back-ground	Full	None
03	Neuro-sis	Fatigue, worry, frustration, inade-quacy, boredom, lack of moti-vation, obstructive distraction, apprehension, or silliness	Back-ground	Full	None
4	Head-ache	Pain, pressure, or other sensation in the head or scalp	Back-ground	Full	None
5	Blank	Emptiness, dullness, or "dryness"	Inter-mittent	Inter-mittent	None
6	Calm	Easy concentration on target of attention with confidence and little effort	Back-ground	Back-ground	Pre-valent
7	Still	Automatic, effortless concentra-tion, no distraction, and "locked-on" sensation	Back ground	Extreme Back-ground	Per-sistent
8	Trance	Unconscious, effortless union or coidentity with attention target	None	None	Automatic Continuous
9	Rap-ture	Timeless and boundless "oceanic" perception of unity of all sense-objects, loss of body-mind-other distinction	← Fused → Into superception		
10	En-lighten-ment	Intuitive full realization of the reality, or truth, of unity of all sense objects, including self-and-field-of-consciousness, and of all the teachings to this effect. Total dissolution from consciousness of all concepts, dialectic, and dicho-tomy.	← Fused → Into superception		

1. Perception is here taken to be synonymous with conscious awareness, or consciousness, and exteroception and interoception are taken to be the external or objective, and the internal or subjective aspects, respectively, of perception. The term superception is coined to designate perception in which there is no conscious awareness of difference between extero-ception and interoception; i.e., between objectivity and subjectivity of sensory stimuli in those very rare instances of the unitary consciousness experience that dissolves the self-other dichotomy.

2. Column IV, self-consciousness, is considered the most significant and useful variable in most attention control exercises because its progressive attenuation from $\mu6$ to $\mu8$ pre-sages that extinction of the sense of separate identity at $\mu9$ that is probably the greatest alteration possible in adult human consciousness. As the degree of this attenuation and ex-tinction varies directly with the degree of attention control, or attentionality, as shown by the attention control index, the efficacy of attention control in producing this alteration is evident.

3. No emphasis is placed here on the emotional content of the various perceptions because it is considered of no importance relative to the progressive diminution and extinc-tion of self-consciousness that is the purpose of such attention control exercises.

A bipolar scale of common perceptual experience in elementary attention control exercises.

λ Attention Control Index	VI Related terms	VII Comments
0	Mentation, Intellection, cognition, conceptualization, recollection, daydreaming, reviewing, planning, anticipating, questioning, deciding	Ordinary, third state or third room (DeRopp) of consciousness
0	Hypnogogic or hypnopompic state (without imagery)	
0	Hypnogogic or hypnopompic imagery (slide-film type)	Zen masters call it makyo and say it is an unstable combination of $\mu 1$ and $\mu 0$.
0	Hypnogogic or hypnopompic imagery (cinema type), hallucination, creative imagery	Same, but more stabilized
0	Unconsciousness	First state or first room of consciousness (DeRopp)
0	Dream consciousness	This second state, or room, of consciousness is distinguished from fantasy and reverie mainly by the difference in quality of awareness of self and of environment.
0	Dysponesis	Definition: "Physiopathologic state composed of errors in energy expenditure that interfere with nervous system function and thus with control of organ function" (Whatmore)
0	Neurasthenia, hysteria	Considered to be an unconscious combination of sublimated $\mu 3$ and $\mu 0$.
0	Dizziness, faintness, vertigo	
0	Torpid, stupid, sterile, paralyzed, anesthesized	This condition usually alternates with $\mu 0$ or $\mu 1$, but occasionally with $\mu 6$ or $\mu 7$.
1	dyhana, sammai, relative samadhi, induced contemplation passive volition, mindfulness	"Access concentration" (Goleman) Initial feedback control. "Pleaseant side of neutral" (Kamiya)
2	Absolute samadhi, acquired contemplation, grace, elation, euphoria	First Jhana of Concentration. Fourth Room of Consciousness. Unconscious feedback control. "Be still and know . . ."
3	Anatta, mu, catalepsy, catatonia	"Body and mind fallen off" (Sekida). Continuous unconscious feedback control. Loss of body boundaries.
4	Mushin, Sunyata, false nirvana, emptiness, void, "Satan's Cave," bliss, ecstasy	Second Jhana of concentration
4	Nirvana, Buddhahood, Cosmic Union, Divine Union, Kingdom of Heaven, Kingdom of God	Third Jhana of concentration. Fifth Room of Consciousness.

4. The 01, 001, 3, 03, 4, 5, 6 and 7 numbers of the μ index could be used as keys of a very simple "existential" tele-typewriter operated by eight fingers, one on each key, to instantly signal changes in perceptual experience as they occur in meditation or biofeedback. Perceptions indexed $\mu 8$ to $\mu 10$ are usually quite obvious from visual observation of the subject's appearance and behavior at the time, and can be verified by psychological and/or physiological examination immediately following. Thus the subject's thumbs would be free to operate two additional teletype keys (right and left) that would signal contemporaneously whether it was words or pictures, respectively, that were the main content of his awareness when he was in $\mu 0$, 01, or 001. Analysis of this information should be useful in determining, among other things, whether his most effective meditation target would probably be words (mantra) or pictures, (yantra), or neither. If EEG were being used, coincidence of $\mu 0$ signals with Beta occurence would be of interest. Conditions $\mu 1$ and 2 can be discerned by visual observation and/or EEG theta activity, but $\mu 02$ only by REM when EOG is used. EOG REM might also give a clue to the degree of Col. III and IV exteroception and interoception present in the $\mu 1$, 01, and 001 states, with a view to determining the extent to which hypnogogic and hypnopompic imagery is "creative" imagination or simply vivid dreaming.

5. Please address comments, criticisms, or corrections that would make the scale more useful in either general or specific applications, to: The Institute of Behavioral Sciences, Suite 203, 1035 University Avenue, Honolulu, Hawaii 96814.

11. Meditation feedback training with yoked high-performance surrogate or partner reinforcement.

12. Experimental environments, as various lighting hues and intensities, temperatures, atmospheric pressures and densities, etc. during meditation feedback training.

13. Electrothermodynamic regulation of pertinent physiological processes during meditation feedback training* in a reversal of the Seebeck and Paltia effects.

14 EEG alpha, theta, or delta direct microvoltage feedback to adjacent electrode sites (such as mastoid and eyelids) in an alert, closed-loop variation of Soviet sleep-therapy experiments.

A neurophysiological foundation for a preventive psychiatry could develop incidentally from current research in voluntary control of internal states or responses (VCIS or Response Ability) through learned control of some previously autonomic nervous responses, especially cognition, if such research can maintain the force and direction originally given it by the formulation of its psychophysiological hypothesis, without dissipation by divergent pressures of popular interest in academic classification and evaluation of so-called altered states of consciousness (ASCs).

The greatest promise of a well-researched preventive psychiatry might well develop in the clinical applicability of its incidental biofeedback or other reconditioning techniques, in a parallel to preventive medicine's immunization programs.

* Feedback of electrophysiological readouts during practice of a meditative exercise such as AT repetitive autosuggestion, yoga breathing concentration, TM or Nembutsu mantra recitation, Zen shikantaza or Koan exercise, etc., similar or identical to the autogenic feedback training technique developed by The Menninger Foundation research.

References

1. Baba Ram Dass. "Lecture at The Menninger Foundation." *Journal of Transpersonal Psychology*, Vol. 2, 1970.

2. _____. "Lecture at The Menninger Foundation. Part II." *Journal of Transpersonal Psychology*, Vol. 3, 1971.

3. Clark, Kenneth. President's address to American Psychological Association, Washington, D.C., 1971.

4. Fischer, Roland. "A Cartography of Ecstatic and Meditative States." *Science*, Vol. 174, 1971.

5. Goleman, Daniel. "Meditation as Meta-therapy: Hypotheses Toward a

Proposed Fifth State of Consciousness." *Journal of Transpersonal Psychology*, Vol. 3, 1971.

6. Green, Elmer E. and Green, Alyce M. "On the Meaning of Transpersonal: Some Metaphysical Perspectives." *Journal of Transpersonal Psychology*, Vol. 3, 1971.

7. _____, and Walters, E. Dale. "Voluntary Control of Internal States: Psychological and Physiological." *Journal of Transpersonal Psychology*, Vol. 2, 1970.

8. Kaufman, Lloyd and Rock, Irvin. "The Moon Illusion," *Scientific American*, Vol. 207, 1962.

9. Kiefer, Durand. "Open Letter to the Biofeedback Research Society." *Psychologia*, 1971.

10. Koestler, A. *The Ghost in the Machine*, Macmillan: New York, 1967.

11. Shaw, George Bernard. *The Future of Christianity*, 1915.

12. Skinner, B. F. *Beyond Freedom and Dignity*. Knopf: New York, 1971.

13. Tart, Charles T. "Transpersonal Potentialities of Deep Hypnosis." *Journal of Transpersonal Psychology*, Vol. 2, 1970.

14. _____. "Scientific Foundations for the Study of Altered States of Consciousness." *Journal of Transpersonal Psychology*, Vol. 3, 1971.

V
Psychic
Research

Since the 1880s, when the British Society for Psychical Research and (three years later) the American Society for Psychical Research were organized, psychic research has been an active frontier in the exploration of consciousness and the relationship of mind to brain/body.

The subject of psychic research is psi (ψ), the term for psychic (extrasensorimotor) phenomena in general. Psychic research—which is not synonymous with the term parapsychology—studies three broad categories of psychic phenomena: extrasensory perception (ESP), psychokinesis (PK), and survival phenomena (θ). (Parapsychology refers to a narrower approach to psychic phenomena, the approach developed by J. B. Rhine, which pretty much excludes the examination of mediumship, haunting, possession, etc., and confines itself to laboratory study of ESP and PK.) ESP (which the Russians call bioinformation) includes telepathy, clairvoyance, precognition, and retrocognition. PK (known as bioenergetics to the Russians) or "mind over matter" covers such phenomena as teleportation, materialization, psychic healing, psychic photography and thoughtography, and out-of-the-body experience (or astral projection). The third area of study includes apparitions, hauntings, mediumship, and poltergeists (although the latter now appear in some cases to be due to unconscious psychokinesis by living persons on the scene).

There is a tremendous amount of activity in the psychic research field. Lectures, workshops, development courses, and home study guides abound—often for mercenary reasons and in irresponsible fashion. The following organizations are well established and trustworthy: American Society for Psychical Research, 5 West 73rd Street, New York City

10023; *Parapsychology Foundation, 29 West 57th Street, New York City 10019; Psychical Research Foundation, Duke Station, Durham, North Carolina 27706; Foundation for Research on the Nature of Man, 402 Buchanan Boulevard, Durham, North Carolina 27708; Academy of Parapsychology and Medicine, 314A Second Street, Los Altos, California 94022; Association for Research and Enlightenment, P.O. Box 595, Virginia Beach, Virginia 23451; Spiritual Frontiers Fellowship, 800 Custer Avenue, Evanston, Illinois 60202; and The Institute of Noetic Sciences, 575 Middlefield Road, Palo Alto, California 94301.*

Just as the psychic research organizations are multiplying rapidly, so are books and magazines concerned with it. The oldest commercial publication in the field is Fate, 500 Hyacinth Place, Chicago, Illinois 60035. The most solid and satisfying magazine is Psychic, P.O. Box 26289, Custom House, San Francisco, California 94126. Most of the organizations listed above also have journals that are available through membership.

Of making many books there is no end, said Ecclesiastes, and that applies to psychic research. But these deserve special mention: The Challenge of Psychical Research *by Gardner Murphy (Harper & Row, 1961);* Parapsychology Today *by J. B. Rhine and Robert Brier (Citadel Press, 1968);* The ESP Reader *by David Knight (Grosset & Dunlap, 1969);* Psychic Discoveries Behind the Iron Curtain *by Sheila Ostrander and Lynn Schroeder (Prentice-Hall, 1970);* The Roots of Coincidence *by Arthur Koestler (Random House, 1972);* The Guide Book to the Study of Psychical Research *by Robert Ashby (Samuel Weiser, 1972);* Psychics *by the Editors of Psychic Magazine (Harper & Row, 1972); and* Psychic Exploration *by Edgar D. Mitchell (Putnam's, 1974).*

9 Tracing ESP Through Altered States of Consciousness

Charles Honorton

> To see the world in a grain of sand,
> and heaven in a wild flower;
> Hold infinity in the palm of your hand,
> and eternity in an hour.
> Auguries of Innocence   William Blake

An important new area of research in parapsychology is the search for "psi-favorable" states of mind. Are there distinguishable states of mind or "feeling states" that are particularly conducive to the manifestation of ESP?

Three lines of evidence converge to suggest that there may indeed be such psi-favorable states. This evidence is drawn from investigations of spontaneous "psychic" experiences, observation of practices such as mediumship, dowsing, automatic writings, etc.—in which psi activity is presumed to play a part—and from controlled laboratory experiments.

Spontaneous Cases

Over the last twenty years, Dr. Louisa Rhine of the Institute for Parapsychology, Durham, N. C., has amassed more than ten thousand case reports, suggestive of psi, from people in all walks of life. Of these, about 65% involved apparent ESP (telepathy, clairvoyance, or precognition) in dreams while only 35% of the cases involved waking psi experiences. Perhaps more intriguing was the fact that psi in dreams seemed to convey more detailed and accurate information than did waking experiences. This analysis suggests that ESP may be more likely to emerge through altered states of awareness such as dreams than during normal wakefulness and that dream-mediated ESP impressions may carry more information than waking impressions.

The Psi Practices

Practices such as mediumship and automatic writing have frequently been associated with dissociation of the personality. Terms such as "trance," "meditation," and "automatism" have been used to describe a special state of mind that the sensitive believes he must enter in order to become receptive to ESP.

In a study of the introspective reports of several gifted sensitives, parapsychologist Rhea White of the American Society for Psychical Research in New York has described several steps that appeared to be consistent among the sensitives in their preparations to elicit ESP impressions: deep mental and physical relaxation; reduction of strain; passivity; and ability to "blank" their minds.

Laboratory Studies

A number of experimental studies using card-guessing tests of ESP indicate that relaxation, passivity, freedom from outside distraction, and lack of strain tend to be conducive to successful psi performance.

Typical of the studies in these areas are two experiments conducted by Dr. Gertrude Schmeidler of the City College of New York. In one study of women in a maternity ward of a hospital, those who were relaxed and accepted the testing situation scored significantly above chance in ESP tests, while women who were not relaxed and who did not accept the testing situation were not successful. In the other study, Dr. Schmeidler tested hospitalized concussion patients and found them to be successful in an ESP test, while other patients, hospitalized for other disorders, were not successful. Dr. Schmeidler suggested that the difference may have been due to the greater passivity and reduced orientation toward external events shown by the concussion patients.

A number of laboratory studies concerning the effects of hypnosis on ESP compared ESP scores while the subjects are in hypnosis or following posthypnotic suggestions with their scores in the normal waking state. In a recent review of these studies, Dr. Stanley Krippner and I concluded that hypnosis does appear to facilitate ESP, although the mechanisms underlying its facilitative effect on psi are—as yet—unknown.

Altered States of Consciousness

These three lines of evidence suggest that successful activation of ESP may be related to a relaxed, passive state of mind, one which is relatively devoid of visual imagery, and in which there is a decrease in externally directed attention, perhaps coupled with an increase in attention toward internal feelings and sensations. One or more of these characteristics appear in a number of mental states now called *altered states of consciousness* or ASCs. A pioneer investigator in this area, psychiatrist Arnold Ludwig, has defined ASCs as:

"... *any mental state* ... *which can be recognized subjectively* ... *(or by an outside observer) as representing a sufficient deviation in subjective experience or psychological functioning from certain general norms for that individual during alert, waking consciousness. This sufficient deviation may be represented by a greater preoccupation than usual with internal sensations or mental processes, changes in the formal characteristics of thought, and impairment of reality testing to various degrees.*"

Typical examples of ASCs are dreams, alcoholic and drug intoxication (including "psychedelic trips"), hypnotic and other trance states, and certain types of meditation. They share at least one common element: a subjectively distinctive mode of functioning different from the type of alert aroused states in which we spend most of our waking hours.

Within recent years, powerful physiological monitoring techniques have been developed that have greatly expanded our ability to study conscious states. A prime example was the discovery of cyclical EEG (brain wave) patterns during sleep and the related periods of rapid eye movements (REMs) which provided—for the first time—an objective approach to the study of dreaming.

Traditionally, most scientific psychologists have been reluctant to study "consciousness" or "experience" because of the unreliability of the introspective report. Now, however, we have evidence suggesting that physiological changes parallel, at least to some extent, the individual's reports of inner experience. For instance, when subjects report dreams in which the action is primarily horizontal (such as watching a tennis match), they tend to have more horizontal than vertical REMs. Active dreams tend to be associated with more REM activity than passive ones.

Such physiological parallels with private experience have led to a renewal of interest in mental activity as a legitimate object of scientific attention.

Dream-Mediated ESP in the Laboratory

ASCs can occur naturally or be induced experimentally. Dreaming is a naturally occurring ASC that is universal in man, and as suggested earlier, seems to be one of the main vehicles through which ESP is manifested in real life situations.

In 1960, Dr. Montague Ullman, in collaboration with Dr. Karlis Osis and Mr. Douglas Dean, began pilot studies that led to the development of an experimental analogue to the spontaneous psi dream. Formal experiments began when Ullman moved to Maimonides Medical Center in Brooklyn, where he was joined by Sol Feldstein, Dr. Stanley Krippner, and later myself. In most of the studies a sensorially isolated agent concentrates on a randomly selected target in an attempt to influence telepathically the sleeping subjects' dreams. The subjects are wired up with electrodes in order to record EEG and eye movement activity throughout the night. As the subjects begin to dream, as indicated by REMs, one of the experimenters signals the agent to "send" the target. At the end of each dream, subjects are awakened and report dreams on tape.

This basic procedure has now been employed in nine studies. In some cases unselected subjects participated one night each. In others, individuals selected for their psychic experiences were used throughout the experiments, usually between seven and sixteen nights. Several outside judges examine transcripts of the dream reports and copies of the target pictures. Without knowing which picture was used on a given night, these judges rate the degree of correspondence between each target-dream report pair. ESP is evident when they assign significantly higher ratings to the correct pairs. Six of the nine studies have yielded statistically significant results.

We have now begun to modify these procedures in order to assess the effects of other factors. For example, in some pilot sessions we have omitted the agent to see if subjects could clairvoyantly incorporate aspects of a target. In one such dream session, the target was a picture of Courier, a United States communications satellite launched in 1960. The subject's dream reports contained the following images, leading the judges to pick the Courier photograph as their first choice: ". . . Some kind of an optical instrument like a *hunk of glass that had crossbars in it . . . a telephone line . . . a globe of glass . . .*"

In another recently completed experiment with English sensitive Malcolm Bessent, we employed a precognitive ESP task. The subject tried to dream about experiences that would be randomly selected for him the following day. The results of this study were highly significant.

With the goal of identifying psi-favorable states, we have begun to compare imagery elicited from several different states. In some of our pilot work, for example, we have elicited reports from subjects during different levels of wakefulness and sleep. In one session with a college student, we obtained imagery reports while the subject was hypnotized, in a hypnagogic state (a borderline state between sleep and wakefulness), dream reports, and from awakenings from deep, nondream sleep.

The target, "Snow Mountain" by Chang Shu-Chi, depicts a mountain with pine trees and boulders dotting the scene and a deer in the distance. The picture contains no vivid colors, only subdued blacks, browns, grays, blues, and greens. The following excerpts illustrate the type of material elicited from the subject in different states:

Hypnosis Report: "Out in the distance sort of a mountain . . . Sort of a square frame . . . *Black, blue,* and *green.*"

Hypnagogic Report: ". . . An *uphill* sloping line . . ."

Dream Report: ". . . I remember having one image sort of a cloudy sky and *a hill with pine trees on it.* Sort of *a steep hill . . . Gray and white and black clouds above this very steep round hill.*"

Deep Sleep Report: "I had been talking about . . . hate . . . *Grays* and *blacks.*"

Post-Sleep Interview: "Seeing *mountains . . .* a *dark black* in the background . . . The entire thing was *rock color,* very *dull* and *shadowy* and *dark . . .* Sort of a *steep hill . . .*"

We are now trying to probe the factors that lead to successful activation of psi in dreams. Some of these studies compare the different ways in which psi is expressed in a variety of ASCs, such as in the preceding

pilot session. Other experiments attempt to assess the subject-agent relationship, different types of target material.

It may take many years to answer all the questions raised by the ESP
dream experiments. The results thus far, however, suggest that this approach may provide us with ESP effects under controlled conditions that
are more similar to "real life" ESP than the traditional card-guessing
approach.

Occasionally, subjects in the laboratory have reported dreams that
appear to relate not to the target but to some external situation. One
subject, a young medical researcher, had a dream in which she was in an
automobile accident while crossing the Verazzano Bridge into Staten
Island. The next day she discovered that her boyfriend had—that night
—been crossing the same bridge on his motorcycle and had a flat tire.
Although not injured, the accident held up traffic on the bridge and the
experience had been a frightening one for him.

When the same subject returned to the laboratory for her second
session, she reported a dream in which her elderly grandmother was
sitting on the floor in a pool of blood. Again—the following day—the experience was confirmed: during the night, her grandmother had fallen,
cutting her head on a corner of the wall. She was found by a relative,
unhurt except for the cut on her forehead.

Hypnotically Induced Dreams and ESP

One problem with attempting to "program" telepathy within the
context of nocturnal dreams is that we are competing with emotion-laden
content that is more relevant to the dreamer. Since dreams serve to work
out powerful needs and motivations for the individual, it is possible
that ESP success in these experiments will depend on the degree to
which the target material fits into the subject's needs and drives.

In an effort to gain greater control of dream content and to increase
its relevance to the ESP task, we have begun to explore the efficacy of
artificial dreams, induced through hypnosis. For many years clinical
psychologists and psychiatrists have used hypnotic dreams as an adjunct
to psychotherapy.

In general, the patient (or subject) is hypnotized and given suggestions to dream—while remaining hypnotized—about some specific topic,
such as a traumatic experience. Although hypnotic and nocturnal dreams

are not actually the same, they often appear very similar in content. Unlike nocturnal dreams, hypnotic dreams can easily be controlled by suggestion.

To simplify the procedure, we decided to use a clairvoyance task, omitting the need for an agent. The subjects, mostly college students, were selected with a test of hypnotic susceptibility. In order to maximize the effect of the dream suggestions we used only those who seemed capable of deep hypnosis. The hypnotized subjects were given suggestions to dream about the target picture in an envelope. We told them it would be as though they were "walking into the picture, becoming part of it."

After the subjects reported their imagery, they were shown the target pictures and attempted to pick the target that best resembled each hypnotic dream. The subjects were able to do this to a statistically significant degree. They picked the correct targets 46 percent of the time compared to chance expectation of 25 percent. The following examples illustrate the type of imagery associated with hypnotic dreams as well as the quality of the target-dream correspondences.

Target: "The Green Violinist" by Chagall. (A green-skinned figure playing a violin. In the background are several buildings and the figure appears to be dancing through the mist that surrounds him.)

Hypnotic Dream Report: ". . . an odd, mottled, leaflike texture of *pale green and dark green* . . . Then—this is the weird part—the *greenish overall perspective* drew me and I disappeared into it and was suddenly in another place—a kind of *misty place* where there was this old *castlelike structure in the background.* And I was *running through the mist* . . . so free and infinitely happy."

Target: "Portrait of Lieutenant Milliet" by Van Gogh. (A full-face closeup of a bearded officer wearing an orange hat. There is a star and crescent in the top-right-hand corner which is gold.)

Hypnotic Dream Report: ". . . I had the impression that this was the *closeup of a face* . . . I tried to see more and I see kind of an *orange* and *gold* cobble."

We have now begun to investigate factors that may favor psi in hypnotic dreams. Is success dependent upon the subjects' susceptibility to hypnosis? Is it related to the depth of the subjects' "trance" or the degree to which the experience is really "dreamlike"? Is hypnosis necessary or could subjects do just as well without it?

These are some of the questions we are asking in our current investigations. Thus far, our results suggest two conclusions. Subjects who are highly susceptible to hypnosis are better able to incorporate psi material in their "dreams" than those who are less susceptible. Further, subjects reporting that they are "in" an altered state, during their hypnotic dreams, are demonstrating a higher degree of ESP than those who report being in a normal state.

Here is a dramatic example of a hypnotic dream report from a subject who was both highly susceptible to hypnosis and reported being in an altered state of consciousness.

Target: "The Adoration of the Shepherds" by El Greco. (The Virgin Mary holding the infant Jesus. Shepherds around the child and green leaves from a tree are visible by an opening in the structure behind the figures.)

Hypnotic Dream Report: "The *Virgin Mary.* A statue and *Jesus Christ.* An old church with two pillars overgrown with *grass* by the church entrance. The *Virgin Mary was holding Jesus as a baby.*"

Conscious Control of Brain Waves and ESP

Meditative practices, especially yoga, sometimes lead to apparent psi occurrences.

Several recent studies of accomplished meditators, including Zen masters, indicate that their meditative states are associated with the increase of one particular EEG pattern—the *alpha rhythm.* Alpha is present in most people when they relax with their eyes closed and are in a passive mental state. It tends to disappear when the eyes are opened. Zen masters, however, can sustain alpha even when their eyes are open.

A number of investigators, notably Drs. Joe Kamiya, of the Langley Porter Neuropsychiatric Institute in San Francisco, and Barbara Brown, of the Sepulveda, California, VA Hospital, have actually trained people to consciously control their brain waves.

Ordinary people can gain conscious control of their brain waves through biofeedback techniques. When the subject produces alpha waves, a special "alpha training" device automatically and immediately provides him with feedback with a tone or a light. As the subject is given more and more feedback he learns to associate the signal with a particular type of mental state and gradually gains control of it.

Alpha-trained subjects report that alpha is associated with many of the same sorts of things Rhea White's gifted ESP subjects reported: relaxation, passivity, reduction of visual imagery, and a decrease in attention toward outside events along with an increased awareness of internal feelings and sensations.

To test possible relationships between ESP and alpha, we performed an experiment with high-school students guessing the standard ESP cards. Before the experiment began, the subjects were wired with electrodes so that we could monitor their EEG activity while they were making their ESP responses. The subjects sat in a soundproof, darkened room, relaxing as much as possible. In another room, a technician monitored the subject's brain-wave pattern while he guessed "down through" packs of ESP cards. (Thus, we were using a clairvoyance type of ESP test.) From the subjects' EEG records we found that those who had relatively high amounts of alpha scored significantly higher in ESP than those who had little or no alpha activity in their EEG record.

Although this initial experiment was very suggestive of a relationship between alpha and ESP, it is still too early to tell whether it will be borne out in further work.

Another parapsychologist, Rex Stanford, Ph.D., of the University of Virginia, attempted to repeat our experiment using a precognitive ESP guessing test. Dr. Stanford found a significant negative relationship between ESP scores and alpha. That is, with his subjects, high ESP was associated with low alpha and vice versa. We do not know whether this disagreement was due to differences between our two experiments or to other—as yet unknown—factors.

Currently, we are investigating changes in ESP performance related to conscious control of alpha. We are training subjects to "generate" alpha on some trials and to "suppress" it on others. Like other investigators, we have found that many subjects are able to learn to control their alpha in a few hours. After the alpha training phase, subjects make ESP responses, sometimes while "generating" alpha and at other times during alpha "suppression." When the study is completed, we may have a better indication of how alpha affects ESP.

Investigators in other laboratories are exploring different approaches to the study of ASCs and psi. Dr. Karlis Osis of the American Society for Psychical Research has, for example, been conducting experiments on the effects of meditation on ESP and has found a number of interesting correlations between ESP and questionnaire responses following meditation.

The two main factors that Dr. Osis and his coworkers have found to relate to psi performance are (1) "A relaxed, non-defensive openness and feeling of closeness to others. A lowering of the boundaries and barriers between group members" and (2) "An intensification of and change in the individual's state of consciousness." The ASPR group is also beginning to investigate the efficacy of biofeedback techniques in training subjects to become deeply relaxed.

Another investigator, W. G. Roll of the Psychical Research Foundation, Durham, N. C., has for a number of years been studying psi effects in mediums and psychic sensitives. Roll has recently begun a program of research that involves looking for EEG changes characteristic of the trance state and successful ESP activation.

The investigation of psi-favorable states is really just beginning. The experiments summarized here are representative of the types of approaches parapsychologists are taking in their continuing search for a greater understanding of the "psychic."

10 Unexplored
Areas of Parapsychology
Charles W. Johnson, Jr.

Organized study of psychic phenomena in modern times goes back a century and academic parapsychology in the United States is almost half that old, but a scrutiny of the vast amount of parapsychology literature published during these two periods suggests that some serious blind spots in the research efforts seem to exist.

For example, Eastern yoga tradition and very limited Western research suggest that psychic phenomena result from overactivation of the *autonomic nervous system.* Shouldn't this interesting neurophysiological clue be followed up in a field so lacking in concrete, material clues? In following up on this clue we come to suspect that psychic phenomena can be stimulated by activation of either branch of the autonomic nervous system. In the emotionally unstable, this overactivation occurs in the sympathetic portion of the autonomic nervous system, and leads to further personality disintegration. In the emotionally stable, the overactivation seems to occur in the parasympathetic portion of the autonomic nervous system and is much more conclusive to healings and accurate prophecies. We should note, with apprehension, that marijuana, LSD, and perhaps yoga exercises produce sympathetic dominance over parasympathetic. We say with apprehension because sympathetic dominance is characteristic of a wide range of negative emotional responses such as hate, anger, lust, greed, envy, guilt. On the other hand, parasympathetic dominance is fostered by serenity, platonic love, unselfishness, faith, hope, repentance. Obviously, we are dealing with something here that is very relevant to religion. Since we have arrived at this point independent of religious dogma, but in quest of parapsychological under-standing and scientific truth, it might be useful to take a look at *religious dogma* to see what light it might throw on our quest. Indeed, we offer *religious dogma* as the second of our unexplored areas of parapsychology.

Almost all religions declare that there is both good and evil in our world, and that good and evil are best categorized by our emotional re-sponses. They then tabulate these responses as we have just done, label-ing as good those emanating from parasympathetic dominance and as evil those emanating from sympathetic dominance. By these religious traditions evil is powerful, but second in power to good. Appeal to the evil power within us is fraught with danger, but can produce valid psychic experiences. We might suspect that a disorganized personality produces his phenomena through sympathetic nervous system overactivation. On the other hand tests have shown that the organized, healing and pre-cognitive personality is parasympathetically stimulated in periods of trance.

Returning to *religious dogma,* we should be able to hope that some of the inspired "truth" proclaimed in this field might prove to be a most fruitful reservoir for parapsychological hypothesizing and exploration. Let's illustrate with two important Christian dogmas.

We have just noted that a close correspondence exists between at-tributes of God and the emotional responses supported by the parasym-pathetic portion of the autonomic nervous system. Christ is represented as divine—part of a mysterious trinity of God. We can assume that he was capable, by will, of having the parasympathetic portion of his auto-nomic nervous system completely dominate over the sympathetic.

But Christian dogma tells us that Christ was the result of a virginal conception, and early Christian tradition claims the Christ's mother Mary was also the result of a virginal conception in her mother, St. Anne. Roman Catholic dogma only refers to St. Anne's conception of Mary as an "immaculate conception"—without "original sin"—or, per-haps, without a dominant involvement of the sympathetic nervous sys-tem—a dominance that occurs in complete sexual arousal.

As scientists, we have to recognize that a virginal conception is pos-sible. Primarily, it requires an atypical response of the *parasympathetic nervous system* (here linked by religious dogma to God in the form of the Holy Spirit), at a critical time in the process of oögenesis or female egg development. The result of a first generation virginal or partheno-genic reproduction must be a female, genetically identical to the mother.

But a second generation human parthenogenic reproduction might be a haploid male. We are in no position to know except that the one alleged result of such a reproductive process, Jesus Christ, was a man and a very unique one.

We do know that some lower species of animal life manifest an alteration of sex with two successive generations of parthenogenic reproduction. But the important fact we want to emphasize for parthenogenic human reproduction is the atypical involvement of the parasympathetic nervous system.

Having tried to establish some concrete scientific case for reexamining the parasympathetic portion of the autonomic nervous system to acquire a better understanding of psychic phenomena and a related better understanding of the concept of God, we might examine another Christian dogma, dealing with the all-important emotional input into the common subconscious that seems to unite us all in some psychic way.

Certainly someone with Christ's control over the events around him, and the emotion within him, need not have died on a cross, and especially need not have died *in pain* on a cross. Dogma tells us that this death, in pain, was atonement for our sins, and to sponsor our potential salvation. In the neurophysiological vernacular we are trying to establish, this would suggest that Christ, by experiencing the pain of the crucifixion, changed a psychic dimension belonging to us all in a way that helps us overcome the ill effects of sympathetic nervous system dominance, (i.e., overcome "sin,") and in a way that fosters parasympathetic dominance (i.e., fosters "salvation").

Our quick look at some fundamental facts about our *autonomic nervous system*, and a seeming tie-in with *religious dogma*, leads us to another inadequately explored area relevant to parapsychology.

We require a massive source of energy to supply the potentially omniscient, telepathic, clairvoyant, prophetic communication channels that seem to exist between us and that are characteristic of our concept of God. Within this energy domain, time and space must be meaningless in the sense that they have meaning to us. From these specifications the physicist might suspect that we are talking about electromagnetic vibrations, but the parapsychologist would know that this type of energy form has seemingly been ruled out by its requirement of space-attenuation not manifest in ESP phenomena.

If we note the interaction of electric and magnetic forces in an electromagnetic field, and note that energy can be interchanged from electric to magnetic and vice versa, we can suspect that nature's pattern for energy wave phenomena should always involve such interacting fields. Is there a psychic energy field interacting with gravity just as a magnetic field interacts with an electric? Can energy be transferred between the gravity and the psychic fields as they can be between the electric and magnetic? Can we thus account for psychic cold spots in haunted houses, and for seeming gravitational anomalies in some earth locations, by such an interaction or energy exchange? Such an hypothesis is needed to explain levitation phenomena and poltergeist phenomena, both of which manifest a localized, partly nullified gravity.

Some useful evidence in this area of speculation might be that offered by H. Forwald in *Mind, Matter, and Gravitation*. He has found a "psychic" field, operating perpendicular to the gravitational or accelerational direction but similar to it. We might note that magnetic fields always operate perpendicular to the interacting electric fields.

We should be especially intrigued with the fact that, with the temperature near absolute zero, physicists can create a condition of infinite conductivity wherein a current will exist forever, but all energy is in the magnetic field. Is there an analogue in the gravity-psychic field wherein proper procedures ("right living") result in "immortality"? The abundant symmetries of science say "yes!"

If there is a real energy wave as yet undetected by organized science, even though strongly predicted by parapsychology and religion, how does man detect it? That is, is there some specific organ, hopefully part of the autonomic nervous system, that is sensitive to this undiscovered energy form? Ancient mystic tradition immediately suggests the pineal gland in the center of the brain. It is certainly relevant to recognize that pineal gland tissue is similar to retina tissue. Retina tissue is sensitive to the narrow band of electromagnetic radiation-energy we call light. The pineal gland should also be sensitive to some energy radiation, perhaps a "psychic" energy. Just as the retina can be destroyed by the wrong kind or intensity of electromagnetic radiation, so, perhaps, the pineal, traditionally held to be the seat of man's immortal soul, can lose its ability to perceive psychic energy by adverse psychic energy radiations. Here again we have a suggestion of the power of right and wrong thought, of right and wrong emotions, in conjunction with autonomic nervous system involvement. We should also note that the pineal's mysterious (to

science) function apparently is involved with puberty and sexual maturation. We are reminded of the postulated importance of sexual behavior
in religion, especially with regard to man's psychic integrity and immortal soul.

For a moment, let us note mysterious, energy influences long enough
to look at *biorhythm cycles*. Biorhythm cycle theory is as old as the
twentieth century. It postulates a 23-day cycle of our physical stamina,
a 28-day variation of our emotional stability, and a 33-day intellectual
influence. These cycles are empirically established. Their cause is not
given as part of the theory. Their validity is more widely accepted in
Europe than in America.

If we note that a sizable volume of the sun, just below the surface
of its equator, rotates with a period of 23 days, and a sizable volume of
the sun near its poles, and again just below its surface, rotates with a
33-day period, we can surmise that an electromagnetic radiation influence
or a gravity-related psychic field influence might be generated by the sun
and might be influencing man's autonomic nervous system. The 28-day
influence might, of course, come from a rotational influence of inter-
mediate sun latitudes. The sun can rotate with different periods at different latitudes and different depths from the surface because it is a big
ball of gas wherein regions can slip upon each other.

It is known, of course, that rotating electric and magnetic fields such
as the sun possesses will produce effects on earth's life.

The biorhythm cycles, in addition to being a potentially valuable
clue to mysterious, energy radiations that affect man, may be especially
useful to parapsychologists. They, therefore, constitute an important
unexplored area of parapsychology. This is true because the 28-day emotional biorhythm cycle affects our intuition and our creative thinking.
The 33-day intellectual cycle also affects these factors. Intuition and creativity are, in turn, correlated with ESP, and we have every right to suspect that the 28- and 33-day biorhythm cycles will influence man's
psychic abilities.

One of the more frustrating mysteries of parapsychology is the sporadic and unreliable nature of the ESP faculty, even in established
psychics or mediums. A check of the variable performance of many "sensitives" who have been studied by parapsychologists with respect to their
biorhythm cycles will hopefully further verify the existence of the 28- and
33-day biorhythm cycles and allow parapsychologists to anticipate cyclic

high and low ESP scoring for an individual. But to verify this would require digging out old scoring records that are buried in individual parapsychologist's files. None of the researchers who have such useful data have published it or examined it for these biorhythm cycle effects.

The next unexplored area of parapsychology does not involve an obscure, empirically established theory but a very common social phenomenon, and probably the most natural manifestation of telepathy. Why hasn't science—especially the science of parapsychology—examined the psychic phenomenon called "falling in love." Whether the attraction is lustful, and the basically sympathetic nervous system activated, or whether it is a Platonic love, involving primarily parasympathetic nervous system activation, there is reason to expect a mutual telepathic transfer and reinforcement of thought patterns. Indeed, if we look for a natural usefulness of telepathy, as we should, the attraction between the sexes is the obvious place to start. The fact that both parapsychology and psychology have given an absolute minimum of attention to this subject is quite mysterious.

Perhaps the close relation of love to another important unexplored area of parapsychology, namely sex, is a cause of the examination of love being inhibited—for surely our study of sex, especially as a primary expression of psychic energy, is inhibited. Surely the process of pro-creativity is the most natural place to look for the most fundamental expression of the psychic energy we have been trying to track down. The fact that God is worshipped as a "creator," and that artistic and inventive creativity are considered ESP related, would seem at least symbolically significant here.

The concept of man having an immortal soul that can be damaged or destroyed by misuse of this creative power is quite likely related to the inhibition in studying this subject area. Unfortunately, this drastically limits our capacity to understand all the rest of the field of psychic phenomena.

Let us assemble some potentially useful data. Let us note that salmon fish, which may require a psychic faculty to find their way back to their place of birth, and honeybees, which also manifest faculties which may be psychic, both mate "till death do us part" by the simple expedient of the male dying immediately after mating. Does the integrity of this psychic faculty, and therefore the survival of these species, depend upon this nature-imposed monogamous mating?

We might further note that the supersimian ape, the jackdaw, the porpoise, often the wolf—indeed the upper level of evolution of most types of animal life—are monogamous. This makes the preachments of Christ and John the Baptist against divorce seem more natural, and adds validity to the claim of most religions and teachers. These all claim that human sexual union involves a uniting of the two immortal souls involved. Because of the dangers thus entailed, many religions extol the superiority of celibacy for spiritual or psychic development.

We should also note the tie-in with previously discussed areas. We have already stated that the pineal gland in the brain, which may be especially sensitive to psychic energy waves, is also, by mystic tradition, the seat of man's immortal soul. Modern science tells us only that the pineal seems to become functionally active at puberty, or sexual maturity —when we develop this soul-uniting sexual capacity?

Perhaps the most relevant aspect of sex for parapsychologists is the tradition that psychic phenomena constitute an expression of re-pressed, suppressed, or sublimated sexuality. Useful or "good" psychic phenomena arise in a "pure" atmosphere. But it is also a matter of tra-dition—in witchcraft, for example—that misuse of the trance state of complete sexual arousal can also produce psychic phenomena, which is further evidence that psychic energy can be tapped for either good or bad usage, seemingly through the parasympathetic or sympathetic parts of our autonomic nervous system.

Now that we have suggested love as a natural expression of telepathy and sex as the most natural expression of psychic energy, and main-tained that both love and sex are among the glaringly unexplored areas of parapsychology, it seems especially appropriate to call attention to a well-explored area of interest that has not yet been accepted by para-psychologists as the obvious psychic manifestation that it is. We refer to UFOs.

Poltergeist phenomena have been examined by parapsychologists and found to be most probably psychic energy manifestations arising from a sexually maturing adolescent whose creative talents and need for love are being suppressed. Poltergeist phenomena can then be tentatively labeled a manifestation of distorted creative energy. Parapsychologists also have studied apparitions of the dead, or ghost phenomena, and found these to arise in cases of painful and unjust deaths. The painful aspect should remind us of Christ's death and its postulated effect upon us. The unjust element introduces the possibility of guilt feelings by the living—a possibly relevant generating source of psychic energy.

We want to relate UFOs to poltergeist and ghost phenomena, but we can also use some evidence from the field of reincarnation phenomena. The best cases of alleged reincarnation constitute powerful evidence for the reality of an ESP faculty, but many profound thinkers accept these phenomena at face value—as proof of reincarnation. We must note that some alleged reincarnation cases are very weak, suggestive of the variableness of all psychic manifestations, or of hypnosis results or, indeed, of the degree of dream "reality." Related to our earlier assertion that psychic phenomena can be good or evil, and our suggestion that parapsychologists might usefully take cognizance of religious dogma, we must note that reincarnation phenomena have been labeled manifestations of the devil by Christian Catholic dogma. This might simply be saying that they arise from an overstimulation of the sympathetic portion of the autonomic nervous system.

Certainly, for our present purposes, we can accept reincarnation phenomena as having valuable symbolism. If reincarnation phenomena, ghost phenomena, poltergeist and UFO phenomena all reflect undesirable or even evil psychic manifestations, parapsychologists need only be wary as they examine these important areas of psychic energy evidence.

Using some of the testimony of reincarnation manifestations, then, for their symbolic evidence, we note the claims of these alleged disembodied entities to the effect that between incarnations they wander about in a void, searching for an appropriate set of parents to further their karmic development. We should be prompted to ask, what happens if the disembodied entity finds such an appropriate set of parents but is foiled in its reincarnation attempt because the chosen couple practices some form of birth control?

Might such a situation occasionally give rise to the distorted form of creativity—the psychic phenomenon—called UFOs? This would just be a "ghost" created at the opposite end of life. With this speculation behind us we now note that UFOs simply aren't sighted in India,* a

* The author's hypothesis may explain some UFO sightings, but at this point he is incorrect. A UFO was seen by hundreds above Srinagar, Kashmir (in India) in 1972. Moreover, "ghosts" don't leave impressions in the ground, or lingering radioactivity, as some UFOs have. Nor do they leave showers of aluminum-silicon chaff as some UFOs have done. *Editor.*

land in grave difficulty for its overprocreativity. We also note that a maximum density of UFO sightings seem to have occurred in the France of a decade or more ago, a France that had sustained a full generation of minimum population growth, and therefore maximum birth control.

That UFOs are psychic phenomena in a class with poltergeist and ghost phenomena seems strongly probable from the odor, light, fire, and electromagnetic manifestations that are common to all three at times. Also common to all, and relevant to autonomic nervous system involvement, are the tingling sensations sometimes produced, the profound fear—even in animals—that is often produced and the psychosis that sometimes develops after experiencing one of these types of psychic phenomena.

We again postulate that UFOs may be psychic manifestations of distorted procreativity with which we are polluting our spiritual environment as we seek to save ourselves from a very real, material, overpopulation problem. Again we have been led to an independent support of an unpopular religious dogma—one cautioning us about unnatural misuse of our procreative faculties.

Obviously, we human beings are in need of guidance. Are people in general, and parapsychologists in particular, ignoring some useful, unexplored discipline that might enhance our capacity for "right" psychic influence and repress our danger from "wrong" psychic influence? The long multicultural, multireligious tradition proposing *fasting* as such a discipline suggests to us that we have come upon another important unexplored area of parapsychology. Fasting has a long history as a religious discipline. This fact supports our suggestion that religion, relating as it does to psychic energy utilization, should be examined for parapsychologically valuable clues. We should also note that fasting has an ancient and even a modern, but ignored, tradition of being related to miraculous cures. Tony, the famous psychic healer in the Philippines, accords fasting part credit for his healing ability, and Upton Sinclair in a 1911 book, *The Fasting Cure*, expounds fasting for the individual who seeks cure of disease, and for better health and rejuvenation.

But fasting also ties in, importantly, with the first unexplored area of parapsychology we mentioned. Because digestion is largely the province of parasympathetic nervous system activity, fasting releases this portion of our nervous system in much of its work, thus apparently allowing its excess energy to dominate over sympathetic nervous system activity. The "divine" inspiration sought by religious leaders through fasting was thus arising, most probably, from some parasympathetic nervous system activity. Of course, the "miraculous" healings produced through fasting also must arise from overstimulation of this part of our neurophysiology, a part which we have tentatively established as being God related, and certainly parapsychology related.

The fact that fasting inhibits the sex drive may also be relevant to fasting's beneficial effects.

We have already discussed psychic energy as being possibly related to the gravitational field and possibly relevant to biorhythm cycles and to pineal gland receptivity. The important point is that psychic phenomena are proof of the existence of an energy not presently known to science, an energy that can be generated by, or at least tapped by, the human mind, an energy that may be omnipotent if religious dogma is correct in its assertion of the power of God.

It is of special relevance, then, to note that after 20 or 30 days of fasting, the faster ceases to lose the pound or so of weight per day that is necessary to provide him with minimal energy for breathing, heartbeat, thinking, and light activity. For a period of up to a week, in the advanced state of fasting, the faster is not getting his energy from body weight loss. We don't know where he is getting it from! Science has been so remiss in studying the discipline of fasting that it doesn't even realize this mystery exists, although Hereward Carrington, Ph.D., tried to tell us about this mystery in 1908 in his book *Vitality, Fasting, and Nutrition*.

In this book, Carrington suggests that energy (psychic?) enters the body during sleep and that the process is accelerated by fasting.

The violation of conservation of mass-energy is repeated when the faster breaks his fast. For several days, he gains weight much faster than food and water intake can account for. Other mysteries involved in the fasting experience are lack of development of any vitamin deficiency symptoms and a marked, reduced need for sleep. Mental clarity and disease resistance are also mysteriously enhanced. Truly, scientists and especially parapsychologists are ignoring a vital area of needed exploration in ignoring the discipline of *fasting*.

The unexplored areas of parapsychology are clear: the *autonomic nervous system* as the probable receptor of psychic energy influence; the *dogmas of religion* as a potential reservoir of clues to truth; *gravity-*

related energy waves as a possible source of psychic energy; *biorhythm-cycle* influence as a practical predictor of time-variable psychic ability; falling in *love* as a primary manifestation of telepathy; *sexual expression and procreativity* as the primary natural psychic energy manifestation; *UFOs* as an unnatural or distorted form of man's creativity, analogous to poltergeists; and *fasting* as a means of enhancing man's psychic potential and more accurately exploring his psychic world.

Why are all of these unexplored areas of parapsychology going begging for attention from parapsychologists? Are the evil forms of psychic manifestations so dangerous that a divine providence is protecting man in general and parapsychologists in particular from a too rapid advance into deadly or soul-destroying territory?

But such protection is needed only if we are ignorant of the facts that are available to us. We should not need to fast to sharpen our intuition and perceive truth and fruitful areas of research, although fasting might well benefit both parapsychologists and the population in general.

We must remember that fasting gains new insights through a heightened activity of the beneficial psychic energy initiator—the parasympathetic nervous system. But alcohol, manijuana, and LSD all produce their effects through heightened activity of the harmful psychic energy initiator—the sympathetic portion of the autonomic nervous system. Our ignorance of the potential significance of these factors may be seriously damaging a significant portion of our younger generation.

The drug problem is only one small area where parapsychology's failure to follow up on vital clues in its area of interest may be damaging the very core of civilization. Certainly a verification of religious dogma, if it be truth, is vital to our continued existence. Does the turmoil on college campuses and in city ghettos stem from psychic disturbances caused by a sexual promiscuity somewhat more prevalent in these areas than in the general population? If so, parapsychology should be telling us so, to reinforce the religious dogmatists, whom we will not listen to.

What we really must know, and soon if we are to survive, is: Are we even worthy of survival? Does man have some contact with an infinite source of energy that gives substance to the potential existence of an immortal soul? Is there an all-powerful spiritual or psychic law of cause and effect, such as all religions have proclaimed, which inexorably rewards us for good actions and brings misfortune for proscribed activities?

We must be acutely aware of the religious dogma that proclaims that "wrong" living will blind us to truth—damage our intuitive approach to any problem we tackle—make us blind to the otherwise obviously distinctive good and evil aspects of psychic energy and psychic manifestations.

The card-guessing and dice-throwing games have served their useful purpose. So have the ghost hunts, the poltergeist investigations, the reincarnation studies. The right and the wrong prophecies have been recorded. But has the understanding of pschic phenomena really advanced in the past one hundred years or is half of the energy expended in psychic research emanating from negative motivations that are cancelling out the potentially forwarding work that constitutes the other half of parapsychological research?

It would be especially ironic if psychic factors that parapsychologists are trying to study were operating to minimize progress in this all-important research area. But how else can we account for *all* these unexplored areas of parapsychology?

References

(Limited to two for each "unexplored" area of parapsychology)

Gellhorn, Ernst. *Principles of Autonomic-Somatic Integration*. University of Minnesota Press: Minneapolis, 1967.

Kuntz, Albert. *The Autonomic Nervous System*. Lea and Febiger: Philadelphia, 1945.

The Holy Bible.

Koch, Kurt E. *Christian Counseling and Occultism*. Krepel Publications: Grand Rapids, Michigan, 1965.

Forwald, Haakon. *Mind, Matter, and Gravitation*. Parapsychology Foundation: New York, 1969.

Witten, Louis, ed. *Gravitation: An Introduction to Current Research*. John Wiley: New York, 1962.

Weraliz, Hans J. *Biorhythm, a Scientific Exploration into the Life Cycles of the Individual*. Crown: New York, 1961.

Thommen, George. *Is This Your Day?* Crown: New York, 1964.

Blanton, Smiley. *Love or Perish*. Simon and Schuster: New York, 1954.

Fromm, Erich. *The Art of Loving*. Harper & Row: New York, 1956.

Malinowski, B. *Sex and Repression in Savage Society*. Meriden Books: New York, 1955.

Ellis, Havelock. *Psychology of Sex*. Mentor: New York, 1954.

The UFO Evidence. N.I.C.A.P.: Washington, D.C., 1964.

Jung, Carl. *Flying Saucers—A Modern Myth of Things Seen in the Skies*. Harcourt, Brace & Co.: New York, 1959.

Shelton, Herbert M. *Fasting Can Save Your Life*. Natural Hygiene Press: Chicago, 1964.

Hazzard, Linda Burfield. *Scientific Fasting*. Health Research: Mokelumne Hills, California, 1963.

VI
Paraphysics

The term "paraphysics" was coined in the nineteenth century by the eminent German researcher Baron von Schrenck-Notzing. But only in the last decade has it gained wide use among scientists. E. Douglas Dean of the Newark College of Engineering defined paraphysics in his 1967 Presidential Address to the Parapsychological Association as "the study of those paranormal phenomena which can be viewed as extensions and generalizations of physical phenomena." It is especially concerned, he said, with the relationships between psychic research and physics, including phenomena such as dowsing, radiesthesia, physical mediumship, and the physical aspects of parapsychological research and of paranormal healing.

Paraphysics seems to be bridging the gap between physics and metaphysics. At least, an attempt is being made to apply the methodology and data of science to man's search for ultimate understanding of himself and the universe. In the process, many surprising discoveries are being made—discoveries that tend to show that ancient concepts from religion, philosophy, metaphysics, and various occult traditions do indeed have a substantial—though prescientific—basis. Astrology, for example, is being supported in some important respects by studies in heliobiology, geomagnetism, and biorhythms. Strong correlations have been found between positions of the sun, moon, and planets, and changes in the state of our body chemistry—changes that subsequently affect mood and behavior. It appears that astrology is on the verge of being transmuted in the same way that alchemy led to chemistry.

So far there are no books solely on the subject of paraphysics. How-

ever, Oliver Reiser's Cosmic Humanism *(Schenkman, 1966) and* Cosmic Humanism and World Unity *(Gordon and Breach, 1974) covers the subject in part. Joseph Goodavage's* Astrology: The Space Age Science *(Signet, 1967) is also a mine of information.* Psychic Discoveries Behind the Iron Curtain *by Sheila Ostrander and Lynn Schroeder (Prentice-Hall, 1970) is useful. In Downton, England, Benson Herbert of the Paraphysical Laboratories edits the* Journal of Paraphysics. *And Edgar Mitchell's* Psychic Exploration *(Putnam's, 1974) has two excellent chapters on the subject.*

11 Plants,
Polygraphs, and Paraphysics
John White

Do plants have feelings? Are they aware of what humans think? Cleve Backster says yes. And he backs it up with demonstrations.

Backster, 48, is a polygraph ("lie detector") specialist. During nearly twenty-five years of polygraph research, he has become a recognized authority in the field. His zone comparison technique for reducing the number of inconclusive polygraph examinations is a standard method taught at polygraph examiner schools. In 1964 he was one of four experts called before Congress to testify on polygraph usage in government. Formerly with the United States Counter-intelligence Corps and the Central Intelligence Agency, Backster now directs a school in New York City for basic and advanced training of law enforcement officers in techniques of polygraph usage. He also heads Backster Research Foundation, Inc., which he founded in 1965. The following year the Foundation's major effort centered upon exploring the phenomenon Backster terms "primary perception." It is primary perception that he demonstrates, using a polygraph to show that plants may well indeed know your most private thoughts.

Primary perception, Backster says, is a yet undefined sensory system or perception capability existing in cell life. Among other things, that means plants can sense emotion and emotional thought in humans and animals, Backster contends, although we don't know how. Moreover, this ability seems independent of presently recognized natural forces. When primary perception occurs, distance appears not to be a consideration. To complicate matters (or, depending on one's point of view, to simplify them) Backster has found that the capacity for primary perception extends at least down to the single cell level. Meaningful reactions can be obtained from fruits and vegetables until they are completely rotten. Researcher Backster cautiously suggests that based on observations using minerals, metals, and triply distilled water, surprises are likely concerning how far below the cellular level "life" really extends.

Earlier this year the *Wall Street Journal* reported that Backster's experiments "seem to indicate that besides some sort of telepathic communication system, plants also possess something closely akin to feelings or emotions. . . . They appreciate being watered. They worry when a dog comes near. They faint when violence threatens their own well-being. And they sympathize when harm comes to animals and insects close to them."

Backster reported his experimental results in the Winter 1968 issue of *International Journal of Parapsychology*. (That is his only published report to date.) Entitled "Evidence of a Primary Perception in Plant Life," the report came to the attention of *National Wildlife*, which investigated the matter and reported it in February 1969. "One thing impressed us immediately," the editor wrote. "He really knows his business, and is pursuing his investigations with great care to avoid any chance of criticism from the doubting scientific community, though he admits that seems inevitable."

Criticism? Well, yes and no. Though Backster has met with a wait-and-see attitude from some scientists, more than seven thousand others have written to him requesting further information. And, he adds, more than twenty universities and research organizations are now attempting to replicate his observations and thereby corroborate them. He feels it isn't time to say which ones. "When work is in progress," he told me, "the best way to stop it is to publicize it. When they get enough information to report, they'll publish it. Until then no purpose is served by pestering them. There's been enough publicity already. What we need now is more hard research."

Backster's investigations began almost by chance on February 2, 1966, when he was doing some polygraph research in his New York City laboratory located near Times Square. After several hours, he felt he needed a break so he started watering a plant. When he finished, he idly wondered if he could use his testing equipment to measure the rate at which water rose from the root area into the leaves.

A polygraph measures three functions in humans: changes in breathing, changes in blood pressure and pulse activity, and changes in the skin's electrical properties. This last measurement is known as galvanic skin response (GSR) or psychogalvanic reflex (PGR) and is Backster's area of greatest expertise. Backster felt he might be able to get a PGR reading on the polygraph. So he placed an electrode on either side of a leaf on a nearby philodendron potted plant and held them in place with a rubber band. The results were indicated on the polygraph's moving paper by an ink pen that swung side to side in accordance with changes in the electrical potential measured by the polygraph.

As far as indications of moisture ascent in the plant, nothing meaningful happened. But after approximately one minute an unusual tracing appeared—a contour, Backster reported, "similar to a reaction pattern of a human subject experiencing an emotional stimulation of short duration."

Backster had never seen this before and it intrigued him. What could explain the similarity of a tracing from the plant and what he knew was a well-verified pattern of emotional arousal in humans? Earlier this year he said to me, "I still don't have any idea of what caused the initial reaction. I wasn't thinking of causing anything to happen or of harming the plant."

But it had happened and he wanted to know why. He decided that the "threat to well-being" principle, which is a clearly recognized means for triggering emotionality in humans, might be successful in triggering a response from the plant. So he immersed a leaf in a cup of hot coffee and waited. The tracing remained steady. Nothing happened.

Then, Backster wrote in his published report, "after an approximately nine-minute interim, the author determined to make a more direct attempt by threatening the cell tissue being tested, i.e., the leaf between the electrodes. He decided to obtain a match to actually burn the plant leaf being tested. At the instant of this decision, at thirteen minutes fifty-five seconds of chart time, there was dramatic change in the tracing pattern in the form of an abrupt and prolonged upward sweep of the recording pen. Because of his relative lack of body movement at that moment, and also his absence of physical contact with the plant and with the instrumentation, the precise timing of the pen activity suggested to the author that the tracing might have been triggered into such action by the mere thought of the harm he intended to inflict upon the plant—

in fact, upon the very leaf between the electrodes. The author theorized that this occurrence, if repeatable, would tend to indicate the existence of a perception capability in plant life . . ."

Months of testing followed this discovery. To remove the possibility of human error or unconscious interference, Backster and a Foundation associate, Robert E. Henson, conducted a series of experimental runs using live brine shrimp and automated equipment. The instruments were programmed to kill the shrimp on a random basis by dumping them into boiling water. Three philodendron plants, each located in separate rooms, were wired to polygraphs. No one was present on the laboratory premises. Then, with no one able to know when the shrimp were actually dumped, the programmer was started by a time delay switch. Everything from the instruments was recorded automatically, and two sessions totalling seven runs were made. The result: five to seven seconds after the dumping of the shrimp the instruments registered a large burst of plant activity that, Backster says, because of the experiment's design can only have come from the shrimp. The statistics of the matter—five times greater than chance—led him to wonder: "Could it be that when cell life dies, it broadcasts a signal to other living cells?"

Since then, Backster has expanded his exploration to include fresh fruit, vegetables, mold cultures, yeasts, and forms of animal cell life (including scrapings from the roof of a human mouth, blood samples, paramecia, amoebae, and even spermatozoa). All observations supported his hypothesis of an undefined primary perception capability. The phenomenon, then, would appear to include a broad range of organisms low in the evolutionary scale, regardless of their assigned biological function. It may be, Backster hypothesizes, that an unknown kind of communication signal links all living things.

The nature of the communications channel linking cells is mysterious. "We know it is not within the different known frequencies—A.M., F.M., or any form of signal that we can shield by ordinary means," he says, "and distance doesn't seem to impose any limitation. I've tried shielding the plants with a Faraday screen cage (which prevents electrical penetration), even lead-lined containers. It seems that the signal may not fall within any known portion of our electrodynamic spectrum." Although, he points out, somewhere in the process the signal is converted to electrical current measurable by a polygraph.

It also seems plants have an ability to discriminate signals and selectively monitor them. In his lab, Backster has been surprised to find a plant providing a tracing that matches in frequency the heartbeat of someone present in the room. For reasons unknown, the plant tuned in to that person's heartbeat alone, among all those present. This tuning-in ability is another property of the phenomenon Backster has discovered. Plants are especially attuned to their caretakers. Good thoughts and a happy mood seem to be major factors in "green thumb" gardeners. But anxiety, depression or—worst of all—hatred can almost guarantee a poor growth, especially if directed at the plants. Except for weeds, Backster jokes. They just don't seem to listen.

Although an explanation is still lacking, this much seems apparent: plants and other simple organisms can detect our thoughts and emotions and respond to them. This is what a minister, the Rev. Franklin Loehr claims for his 1959 experiment recorded in his book *The Power of Prayer on Plants.* Loehr tells of planting two beds of flower seeds. The conditions were identical in all respects and the plantings were cared for identically, with a single exception. One of the plantings was prayed over for a few minutes every day. The flowers that were prayed over grew faster and taller and seemed healthier.

There are many other anecdotal reports offering some degree of support for this and Backster's work.

Results similar to Loehr's were reported in *Psychic's* April 1972 issue by Robert N. Miller, an industrial research scientist and former professor of chemical engineering with a Ph.D. in his field. Dr. Miller conducted his experiment with instrumentation for measuring plant growth accurately. During a five-minute period, he reported, a blade of rye grass increased its growth 840 percent over the growth rate for the day preceding. The only variable during the five minute period was that two famed psychic healers—Ambrose and Olga Worrall of Baltimore—"held the seedling in their thoughts" during a prayer session.

If plants are constantly attuned to living things, why aren't they in a perpetual state of frenzy? For example, what about the lobsters that are being dropped into boiling water at restaurants all over town? Wouldn't they interfere with experiments? Backster has been asked about this possibility so often that he calls it "the Chinese restaurant question."

He answers it this way: "There appear to be two basic categories of perception. One, the plant is fantastically attuned to all things going on in its immediate environment—the laboratory space or the house or whatever. Two, they can tune in to something in a very selective manner. Once a plant is attuned to you, you can be anywhere and it can follow you as if there were nothing separating you." Theoretically, of course, it should be picking up everything in between. But apparently it doesn't work that way.

"In order to get any idea of how it can do this, I think you have to get into quantum mechanics," he says.

Probably so. Backster expresses interest in a characteristic of nature often claimed in Eastern philosophy and teachings, namely, the existence of a near-nontime-consuming communication capability, regardless of distance.

Says Backster, "I'd like to get the space people to do something with a space probe to show that distance doesn't limit primary perception." If possible he would put a plant wired to a polygraph on a space satellite and then station a person to whom it is attuned in Ground Control at Houston. Then he would cause the person to experience some unusual emotion—perhaps shock him with electricity—and have the polygraph data telemetered back to earth. That way the speed of propagation could be determined. "I suspect," he says, "that this signal would return in half the normally expected time." In other words, the time involved would be just what is normally required for the telemetric signal to travel from the space probe back to the receiving instrument, as if it had nearly instantaneously traveled from the person to the space-bound polygraph. "If it did that," Backster says, "you'd have evidence supporting a non-time-consuming form of communication, a phenomenon not falling within the electromagnetic spectrum, at least as we now understand it."

What work does Backster now have in progress at the Foundation? Two projects just as amazing: feelings in eggs and plant memory.*

The experiment involving eggs began from another "chance" circumstance like the first one when Backster was watering his plants. In this case, it was a pet Doberman Pinscher that Backster kept in the lab and sometimes fed raw eggs to make his coat glossier. On one occasion, when

* Backster recently granted a film interview and demonstrated his latest work in 16 mm. color movie entitled *The Ultimate Mystery*. For information contact Hartlay Productions, Cat Rock Road, Cos Cob, Connecticut 06807. *Editor.*

following this routine, he noticed that the plant connected to a nearby polygraph reacted strongly when the egg was broken.

Again Backster wondered what would happen if he hooked an egg to the polygraph. So he did, and part of a one-hour recording showed something amazing: what seemed to be the heartbeat of an embryo chick. The recorded cycles indicated a frequency of approximately 170 beats per minute, which is appropriate for a chick embryo three to four days in incubation. Yet the pulsation was coming from a nonincubated fresh egg. When Backster later dissected the egg, he found that it had no physical circulatory system to account for the recording.

This observation raises new considerations in that old question: Which came first—the chicken or the egg? Is there, Backster wonders, an "energy field blueprint" providing a rhythm and pattern about which matter coalesces to form organic structures—a force field that hasn't been known to exist? Does the "idea" of an organism precede its material development? Perhaps this is evidence for what the Bible and Plato say: In the beginning was the Logos—the structuring principle or thought-form of the entity-to-be.

The other planned experiment—plant memory—will use trolley wires to which six small cups are attached.

In its preliminary form, the wires are in a pulley system, driven by an electric motor so the cups make the rounds in a horizontal plane. Each cup will have a plant seedling in it and each seedling is a different plant variety from each other and from the plant being tested. When one randomly selected cup passes the plant, a light will shine on the plant, as an intended reward. Backster thinks this may condition the plant to "remember" that particular seedling and react later on without the light. A polygraph connected to the plant by a light-conducting electrode will record the entire run. The big question: Will the plant react similarly when the cup passes but no light shines?

Backster has had indications of memory in plants during earlier observations. A followup report by *National Wildlife* in November 1971 mentioned one in which six of his polygraph students participated. "One was chosen by lot to destroy a plant. Keeping his identity from Backster, the 'criminal' committed his deed secretly, with only another plant as witness. Then Backster hooked a polygraph up to the surviving plant, and the six suspects paraded into the room in turns. Five of them caused no noticeable reaction in the witness-plant, but the sixth, the killer, sent it into a tizzy."

Other men before Backster have explored the strange realm of electrical measurements in vegetation. One of the earliest was the Indian scientist inventor Sir Jagadis Chandra Bose (1858–1937). According to *Encyclopaedia Britannica* Bose's work in the field of animal and plant physiology "was so much in advance of his time that the precise evaluation of it was controversial." There was no question about the results of his mechanical inventiveness, however. In 1917 he was knighted for his devices, especially the crescograph, an instrument that could magnify objects as much as ten million times.

Bose is the modern discoverer of "feelings" in plants—"modern" because the phenomenon was first recorded (in obscure language) thousands of years ago in Hindu scriptures.* What Bose did was bring technology to bear on the phenomenon. In doing so, he found "mental" responses in plants. For example, when a raw carrot is pinched or pierced, he said, it gives a violent electrical "cry for help." The story of Bose's work is told with some detail in Paramahansa Yogananda's *Autobiography of a Yogi.*

Yogananda's account is based on visits to the scientist at his research center, the Bose Institute, in Calcutta. There Bose told him: "The telltale charts of my crescograph are evidence for the most skeptical that plants have a sensitive nervous system and a varied emotional life. Love, hate, joy, fear, pleasure, pain, excitability, stupor, and countless other appropriate responses to stimuli are as universal in plants as in animals."

Another investigator of plant physiology is Dr. Harold Saxton Burr, formerly of Yale Medical School. At eighty-two, Burr is still researching actively from his home in Old Lyme, Connecticut.† He has spent nearly sixty years studying the electrical characteristics of living organisms from plants to man. It was Burr who discovered that bioelectrical fields could

---

* Backster learned of Bose's work after his initial observations. However, Backster is the first to point out the capability in vegetation to sense remote stimuli in an apparently extrasensory manner. In fact, his use of the term "primary perception" is a synonym for "extrasensory perception" except in Backster's view there is nothing "extra" about it. Rather, this capability is basic or primary to the specialized senses of higher organisms. But Backster acknowledges Bose fully and cites one of his 20 works in the bibliography of the "Evidence" report.

† Dr. Burr died in 1973. *Editor.*

be measured. Using a microvoltmeter and other commercially available instruments, Burr has been mapping the distinctive electrical field patterns that man, animals, and vegetables have. Spearman Ltd. of London recently published his magnum opus, *Blueprint for Immortality*, which deals with the basic properties of all protoplasmic systems and their inherent electrodynamic fields.

Burr points out that every living system is made up of protoplasm, which is a reactive tissue. In that sense, every organism has the progenitor of a nervous system because it, too, is made of protoplasm. Furthermore, there is a universality to the field phenomena. "It's everywhere," he told me, "all through the universe and all through you and me and plants—a field that can be measured by electrical instruments."

Despite that stance, Burr feels that his work and Backster's are in somewhat different areas. "As far as I know, there's no relation between the research we've done and Backster's. He's on the fringe of science with that kind of research—and he may be right. He's been in my laboratory and I enjoyed talking with him. The real problem is: How are you going to interpret all the physical evidence? I've been in this too long to think there's only one answer and I've got it. Backster may be completely correct. But for my money, valid evidence is not obvious. I don't *know*—that's all I can say."

A more affirmative view of Backster's work comes from Dr. Aristide Esser, a Dutch-born medical doctor who works at the research center of Rockland State Hospital in Orangeburg, N.Y. In 1968, he and fellow researcher Thomas Etter, a physicist, ran several experiments with plants to test Backster's discovery. "We had some fantastic results," Dr. Esser says. "We didn't test as long as we wanted because we ran out of funds. So our results were more qualitative than quantitative. But they were really stunning. We indeed saw that the plants reacted to emotion, and I can say without hesitation that in the cases of those preliminary tests, I corroborate that particular observation by Backster."

I asked Dr. Esser if some other explanation was possible for what he observed. His reply was an emphatic no. "This is very simple. You put an electrode on each side of a leaf, put a slight current on them and then measure the resistance. After things are stabilized, what you get as a readout on the pen recorder is a straight line with a little waving back and forth. Once you have this, you can tap at the leaf, blow on it, wiggle, even burn it—and nothing happens. But then if you take the owner of the plant or if you bring in somebody—but you don't let him know what you're doing—and you put him under pressure so he gets quite upset, all of a sudden the pen recorder begins to show tremendous deflections that are coincident with the time of giving the emotional stimulus to him. Immediately afterward, if you do any of the things you did before, nothing will happen. The deflections are synchronous with the stimulus emotion aroused in the person. So I don't see any possibility of them being artifacts because if that were so, you could find them at other times when the plant is hooked up but the owner isn't around. But we didn't find any."

The 21 March 1969 *Medical World News* reported briefly on Dr. Esser's plant experiments as part of a longer article on his work in parapsychology. Although he has not been able to fund further experiments, Dr. Esser hopes that someone will pick up where he ended. "It's a very important thing," he says.

Dr. Esser traced scientific interest in the subject to the book *Germs of Mind in Plants* published in 1905 by a Frenchman, R. H. Francé, who speculates on the nature of perception in plants and elaborates on Darwin's theory that plants have a nervous system. While making observations in the field, Francé saw things such as plant reactions to bees that were not even in sight of the plant.

Darwin in his *The Power of Movement in Plants* observed the same thing in plants: they have sense organs and "some sort of a nervous system." He cites many examples in support of his thesis. Among them is that of the mimosa plant, commonly called "Sensitivity." Touch one leaf on the mimosa and all the leaves fold down as if it had a nervous system, although these "plant nerves" are something "quite different from those of animals, since they must be adapted to the peculiar life of plant bodies." Nevertheless, Francé concludes, "the sense-life of animals is only a higher developed state of that of plants."

Does Dr. Esser have an explanation for primary perception? "I read an article by Albert Szent-Gyorgyi on bioelectronics (*Science*, 6 Sept. 1968) which speculates about the energy needed to set up an enzymatic reaction in a plant leaf," he says. "Apparently it's in the quantum range and the displacement of just one quantum of energy would be enough to set in motion an enzymatic system of a plant and thereby set a reaction in motion which would change the pH (acidity-alkalinity) of a plant, or something like that, which in turn would change the electrical conductivity of the leaf. As a result, you would get a difference in potential—or whatever it is—between the electrodes. Now it's conceivable that emotional states in a living organism may generate or release some sort of subatomic energy. So this is the farthest we've come in speculating about a possible mechanism: a specific release of quantum energy during an emotional state, with the plant for one reason or another being able to pick that up and convert it to an enzymatic reaction. Once you have an enzymatic reaction, you can get a tremendous potential difference. But we don't really know whether Backster's effect is a diminishing of conductivity or a heightening of potential. Those are things that have to be figured out."

Dr. Harold Puthoff is one of those doing some figuring about the Backster effect. Dr. Puthoff, a laser physicist at Stanford University and Stanford Research Institute, hypothesizes that the Backster effect may involve tachyons, the subatomic "particle" postulated in 1967 by Columbia University physicist Gerald Feinberg. Tachyons are theoretically supposed to travel faster than light but so far have not been experimentally detected.

Dr. Puthoff has been funded by Science Unlimited Foundation of San Antonio, Texas, to determine, first, whether the Backster effect is a *bona fide* phenomenon, and second, what the mechanism is. Dr. Puthoff notes that his hypothesis rests on "a sort of overall correlation of what Backster says about his result and what I know about tachyons." This might be considered a "flimsy basis" by some physicists, he admits, and adds that he doesn't want people to think this hypothesis is a strong one. "I don't want to push the tachyon hypothesis as having a higher probability than any other until the experimentation indicates something."

Testing will begin soon. The experiment will use lidar (lasar radar) as a comparison signal with the Backster signal to get a comparative measurement on the velocity of propagation. Such a measurement would determine the time delay of signal propagation and thereby reveal whether the signal is slower, equal to, or greater than the velocity of light. If it's slower, Dr. Puthoff says, that will be an indication to look at electromagnetism or perhaps low frequency sound as the carrier. But if it's faster, then tachyons may be the mechanism involved.

Another scientist who supports Backster is IBM chemist Marcel

Vogel. With forty years in science and an authority on the structure of liquid crystals, author-inventor-researcher Vogel says that he, like Backster, has proved that plants respond to human emotions.

Humans have very weak electrical fields, Vogel explains, and because of moving protoplasm, plants do also. When man's electrical field penetrates that of the plant, a measurable response can result. Thinking intently about burning a plant is sufficient stimulus to get a plant reaction. "Plants are very sensitive instruments for measuring the emotions of men," he says.

Vogel has a novel use for primary perception in plants: a catalog of aberrations in people. In conjunction with three medical doctors, he is using plants to analyze human mental conditions and develop standard reactions to them. Persons with diagnosed psychological problems are exposed to a standard plant-polygraph combination. The resulting readings are then used in preparing a catalog of polygraph readings that are the characteristic signatures of schizophrenia and manic-depressive states, drug and alcohol dependency, etc.

This is only one of the awesome projects Vogel is working on. "I've gone much deeper than that," he told me. "I'm getting now what I could call thought spectrograms—recordings of the very process of thinking. They are not the same as electroencephalograms. They are recordings of the fields that the body radiates under a thought or a strong emotion or in deep meditation."

It can get lonely when you're way out front. Backster has learned that from experience. But stick-to-it-iveness is the name of the game in science, and today Cleve Backster stands among a growing number of daring and imaginative scientists who are bringing about what has been called "the emergence of paraphysics."

In this new field, modern and sensitive instrumentation is being used to investigate the bioenergetic nature of man and the universe. You might say it's on "the fringe of science" but it seems more likely that history will describe it as "the edge of science—the leading edge."

Among those contributing to the emergence of paraphysics are: James Beal, a physicist for NASA at Huntsville, Alabama; Brendan O'Regan, an Irish brain chemist at Buckminster Fuller's Design Science Institute; Ottmar Stehle, a West German scientist; Prof. William Tiller of the materials science department at Stanford University; the Soviet physicist, Victor Adamenko and his biologist colleague E. K. Naumov;

the recently deceased George De la Warr and his wife, who established their own laboratory at Oxford, England; and Andrija Puharich, M.D., a neurophysiologist and inventor in Ossining, New York. Brilliant theoretical conceptualization is being done by scientist-philosophers such as Oliver Reiser at University of Pittsburgh (*Cosmic Humanism*), Preston Harold (*The Single Reality*) and Robert Smith at University of Alabama. In Downton, England, Benson Herbert of the Paraphysical Laboratories edits the *Journal of Paraphysics*.

Through the work of these people and others, along with Backster, Vogel, and Esser, paraphysics is thought by some to be pointing toward a convergence of science and religion—because the "Backster effect," seen in a metaphysical light, implies that all life is one. Apparently a signal linkage exists among all things, indicating a subtle unity to all creation. From physics to metaphysics—through paraphysics.

If this is so, it is ironic but appropriate for our age that sophisticated technology is demonstrating the short-sightedness of materialism and is aiding a rebirth of man's spiritual life.

What does Cleve Backster think of the implications of his discovery?

"Before all this started, I used to be pretty much a disbeliever—an agnostic who didn't take the trouble to be an atheist. But now if you asked me, I'd have to reflect newly acquired insight regarding what higher levels of spirituality really entail. I feel that avenues are now apparent for scientific exploration of previously elusive phenomena such as meditation and prayer. But even more important, it is my belief that such research can give some overdue meaning to one's concept of the soul. It's already done this for me."

12 Messages to
and from the Galaxy
Oliver L. Reiser

A Cosmic Humanism Emerges

In years gone by, the writer sailed under the banner of "Scientific Humanism." Individuals in this "movement" included a number of thinkers, the best known of whom is Sir Julian Huxley. Later on, this philosophical development was joined by some who, in their attitude toward religion, were either agnostics or atheists. This, of course, was (and is) their prerogative and I do not quarrel with their right to that variety of what is now termed "secular humanism."

But because my own world view has taken on an increasing impetus toward a pantheism reminiscent of the philosophy of Pythagoras, Giordano Bruno, Spinoza, and Einstein—to mention only a few—I have found the label of scientific humanism less and less satisfactory. When Dr. Charles Francis Potter proposed the term Cosmic Humanism as a proper label for the philosophy of Albert Einstein, I adopted this immediately as the best term to designate my own world view—especially after Dr. Einstein assured me (by letter) that "your view is very close to my own." Now, however, this philosophy needs to be modernized at some points, and this is what I am here attempting to do.

Most philosophers today have little interest in a revival of pantheism as a cosmology. But for some of us, the so-called radical theology of the "death of God" is as superficial as the traditional anthropomorphic notion of God. Both are obsolete. However that may be, from here on my own efforts at the "integration of human knowledge" (to use the title of one of my works) will be devoted to establishing Cosmic Humanism as the best substitute for the outmoded theistic-atheistic viewpoints. Henceforth, and as a part of the program of a "creative semantics," I shall avoid the use of the term "God," so far as possible, and speak of the "Cosmic Imagination" and the "Cosmic Lens" as the appropriate realities of this developing form of Cosmic Humanism.

There are many facets to this world view. It involves an epistemology, a physics and astronomy, a theory of biological evolution, a theory of the nature of man, and an ethics and a political philosophy. My special concern on this occasion is to explain the theory of human consciousness that is emerging from this cosmology. This leads to what is termed a *bipolar theory of human consciousness.*

The essential idea involves the rejection of what has been called the "under the hat" theory of consciousness—that human consciousness is identical with the bioelectric processes ("brain waves") that issue from the nervous system.

According to our view, human consciousness is a synergistic result of a feedback circuitry between the field influences of the cerebral hemispheres and the cosmic field—the hydrogen-helium plasma of the galactic disc. Here the galaxy ("Cosmic Lens") is treated as a whole, a cosmic gestalt and in resonance with the cerebral lobes, which generates a novel emergent, the *psychosphere.*

The Cosmic Lens

In order to theorize within the limits of the foregoing general principles, and at the same time move toward the desired synthesis, it is necessary for me to return to the ideas previously conveyed to me by Dr. Andrija Puharich. This takes us into the field of nuclear physics as applied to biological phenomena.

Working together on this, Dr. Puharich and I have come to advocate the hypothesis that quantized spin states in biophysical systems are the source of "information," so that in human beings the signal detection system is to be found at the atomic level (not the molecular level) in the hydrogen bonds that are suspended in the protein $C = O\text{-}H\text{-}N$ system. On this foundational level, therefore, the explanation of coherence in terms of magnetic moments, orientations, and polarizations is provided by the elements of atomic spin, precession, and so on.

So much for the biophysical basis. Next, moving out to the wider cosmic system, we note that over 90 percent of the galaxy is composed of hydrogen. This hydrogen is fairly evenly distributed throughout our Milky Way—the galactic disc—so that in reality we human beings live in a galactic hydrogen field. Given that, the just-mentioned quantized spin orientations of the protons of the field and their various states in geometrical configurations thus provide the equivalent of the Lens of the Cosmic Imagination, which—as we propose—can and does utilize this mechanism to influence events in biological systems here on the earth. Clearly at this point the phenomenology of our spiral galaxy begins to resemble the supposed causal influences of astrological doctrines. Here, if anywhere, is where the zodiac of astrology finds its place in a Cosmic Humanism.

To continue the story, let us turn to the source of hydrogen atoms in the galactic disc. The astrophysicists inform us that hydrogen pours into the center of the rotating galaxy in the region of the constellation Sagittarius, which is near the center of the galaxy. The astrophysicists also report that the hydrogen spurts out from the core and takes the form of the S-shaped pattern of the spiral arms. Something remarkable is happening in the galaxy's nucleus to replenish the hydrogen clouds and also transmute hydrogen into helium—something, perhaps, that transcends presently known laws of physics. This "rain of hydrogen" may be related to the galactic halo, and this reminds one of the earlier suggestions of Sir James H. Jeans that the hydrogen comes from outside the galaxy, as if from a higher dimension.

Galactic Psychodynamics

The poet has said that life is a dome of many-colored glass that stains the white radiance of eternity. If one were to translate this visual imagery into the language of music—and this is possible, as we shall see—we could rephrase this and propose, in all seriousness, that our spiral galaxy may utilize laser beams in a kind of musical consonance to weave the warp and woof of the cosmoplasmic ("magnetohydrodynamic") waves. These waves in turn create the dynamogenic holograms that constitute the Platonic archetypes of the spiral stairway of emergent evolution.

That is to say, what is here being proposed is that we explore at greater length the possibilities inherent in the analogy (homomorphism) between the human brain and the spiral galaxy, thus transforming the galactic disc into the Cosmic Lens by endowing it with the generative capacity that the brain of man possesses. This, if valid, would mean that both galaxy and brain can serve as time-spanning (intelligent) guidance systems for their respective sensoria.

In this projected synthesis the implications are still to be exfoliated. What additional functions the galaxy—now the Cosmic Lens—may have with respect to other planetary systems of the Milky Way wherein life may take its "lactic" nourishment are still to be investigated.

In proposing this analogy we are, of course, in the eyes of the Positivists, committing the odious fallacy of "anthropomorphism," the analogy being perhaps the most "outlandish" since Johannes Kepler. You recall that after discovering his three famous laws of planetary motion, Kepler exclaimed ecstatically: "O Lord, I think Thy thoughts after Thee." Well, if Kepler's Lord did not object, why should others quibble over something that boggles the mind only of unimaginative pedants?

The reader will note that in the above philosophical extravaganza there are two themes, both of which deserve further explanation. First of all there is reference to laser beams, and second, there is mention of holograms. These two, in the present scheme, can be joined like Gemini configurations of the zodiac, and we must consider this conjunction in detail as we follow the implications of the gleams.

That both lasers and holograms must occupy an important place in our cosmology is not obvious at first sight. It is only when their functions are related to the psychosphere that the potentialities for synthesis become more evident. One idea that has served as a catalyst of synthesis is the suggestion that helium, when supercooled, has the properties of life and consciousness.

Laser Light and Holograms

The topic of laser beams is one that has lately been so much in the limelight that one has justification for assuming that the reader has some knowledge of the subject.

Most individuals know that the term "laser" is an acronym for "light amplification by stimulated emission of radiation." The more technically trained also know that a laser is an optical maser. Spontaneous light (photons) travels in all directions; but lasers give off "coherent" light rays. That is, rays of focused energy produced by atoms that emit their waves "in step" or "in phase." In this manner a narrow beam of very intense light is generated. The laser apparatus consists of a tube with reflecting mirrors placed at proper distances apart so that light waves of characteristic length (monochromatic rays) are reflected back and forth to reinforce them, and thus they are emitted as coherent beams for each type of laser.

The principle of "stimulated light" was described by Einstein in 1917, but it is only recently that most of the practical applications have been made. Many obstacles remain to be overcome before the full advantages of this "miracle light" can be exploited. But even now we hear talk of "deathrays" from "ray guns," "miracle surgery," interplanetary television and telephone calls, tracking satellites, power transmission via lasers, and many other marvels from this new "Aladdin's lamp of science." Perhaps the most revolutionary of all the pioneering efforts in the uses of laser technology is in the field of the control of thermonuclear fusion, i.e., "taming the hydrogen bomb" for limitless, cheap, and pollution-free energy for mankind. Thus the light that is intense enough to drill a hole through a steel plate may eventually be harnessed to a propulsion system for "space ships" that journey into celestial realms. Such a vehicle has been called "Unibutz" by Robert A. Smith, III, of the University of Alabama.

Among the novel applications of lasers, of special interest to us here, are the applications in holography. Let us therefore turn to this topic for a moment.

The new field of holography is one of the byproducts of laser technology. This is a method of making three dimensional pictures by illuminating an object in such a way that both the light reflected from the object and from a mirror are recorded simultaneously on film. Thus the record of the object is a record of the reflected light waves—a diffraction or an interference pattern that can be projected upon a screen so that the 3-D effect is clearly visible. In this manner the reconstructed array of wave-fronts is "frozen" and the hologram, the whole picture, is available. What is astonishing is that the optical image can now be translated into an acoustic "image," as we shall see. In a similar way, if one but put consciousness at the right spot in space-time, would he not be on the way to some new kind of synesthesia—a kind of "cosmic consciousness"?

Among the more recent applications of lasers to holography is the development of a "holographic memory" to replace the magnetic tapes in their large computer consoles. This invention of the memory holograph may revolutionize the field of computer data processing. Add to this the development of new lasers that can operate at room temperatures, instead of only at extremely high temperatures, and it becomes possible to employ lasers for the transmission of voice and other data in high capacity optical communications systems. Among other things, the "Photophone" will in time become available at low cost.

Returning to the earlier point that the optical image can be transposed (as the gestalt theorists would say) into an acoustic image, and recalling also our supposition about the psychosphere emerging from the galaxy and the circumglobal layer that is attached to the earth, we then venture further into the hinterlands of science fiction and ask the question: Are we about to emerge into the kind of consciousness that has been described as the "mystical experience"—a "total awareness"?

What is so marvelous in all these startling developments in astrophysics and paraphysics is the way in which we gain glimpses of how consciousness acquires a supporting cosmic frame and also how light is shed on the origin of life itself. The amazing idea that "an exotic form of amplification," such as maser action, is occurring in the galaxy, and that this could be responsible for the stimulation of the energy levels—this maser-type function serving to amplify the original signal— is now being studied by those radio astronomers who are investigating the interstellar molecular species that are familiar in the domain of organic chemistry.

The interconnections here are no clearer than the grammar that seeks to describe the thoughts. Perhaps it really does not matter where we start this cosmic cycle—a celestial-terrestrial feedback—except that, as we know, the galaxy in its origin did precede the birth of the earth by perhaps ten billion years. With this in mind, we propose the sequence: cosmic matter → galactic mind → organic molecules in space → living cells on earth → circumglobal helium layer → genus *homo* → psychosphere. Do we have here the oriental image of eternity: a serpent swallowing its own tail? Is the Cosmic Imagination supplying the images

to the Cosmic Lens, utilizing the radiation it eats and disgorges to produce its own illuminated journey through the spiral forms of time and
space? If so, it appears that we still need the laser or maser, the cosmic
rays, and perhaps the holographs also, to provide the "inspiration" for
the cosmic cinerama.

To be sure, the explanation of the origins of cosmic rays and radio
waves that are so essential to a complete understanding of the ongoing
cosmic processes are still awaiting agreement. I would say that the un-
raveling of this mystery is irrelevant to our discussion at the present
moment, except that in this marvelous tapestry of galactic psychody-
namics one no longer knows what is "relevant" and what is not. We
therefore pause for a moment to have another look at what we have
ignored.

Synchrotron Radiation

The idea that cosmic radio waves are emitted by the so-called syn-
chrotron process was first proposed by astrophysicists K. O. Kiepenheuer
and Hannes Alfvén. This refers to the radiation process whereby charged
particles emit radiation as they spiral in a magnetic field. One important
property of radiation emitted by this process is that it is linearly polarized.
This means that the image of an object radiating by this mechanism
will look very different as one rotates a piece of polarized light in front
of the image plane. This remarkable idea was successfully applied to the
origin of the tremendous energy supply of the Crab Nebula, which contains a vast number of high-energy electrons spiraling about the magnetic
field that permeates the nebula. Thus the Crab is a gigantic cosmic ac-
celerator, producing cosmic rays that spread through the galaxy and also
bombard the earth.

Later on "pulsars" and "neutron stars" were discovered in the Crab
Nebula, the former sending out pulses of light at the rate of 30 times
per second. These rotating stars send out beams like a gigantic rotating
lighthouse beam, except that the beams are x-rays, light and radio pulsations. The energy generator in the Crab has a strong magnetic field and
the pulsar is a gigantic rotating magnet, rotating about 30 times per
second. There are theories about the possible cause of the periodicity,
but many aspects are not yet understood.

Plasma Music

The subject of "magnetohydrodynamic waves" (Alfvén waves) plunges us into the ocean of the cosmoplasma. And that introduces us to the newest member of the cosmic symphony—plasma music—something we are going to hear more of as time passes.

In discussing "superconductivity" as a manifestation of the behavior of supercooled helium acting under the influence of magnetic fields, we must note that the "particles" of the helium plasma have been compared to a string of pearls on a cord under tension. One consequence of this is that just as ordinary sound waves (acoustics) can be elicited from a stringed musical instrument, such as a violin, so the magnetohydrodynamic waves can be set up in the plasma from the strung-out series of particles. As one writer has pointed out, there can be a kind of plasmic counterpart of music.

But if we go further and postulate that there is indeed an improviser at work in the Cosmic Temple of Consonance, we then have the Conductor of the cosmoplasmic symphony. Would this be the "mind" of the galaxy? But does the galactic disc (Lens) have a "mind"?

For my part, I see no reason why, if the mind of man can be conscious of its own body, the galaxy—if it is an integrated unit—cannot also. This is only panpsychism carried to its highest level.

The possible benefits of a holistic sensorium are enormous. Let us suppose that man has mastered the art and the science of resonance or synchronicity with the psychosphere. He could then compose music for the cosmoplasma—a Pythagorean "music of the spheres" of galactic proportions. It might parallel the achievement of Dr. Joe Kamiya, who has constructed an electronic device that facilitates the production of alpha brain waves so that—some researchers think—by applying this new biofeedback technique it will be possible to translate brain signals into acceptable music harmonies. This "music of the hemispheres" strangely resembles our "global hemispheres" music and the music of the cosmoplasma. Cosmic alphaphones, no less!

We have previously referred to the research of Hannes Alfvén in the area of "magnetohydrodynamics" (MHD), for which he received a Nobel prize. The applications of his work seem endless. It turns out that these Alfvén waves may provide one method for generating electrical energy. Here coal is converted into gas; this gas is seeded with tiny particles to make it more conductive; and then it is forced through a stationary magnetic field—plasma physics once again. If scientists also learn how to utilize laser beams to fuse hydrogen atoms, it should then be possible to produce the thermonuclear reaction in the sun that releases the prodigious explosive energy of the hydrogen bomb. And if, as Professor Moshe J. Lubin of the University of Rochester hopes, it then becomes possible to inject frozen pellets of hydrogen into a cavity (a kind of small-scale replica of the galactic "refrigerator" for bonding organic compounds) and bombard them with a laser beam and set up a thermonuclear fusion reaction, this laser generated thermonuclear fusion, if it could be controlled, would provide the energy for the propulsion of space-vehicles to explore the other planetary systems of the galaxy.

But everything depends upon knowing how to control the processes so as to avoid catastrophe—guidance problems again. This, of course, is the story of man as the plasma music rises to a climactic crescendo: cremation on the earth—incinerated as wars rise in temperature from "cold" to "hot"—or man's peaceful journeys to other parts of the cosmos.

If, on the human level, we can "synchronize the power of resonant thought," we can get human minds to focus on the problem of the future evolution of consciousness, and we might then come up with the correct "interference pattern," creating, in time, a lovely Platonic Hologram. In that day we will be able to write the score and the equations for the symphony of wave actions that course through man from the spin precessions of the lowest level electron within himself to the plasma waves that originate in the galactic system that, sooner or later (probably both), act in and through mankind.

Man's Message to the Galaxy

In our earlier version of the bipolar theory we conjectured that at the other pole of human consciousness, outside the cerebral lobes, was the circumglobal helium layer known as the heliosphere. However, more recent studies suggest that the resonance, or feedback circuit, operates between the brain and the galactic plasma that is beyond the pulsing ionosphere, heliosphere, and magnetosphere, but circumscribing and penetrating these in an all-inclusive cosmic field. In this fashion we reinstate the ancient vision of the microcosm-macrocosm homology—the mirror-image dualism of man and the cosmos, brain and galaxy. This must be so if the spin resonances, precessions, and angular momenta in biophysical systems exhibit coherence with respect to orientations and polarizations of cosmic counterparts. By analogy, therefore, we may expect that the human brain in action—as in memory and visualization—exhibits a parallelism between the domain of matter when its contents are observed as *particles, atoms, molecules,* and *macromolecules* (including DNA-RNA genetic units) and the domain of mind when its contents are experienced as *percepts, concepts, images,* and *higher mental organizations.* These latter, as we have indicated, are also functions of complexity of "interference" patterns. Here, too, the wave-particle complementarity principle reappears, but on a higher level of emergent evolution, as we step up the rungs of the ladder of emergent evolution from the "inorganic" through the "organic" to the "superorganic."

What is important to note here is that there are two ways in which the "reunion" of man and the cosmos can come about: in the first place, by astronauts journeying into the wider world of planetary and stellar systems; and second, by man staying where he is, here on the earth, and learning to resonate with the pulsations and rhythms of the cybernetic feedbacks that build up the *psi*-field potentials in the hydrogen-helium plasma. Perhaps these two are parallel paths and will go along together.

At the end of the journey, the "archetypal hologram" will appear as a *visualization of the Cosmic Imagination.* This is now the full meaning of what was projected in my earlier essay "Cosmecology."* The message is clear and simple: out of the galaxy man is born; by the light of the galaxy man lives his life; and to the galaxy man will return. This is the samsara of Emergent Man's celestial voyage. As Robert Smith puts it: The majesty of cosmic space and the majesty of man's cosmic mind form a single reality, and the synoptic vision thus engendered provides the new womb for humanistic gestation, the cocoon for metamorphosis, to allow man to see his own exosomatic heredity evolving through a Cosmic Lens projected from an image in the Cosmic Imagination. Thus, Emergent Man's new image of man provides the morphogenetic force for the New Earth and the New Humanity. This is man's message to the galaxy.

* "Cosmecology: A Theory of Evolution." *Journal of Heredity,* Vol. 28, 1937.

VII
Biotechnology

Biotechnology is one aspect of the interface between man's psychoenergetic existence and his technological creations. It arises from the discovery —among many—that cells and other biological components have various electronic solid state physical properties such as semiconduction, capacitance, and microwave transmission.

Perhaps the first form of biotechnology was acupuncture. Today the term includes biofeedback machines, stimoceivers implanted in the brains of Dr. José Delgado's monkeys that allow computer-controlled direct radio communication to bypass the sensory systems, negative ion generators (see James Beal's article), pacemakers, thought-controlled mechanical limbs, Kirlian photography, the tobiscope (a Russian device for detecting acupuncture points), the esoteric inventions of scientist-occultists such as de la Warr, Hieronymus, and Reich, and a host of other devices that promise to extend man's knowledge and control of himself. One possibility on the horizon: a machine for regenerating organs and limbs through electrical stimulation of cells. Another: curing cancer via the Priore device, an electromagnetic instrument now the center of a scientific controversy in France.

The ultimate development, of course, would be to achieve that degree of consciousness that does away with the need for technology. The human frame (called "the human transducer" by Dr. Andrija Puharich, who invented an electronic device for restoring hearing to the deaf) and its associated energy systems would be all we need to produce, transport, or otherwise effect our wishes. Psychic powers seem to be the beginning of that development, but by no means the end (because those states of consciousness described as bestowing "lasting happiness" or "peace of mind" are beyond the reach of psychic faculties).

It is important to keep our technological inventions in perspective. They should be aids to growth and well-being. But like all our technology, there will undoubtedly be opportunity for misapplications in crime and warfare, and opportunity for us to become dependent on them rather than using them to achieve a greater degree of freedom. James Beal points out in "Paraphysics and Parapsychology" (Analog, April 1973) that many operators of various occult devices such as dowsing rods, aura meters, radionics machines and so forth eventually dispense with the equipment and perform the function directly. "The human body/ mind system is part of the circuit," he writes. "The machines perform no understood function by themselves." This is a valuable observation to bear in mind as man strives to move through science toward omniscience.

Resources for further exploration in this area are few. Two articles easily available to the general public are Albert Szent-Gyorgyi's "Bioelectronics" (Science, 6 September 1968) *and Robert O. Becker's "Electromagnetic Forces and Life Processes"* (Technology Review, December 1972). *William Tiller's "Radionics, Radiesthesia and Physics" is contained in* The Varieties of Healing Experience *and can be obtained for $5 from the Academy of Parapsychology and Medicine, Los Altos, California 94022. David V. Tansley's* Radionics and the Subtle Anatomy of Man (Health Science Press, Rustington, Sussex, England, 1972) *is an excellent introduction to the field of radionic diagnosis and therapy.*

J.W.

13 The New

Biotechnology

James B. Beal

Today, from the space program, we are learning there is no absolute "up" or "down" but only an "outward" and "inward."

In the space program, in exploring the heavens, we see an activity that probes outward into the cosmic design to bring about an understanding of its events, its laws and principles; and inward to comprehend the basic "building blocks" of life. In the perspective of history, the objectives of the space program are as old as man himself, constituting a search into the essential nature of existence and of man's place in it.

Much of what goes on in space, especially in the earth-sun relationships and cosmic rays from deep space, affects our environment and ecology, even our biology. It is wise and prudent to learn the mechanism of these relationships and radiation, and what trends they may be causing in the earth's evolution, climate, and ourselves.

The scientists of the renaissance gave man an impetus toward total awareness that has carried him beyond the earth as well as toward the center of life. We are beginning to understand the basic structure of life. A new renaissance will enable man to understand the structure of mind [1].

The brain and its vast web of nerves operate with electrical signals— a fact that has been known for decades, even to high school biology students. It would seem logical, therefore, that the artificial application of electrical impulses (or fields) could produce all kinds of potentially beneficial effects on the nervous system and the body.

This is a thesis that has been bandied about among medical researchers for many years. And with few exceptions—such as electroshock treatments in mental hospitals and electric pacemakers for the heart—this approach has been greeted by extreme skepticism and even derision from the medical community.

Today, however, there is evidence that much of the skepticism is beginning to disappear. A host of current research projects, many of them conducted with human patients, involve the application of electrical signals (and fields) to the nervous system in attempts to reduce pain, put insomniacs to sleep, relieve asthma, ulcers, and high blood pressure, and improve performance and disposition. Scientists say they are providing more than a glimmer of hope that "electromedicine" may soon emerge as a major new approach to many diseases [2].

The human brain is the most complicated structure in the known universe, but as practically nothing of the universe is known, it is probably fairly low in the scale of organic computers. Nevertheless, it contains powers and potentialities still largely untapped and perhaps unguessed at. Probably 99 percent of human ability has been wholly wasted; even today, those of us who consider ourselves cultured and educated operate for most of our time as automatic machines and glimpse the profounder resources of our minds only once or twice in a lifetime [3].

Until comparatively recently (the 1950s) biologists regarded a cell as a minute bag of fluid that was relatively simple in structure. But under the electron scanning microscope, cells were seen to be exceedingly complex. What earlier seemed to be a "simple cell wall" was likely to be folded and convoluted—precisely the right kind of structure to serve as a semiconductor. And components of the cell are likely to include organic semiconductors such as liquid crystals, a material that is hypersensitive to temperature changes, magnetic and electric fields, stress, radiation and trace contamination. To complicate matters even more, many cells have a double outer membrane; electrically, such a membrane functions as a capacitor with the characteristics of a leaky dielectric [4]. It should also be noted that at low frequencies the permeability of the cell membrane to ions is enhanced, thus promoting electrochemical interactions. Nerves and muscle actions are also accompanied by electrical activity involving flow of ionic currents.

It is certainly reasonable to assume that refined detection of minute magnetic and electrostatic fields that accompany biological activity may lead to interesting and useful applications in the future . . . possibly monitoring effects of mind on body physiological processes and early diagnosis of specific diseases.

Viewed as a minute but extremely elaborate electrical system, the living cell (like all electrical systems) is obviously subject to the influence of magnetic and electric fields. And these fields may induce not just one but a complex system of currents, as well as act as indicators of environmental conditions. Small wonder, therefore, that reported field effects at the cellular level are diverse and debatable; the effects will depend upon the components of the system and its organization.

A space scientist at the NASA-Langley Research Center, Dr. Cone, has devised and demonstrated a theory that helps to explain the source of uncontrolled malignant growth and indicates short cuts to development of chemical countermeasures against cancer. Dr. Cone specializes in the investigation of space radiation effects on the blockage of cell division. The Cone theory proposes that the division of body cells (a normal process that goes on continuously) is controlled precisely by the pattern of ion concentrations on the surface tissues of cells. The pattern is formed by the electrical voltage that normally exists across cellular surfaces and varies from one part of the body to another. This theory has provided, possibly for the first time, an explanation of the functional connection between the two major pathological features of cancer—uncontrolled growth of cells and the spread of the disease in the body. The theory implies that the basic deviation from normality producing both of these conditions lies in an alteration of the molecular structure of the cell surface [1, 5].

Dr. Barry Allan and Ralph Norman of U.S. Army Missile Command, Redstone Arsenal, Alabama, indicate in their description of bioelectricity and biowater that a living organism is delicately balanced, especially chemically and electrically. It seems predictable that the highly structured water (biowater) within the cell could, by the exclusion of conducting ions, form the insulation channels of the organism. Further, semiconduction and conduction phenomena might be expected if certain chemical modifications to a highly pure, immobile layer of water were made by life processes. Conduction could easily occur in the less structured aqueous solutions and any mechanism that disrupts the biological water structure will certainly disrupt the biological transfer of electrons. The need for understanding bioelectricity is most fundamental, and research in bioelectricity and biowater and their mutual dependence will yield enormous dividends [6].

A tie-in here should be made with some of the work that Dr. Shafer, formerly of General Dynamics Life Sciences, has done with mice inoculated with virulent lymphatic cancer, then exposed to a high negative ion field (negative ions could be considered "supercharged" oxygen atoms with a surplus of electrons looking for chemical reactions to stimulate). Dr. Shafer noted a slowing down of cancer spread, some complete remissions, some holding constant. Lifespan was greater than other mice remaining as a control group outside the charged ion environment. See also references [4, 7, 8].

It has been established that an electro-power field between the earth and atmosphere exists that, relative to the earth, is normally positive. This is not a recent discovery; the existence of this natural electric field was discovered in 1752. The usual mean strength of this field is on the order of several hundred volts per meter positive polarity, although there are wide fluctuations due to geographical location, weather, artificially induced shielding, etc. For example, in buildings, automobiles, aircraft, and other structures that, due to their metal-containing construction, are shielded and thus have the physical qualities of a Faraday cage, this natural electric field does not exist. Indeed, the extensive use of plastics (almost all have a highly negative electrostatic field) inside buildings and vehicles can provide a strong negative field that augments fatigue, irritability, and natural apathy. This statement leads to an intriguing question: *Are we also electrically polluting our environment?* This seems a distinct possibility. Have you noticed how your new plastic-containing clothing sticks to your body in cold, dry weather? The body field is positive and the plastic is negative, thus creating this uncomfortable effect [9, 10, 11].

Over 150 years ago it was determined that this natural positive electric field around the earth was an important factor in the development of life and that the normal and healthy course of life, especially for vertebrates, including man, is very dependent upon its presence. On the other hand, it was determined before the turn of the century that the absence of this positive electric field has a disadvantageous and negative effect on the vitality of man and influences his fertility.

Experiments and investigations that have been conducted suggest that this electric field produces electrical current in the body that excites the entire organism and its nervous system, which in turn increases the impulse rate to the wakefulness center of the brain. Various biological clocks are also activated. Modern biological theories tend to indicate that the brain receives inputs from the nervous system by means of electrical pulse generation and transmission through the nervous system. One theory of wakefulness and sleep suggests that the number of electrical impulses reaching the brain influences the state of alertness (an increase in beta wave EEG activity occurs). Recent brain wave experiments indicate that artificial electric fields can influence the rate of spontaneous electrical impulse generation by the nerves. Other recent tests have demonstrated that brightness discrimination improves under the influence of artificially created electric fields [10, 11].

The beneficial effects of electrical fields are apparently the results of the combined action of the positive field and the suspended negative ions in the air. The electric field is the force of motion and the ions are the carriers of electrical charge. This is apparently the explanation why investigations of the effects of positive and negative ions on individuals without the presence of a proper electric field have shown negative or no effects. On the other hand, tests have been conducted to determine the effects of positive and negative ions on individuals where a natural electric field was present. The gross results were as follows [12]:

Item	Negative Ions	Positive Ions
Performance	Improved	Decreased
Work capacity	Increased	
Disposition	Cheerful	Depressed
Reaction time	Decreased	Decreased
Equilibrium	Improved	
Vitamin metabolism	Enhanced	
Pain	Relieved	
Allergic disorders	Relieved	
Burn recovery and healing	Enhanced	

Air ions are the result of atoms, molecules, and particles that become charged by either loss or gain of electrons. The principal sources of air ions, both natural and artificial, are high-energy particles such as alpha and beta rays from radioactive sources, cosmic rays, ultraviolet rays, coronal discharges, charge separation from rapid relative movements of surfaces, and thermionic emission. Ordinarily, only about one molecule in ten [16] is ionized or charged and these frequently clump together forming groups.

Unipolar, small air ions have been shown to be biologically active under certain conditions. Molecules and perhaps atoms of O_2 in the air have an affinity for electrons, and thus form negative ions. Only fluorine and chlorine molecules seem to have the same capacity for forming negative ions as do the O_2 molecules. Positive ions are formed primarily by CO_2 molecules.

Although systems for generating artificial electric fields and negative ions already exist and have successfully demonstrated beneficial physiological and psychological effect in combatting fatigue, allergies, etc., such systems have not yet been employed in the classroom for extended periods of time (so far as is known by this author). Development of such a system for the classroom could perhaps minimize other problems associated with student behavior, seasonal allergies and weather changes, and even housekeeping.

Incidentally, an interesting earth field effect perceived by animals is the "earthquake alarm." An earthquake causes a drastic change in the earth's magnetic and electric fields. This field change is of a characteristic "signature" pattern and propagates at the speed of light, while the earthquake travels at about the speed of sound or slower; hence, the animals sense a sudden change in the usually stable, slowly changing environmental background electrostatic field. This is unusual, so the animal is alerted, nervous, and prepared for danger [9].

Of particular environmental interest to those in the mid-East and pertinent to the educational environment is the khamsin wind that moves up out of the desert each spring and fall. It picks up hot air and dust as it sweeps across Africa and the Sinai Peninsula, bringing a variety of afflictions in its northerly thrust. The moistureless air causes feet to swell painfully, noses and eyes to itch, and asthmatics to gasp for breath. Automobile accidents, crime rates, and mental cases increase. Other countries suffer from such hot dry winds containing an excess of positive ions. Italy has the sirocco, southern Europe has the foehn, France has the mistral, and the United States has the chinook and santa ana winds. Young people become tense, irritable, and occasionally violent; older persons become fatigued, apathetic, depressed, and sometimes faint. Professor Felix Gad Sulman of the Hebrew University's Department of Applied Pharmacology in Jerusalem has conducted a nine-year study involving five hundred people using drugs such as monoamine oxidase (MAO) and negative ion generators, which readily bring relief to khamsin victims.

Tests made on animals eighty years ago showed that a negative electric field markedly reduced vitality and fertility of animals, whereas a positive field stimulated respiration, digestion, and metabolism in general. Forty years ago, European research revealed the effect of the absence of a positive field on plant growth and on human performance [13]. The author of this paper also performed some experiments with plants using equipment radiating 10,000 volts per meter. A four-day earlier germination resulted for the bean plants 15 cm from the antenna, compared to the control group. The same equipment is now in use on a child with recurrent monthly asthma attacks requiring hospitalization. In the two months since the equipment flat plate antenna was installed 1.5 meters over his bed, there have been no further attacks.

Since the mid-East has up to a hundred and fifty days of khamsim wind a year, and there will be a deficit of natural negative ions in the air, the optimum environment for well-being would involve use of a negative ion generator in combination with a positive field device to keep the ions moving and distributed, as in the natural earth environment. Recent tests on airplane pilots showed that introducing a strong positive field into the cockpit improved brightness discrimination. Typing efficiency, mental/light mechanical tasks and auto driving response all showed improvement in efficiency and delay in onset of fatigue [11]. As a note of interest, Dr. Kornblueh of the American Institute of Medical Climatology studied brain-wave patterns and found evidence that negative ions tranquilized persons in severe pain. Northeastern Hospital in Philadelphia has a windowless, ion-conditioned room for burn patients. In 85 percent of the cases no pain-deadening narcotics are needed, and the burns dry and heal faster with less scarring, plus the patient is more optimistic. Dr. Albert P. Kruger at the University of California predicts that we shall some day regulate the ion level indoors much as we now regulate temperature and humidity.

Ironically, many of today's air-conditioned buildings, trains, and planes frequently become supercharged with harmful positive ions because the metal blowers, filters, and ducts strip the air of negative ions. This explains why so many people in air-conditioned spots feel depressed and have an urge to throw open a window [14].

The recent advent of solid state physics and field effect transistors have made possible inexpensive, portable instruments (electric field intensity meters or scanners) that can now monitor the environment and keep it optimum for physiological and mental tasks [15]. The availability and sensitivity of these instruments have led to some interesting spinoffs. For example, it has been known since at least 1949 that intensities of the biological electrostatic field could be detected by suitable instruments, but the equipment and technology were not sufficiently advanced for economical study [16]. Detection and interpretation of biological electrical field radiation is reported to be under intensive investigation in Russia for bio-med applications. Equipment described has the same characteristics as laboratory field effect electrometers equipped with a field mill "chopper." The equipment will detect and amplify minute electrical and electrostatic fields inherent in nonconductors (plastics and insulators) and traveling through conductors (metals). The fields can be detected, the field strength determined in volts per meter, and the polarity of positive or negative established. The equipment output can be fed into a conventional "X-Y" area scanning system and then into a facsimile recorder to produce a two-dimensional plan view of the electrostatic field potentials around the object or person. Variations in the shades of gray or color indicate the intensity of the field in volts/meter.

It should be noted here that the recent application of infrared equipment and heat-sensitive liquid crystals to the analysis of body pathological conditions have yielded color readouts of much value to the medical profession [9]. Preliminary investigations into body field variations indicate that the natural body field is positive, while certain types of malignancies are negative; other pathological conditions produce drastic changes in body potential of a peculiar "signature." Further work remains to be done toward interpretation of received data. Recording and control of environmental factors to constant levels are also required so that the very minute signals of interest can be sifted from all the internal, external, and emotional "noise" present. Note the tie-in of body electrostatic field potential variations mentioned above with Dr. Cone's discoveries of cellular bioelectric characteristics discussed earlier.

There is no doubt that a need exists to obtain physiological data without the necessity of restraining the individual either by sensors, wires or rigid confinement. A noncontact means of detecting heartbeat (EKG) has also been developed by Dr. Shafer, who was mentioned earlier.

Known as the Field Effect Monitor [17, 18] and now on the market, this equipment consists of a copper plate sensing antenna, an isolation amplifier (using FET electronics), filter systems, main amplifier section, and readout devices. Acceptable EKG signals have been received at a distance of two to three feet. Recent improvements in antenna design have neutralized local field effects (60 cycle components) and improved signal to noise ratio by over 20 times. Dr. Shafer feels confident that he can also monitor brain waves (EEG) noncontact by changing a few elements of his filter circuit. EKG tracings have been made through intact space helmets or pressure suits. Use of Dr. Shafer's EKG equipment in the school clinic, for example, would provide more freedom of movement and comfort for the student, avoid anxiety, and save time, since clothing does not have to be removed or the student even aware of equipment use.

You can build and experiment with a somewhat similar instrument known as the "Amazing People Detector" [19]. This is basically a very sensitive electrometer or "rate meter" that measures a changing or varying field. In order to detect electrostatic fields, an additional device is needed that rotates, reciprocates, or swings so that the field is interrupted periodically (chopped) into a form of alternating current that can be transformed and amplified. This basic instrument, however, is extremely sensitive to moving electric charges and can give a "feel" for effects in this area around TV sets, rugs, clothing, people, animals, plants, etc.

The magnetic field of the earth averages about 0.5 Gauss and has a particular configuration, intensity, and mode of behavior. It is subject to continuous pulsations of low magnitude at frequencies ranging from 0.1 to 100 cycles per second, with the major components at about 8 to 16 cycles per second, peaking around 10 cycles per second. It is interesting to note that the average frequencies of brain waves, as manifested by the typical 8 to 14 cycle alpha pattern recorded on electroencephalograms (EEG) fall precisely in this range, and indeed, a relationship between these phenomena has been more than once suggested [20, 21]. This falls into the area of biological entrainment of the human brain by low frequency radiation [22]. Note that certain light and sound frequencies can trigger epileptic fits, induce hypnosis, and cause nausea.

The step from external sensory stimuli to subconscious electromagnetic stimuli in entraining cerebral rhythms is not a radical concept [10, 21, 23]. It is fast approaching reality with such items as medical equip-

ment for treatment of nerve deafness now in the developmental stages
by two companies in the United States [24]. The type of equipment being developed stimulates hearing electrically (and was first discovered by
Volta in 1800). Put the disc-shaped radio frequency radiating antenna
plates near the central nervous system and hear! The antenna is placed
near the spinal column or on the head. The device usually contacts the
skin, but can transmit into the body from a short distance. With two
discs, one on each side of the head, you can get stereo that's out of this
world! For more than a century there have been sporadic reports of
"hearing" aurora displays and meteors entering the earth's atmosphere.
Since meteors travel far faster than sound, and other persons present did
not hear any sounds, these reports have until recently been dismissed as
unfounded [25].

With the discovery that certain individuals are extremely sensitive to
the sounds and other as yet undefined effects of electrical and electromagnetic fields to which they are exposed, studies have been made by
many members of the scientific community to determine the source of
these effects, how they are generated, and how the effects are manifested
in man [26, 27].

The ability of many individuals to "hear" radar waves has been well
documented and is generally described as a "buzzing like bees." In other
examples, individuals have been forced to relocate their homes because
of "noise" that was beyond the normally audible range. The development of portable, highly sensitive detection devices provided the capability to verify the existence of these electric field and radio frequency
noises and to pinpoint their source. Nurses who work in mental institutions describe patients who were always complaining and trying to get
away from "the terrible noise." Cotton in the ears did no good, but certain rooms or areas were more quiet for them (an electrical field null
point?). How many people are now in mental institutions or psychologically affected because they are afflicted with hypersensitivity to electric
fields and hear voices, buzzing sounds, and strange signals? This is a vital
thing to consider in this age of increasing mental tensions [27]. Testing
by the Russians indicates that the most sensitive area of the brain to
field effects is the hypothalamus. Damage to the hypothalamus can increase the sensitivity to field changes many times [28].

Here's another one: a bar magnet at 60 cycles and 8,700 Gauss magnetic flux density held to the temple gives rise to a light sensation in per-

fect darkness as well as in a brightly lit room. This is known as the "phosphene" effect and can also be induced by electrical, chemical, fasting, meditation, or fatigue. No one has a reasonable explanation why, but it is known that a person under hypnosis or in a state of mescalin intoxication can often perceive a static magnetic field—through modification of visual images. A flicker effect is associated with a varying field. Patterns such as spirals and geometric shapes are often observed that are strikingly similar to the pictographs left by ancient man in all parts of the world. It appears there may be some potential clues for electronic stimulation (or simulation) of vision in the above areas [4, 29].

Research has established that some aspects of the human brain's electrical activity are related to intelligence. Sensory stimulation such as audio or visual signals cause nonrandom change (evoked response) in this electrical activity (EEG). An instrument called the Neural Efficiency Analyzer measures the ability to learn, as indicated by the efficiency (speed) of information transmission within the brain due to a flashing light stimulus. The neural efficiency "score" is the average time delay in milliseconds between the flash and each of two particular electrical responses of the brain. The lower the number you score, the higher your neural efficiency. Tests of thousands of children and adults reveal a significant correlation between neural efficiency and intelligence quotient with high neural efficiency a factor in high intelligence. Now in production after a dozen years of research and development, the Neural Efficiency Analyzer is the invention of Dr. John Ertl, director of the Center of Cybernetic Studies at the University of Ottawa. Someday this five-minute electronic test of the ability to learn may be in general use in our schools—perhaps even replacing traditional pencil-and-paper IQ tests. Unlike standard intelligence tests with their built-in cultural bias, the Analyzer doesn't penalize so-called "culturally deprived" children. The subject doesn't have to read, write or even speak to take this test, which also makes it ideal for testing handicapped persons. This is a culture-free technique that can be used for identification of youngsters with learning or primary reading problems; motivational factors are not important and potential high or low achievers can be identified immediately and put in special classes [30, 31].

Additional aspects of brain wave evoked response in the audio stimulus area are being investigated for early detection of hearing loss or total deafness in children before serious learning difficulties are encountered.

The electrical stimulation of hearing (or electrophonics) technique, mentioned earlier, may have some interesting application potential here, since it may work if hearing loss or deafness is indicated with the normal audio stimulation techniques.

To enhance the learning process we have many promising new tools or methods we can use such as computers, educational closed circuit, and satellite TV, perceptual test and enhancement equipment (advanced simulators), random access audio and visual retrieval and recording systems, and programmed instruction, to name just a few. We can talk all we want about these important learning methods, equipment, and capabilities we are creating—capabilities that are basic to much of what the public wants done in education—but it means exactly nothing to most of them. We are a world with the greatest total awareness potential ever known. We have reached goals formerly considered unattainable, in spirit and in fact—new worlds! Unfortunately, people seldom relate science and technology to the everyday business of living, fighting the daily traffic, getting the kids off to school, and buying the groceries. If they do, they are apt to curse it, particularly when it comes to new ideas to improve education quality, quantity, and environment. Far too many do not understand, or care little, what education their children get (except when the kids bring it home to threaten parental authority with a little "future shock" item that upsets the cultural status quo).

We can point in vain to communications and weather satellites that are revolutionizing worldwide telephone, television, education, and weather-forecasting techniques. People simply yawn. They rarely ever phone overseas, they can still catch their favorite game shows on TV, and they still get caught in sand or snow storms.

So, who needs any more science and technology? We've got too much already—look at the shape the world is in!

Few seem to realize that civilized man cannot long survive on this planet without increased creation of new knowledge and its enlightened use to handle the fantastically complex interrelated and synergistic challenges of the future.

Our difficulty is that as a world of short-term pragmatists, we are not geared mentally to long-range planning and some of the cultural changes and benefits resulting from advanced science and technology programs.

Concepts of man and the universe and man-in-the-universe motivate our thinking and actions on earth. Are contributions to such concepts unimportant to the quality of life we strive for today? On the contrary, I think they are basic to the definition of what we mean about quality in life. Without a growing precision of our definition of the universe, external and internal, objective and subjective, material and spiritual, and the elements involved, we cannot hope to improve more than the physical aspects of day-to-day living.

The *total human being* must be considered. We can't just sum up the inputs and say this is all there is to this or that person. It is how the inputs are combined that counts, and how the combinations act in symbiosis with the environment. Consciousness itself appears to be a kind of synergistic physical process devolving from the nature of mind. It will not be understood by studying the individual sensing systems, conscious and unconscious—i.e., putting each body input in its own "little black box" and specializing in a narrow range of view. The general systems approach is necessary.

The potentialities of the individual human being are far greater in extent and diversity than we ordinarily imagine them to be, and far greater than currently negative in-vogue models of man would lead us to think possible. We are finally beginning to discover some of these potentialities through the newly emerging Science of Subjective Experience that involves monitoring of unconscious processes, through biofeedback, and increasing our awareness of external and internal effects on our mind and body, so that we can become optimum persons; thus understanding ourselves and others better. The broadest possible overview of our effects on our environment, environmental feedback and the mental/physical result is needed for realization of our potential as a total human being [32]. Thus, as a product of the cosmos we are all "tuned in" and our biorhythms react accordingly (though subtle in effect) to electromagnetic and electrostatic fields, low frequency radiation, ions, and perhaps other unknown factors [33].

There are many systems, natural and manmade, that are synergistic in nature—i.e., the total effect is greater (or different) from the sum of the effects from individual components. The end effect cannot be ascertained by a study of the discrete components. The brain may be the highest form of synergistic structure now known to exist. The phenomenon of consciousness (and learning processes) needs more objective study; however, this may prove a tough objective, since the consciousness or mind has only itself to study itself with! When the sum of all sense-acquired data has been ordered and formulated, the picture that is presented can never be more than cone confined to a particular grade of significance. Higher significant data can only be acquired by going into ourselves—for we are the observers and the interpreters of the world [34].

Man used to say that man the scientist brought order out of chaos. Scientists are now rapidly discovering that all that was chaotic was in man's illiterate and bewildered imagination and fearful ignorance.

Our knowledge of the universe at present is only measurable in dimensional units of energy, time, and space. These are mostly above or below the narrow dimensions man is accustomed to detecting by direct sensing and by conscious awareness [35]. Recent extension of our perceptions to other areas such as radio, microwave, X-ray and beyond has shown that new information is gained wherever man looks, without bias, whether it be inner or outer space.

It is difficult to comprehend the true effect of modern technology upon our lives. Other technologies have risen, made their mark, and in the actual march of time have been eclipsed. The age of the railroad, the steamboat, the automobile, and the airplane—each of these brought new advances in science, created new jobs and higher standards of living. So it shall be with the space and computer age. We have seen some of the dividends already returned to education by the new technologies and we are only at the beginning. Space is the most complex problem that we have ever put our mind to. Its solution will bring the mysteries of our physical world, body, mind, and environment, into sharper focus and will lead to many useful benefits—primarily increased knowledge/awareness and understanding of the universe and its complex synergistic actions, which, whether we like it or not, affect us all [1].

References

1. Beal, James B. "Space—For All." Presentation at Mankind in the Universe Conference, Southern Illinois University, April 1971.
2. Shaffer, R. A. "Shock Treatment— Use of Electricity to Treat Many Ills Gains More Credence." Wall Street Journal, 27 March 1972.
3. Clarke, Arthur C. Profiles of the Future. Bantam: New York, 1967.
4. Garrison, Webb. "Magnets and Human Life." Science and Electronics, August-September 1969.
5. Cone, Jr., C. D. "Unified Theory on the Basic Mechanism of Normal Mitotic Control and Ontogenesis." Journal of Theoretical Biology, 1971.
6. Allan, B. D. and Norman, R. L. The Characterization of Liquids in Contact with High Surface Area Mate-

rials. *N.Y.A.S. Transactions*, Vol. 204, March 1973.

7. Kolin, Alexander. "Magnetic Fields in Biology." *Physics Today*, November 1968.

8. Barnothy, M. F. *Biological Effects of Magnetic Fields*. Plenum Press: New York, 1964.

9. Beal, J. B. *Recent Developments Associated with Bio-Electric Field Effects*. September 1971 (unpublished).

10. Presman, A. S. *Electromagnetic Fields and Life*. Plenum Press: New York, 1970.

11. Carson, R. W. "Anti-Fatigue Device Works by Creating Electric Field." *Product Engineering*, 13 February 1967.

12. Hardy, J. D. *Physiological Problems in Space Problems: Air Ions*. C. C. Thomas: Springfield, Illinois.

13. "Curing an Ill Wind." *Time*, 14 June 1971.

14. O'Brien, Robert. "Ions Can Do Strange Things to You." *Reader's Digest*, October 1960.

15. Sources for Electric field intensity meters:
Electrofields, Inc., 9860 S.W. 40th St., Miami, Florida 33165, (305) 221-4005.

Monroe Electronics, Inc., 100 Housel Ave., Lyndonville, N.Y. 14098, (716) 765-2254.

Kleinwächter, D-7850 Lörrach 2, Kreuzstrasse 105, West Germany.

16. Burr, Harold S., and Langman, Louis. "A Technique to Aid in the Detection of Malignancy of the Female Genital Tract." *American Journal of Obstetrics and Gynecology*, Vol. 57, No. 2, February 1949.

17. Schaefer, W. A. *Further Development of the Field Effect Monitor*. Report GDC-ERR-AN-1114, General Dynamics Convair Division, October 1967.

18. *Field Effect Monitor*. Brochure from General Dynamics Convair Division, 1971. Contact Dr. Armstrong, Dept. 592-0, P.O. Box 1128, San Diego, California 92112, tel. (714) 277-8900 ext. 1340.

19. Garner, Jr., L. E. "The Amazing 'People Detector.'" *Popular Electronics*, June 1968.

20. Graf, E. R. *Radiation Noise Energy and Human Physiology in Deep Space*. American Astronautical Society National Symposium, June 1967, Document AAS67-322 (EN-2)-1.

21. König, H. "Biological Effects of Extremely Low Frequency Electrical Phenomena in the Atmosphere." *Journal of Interdisciplinary Cycle Research*, Vol. 2, No. 3, 1971.

22. Dewan, E. M., "Rhythms." *Science and Technology*, January 1969.

23. Hamer, J. R. *Biological Entrainment of the Human Brain by Low Frequency Radiation*. Northrup Space Lab Technical Memo 532-65-45, January 1965.

24. Companies doing research in electrical stimulation of hearing:
Intelectron Corp., 432 W. 45th St., New York City 10036, (212) 265-5375; Listening Incorporated, 6 Garden Street, Arlington, Massachusetts 02174, (617) 643-4100

25. Sullivan, W. "Space Sounds Old Mystery." *New York Times*, 6 December 1964.

26. von Gierke, H. E. and Sommer, H. C. "Hearing Sensations in Electric Fields." *Aerospace Medicine*, September 1964.

27. Wieske, C. W. *Human Sensitivity to Electric Fields*. Laboratory for the Study of Sensory Systems, Tucson, Arizona, 1963.

28. Kholodov, Y. A. "Effect of Electromagnetic and Magnetic Fields on the Central Nervous System." *Foreign Science Bulletin*, February 1967.

29. Knoll, Kugler, Höfer and Lawder. "Effects of Chemical Stimulation of Electrically-Induced Phosphenes on their Bandwidth, Shape, Number and Intensity." *Confinia Neurologica*, Vol. 23, 1963.

30. Callaway, E. and Stone, G. C. "Evoked Response Methods for the Study of Intelligence." *Aggressologie*, Vol. 10, 1969.

31. Ertl, J. P. "Evoked Potentials, Neu-

ral Efficiency and IQ," in *Biocybernetics of the Central Nervous System*. L. D. Proctor, ed. Little, Brown: Boston, 1969. Further information may be obtained on the Neural Efficiency Analyzer by directing inquiries to:
Associates International, Inc., Suite 320, Johnson Building, Shreveport, Louisiana 71101 (318) 425-4259.

32. Harman, W. "The New Copernican Revolution." Center for Study of Social Policy, Stanford Research Institute, Menlo Park, California, 1971.

33. Luce, G. G. *Biological Rhythms in Psychiatry and Medicine*. National Institute of Mental Health, 5454 Wisconsin Avenue, Chevy Chase, Maryland 20015, Public Health Service Publication No. 2088, 1970.

34. Beal, James B. "Methodology of Pattern in Awareness." *Fields Within Fields . . . Within Fields*. The World Institute, 777 United Nations Plaza, New York City 10017, Vol. 5, No. 1, 1972.

35. Fuller, R. Buckminster. *No More Second Hand God*. Southern Illinois University Press: Carbondale, Illinois, 1963.

One of the most extensive and up-to-date bibliographies on biomagnetism available may be obtained by directing inquiries to:
Biological Sciences Communication Project, The George Washington University Medical Center, 2001 S. Street, N.W., Washington, D.C. 20009, (202) 462-5828
Request *Biomagnetism: An Annotated Bibliography* by Louise A. Manganelli, February 1972.

14 Energy Fields
and the Human Body
William A. Tiller

In the following pages I will project a model of substance that includes unconventional energy fields, or as I prefer to term them, nonphysical energies. This model provides a framework for discussing how many of the nonphysical energies come into play and begin to interact with each other and with the physical, including the human body.

A model can be thought of as a working hypothesis. It is a conceptual framework from which we can start to try to understand some aspect of nature. It is a target at which we can start throwing experiments. In the beginning, it is the first discrimination of ideas into some format or structure that gives one a feeling he is starting to grapple meaningfully with the particular unknown area under consideration. As one begins to model the phenomenon, one is able to formulate the right kind of experiments for testing the hypotheses, and then can perform the experiments and can obtain feedback of new and pertinent information. This allows one to check out whether a particular aspect of the model is correct and subsequently to make corrective changes all through the model as need be as time goes by. However, to do this, one must have a place to start. Thus, models are like the rungs of a ladder from which one climbs from one level of understanding to another. Most models are eventually wrong in detail, but they serve the tremendous function of allowing one to climb from one position of understanding of the universe to a more enlightened position of understanding.

If we look carefully at the human body with electromagnetic detectors, we are able to see EM energy radiated from the body not only as a result of electron orbit changes but also as a result of physical rotations and vibrations of the molecules, cells, etc. In time, we may even come to detect natural X-rays and gamma-ray emission from certain regions of the body. In addition, if we carefully scan the body with sonic detectors, we will detect a unique sound spectrum associated with actual physical movement of cells and body systems—another fingerprint. In time, we can expect to find many such fingerprints radiated from the physical body.

Perhaps one of the most striking techniques for revealing some of these energies is the use of liquid crystals. By painting a person's body with liquid crystals, color patterns can be readily seen. Here, the liquid crystals act as a transducer to turn the body's radiations into an optical manifestation that can be readily seen.

These are the types of radiation we know at this point in time, and we are trying to use this as a guideline for understanding certain uncommon phenomena. We hear of psychometry. We hear of dowsing. We hear of clairvoyance and clairaudience and prophecy and various kinds of channeling (mediumistic) activities. We hear of radionics, vivaxis, and many other unconventional methods of gaining information about our environment and about ourselves. Although we think about such communication conventionally in terms of the visual (which is electromagnetic) and in terms of the sonic, we should anticipate that nature is filled with many other kinds of energies. As we attune to them and discriminate them, then we are obtaining additional information about our environment.

Our present understanding of human energy fields is inadequate to account for the phenomena mentioned above, and others. So many things seem to happen that are not explicable in terms of electromagnetic energy or sonic energy that, by trying to squeeze all these new aspects into that very small mold, we shall get lost (because they just will not fit). Thus, the place where I have started is to take the yogic philosophy of the seven principles operating in man and hypothesize that this really means that there are seven different levels of substance, and that these different substances are unique and have different types of configurations.* They obey entirely different kinds of laws and they have

* W. A. Tiller, "Radionics, Radiesthesia and Physics." *The Varieties of Healing Experience,* 1972, Academy of Parapsychology and Medicine, Los Altos, California 94022.

unique characteristics of radiation (absorption and emission). I further postulate that they operate in different kinds of space-time frames in the universe and so are distinct from each other. The seven levels of substance, from the coarsest going toward the finest, are: 1) the physical level that we are familiar with; 2) the etheric level (the Russians call this the bioplasmic body or the energy body); 3) the astral level; three levels of mind termed 4) instinctive, 5) intellectual, and 6) spiritual mind; and 7) another distinct level that is spirit.

There is said to be a level beyond these seven that is called the divine. However, for our purposes here, we can think just in terms of the seven levels of substance.

These seven substances interpenetrate each other in nature and may interact with each other. They, through the polarity principle, form atoms and molecules and configurations of these. One can apply the metaphysical principle "As above, so below; as within, so without" and realize that what we see in the physical may be used as a model, that this same kind of modeling understanding may be extrapolated through the other levels of substance, differing somewhat in detail from the physical, and that we may begin conceptually to grapple with these other levels. The substances interpenetrate and their relationship may be visualized by considering the situation in our own bodies. To visualize our seven bodies, think of seven transparent sheets of paper, and on these sheets, using pens of different colors, draw circuitry of one color on one and on another draw circuitry of another color, and so on through the seven colors. Then, put these sheets all together and look through them, and you will see an organization of substance at the various levels within the bodies of man. That, basically, is the model I wish to project.

In general, these substances do not interact with each other very strongly. However, they can be brought into interaction with each other through the agency of mind, and it is really at the point of mind that one can bring about changes in the organization of structure in these various levels of substance. That is, through mind forces one can create a pattern, and that pattern then acts as a force field that applies to the next level of substance. In turn, that force field is a force for organizing the atoms and molecules into configurations at that level of substance. That pattern of substance at the etheric level, then, is in a particular state of organization and it has its own radiation field—its own force field, if you like—and that force field, then, is a field for the organization of matter at the next level of substance, the physical level. These etheric forces, then, bring about the coalescence and organization of matter at the physical level of substance.

Here we see something that I have chosen to call "the ratchet effect." One can see an action beginning at the mind level and working its way down through to produce an effect on the physical level (and vice versa).

As an aid to visualizing this model, consider Fig. 1. For these seven levels of substance it is meaningful to draw a plot of the intensity of the radiation versus its frequency. Now, the thing we have to realize is that this particular representation of Fig. 1 is purely for coming into contact with the idea and is not a scientifically correct representation, since these levels of substance represent entirely different kinds of energy, entirely different kinds of physical laws, and they really should be represented on different axes—i.e., different coordinate vectors of phase space. That would be a more proper way to do it. And in fact, along any one of these coordinates, there may be many different kinds of energy that should be represented (just like electromagnetic, sonic, gravity, etc., energies in the physical). But, at least for us to conceptually see the simplest outlines of the model, it is worthwhile to represent it this way: the physical,

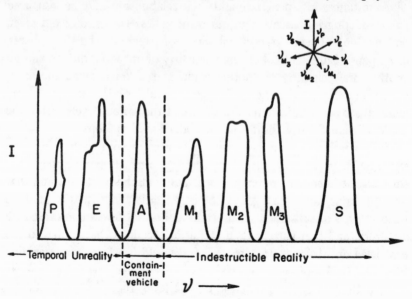

1. Schematic spectral distribution curve illustrating, along one coordinate, relative radiation characteristics of the seven levels of substance.

etheric, astral, mind levels and the spiritual level on one axis. Through focusing attention on the mind and spirit levels, we see the true essence of man. This is the indestructible reality of man and is the on-going man. These levels of energy function (or appear to function) in a nonspace, nontime frame of reference—that is, the patterns of intelligence (in that frame of reference) are not represented on coordinates which relate to space and time.

The astral function is largely as a containment vehicle, it appears, to keep this human essence in a compact form between incarnations. Looking further to the left, we come down to the temporal reality associated with this kind of physical existence—i.e., a vehicle that is suitable for experience in this earth plane (the etheric level and the physical level). In the case of the physical, we have the space-time frame (the Einsteinian frame) which we know a great deal about. The etheric level is a companion level and it operates again in a space-time frame but in a different space-time frame from the physical, and yet these two are complementary. That is, as time goes on, for the physical the potential decreases and entropy increases, whereas for the etheric we have the reverse situation: the potential increases and entropy decreases. A characteristic of the physical frame is one of disorder. A characteristic of the etheric frame is one of the organization of matter. The physical is primarily characterized by electric effects. The etheric is primarily characterized by magnetic effects.

This is the way in which I have come to look at these various energies—i.e., that there are radiations associated with these different levels, and these radiations give rise to the phenomena that we can call psychoenergetics. The majority of these phenomena deal with the etheric vehicle. That is, we have a sensory system in this vehicle that connects us to the psychoenergetic phenomena just as our five physical senses connect us to physical phenomena.

In my model, God created the universe, and He created it as a hologram! A hologram, basically, is a pattern of coherent energy and that pattern has a three-dimensional character in a space-time frame and it represents particular information. The first hologram beyond the divine was a hologram of spirit substance that organized itself, and the organization, at that level, had coherent radiation centers that radiated a pattern that was a hologram at the spirit-mind level. Then the substance organization at this level occurred that, in turn, contained coherent radiation sources that led to the radiation patterns for organization of the intellectual mind. That, in turn, led to organization and coherent radiation to form a hologram for the organization of instinctive mind, and so on down the line. I think we can see the first and simplest representation of this with the cut leaf experiment performed by Soviet researchers using Kirlian photography. They demonstrate that when a part of the physical leaf is cut away, an energy manifestation presumably from another level of substance can still be detected. In my model, this is suggested as evidence of the hologram penetrating to the physical level from the etheric level.

Now, there are several things that are important to note about a hologram. One is that if you take any piece of the hologram, you may recreate the entire hologram, and it is through this that we can understand what was meant when Edgar Cayce said: "Man within man is all representation of the universe. Within a cell of man is a representation of the entire universe—within an atom is a representation." If, in fact, the hologram model of the universe is correct, then this is exactly what we should expect.

A second thing that is important to note about this hologram, if this is the way creation took place, is that the divine pattern produced initially created patterns at the mind level of nature for the development of man in a harmonious way. This results from the coherence in the energy pattern. However, man has free will, and if with that free will he polarizes from an ego-mind aspect, he creates mental patterns that are not consistent with those initially set and they do not reinforce them. This, then, produces an anomaly or disharmony in the initial pattern and that disharmony in the initial mind pattern affects both the individual and mankind in general, so that disease really would start here. That is, the thoughts that one creates within himself and within society at large generate patterns at the mind level of nature. These patterns are superimposed upon the existing divine pattern. They then produce cause and effect relationships all the way down through the various levels of substance, and so we see that our illness, in fact, eventually becomes manifest from the altered mind patterns through the ratchet effect—first to effects at the etheric level and then, ultimately, at the physical level. Here, then, we see it openly as disease at the physical level, and if we begin to sense the etheric level, we will see it also as disease at that level.

What is the way to cure it? Even though we bring about medical changes at the physical level, we do little at these deeper levels, so that the disease will eventually recur. We would be a better doctor if we could produce correction at the etheric level, because then the cure would last longer. However, it will not be permanent because we have not altered the basic hologram at the mind and spiritual levels. We have to change at the mind and spirit levels to change the mental patterns, so that we can produce, if you like, an annihilation of disharmonious elements at this level of the hologram. Then, nature will just go forward in its harmonious way and man will not create and manifest disease!

Let us consider the physical and etheric levels. Think of these, if you like, as a type of transformer association with the etheric as the primary, and the physical as the secondary. The primary circuit always contains the greater quantity of energy, and the secondary circuit manifests a stepped-down condition, so that there is less energy generally. In the physical energy circuit, we see the acupuncture meridians. There is, I anticipate, an analogous circuitry at the etheric level of the system. I am not quite sure of its pattern yet, but I anticipate that there is an inductive coupling between these two companion circuits. Perhaps the one aspect of this relationship that we know most about is that in the physical body we see the endocrine glands as being the important spiritual centers (energy centers) of the body, and have come to learn how strongly their functioning relates to the whole chemical and physiological functioning of the body. At the etheric level we have heard for such a long time about the chakras (psychic energy centers). The chakras and the endocrines appear to be at the same spatial location within the body, and my feeling is that they act as coupled or companion glands—i.e., as chakra-endocrine pairs—and we should begin to think of them as a type of transformer or transducer, if you like.

In Fig. 2 we see the location of the various chakras and we see the endocrine glands located basically at the same physical location. In Fig. 3 we have a representation of a chakra-endocrine pair as a tuned circuit via which one may tap energy from the cosmos. One can tune this circuit to absorb energy and produce current flow in the etheric circuit; i.e., some type of current, whatever it is. There is thought to be inductive coupling of some sort between the etheric body and the physical body that produces various energy current in the physical body and the transmission of energy out into nature, both directly from the physical body and back through to the etheric level, and then out into the environment.

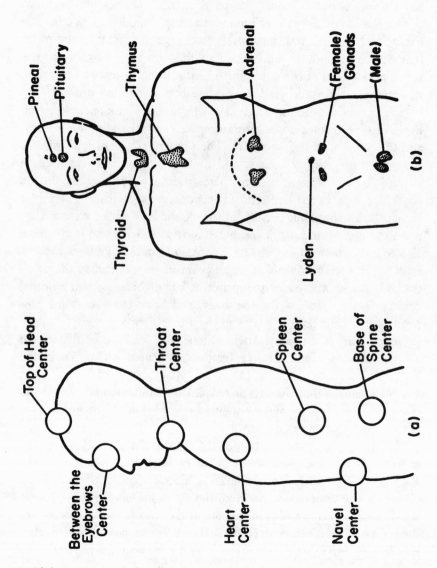

2. (a) Location of the seven major chakras at the etheric level of substance. (b) Location of the seven major endocrine glands at the physical level of substance.

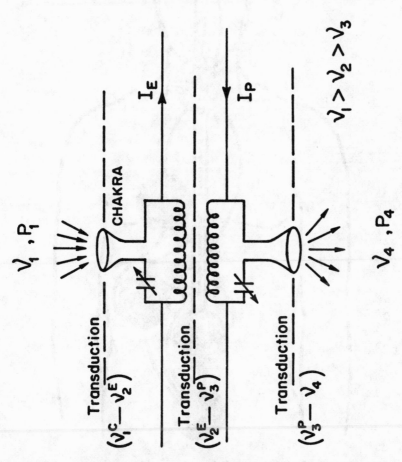

3. Schematic illustration of tuning and transduction aspects of a chakra/ endocrine pair for tapping power from the cosmos.

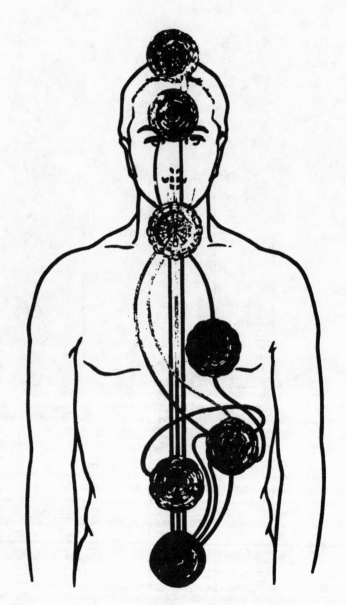

4. Front view of the major chakra system illustrating a morphological character to the energy centers (Leadbeater).

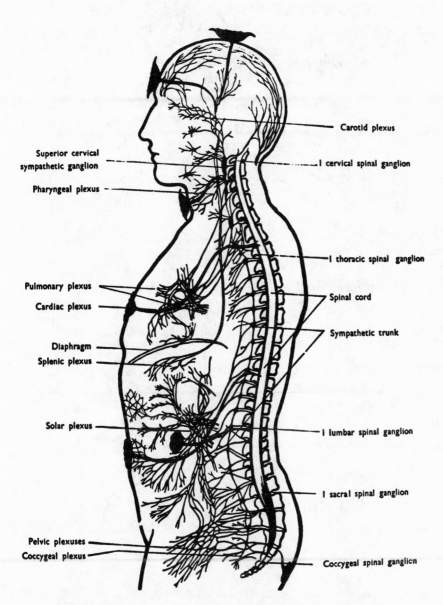

Carotid plexus

Superior cervical
sympathetic ganglion

I cervical spinal ganglion

Pharyngeal plexus

I thoracic spinal ganglion

Pulmonary plexus

Cardiac plexus

Spinal cord

Sympathetic trunk

Diaphragm
Splenic plexus

Solar plexus

I lumbar spinal ganglion

I sacral spinal ganglion

Pelvic plexuses
Coccygeal plexus

Coccygeal spinal ganglion

5. Side view of chakra system and the nervous system (Leadbeater).

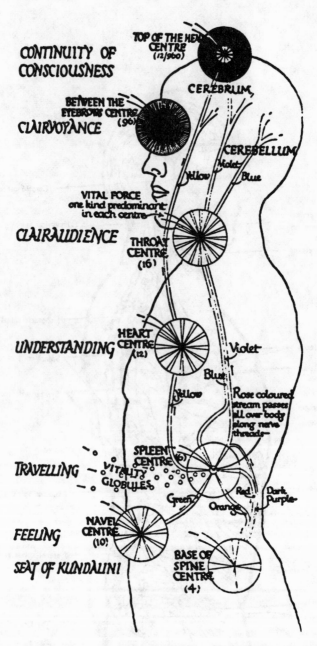

6. Man and his etheric centers illustrating the types of psychoenergetic phenomena associated with each center.

Fig. 4 illustrates a front view of the chakra network in the body. Fig. 5, from the same source, illustrates a side view of the chakra system. We see that, although the chakras have their centers located as indicated in Fig. 4, their seats or root stems appear to be in the locations closely related to those of the endocrine system. In Fig. 6 we note the types of psychoenergetic phenomena said to be associated with each center.

The next step in the progression of our understanding relates to the various psychic manifestations of psychokinesis, telepathy, and so on. For this, I anticipate that we must begin thinking of these chakra-endocrine pairs as coupled units and operating very much in what I would call a laser mode. That is, one must start thinking of these various centers working in synchronization with each other to manifest coherent energy and then radiation from these centers. Thus, if we want to investigate these phenomena, we must monitor the body in such a way that we are reading energy changes from these centers.

The lasing aspect of these centers is very important to understand. If one takes a 10-watt bulb, we know there is only a small amount of illumination radiated from the bulb. It, indeed, sheds some light but it is not a great amount of light, and that is because the conventional light that we use is incoherent and its energy content is not very effective for illumination purposes. Incoherence means that the rays of light are all out of phase with each other, so they cancel, and we get what is called destructive interference of the light waves. Thus, although one gets some illumination, one does not get much. However, if one can arrange for those individual photons of light to all be in phase, then one obtains constructive interference of the light waves—i.e., the resultant wave becomes very large in amplitude. When that happens, you have a laser; you have coherent light and that same 10-watt bulb can now produce an energy intensity over an area of about one square inch that is far greater than that found at the surface of the sun. This is a far more effective use of the energy! From that same total energy, the same basic stuff, by rearranging it in the right way to make it more coherent, one is able to develop a fantastic tool capable of doing many things. That's what I think happens here in the body!

I propose that the manifesting of psychoenergetic phenomena is associated with taking the primary energies in the body and making them coherent. In my modeling, I suspect that if we took all the energy in a single human body and made it completely coherent, there would be at least enough energy to create our entire universe at the physical (incoherent) level. You see, the basic energy is already there; it is just that it is in an incoherent form, and our job is to make it coherent. This we do by developing attunement with nature through our meditation, our thoughts, and our actions—i.e., it takes work. That is when these powers become manifested, and they are manifested through these various mechanisms. Some people seem to have a head start via the structure of their genes, but others can catch up and surpass by muscle-building at these internal levels of self. . . .

VIII
The Neurosciences

The neurosciences—neuroanatomy, neurochemistry, neuroendocrinology, neuropharmacology, and neurophysiology—occupy a point midway between philosophy and the psychological-behavioral sciences. If we ask the philosophic questions "What is mind?" and "What is life?" the neurosciences must be consulted. If we ask the psychological-behavioral questions "How does mind relate to brain/body?" and "How does the life force—the psyche—function in humans?" again the neurosciences must be consulted.

The nervous system is the body's link with consciousness. Although human consciousness can function external to the body—as the evidence of psychic research demonstrates—most of the time it is mediated by and dependent upon the nervous system. How do physical sensations coming through the sensory organs become mental events? How does electrochemical action in the brain's neural networks become the cognitive process called thinking? Where does memory reside? Instinct? Emotions such as love, fear, boredom?

If the mind is its own greatest mystery, the brain is the second greatest. To "know thyself," science has developed a powerful array of instruments to look at the components of man. The electron microscope, the ultracentrifuge, and the on-line computer are helping to probe the secrets of the brain, central nervous system, and peripheral nervous system. Scientists are now beginning to track neural networks through the brain and to observe changes that take place as a result of both nature and nurture. Some animal studies indicate there is a genetic programming behind the development of the brain and nervous system which pro-

ceeds on a well-defined schedule. But at certain critical points in that program, unless the environment provides the proper input, further development will be arrested. The heredity vs. environment question rages on, even at a cellular level.

But neuroscientific evidence makes clear that experience can and does change the nervous system. Therefore if those experiences are deliberately chosen and directed, as in psychotherapies and spiritual disciplines such as meditation, then mankind may be able—to some still undetermined degree—to reconstruct the somatic aspect of mind. By enriching neural networks and developing more efficient supportive processes for nervous system functioning, consciousness can be expanded, awareness deepened, and mind-body integration strengthened.

Information about the neurosciences is widely available. There are many good introductory texts on the nervous system, psychophysiology, and related areas. The most comprehensive summary of current scientific knowledge is The Neurosciences, *edited by Francis O. Schmitt (Rockefeller University Press, 1970). The Brain Information Service at UCLA provides free bibliographies, conference reports, and other materials to researchers interested in all areas of the neurosciences except the diagnosis and treatment of neurological disorders. Write to: Brain Information Service, UCLA Center for the Health Sciences, Los Angeles, Calif. 90024. The Brain Revolution by Marilyn Ferguson (Taplinger, 1973) is an excellent general survey for nontrained readers.*

                                                                                    J.W.

15 Life,
Death, and Antimatter
Henry Conway

The human psyche is one of the deepest enigmas, but discoveries in physics and medicine are giving man some understanding of the nature of the psyche and its apparent existence in a province of expanded time beyond the physical plane of time and space.

Among the many facts known about the psyche are:

A. As a human passes from consciousness into death, the psyche retreats inwardly from occupying the whole physical body to disappear into the anterior end of the cerebral aqueduct and the posterior end of the fourth ventricle. The complex formed by the cerebral aqueduct and the fourth ventricle (Figure 1) is the first internal structure of the body to appear in pregnancy. It forms the center from which all of the body develops. This retreat into the cerebral aqueduct-fourth ventricle is known as "the stages of anesthesia" and it has been found to follow the reverse path of prenatal growth and evolutionary development [2]. In the brain the progressive loss of functions indicates that the retreat is along the brain ventricles.

B. As or approximately as the psyche disappears into the cerebral aqueduct-fourth ventricle, the physical body has been found to have a small loss of weight (½ to ¾ oz.) which is instantaneous and since its discovery in 1907 has not been explained in terms of loss of physical matter [7].

C. Also approximately as the psyche disappears into the cerebral aqueduct-fourth ventricle during drowning and other, near-fatal, accidents, victims often report reliving their entire lives within a second or

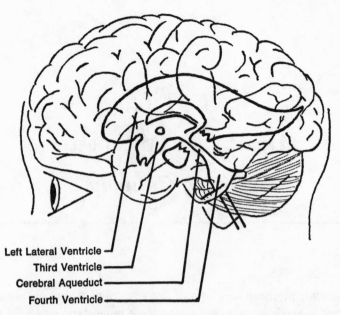

Left Lateral Ventricle
Third Ventricle
Cerebral Aqueduct
Fourth Ventricle

Figure 1. Ventricles (canals) of the brain with part of the temporal horn of the left lateral ventricle removed to see the third ventricle. The central canal of the spinal cord continues directly with the fourth ventricle.

so, often in segments. This expanded time phenomenon has been reported by some psychedelic drug users [22], by some subjects during the electrical stimulation of the pituitary area [12], and by Penfield when he stimulated with an electrical probe the brain of patients and evoked experiences of many years previous [25]. If the psyche retreats only to the extent that consciousness disappears, apparently into the forward end of the cerebral aqueduct-fourth ventricle, then sleep—not death—occurs. But still the conscious segment of the psyche may experience the expanded time phenomenon, since some researchers have found that in some cases even long dreams are, or almost are, instantaneous [17]. Mark Twain told of a long, romantic dream episode with a young woman in Hawaii, which occurred within two steps or less and without any lapse in conversation while he was walking on a street in lower Manhattan many years ago [35].

The difference between the fleeting memories of dreams and the vivid memories of death panoramas seemes to depend on the metabolic segment of the psyche. This segment stays in the physical body throughout life and appears to contain whatever is the memory organization. We can suspect the location of memory to be in the circulatory system because hardening of the arteries decreases the capacity for new memories without affecting memories of even the long past [21]; also memory drugs are circulatory-related [3]. Research indicates dreaming occurs only during light sleep; this would be when the conscious segment of the psyche would be just on the other side of the cerebral aqueduct-fourth ventricle in expanded time. The conscious segment of the psyche would still be close enough to the physical body for its sleep experiences to be recorded by the memory processes in the body, but in deep sleep the conscious segment of the psyche would be too far into expanded time for the memory processes in the physical body to keep in contact and record the sleep experiences. In death the metabolic segment passes into expanded time with the rest of the psyche and could readily record the experiences of the psyche in that domain.

Also rapid eye movement (REM) that occurs in light sleep could be caused by the conscious segment of the psyche immediately on the other side of the cerebral aqueduct interacting with the sleeping body—the conscious interacting with the autonomic, et cetera.

Whatever this psychological thing is that disappears in sleep and death, it has antimatterlike characteristics. Dirac found that antimatter had the opposite electrical characteristics to matter [29]. The psyche has the same pattern of opposite electrical characteristics to the body; the psyche is electronegative and the human body electropositive. These opposite electrical characteristics occur whenever the psyche is active in the body—whenever thought, feeling, will, or growth activities are manifest in the body. Consciousness is a necessary state for thought and is inexplicably bound up with thought. When a person is conscious, the surface of the head is electronegative to a small area at the top rear of the scalp (Figure 2), and as a person becomes unconscious this is reversed [4, 5]. The voltage is very small—about 20 millionths of a volt.

If a person is conscious and this electrical relationship is reversed using an electrical circuit, the person is promptly rendered unconscious [30]. Feelings are manifest by the electrical activity on the skin of the hands, et cetera. This is part of what lie detectors measure. Increases in feelings appear as increases in negative electricity. The will is manifest by nerve impulses that pass into the muscles and cause movement. The portion of the nerve impulse that causes this movement is electronegative [23]. The growth activities of the psyche are manifest in pregnancy, in wound healing, and in the regeneration of limbs in lower animals.

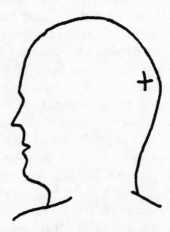

Figure 2. Approximate location of the electron sink (point of lowest voltage) on the scalp. When awake this sink is electropositive to the rest of the scalp. This polarity is reversed as sleep occurs. When the conscious polarity is reversed by an external electrical current applied to the head, sleep (electro-sleep or electro-anesthesia) occurs.

These activities are always electronegative. During gestation the uterus containing the child's body is electronegative to the exterior abdominal wall of the mother's body [6]. As a wound heals the activity is progressively electronegative, especially in the latter stages when cells are differentiating [4], and this process can be improved by increasing the amount of negative electricity [28]. When a new limb is being grown by a lower animal, it is progressively electronegative, and especially when cells are differentiating in the later stages of regeneration, the limb can be increased by as much as 25 percent by increasing the negative potential [4].

Some drugs apparently act by changing the electrical characteristics of the psyche. Thalidomide, the tranquilizer that caused many babies in Germany to be born with birth defects, probably acts this way because it is a fairly strong absorber of negative electricity. It probably tranquilizes the mother by reducing the negative electricity that appears on the head during consciousness, and in the body of the baby growing within the mother it probably reduces the negative electricity of the psyche that forms the baby's body. Gestation and tumors are very similar processes and by reversing the electronegativity, tumor growth has been retarded and often completely aborted [16]. Retarded prebirth growth of thalidomide babies closely parallels tumor growth retarded by reversed electropolarity. The data available on the electrical characteristics and activities of the psyche and the physical body are not extensive, but what there is seems constantly to show the body electropositive and the psyche electronegative following the electrical characteristics of matter and antimatter.

Antimatter in the mineral kingdom apparently has the capacity to synthesize biochemicals produced by metabolism. Antimatter seems mostly or possibly always to penetrate the world of physical matter thru spirals, especially geometric spirals, at the center of which the threshold between time and antitime apparently exists. Energy appears to move both ways across this threshold. In weather patterns, and especially in large storm patterns, incalculable amounts of energy evidently pass into the physical world. Often these storms increase the amount of vitamin B-12 in the atmosphere [24]. Also numerous biochemicals have been detected in the galaxies. In our galaxy the concentration of hydroxyl molecules increases as the center of galaxy, where antimatter possibly exists [15], is approached [34].

The very potent effects from microvoltage, et cetera, in metabolism are another indication that the psyche is antimatter. When matter and antimatter meet in large quantities, they apparently annihilate each other, but large amounts of one and a very small amount of the other apparently can mix without annihilation [15, 32], yet there is possibly a strong interaction of some sort. This is possibly what happens in metabolism; microvoltages, equivalent amounts of magnetism, and even possibly smaller amounts of light cause biochemistry that in vitro would require a million or so times as much of these forces. This highly potent biological control of physical matter may extend into the atomic nucleus, since in glucose tolerance tests the exhaled air has a lower ratio of carbon-13 to carbon-12 than the ingested glucose [19], which means a neutron could have been removed from the nucleus of one isotope or added to the nucleus of the other isotope.

Dirac proposed antimatter moving back in time (antitime). Antimatter is relatively easy to test; it has been fairly thoroughly investigated and has been found to exist [1, 29]. Antitime is far more elusive and has had little study. Not even its basic definition is clear. There are no scientific precedents by which this expanded time phenomenon of human experience can be tested for or identified as antitime. However, the disappearance of substance from the physical world is not unique to human death—it is very common. It is the rule rather than the exception and is at least sometimes associated with suspected antimatter areas. The "black holes in space" theory is an effort to find where perhaps as much as 80 percent of physical matter has disappeared. The centers of the galaxies appear to contain very large "black holes" [27]. Fred Hoyle and Russian satellite observations have given evidence that the centers of galaxies are also antimatter areas [15]. Time at the centers of "black holes," when analyzed mathematically, is infinite. *All time exists at once* [26]. Thus in the area of the physical universe where science is most sure antimatter exists, time is expanded to the infinite; this indicates that antitime is all time existing at once and that the expanded time phenomenon of human experience is a variety of antitime.

Time and antitime are puzzlingly bound together in light [32]. This dichotomy has puzzled Einstein and others in science because light always had the same speed regardless of the relative speed from which it is observed. It is apparently a facet of antitime.

Kozyrev, a Russian researcher, has investigated time, employing both mathematics and laboratory tests involving torsion balances, pendulums, and gyroscopes [18]. Among Kozyrev's findings are: A) time is denser near mechanical action—e.g., the stretching end of a rubber band—and near at least some chemical reactions—e.g., burning sugar; B) there are many factors that will affect time density, including thunderstorms, weather in general, season changes, day and night, gravity, and all living things; C) apparently time has a positive levorotatory flow that removes weight from physical matter and a negative dextrorotatory flow that adds weight to physical matter; D) optically active chemicals affect time rotation.

The author found similar rotatory characteristics in the psyche as it is affected by drugs. In early 1961, after observing similarities in structure and functioning, the author theorized that the psyche was an electromagnetic wave organization of a special variety and occupied the brain in a manner similar to electromagnetic waves in a wave guide. Laboratory tests run on a rat in 1964 and on a rabbit in 1967 showed light to be a constant activity in the living brain and to vary characteristically with sleep, consciousness, sight, smell, and so on. In both laboratory tests Hoffman Electronic EA7 series photovoltaic needles were implanted in the cerebral cortical sight area [8]. These photovoltaic needles convert light into electricity and were the same series used in the experiments that showed that exterior light penetrates deep into the living or dead brains of a variety of animals.

A study of brain drugs showed considerable evidence that such drugs act on the psyche by changing its light characteristics [9]. Generally, stimulants fluoresce strongly and in the red and yellow portions of the spectrum. Tranquilizers and other calming drugs fluoresce in the blue or reduce the fluorescence of certain brain molecules. Anesthetics have high refraction indexes (slow transmission of light) and/or fluoresce in the ultraviolet. Narcotics such as morphine, and psychedelics such as LSD, fluoresce strongly and across broad areas of the visible and ultraviolet spectrums; these two types of drugs also generally rotate polarized light in opposite directions [31]. The cerebrospinal fluid fluorescence, the glucose (apparently the only brain fuel [14]) utilization fluorescence, the scoptic absorption curve, et cetera, generally approximate each other and span the visible spectrum. Endogenous chemicals, which in abnormal quantities can cause "illusions," usually have spikes or other components of fluorescence in the ultraviolet. This and other evidence indicate consciousness spans the visible spectrum as its activity, while the semiconscious and the unconscious span part or perhaps all of the ultraviolet and the other shorter wavelengths as their activity. Nerve impulses can cause chemicals to fluoresce [33]; apparently morphine, LSD, et cetera, act by their ultraviolet fluorescence lighting up the subconscious and the unconscious to the adjoining conscious view *to form a single abnormally broad consciousness.* LSD-type drugs generally differ from morphine-type drugs in their effects on the psyche and in that they rotate polarized light *in opposite directions. It is here that Kozyrev's patterns of time rotation, direction, and possibly polarity are apparent.*

The human body is composed of three major spirals oriented around the cerebral aqueduct and the fourth ventricle (Figure 3). Two of these spirals are formed by the third and lateral ventricles, which early in pregnancy grow out of the forward end of the cerebral aqueduct to form the forebrain with its massive cerebral hemispheres. The third spiral is the somite body—the body from approximately the neck on down—which early in pregnancy grows rearward from the fourth ventricle and the rest of the hindbrain and in segments called somites or metameres [11]. The third spiral is evident in the skin areas (dermatomes) which the various spinal areas or possibly nerves serve [20]. The third spiral is

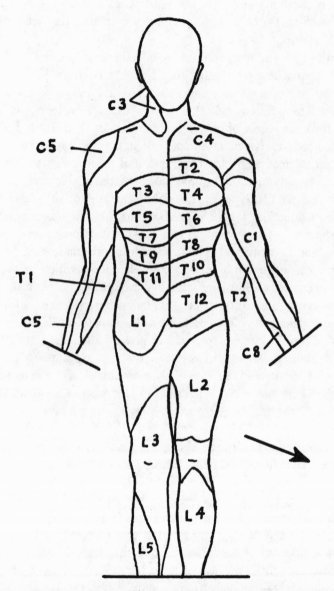

Figure 3. The Third Spiral of the Human Body Schematic of skin areas (dermatomes) found by Foerster when he severed posterior root spinal nerves. This spiral pattern generally also occurs on the back, hands, and feet. (C-cervical, T-thoracic, L-lumbar). T. Lewis, *Pain*, 20–21, Macmillan, 1942.

complex but it has an overall lefthand rotation; this possibly accounts for such phenomena as the left testicle being characteristically lower than the right and the left leg frequently being slightly longer than the right. The rotation of the cerebral spirals is not so clear, but they are probably opposite to that of the somite spiral. Since the brain grows from the animal pole surface of the germ disc and the somite body grows from the opposite surface [11], there should be a coriolis relationship. There is probably some evidence of this relationship in the homunculus patterns of the sensory and motor cortical areas [11, 23]; the cranial nerve homunculus is upright, but the somite homunculus is a mirror image. It is upside down and on the opposite side of the brain to its location on the body. LSD and other "hallucinogenic" drugs are generally dextrorotatory and apparently follow Kozyrev's dextrorotatory time pattern, expanding consciousness inwards (centripetally) beyond the cerebral aqueduct into the expanded time of sleep and death—apparently into the world of antitime and antimatter. The "hallucinations" of these drugs are often characterized by experiences back in time, bizarre "phantoms" of humans (living and dead), animals and plants, and by "understanding" nature on a vast cosmic scale [22]. Morphine and other narcotic drugs are generally levorotatory and apparently follow Kozyrev's levorotatory time patterns, expanding consciousness outwardly (centrifugally) and especially into the somite spiral—down into digestive, sex, et cetera, organs. These drugs are generally characterized by greatly enhanced appetites as for food and sex. The electrical polarity of Kozyrev's time patterns possibly also fits the electrical polarities of the psyche and the body. But conclusions such as these are only tentative because the United States Government translation of Kozyrev's paper [18] is difficult, not a good translation, and none of the test equipment drawings are included. There is apparently no study in the technical literature covering Kozyrev's time patterns with gain and loss of weight in the human body, but Hauschke claims that laboratory tests show that plants routinely move matter in and out of physical existence [13]. This is possibly the source of carbon isotopes in flora and fauna.

The data on time, antitime, antimatter, biological and galactic spirals, and so forth, which Dirac, Kozyrev, Hoyle, and others have given us, closely parallel the three baffling biological phenomena cited at the beginning of this paper: (a) the inward retreat and disappearance of the psyche in sleep and death, (b) the loss of weight at death, and (c) the "expanded time" of sleep and death.

The "unknown" beyond consciousness and earthly life is deeply puzzling; it begets doubts, fears, hope, faith. Some people, including many scientists, reject all and everything about this unknown. No amount of scientific evidence can induce them to accept the nonphysical. Other people are completely gullible. They accept all and everything of the "occult" without rational evidence. But for anyone who rejects both impervious skepticism and complete gullibility, scientific data shows man's psyche to be of a nonphysical nature—evidently antimatter—and shows that in sleep the conscious segment of the psyche and in death the whole psyche passes through the cerebral aqueduct-fourth ventricle* into a world of expanded time—evidently the world of antitime and antimatter.

* This statement has striking similarity to reports from the yogic tradition saying that at death advanced yogis voluntarily pass their consciousness out of the body through the *sahasrara*, the seventh chakra, at the top of the cranium. *Editor*.

References

1. Alfvén, H. *World-Antiworlds*. Freeman: San Francisco, 1966.
2. American Medical Association, *Fundamentals of Anesthesia*. Saunders: Philadelphia, 1962.
3. Arehart, J. L. "Retaining Memory in Older People." *Science News*, Vol. 101, 18 March 1972; "The Role of Hormones in Learning, Memory and Behavior." *Science News*, Vol. 101, 20 May 1972.
4. Becker, R. O. "The Direct Current Field: A New Data Transmission and Control System in Living Organisms." Veterans Administration Hospital, Syracuse, New York, 1961 (unpublished).
5. ———. et al. "The Direct Current Control System—A Link Between Environment and Organism." *New York State Journal of Medicine*, 15 March 1962.
6. Burr, H. S. and Langman, I. "A Technique to Aid in the Detection of Malignancy in the Female Genital Tract." *American Journal of Obstetrics and Gynecology*, Vol. 57, 1949.
7. Carrington, H. "Dr. MacDougal's Experiments." *Archives of the American Society for Psychical Research*, Vol. 1, 1907.
8. Conway, Henry. "The Rational Faculty of Man as an Energy Organization," 1968 (unpublished).
9. ———. "Optical Characteristics as a Basis for a System to Design and Evaluate Brain Drugs," 1968 (unpublished).
10. Ganong, W. F. et al. "Penetration of Light into the Brain of Mammals." *Endocrinology*, Vol. 72, 1963.
11. Gray, H. *Anatomy of the Human Body*. Lea & Febiger: Philadelphia, 1959.
12. Grinkler, R. and Serota, H. "Studies

38

on Corticohypothalamic Relations in the Cat and Man." *Journal of Neurophysiology*, Vol. 1, 1938.

13. Hauschke, R. *The Nature of Substance.* Vincent Stuart: London, 1966.

14. Hoagland, H. "Brain Metabolism and Brain Wave Frequencies." *American Journal of Physiology*, Vol. 123, 1938.

15. Hoyle, F. "Speculation on the Nature of the Nuclei of Galaxies." *Nature*, Vol. 224, 1 November 1969. See also Shebad, T. "Soviet Space Tests Hint a Universe of Matter and Antimatter." *New York Times*, 13 July 1969.

16. Humphrey, C. E. and Seal, E. H. "Biophysical Approach Towards Tumor Regression in Mice." *Science*, Vol. 130, 1959.

17. Kleitman, N. *Sleep and Wakefulness.* University of Chicago Press: New York, 1963.

18. Kozyrev, N. "Possibility of the Experimental Study of the Properties of Time." U.S. Department of Commerce, Joint Publication Research Service Document No. 45238, May 1968.

19. LaCroix, Marcel et al. "Glucose Naturally Labelled with Carbon-13." *Science*, Vol. 181, 3 August 1973.

20. Lewis, T. *Pain.* Macmillan: New York, 1962.

21. Lyght, C. E. et al. *The Merck Manual.* Merck & Co.: Rahway, New Jersey, 1966.

22. Masters, R. E. L. and Houston, J. *The Varieties of Psychedelic Experience.* Holt, Rinehart & Winston: New York, 1966.

23. Morgan, C. T. and Stellar, E. *Physiological Psychology.* McGraw-Hill: New York, 1959.

24. Parker, B. C. "Rain as a Source of Vitamin B-12." *Nature*, Vol. 219, 10 August 1968.

25. Penfield, W. "Some Observations of the Functional Organization of the Human Brain." *Annual Report of the Smithsonian Institution*, February 1955.

26. Penrose, R. "Black Holes." *Scientific American*, Vol. 226, May 1972.

27. Ryan, M. P. "Letters," *Journal of Astrophysics*, 15 October 1972.

28. Schulte, H. F. "A Review of Air Ionization and Its Effects on Living Systems." *Proceedings of the National Electronics Conference*, Vol. 18, 1962.

29. Serge, E. G. "Antimatter," *McGraw-Hill Encyclopedia of Science and Technology*, Vol. 1. McGraw-Hill: New York, 1968. See also "Antimatter." *Encyclopaedia Britannica*, Vol. 2. William Benton: Chicago, 1968.

30. Smith, R. H. "Electroanesthesia—A Review." *Anesthesia and Analgesia*, Vol. 46, January-February, 1967.

31. Stecher, P. G. et al. *The Merck Index of Drugs and Chemicals.* Merck & Co.: Rahway, New Jersey, 1960.

32. Steigman, G. "Antimatter and Cosmology." *Nature*, Vol. 224, 1 November 1969.

33. Tasaki, I. et al. "Fluorescence Changes During Conduction in Nerves Stained with Acridine Orange." *Science*, Vol. 163, 14 February 1969.

34. Turner, B. E. "Interstellar Molecules." *Scientific American*, Vol. 226, March 1973.

35. Twain, Mark. "My Platonic Sweetheart." *Reader's Digest*, November 1953.

16 Of Time and Mind:
From Paradox to Paradigm
Keith Floyd

To think about thinking, to wonder about wondering, to feel strongly about feeling strongly: these are perhaps uniquely human forms of awareness. This capacity to reflect upon itself—i.e., reflection upon reflection —appears fundamental to the nature of human consciousness. This thinking about thinking about thinking Arthur Koestler has called "the paradox of the ego spiral" [2]. It is at once our triumph and our tragedy, for in this very human process reside equal potentials for ecstasy and anguish. The moment one thinks a thought, the thinker (subject) and the thought (object) may be experienced as one in the unitary process of thinking. When this occurs, it is as if two mirrors have been opposed and each reflects the other into an infinite regression of reflective depth —past the speed of light, out of time altogether. It is an immediate, direct experience of the infinite within one's own consciousness. On the other hand (the right), just as we possess the capacity for experiencing the ecstatic heights of union and wholeness in that reflective depth, so do we have an equal capacity for fragmentation and the schizoid splitting of ourselves into thinker and thought, body and mind, feeling and action. This split-up condition of the human psyche is what is commonly known as "normalcy." And as R. D. Laing has so poignantly put it, "What we most need is to be cured of our blasted normalcy." [3]

The mind is perhaps the deepest mystery, the most profound paradox,* of all existence. It may truly be that "darker than any mystery,"

* As Alan Watts has so well said, "Paradox is just the truth standing on its head to attract attention."[9]

to use the words of Lao-Tzu [8]. There is, however, yet another paradox that must be confronted prior to our attempt to formulate a theoretical model of the mind. This preliminary problem concerns the nature of time.

Given our apparently linear, sequential experiencing of past, present, and future, we quite naturally interpret time as a constant instead of in terms of a construct, despite Einstein's gentle proddings to the contrary.

Contrary to common conviction, we may all rest assured that nothing has ever happened in the past and that nothing will ever happen in the future. Everything that happens, happens at the moment of being, right now, or not at all. We have memory traces that we conveniently refer to as "the past," and we have anticipations that we confidently regard as "the future," but *being* itself is of the present, and ever was, is, and shall be. *Now* is none other than that inconceivably subtle (nonexistent?) interface between "past" and "future." Paradoxically enough, our present is indeed a generous gift—of absolutely everything and nothing.

Perhaps we had best pause at this point for a somewhat more concrete treatment of these confusing abstractions. Ready? Five seconds ago we think of as residing in the past, right? At approximately that time you were perhaps reading the word "Perhaps" at the beginning of this paragraph. But at the time you were first reading it, of course, it had to be happening in the present. Five seconds from now will be in the future, right? All right, beginning *now*, please check your watch and together we'll find out what it is like to arrive in the future. One, two, three, four, five; here we are in the future, right? Well, hardly. To repeat this elementary consideration, nothing has ever happened in the past and nothing will ever happen in the future. All that happens, happens in the present or not at all.

Now we must address ourselves to the problem of the present. If it is true that five seconds ago may be considered the past, and five seconds from now will be in the future, then it must be equally true that a thousandth of a second ago must also be viewed as the past, for it is no more. And a thousandth of a second on the other side of this exceedingly fine line we call the present must be thought of as the future, for it is not yet. Between the "no more" and the "not yet," occupying infinitely less than a billionth of a second, lies that eternally present, yet absolutely absent, timeless time zone within which everything that has happened has happened. But it's beginning to seem as if there is no time left in which anything could possibly be happening. There would appear to be no time at the interface. As Paul Tillich expressed it in his brilliant and moving little book, *The Eternal Now,* "The riddle of the present is the deepest of all riddles of time" [7].

The profound paradox of the present is that it both is and is not, all at once, just as the infinite exists only because it doesn't, and it doesn't only because it does . . . (and so forth, ad infinitum, appropriately enough).

To extend the paradox one step farther: if all awareness occurs within this infinitely fast moment of being known as the present, then, as Zeno long ago insisted, motion is impossible. A photograph of a racehorse in action snapped at a thousandth of a second yields an image of the horse frozen in a fixed position within that single, still frame. Yet we may liken the instant of awareness in the present (for, remember, there is nowhere else for awareness to occur) to a camera that is set infinitely faster than a billionth of a second. If we pan the racehorse and snap the shutter at that speed, we shall have captured stillness indeed, a picture of perfect motionlessness.

Our whole notion of time grows out of what we sense and interpret as motion. Apart from the experience of what *appear* to be sequential, still frames of awareness, giving rise to the illusion of motion, there can be no concept of time.

This principle is readily apparent in regard to motion pictures, but is generally unapparent when it comes to our "ordinary"† awareness. Sitting in a darkened theater viewing a scene on the screen, we perceive continuous motion, just as is observed outside on the sidewalk. Yet in the case of the former, we are aware that what we experience is merely the illusion of motion created by a sequence of separate still pictures flashing on the screen at the rate of approximately twenty-four frames per second. At that rate—within the range of our own waking, beta brain-wave rhythm, incidentally—we are unable to perceive the separate stills, as the brain insists on interpreting the unfolding scene in terms of smooth, flowing motion.

By way of setting up an analogy that will be useful in a moment, imagine if you will that the projectionist has slowed the projector so that the frames are passing between the light and lens at only half the

† What we think of here as ordinary being most extraordinary!

normal rate. Obviously, the viewer would then observe the scene on the screen unfolding in slow motion, half as fast as before. At sixteen frames per second, he begins to be aware of a flicker effect, and at eight frames per second observes choppy, pixilation movement as in old-time movies. For future reference, please keep in mind that eight frames per second would correspond roughly to the lower threshold of the alpha rhythm of the brain. Suppose the projector were then switched to a rate of five frames per second, corresponding to the middle range of our theta rhythm. The viewer could then begin to distinguish the separate still photographs out of which the illusion of motion is created. Further slowed to two frames per second, one's awareness of the paradoxical moving stillness would become even more pronounced. This would, of course, correspond to the delta rhythm that our brains ordinarily produce only during deep, dreamless sleep. Then if the film were suddenly to stop rolling, one would see a single still picture projected on the screen.

Needless to say, it would be quite a revelation for someone having no knowledge of the cinematographic process were he exposed to the above sequence of events. At somewhere around four-and-a-half frames per second, we would probably hear him exclaim, "Ah, ha, now I see how the tricky devils do it!" And the moment the sequence came to a stop on one still frame, the entire process would be revealed in perfect clarity.

Still, our friend most likely fails to understand that essentially the same process will continue to function in his own consciousness as he leaves the theater and strolls down the street. It will be no more apparent to him than was the other when he was viewing twenty-four frames per second, for his brain will be processing the pictures‡ that comprise his awareness at a continuous rate approximating twenty-four frames per second, assuming he is in the normal, waking, beta state.

Let us suppose, however, that our friend approaches an intersection and stumbles onto a teacher of sorts who takes him aside and instructs him in one of the various disciplines that point one toward achievement of "the quiet mind," as they say. Let us further suppose that day in and day out he conscientiously devotes himself to the monumental task of simply sitting quietly and doing nothing. Having struggled to so sit

‡ The total event—not limited to the visual mode, obviously.

through several years of seemingly self-defeating effort, suppose now our friend is sitting crosslegged in a dimly lighted room, with his spine straight, his ears in line with his shoulders, and his nose in line with his navel. With this picture clearly in mind, imagine that his eyes happen to fall inadvertently upon the illuminated face of a nearby clock.

Having just begun his meditation practice for the evening, he is probably firing beta (approximately 14–30 bursts of neural energy per second) as his predominant brain-wave rhythm. In that state of normal awareness, he observes the clock's second hand sweeping around the dial at what appears to be its usual speed. As he continues quietly sitting, thoughts and words, concepts and images slowly begin dropping away from his consciousness. Evidently, his rate of brain-wave flashing is gradually decreasing. After a few more moments of this disciplined letting-go, as it might be described, an electroencephalograph would reveal that he is consistently firing alpha (within the range of approximately 8–13 flashes per second). At a constant 10 flashes per second, he experiences not only a blissful, serene state of consciousness, but notices also that the second hand on the clock appears to have slowed to approximately half its former speed. "A very interesting subjective effect," he thinks, in a temporarily jarring burst of beta. And he notices without thinking that a barely perceptible on-off flickering of light has begun to punctuate his awareness, as if he is opening and closing his eyelids at a rapid clip.

Another three minutes of this sitting in tense relaxation brings him yet closer to the stillness within, and he drops down into theta rhythm (approximately 3–7 flashes per second). In this altered state of brain functioning, he experiences a number of highly interesting effects. First he is aware, without verbalizing it internally, that the blissful serenity of alpha has increased so markedly in intensity that it could only be called a state of ecstasy. He finds his mind flooded with creative insights, as if it has established direct contact with every mind that has ever been or ever will be. It could almost be described as a dimension of awareness beyond space and time. His consciousness is expanding and he feels himself at the threshold of what has been called "cosmic consciousness." And the flickering light pulsations observed earlier have now become much more pronounced. It is as if a strobe light set at around 5 flashes per second, the basal rate at which his brain waves are firing, is flashing in the darkened room. He notices the choppy, pixilation movement of the second hand on the clock and observes that it corresponds precisely to the stroboscopic rate of flashing. The flickering light he recognizes unmistakably as the flashing of his own brain waves. It now seems to take the second hand from 15 to 20 seconds to cover a 5-second span on the face of the clock.

Next his brain-wave activity drops down to the middle of the delta range, in the area of 1.5 flashes per second. The clock's second hand now "moves," if one could call it that, in imperceptibly shifting still frames, and the ecstasy of waging delta becomes virtually unbearable. Then the strobelike flashing slows, slows and stops, and in that timeless instant the second hand on the clock stops dead still. He is astonished to discover that with the stopping of his own brain waves, all motion in what passes for the physical universe has stopped dead still. Prior to this "moment of the slack jaw," he had always thought of his perceptual apparatus as a sort of sound-camera, a recorder of events, but now he has glimpsed for the first time that he is also the projector. He has seen that when one's brain-waves stop flashing, birds freeze in flight, people cannot move, and the entire universe stands still. The "out there" of external reality has suddenly been seen in a whole new "inner" light. Distinctions such as "inner" and "outer" all vanished in a lightning flash, and he realizes what Lao-Tzu must have meant when he suggested, "It is due to making distinctions that its Suchness is lost sight of." [8] Even the perfectly nonsensical Hindu hint *Tat twam asi* ("You are that") has suddenly made sense beyond sense, and he knows he will never be the same again (he may even rightly wonder if he will ever be "sane" again). With the intrusion of that disquieting thought, the brain waves again begin flashing, slowly at first, then picking up speed, and the observed "movement" of the second hand on the clock corresponds precisely to the rate of flashing.

Back to beta and the flicker-fusion of smoothly moving images once again, our friend reflects on the implications of the madness he has just experienced. He sees, first of all, that what we think of as time is merely a function of one's basal brain-wave rate, a convenient and fascinating fabrication of the conscious mind. Looking even more deeply, he thinks he may see a clue to the nature of what we are pleased to call "death." Clinically considered, he knows that death occurs upon the cessation of brain-wave activity, and that the cessation is usually preceded by a slowing-down process. Assuming his experience may be taken as a fleeting glimpse into the nature of things, he anticipates that his own "death" will be preceded by observations of activity perceived in increasingly slowing motion as the moment approaches—people moving about, voices, all sights and sounds inexorably slowing, slowing, and finally stopping, stopping "dead still" (an apropos expression if ever there was one). And he strongly suspects that in that inevitable moment one cannot but catch the biggest joke of all, the one Wei Wu Wei has so cleverly called "the joke that made Lazarus laugh." [10]

When brain waves are still, time stands still, and when time stands still, the illusion of motion becomes impossible, and with the impossibility of that illusion, the fundamental illusion of separate selfhood is in double jeopardy.

Having seen that time (and/or motion) goes slower, the slower the brain-wave rhythm, it would not be at all surprising to discover that those with superior skills—great athletes, for example—may merely be blessed with basal brain wave firing significantly slower than that of the general population. This may prove to be the critical difference between the "star" and the "superstar." The baseball player firing alpha, for instance, might perceive the ball at no more than half the speed perceived by his teammate firing beta. One firing theta could carefully observe the approach and spin of the ball, examine the stitches, read the label, and have up to four times as much "time" to regulate the swing of the bat and make his moves. The player with the slower brain-wave rate could more nearly come close to observing the individual units of motion just short of pixilation. Stopping just short, he would be unaware that his perception differed radically from that of others on the field, but he would clearly have a definite advantage over his fellows. In the January 1973 issue of *Intellectual Digest* [5], John Brodie of the San Francisco 49ers football team described precisely this effect and indicated that he and others occasionally experience it during critical plays of crucial games. It might well be that anyone who could produce delta waves at will could pick up a Ping-Pong paddle for the first time and promptly become the greatest Ping-Pong player in the world. With the ball perceived as moving at less than one-tenth its usual speed, one would have more than ten times as long to observe and plan and act. You are invited to fantasize freely, Walter Mitty style, and dream up additional applications of this intriguing principle.

While the hypothetical experiences of our friend may be written off by many as pure fantasy, increasing numbers of people know from personal experience that time is an entirely flexible function of their own minds. In various altered states of consciousness, time may be slowed down, speeded up, leapfrogged, or even run backward. One who insists such things are impossible is presuming a great deal about the nature of reality. The limits of reason, we may reasonably surmise, hardly define the limits of reality. Nature is not bound by the limits we impose upon ourselves. Presumably, whatever obligations She cares to assume are assumed strictly for the sake of Her own amusement.

To help solder the connections between time, motion, brain waves, and the material that follows, you will need to secure the equivalent of about a dozen 3″ x 5″ note cards. The only other equipment required for this demonstration is a floor, in lieu of the actual ground, and a willing spirit. Assuming you were conscientious enough to secure the cards, let us proceed.

Please imagine that each card represents what we shall hereafter refer to as an "on phase," a flash of brain-wave activity. This we might view as the level of operation of the conscious mind. Imagine also, if you will, that the floor, or ground (for those of you who are really serious about this), extends infinitely in every direction and represents the dark, deep unconscious, the "Ground" of the conscious mind, out of which come the spheroid bursts of light represented by the note cards. It is roughly the equivalent of Jung's "Collective Unconscious," or "Objective Consciousness," as he later came to prefer calling it [1].

Now, with cards in one hand and this book in the other, please line your cards up end-to-end across the floor. That done, you are asked to consider that, as with your abutting cards, the flashes of our conscious awareness ordinarily appear as a continuous stream of experiencing with no spaces between flashes, and thus, no perception of separate flashes. We are simply unaware of the dark gaps between flashes, that is to say, we are unconscious of the unconscious (but, after all, that is what makes it the unconscious). Just as an alternating current appears to produce a continuous stream of light in a turned-on bulb, so it is with our conscious awareness. But in both cases it is nothing more than an apparent§ sequence of stroboscopic on/off pulsations of electrical energy that are simply flashing too rapidly to permit the perception of separate

§ Exactly how and why the "sequence" is only "apparent" will be dealt with momentarily.

flashes in our field of ordinary awareness. Cards separated by no more than a millimeter would correspond to our normal, waking beta rhythm.

Reducing the rate of flashing, as in meditation, sensory isolation, psychedelic experience, and other forms of brain-wave alteration, we begin to be subliminally conscious of separate flashes. This is preliminary to our conscious awareness of the spaces between flashes. In the language of the street, we are talking literally about getting "spaced out."

Returning once again to your continuous stream of cards laid out across the floor, it would be helpful if you would now separate each card from its neighbor by a distance of about one inch. What you are invited to see in this modified arrangement is suggestive of what one experiences while tuning in the alpha rhythm, as happens in the early stages of most forms of meditation. One begins to become aware of the dark gaps (off phases) between flashes (on phases). With this awareness, one cannot but feel a deep sense of peace and serenity, although one may be completely unaware of why it is happening. Let me suggest that it is because one is on the verge of seeing through the dark gaps into the infinite depths of the unconscious, the ground of one's being. And this inexpressible merging of the conscious mind and the unconscious has all the earmarks of union and communion with the "Ground of Being."

Spreading the cards further apart—say, five inches apart—you may now notice that one has equal amounts of "time" in which to be aware of the on phase and the off. This might be seen as corresponding to the upper threshold of one's theta rhythm. It is in this state, you'll recall, that creativity abounds, as one's consciousness is experienced as One with a limitless ocean of Consciousness. As a single process, the conscious mind plunges into the infinite depths of the unconscious and/or the unconscious breaks through from the depth to envelop the conscious mind.

Further slowing the rate of firing (as represented with cards perhaps 12 inches apart) one now has "all the time in the world," as they say, in which to be absorbed and assimilated into that fathomless depth. Then the flashing stops dead still (quickly, pick up your cards!). In that instant, all motion ceases, one is out of time, beyond the relative world altogether. Nothing stands between oneself and the Ground. The conscious mind and the deep unconscious are One, as was always so, but was simply unrealized. And up until the moment the flashing re-

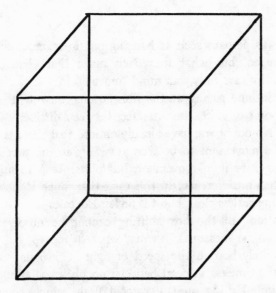

sumes, one is perfectly content, as Camus expressed his highest aim, "to remain lucid in ecstasy."

We must now address ourselves to the problem raised by the necessity for qualifying "sequence" as nothing more than an "apparent sequence." As was suggested earlier, past and future are purely subjective operations and have no objective existence in reality.* Reality knows only the single still frame of the moment of being. Subjective memory and expectation make possible our interpretations of "before" and "after," and give rise to a sense of motion derived from the appearance of a sequence of still frames. It is this apparent sequence that makes possible the illusion of motion. If past and future do not, in fact, exist, there can be no motion. And if motion does not exist, there can be no time. And if time does not exist, space and matter become very tenuous propositions indeed.

To illustrate what appears to occur in the processes of perceived motion, let me begin by presenting above my favorite demonstrator of perceptual shift, the classic Necker cube.

If you will gaze at the above configuration of connected lines for a few seconds, you will suddenly observe that the figure-ground relationships have shifted and you are viewing what appears to be a quite different box. First it may have seemed to be resting on a flat plane,

* The question remains, of course, whether anything exists "objectively" in reality.

and then it was perhaps seen as hanging out in space. Something apparently changed, but what moved to make that change possible? Obviously, in this case, only your mind "moved."

As you continue gazing at the illustration, you might attempt to discern the point of shift, the interface, between distinctly interpreted perspectives. No doubt you have already noticed that there is apparently no perceptible movement to be seen anywhere in the process. Where there is change, we infer movement, but please keep in mind that it is no more than an inference. In this case, that much is clear; in other cases it may appear less clear, but it is no less the case.

The "motion" of the box shifting cannot be observed, and its "speed" cannot be measured, because what happened, happened out of time—infinitely beyond the speed of light. The figure-ground shift occurred in the timeless interval between on phases (flashing) of your conscious mind. During one interpreted flash, which comprised the totality of your awareness in that instant, you observed a single, stable configuration of the cube. Then came an off phase (the dark gap between flashest), and the next on phase revealed the box in a new perspective. The off phase is of the unconscious, that timeless, limitless dimension, while the on phase is a manifestation of the conscious mind, the surface-level at which we carry on our multifarious (if not nefarious) business of the relative world.

All that we perceive as motion (which is also all that we experience as time—and space, for that matter) is exclusively a function of consciousness shifting figure-ground relationships to create the "next" picture in the perceived "sequence." That "motion" is the no-motion at the point of shift (that infinitely subtle nuance), which only seems to be made up of one still frame after another. Our everyday perception of sequential motion is precisely analogous to the shift in perspective of the Necker cube. As we observe the shifted perspectives, we might be inclined to believe the shift simply happened too quickly to perceive, yet it is actually of a dimension beneath the level of conscious awareness. Neurologically speaking, we have an "on flash" of brain-wave activity (conscious mind) in which we perceive one perspective, then comes the off phase in which the figure-ground pattern is shifted to appear as the next picture in the perceived sequence, and so on, ad infinitum. With

† Kindly remember that the idea of an actual sequence of flashes is nothing more than a conceptual convenience and should not be taken literally.

every perceived shift in figure-ground relationships we have a new ambiguous pattern presented for interpretation at the conscious level. So
the conscious mind and the unconscious, again, shift like the Necker
cube, the off phase being the phasing itself between distinctly interpreted
perspectives that give every appearanceof unfolding sequentially in time.

Another interesting property of this fascinating process is that any
number of figure-ground shifts may be perceived in any given amount
of "time," since time is not actually a factor. What we might think of
as a billion shifts in the perceived motion-picture sequence may seem
to happen in what we would call a billionth of a second, or one shift
may take a billion years. This might help account for the experience
of countless individuals near death who have reported seeing their whole
lives in a flash, as if unrolled on a scroll. When the flashes of neural energy
slow and stop, all the still frames are there to see simultaneously and instantaneously for there is no more time out of which the illusion of sequence can be fabricated. We are not looking at frames rolling by with
the past being taken up on a reel to the right and the future unreeling
from the left—we are viewing at a tangent to the linear plane, peering into
the infinitely reflective depth of a single still frame. All frames are of the
one frame.

In what we observe to be the on-off flashing of brain-wave activity,
apparently the flash itself is only the moment of awareness of a shifted
perspective of the figure-ground relationships in an ambiguous pattern
comprising the screen of conscious awareness. Both the point of shift
and the flash (the dark and the light, the figure and the ground) evidently occur in no-time, but Consciousness conspires to create the appearance of separate, sequential flashes or frames of awareness. Since
there is no time between flashes (the shift requiring none, as was seen
with the Necker cube) there is nothing to separate flash from flash, or
flash from no flash. The one flash of dark/light is merely the light/dark
of Consciousness playing as though the illusion of time/motion is for
real and forgetting it is playing a trick on itself just for fun.

What before we perceived in terms of a dualistic on/off, light/dark
sequence of brain-wave activity, we may now wish to view instead as
a unitary dark/light pattern of a single frame within which all awareness manifests itself, and out of which any form may be created. The
shifting of figure-ground relationships alone creates distinctions such as
on and off in our field of consciousness. This should come as no great

surprise, as our Buddhist neighbors have for centuries been trying to tell us that nirvana (the Infinite Unconscious) and samsara (the day-to-day activity of the conscious mind) are one and the same. The unconscious is as readily apparent in every off phase as the conscious mind is in every on phase of the cycle, but we fail to see the former because of our lock-step habit of paying attention only to the latter. When brain waves are slowed to the range of perceptible flicker, we begin perceiving with equal clarity the off phase and the on phase (nirvana and samsara) and we realize the essential oneness of the cycle, i.e., that there is no on without an off and no off without an on—each creates the other and is the other. Every wave has a crest and a trough; every brain wave has an on and an off.

To repeat once more, the unconscious is manifested in every off phase of the on-off cycle. It is as if one shoots down (or opens up) at a tangent through the dark gap between on phases, and that tangent extends infinitely in every direction into the deep unconsciousness. But it must be remembered that there is no time or space, and so, no directionality in the unconscious.

In our "ordinary" consciousness we fix our awareness only on the on phase of the cycle. In our "high" moments, we see through the surface screen and see that which cannot be seen. This is like God playing hide-and-seek with himself, as in the Hindu Vedanta scheme of things. There can be no on phase without an off, but there can be an off without an on. Before the beginning (of "time") there was an off (Void) that wasn't even that, for it wasn't an off relative to an on or to anything at all. "And God said, 'Let there be light'" (an on flash), and the cycle was established. At "death" the on phase ceases along with the relative off, but not the Absolute Off, the Ground of All Being. Once one has awakened to even a partial realization of the deeper Nature of his Being (i.e., "catches a glimpse into his Self-Nature," as they say in Zen), then the idea of death has forever lost its sting.

It is as if all that we see as comprising our separate selfhood is drawn on an infinite sheet of paper (infinite in every direction, unimaginably enough), and we learn to think of ourselves as contained within the outline of the drawing. We neglect to notice that the outline appearing to circumscribe our entire being is the same line as the inline of everything else. And that inline delineates and defines our apparent individuality as precisely as does the outline. They are, in fact, the same line; it is just a question of shifting perspective. We naturally fail to see that all that surrounds us and gives us our sense of selfhood is everything that is—and that includes ourself. At the moment of what we term "death," it is as if the line, the most superficial aspect of our case of mistaken identity, is merely erased. There is as much "self" as ever left within the former boundary line, but now we see the whole idea of a separate self was no more than the illusory feeling of separation itself.

To illustrate it somewhat more poetically, we are rather like a plastic bag of seawater sinking into the fathomless depths of some infinite ocean. At the moment of "death" and/or "ego death," the plastic bag, by which we maintained all sense of our separate seawaterness, suddenly disintegrates and disappears leaving no trace. The water we had identified as our "self" may appear forever lost, or the whole of the warm and boundless Sea of Being may be seen as gained. Again, it is all a question of shifting perspective. Clinging to the unreal sense of separate selfhood past that ultimate point would quite literally be one hell of a fix, figuratively fraught with no little weeping, wailing, and gnashing of teeth. Conversely, letting go to flow freely beyond that infinite point could be nothing less than a perpetual state of ecstasy.

This way of looking at our Self-Nature might go some distance toward explaining various forms of psi phenomena that otherwise may seem to defy both "natural law" and rational explanation. If the deep unconscious is continuous with everything that is (or *is* what everything is!), then what we think of as our consciousness is one with all the Consciousness that is, has been, or shall be, to put it in temporal terminology. From this perspective, it would be expected that ESP is not limited by the speed of light, for Consciousness has nowhere to go—it's already there! It should not seem surprising when a mother dreams her son's plane crashes on the other side of the world at the precise instant of the actual event. After all, is it not the same Consciousness in which they live and move and have their Being? Being in the here and now knows no separation, no split, in time and/or space. Precognition and retrocognition would be seen as natural phenomena, and not at all astounding, once one recognizes the absence of even the concept of time in the deep unconscious. Distance and duration are exclusive properties of the relative space-time frame of reference. It is encouraging to note that the idea of the Oneness and Allness of one and all, once thought the drink of wild-eyed mystics, is fast becoming the meat of clear-eyed modern physicists.

In Consciousness, the one frame is every frame, storing an infinitude of images in an infinitely creative pattern of pure and perfect ambiguity. As in the enormously exciting process of 3-dimensional lensless photography known as holography, a vast amount of optical information —many pictures—may be stored within, and retrieved from, a single holographic plate, depending on shifts in angles in the exposure and reconstruction of images. To extend the parallel one step farther, it is interesting to note that any single fragment of the hologram is seen to contain the entire image stored within the complete holographic plate. Each part is at once the whole and the whole is every part. It does appear modern science and ancient mysticism are about to meet at the crossroads. Perhaps neither will be too surprised to discover each is but a mirror image of the other.

If we are to succeed at this point in developing a holographic model of the structure of consciousness, it will be necessary to assume for the time being the philosophical posture of commonsense realism. In other words, we must proceed as if we accept at face value the objective existence of external reality in general, and of the physical brain in particular. The built-in limitations of our dualistic language structure will also no doubt continue to bedevil us.

All that we experience as external reality is apparently nothing more than patterns of neuronal energy firing off inside our heads, yet these patterns have the capability of representing (or reflecting?) a broad spectrum of sensory, nonsensory and extrasensory experiences. A free (and freeing) translation from an ancient Sanscrit manuscript has provided the rules for the game: "Gracious one, play your head is an empty shell wherein your mind frolics infinitely."

Increasing numbers of neuropsychologists and neurophysiologists are coming to regard higher brain functions in terms of an optical system processing a form of bioluminescence (light in the midst of the darkness of the skull). To briefly summarize my own tangent in this general line of speculation, let me suggest that brain functions such as perception, memory, imaging, and so forth, are beginning to appear most clearly explainable on the basis of a holographic model.* The "screen" of awareness may turn out to be an organic form of a holographic plate that processes 3-dimensional perceptions and reconstructed images with equal facility.

Although laboratory evidence is just beginning to accumulate, and introspection remains suspect, it may not be premature to hypothesize that the area of the midbrain immediately posterior to the optic chiasma will be found to be the locus of a neural holographic plate. The pituitary gland, hypothalamus, thalamus, and pineal body in particular appear to be intimately associated in the theater of conscious awareness. The discovery that the pineal body, long thought by many a vestigial sensory organ, is partially composed of light-sensitive tissue similar to that found in the retina of the eye, seemed to lend support to the speculation that it might serve as the "grid" of patterned ambiguity on which perceptions are constructed and memories are reconstructed. This seemed too much to hope for, of course, inasmuch as this pea-sized organ has for so long been regarded in the East as the "third eye," and considering that Descartes and others had so long designated it "the seat of the soul."

In attempting to work through the interrelationshpis of the organs of the midbrain, all that seemed clear at first was that the thalamus apparently radiates neural energy to the opposing cerebral hemispheres and possibly organizes incoming impulses into more coherent wave forms. In this process, it was also suspected that the thalamus may serve as the source of the alpha rhythm, as a regulator of brain-wave frequency and intensity, and may play an important role in the scanning and retrieval mechanism(s) of the brain. It appeared, however, that if the pineal body did play a primary role in perception and memory, its excision would be seen to produce profound, if not total, disruption of these functions.

Such, of course, has not been shown to be the case. The removal of the pineal body in rats disrupts the circadian rhythm, the biological clock of the organism, and similar effects have been observed in humans. Further reflections on the process suggested that the "screen," the holo-

* If you wish to explore the fascinating field of holography in more depth and detail, note especially Leith and Upatnieks' excellent article, "Photography by Laser," [4] and Karl Pribram's chapter, "Holograms," in his monumental work, *Languages of the Brain* [6].

graphic plate that I had so long been attempting to identify with an organ, may actually be a function of an area instead of an organ. It began to appear that the pineal body occupies the midpoint at the center of a neural energy field, at which point occurs the burst of light that is experienced as the screen of consciousness on which shifting figure-ground relationships represent external reality. This would be the same point at which the sense of time and/or motion manifests itself, and so it should not be surprising to discover that the removal of the pineal body strips the gears of the biological clock. This would simply mean that the monitoring mechanism of the sequential bursts of light goes when the pineal body goes. The flashes persist in the same area, at the same point, even though the organ at which they had occurred has been removed.

It now seems highly plausible that the "seat of consciousness" will never be found by a neurosurgeon, because it appears to involve not so much an organ, or organs, but the interaction of energy fields within the brain. These patterns of energy would be disrupted by surgical intervention, and have long since disappeared in cadavers. Neurophysiologists will not likely find what they are looking for outside their own consciousness, for that which they are looking for is that which is looking.

In terms of the model under consideration, this mysterious area of the midbrain would evidently function as a transducer in the processing, or impedance matching, of "external" (physical) and "internal" (neural) wave energy. Patterns of brain waves would be activated in the contralateral cerebral hemispheres (each being a mirror image of the other) based on the holographic image perceived. Memory would involve enervation of the originally fired neuronal circuits, a reactivation of the brain-wave patterns that were interpreted as the original experience, a convergence of interference waves reflected from the contralateral hemispheres, and a reconstruction of the original hologram. What we term "memory" would be seen as the conscious-level interpretation of the otherwise ambiguous figure-ground pattern appearing on, or within, the holographic plate, the locus of conscious awareness. Coherent wave energy may also be found essential to the process, just as coherent light produced by the laser is necessary in holography. Perhaps the neural energy must be polarized and made coherent for the system to function efficiently. As is true of the holographic process, the more coherent the light, the clearer the reproduction of the holographic image. The degree of coherence of the wave forms might well determine the relative degrees of efficiency in both the storage and retrieval processes.

In all fairness, it should be remembered that the foregoing summary of personal speculations is based on the perhaps groundless assumption of the brain in a general scheme of commonsense realism. Still, it will surely do us no harm to recognize and acknowledge our assumptions as assumptions. We might even go so far as seriously to consider that, contrary to what everyone knows is so, it may not be the brain that produces consciousness, but rather that it is Consciousness that creates the appearance of the brain, matter, space, time, and everything else that we are pleased to interpret as the physical universe. All we can possibly know for sure is that something very interesting is going on. Exactly how, why, or what it's all about, God only knows! And the biggest paradox of all may well turn out to be that there's not a paradigm's worth of difference, so to speak, between Him and you.

References

1. Jung, C. G. *Memories, Dreams Reflections*. Vintage Books: New York, 1963.
2. Koestler, Arthur. *Arrow in the Blue*. Macmillan: New York, 1952.
3. Laing, R. D. *The Politics of Experience*. Ballantine Books: New York, 1967.
4. Leith, E. and Upatnieks, J. "Photography by Laser." *Scientific American*, June, 1965.
5. Murphy, Michael and Brodie, John. "I Experience a Kind of Clarity." *Intellectual Digest*, January, 1973.
6. Pribram, Karl. *Languages of the Brain*. Prentice-Hall: Englewood Cliffs, New Jersey, 1971.
7. Tillich, Paul. *The Eternal Now*. Scribner, New York, 1963.
8. Waley, Arthur. *The Way and Its Power*. Grove Press, New York, 1958. (A superb translation of Lao-Tzu's sublime *Tao Tê Ching*)
9. Watts, Alan. *The Book*. Collier Books, New York, 1966.
10. Wei Wu Wei. *The Tenth Man*. Oxford University Press: London and New York, 1966.

IX
Ecological
Consciousness

This section might also be titled "The Evolution of Consciousness" because as man grows to know himself, he becomes aware of his "self" as a
dynamic pattern of events extended through time and space—a process,
not a thing. As Buckminster Fuller puts it, I seem to be a verb. Since
we are products of our biological past, the expansion of consciousness
means incorporating information about our evolutionary heritage into
our awareness. That is, we must accept and understand our animal origins. In the spatial dimension of our existence, expanding consciousness
means becoming aware of how we interact with our environment. Thus
we gain greater self-control and freedom when we become aware, for example, of how atmospheric ions, lighting conditions, sunspot activity,
geomagnetism, barometric pressure, blood sugar level, and chemicals in
food affect our moods, thought and behavior.

But we are not rigidly bound to our animal origins or environmental
conditions. Knowledge is power, and as we grow in self-awareness, we
reduce the degree to which our mental life and behavior are conditioned
and determined by heredity and environment. Aristide Esser's article
considers the evolutionary development of the human brain and suggests what we may do to overcome the so-called instinctual behavior that
leads to aggression and conflict.

Complementing Dr. Esser is an article by Robert A. Smith, III, who
suggests that general systems theory is our passport to the evolution of
greater consciousness. "General systems thinking" and "a general systems
view of the world" are a mode of awareness that sees things integrated
and whole—not fragmented. It sees interrelated hierarchies in nature and

society whose patterns tend to remain invariant although the content changes. It attempts to build newer, more comprehensive models of reality—metamodels—to replace the ones that no longer are adequate. This approach provides new insights into the general patterns of existence: fusion instead of confusion.

The Society for General Systems Research has members around the world. Information about the society is available from the Secretary, Joseph Henry Building, Room 818, 2100 Pennsylvania Avenue N.W., Washington, D.C. 20006.

Several texts are available to guide you into the larger view of life that is general systems thinking. General Systems Theory *by Ludwig von Bertalanffy (Braziller, 1968) is the classic. Von Bertalanffy is recognized as the "father" of general systems theory.* The Systems View of the World *by Ervin Laszlo (Braziller, 1972) is a brief work for the general public, while his* Introduction to Systems Philosophy *(Gordon and Breach, 1972) is a comprehensive, technical survey of general systems theory's application in science and philosophy. Gregory Bateson's* Steps to an Ecology of Mind *(Chandler, 1972) is a thought-provoking collection of essays related to this subject.*

J.W.

17 Our Passport
to Evolutionary Awareness
Robert A. Smith, III

> ... *The New Science (General Systems) attempts*
> *to overcome the limitations of the mechanistic view,*
> *and in the very process, to reintroduce the human or*
> *humanistic element which was lost. It tries to give*
> *new answers to old questions and to control mistakes*
> *we obviously made in our scientific world view and*
> *civilization.*
>> —*Ludwig von Bertalanffy, "System, Symbol and*
>> *The Image of Man," in I. Galdston,* The In-
>> terface Between Psychiatry and Anthropology.
>> *(New York: Brunner/Mazel, Inc. 1971.)*

Man does not necessarily live by his volition but we, as humans, "are
lived by a force that we call evolution" [1]. This evolution force has
been influenced by (a) the Agricultural Revolution, (b) the Scientific
Revolution, (c) the Industrial Revolution, (d) the Knowledge and
Cybernetic Revolution, and now (e) the Ecological Revolution. Problems associated with this last revolution have accelerated significantly
since World War I and have become global in scale, potentially affecting the physical balance of all life on earth. But as John McHale, the
futurologist, maintains, technology itself is not the awesome monster;
rather it is the conceptual approaches and social attitudes that determine
how technology will be employed that create the problems of "Big Science" and many of our ecological problems. Perhaps the major problems
resulting from "Big Science and Technology" emerge primarily as a
consequence of their vast complexity and machinelike interdependence.

Attempts to overcome the negative effects of "Big Science and Technology," unfortunately, have led to mechanistic and organismic rather than organic solutions. It is unfortunate that the computer, which could simulate possible social organizations, has taken on the manichean methodology of national military establishments in so many cases [2]. Too, the tendency to recapitulate the ideological utopias of the past through machine programming does not enhance the computer as a truly progressive social instrument [3]. Yet Herbert Simon and Buckminster Fuller do indeed demonstrate that "if computers are organized somewhat in the image of man, then the computer becomes an obvious device for exploring the consequences of alternative organizational assumptions of human behavior" [4]. A visit to Southern Illinois University* and Bucky Fuller's World Game display—computer simulation and the enthusiastic young guides of the Game, amply demonstrate the truth of a humanistically programmed computer. If synchronicity were properly connected with synergy, then we would find Fuller, Forrester, Simon, and others individually but jointly working on mutual problems.

As Simon elaborates, "A man viewed as a behaving system is quite simple. The complexity of his behavior over time is largely a reflection of the complexity of the environment in which he finds himself" [5]. Ronald Laing, the controversial British psychiatrist; Bion, Harry Stack Sullivan, William Gray, Nicholas Rizzo, Arieti, and other interpersonal psychiatrists strongly support Simon's observation. But here we come to our main premise—overspecialization and its inevitable consequence of the impersonal as opposed to the real need for the intrapsychic, interpersonal, and transpersonal. Specialization naturally tends to lead to "immaculate perception" or the filtered perception caused by overly trained capacity and underly trained connectedness. Lancelot Law Whyte stated our goal: "Unity in diversity and continuity in change."

At this point, I think it would be wise to address myself to that old Western problem—dualistic thinking. Roy Grinker maintains that "dualistic thinking . . . is static and oriented toward stability and permanence" [6]. Taoism offers us some real clues on how to overcome the destructive effects of dualism. The yin and yang of Taoism becomes the microcosm of the vaster universe. Yin, like earth, possesses Jung's *anima* qualities such as tenderness, receptiveness, and quiescentness, while yang, like the

---

* Since this article was written, Buckminster Fuller has relocated the Design Science Institute in Philadelphia. *Editor.*

sky, possesses Jung's *animus* qualities such as strength, activeness, positiveness, and creativeness. And as Lee points out, "The characteristic of the yin and yang interplay is the complementary relationship between the opposites. They are not in dichotomy but complementary" [7].

It seems to me that Lee is wisely leading us toward true relativity—the ever forming when opposites unite—the past and future to form the infinite present or a movable synthesis of life [8]. It is this movable synthesis of life that we are missing.

R. G. Studer explicitly outlines the problem we are dealing with in this paper in these significant words [9]:

> The various subsystems which make up the human environment (e.g., transportation, housing, medical, educational) are considered discrete, requiring specialists to deal with them. Indeed vast, complex bureaucracies have evolved which insure that these subsystems are neither redefined nor properly interrelated. The economy of effort and sheer cost of maintaining such systems is clearly untenable, as every urbanologist knows, and the problems of management seem insurmountable as the fragmentation and deterioration continue.

Studer suggests that we can overcome this fragmentation and deterioration if we make plans for resolving social, biological, and environmental deficiencies. He maintains that the "task of the human systems designer is to arrange the environment so as to maximize autonomy in the context of collective goals, and minimize the probabilities of exploitation of the many for the benefit of the few. In short, planning and design is not antithetical to human freedom; it is absolutely essential to insure it" [10]. Although "the techniques of simulation are not highly developed where the vicissitudes of human behavior are concerned . . . such techniques provide an important resource for realizing a modelled human system in the real world. Certainly it is not guessing" [11].

Research in general systems theory tells us that a fundamental distinction must be made between closed and open systems. Closed systems are isolated from their environment, whereas open systems are not. The biologist Waddington has illustrated in brilliant and vivid fashion the operation of an open system with its environment. He calls it the *epigenetic space*, or that position between genotype and phenotype space. The epigenetic space is the arena where the already formed goes through a forming process and emerges re-formed. But this is a continuous process—a movable synthesis or a constant complementarity of the yin and yang for the individual, the generation, the institution and, carried to the highest level, the universe [12]. Perhaps Arthur Koestler states it succinctly: "The single individual constitutes the apex of the organismic hierarchy, and at the same time the lowest unit of the social hierarchy" [13].

I have attempted to demonstrate the folly of specialized polarization. Polarization is a loss to all, particularly the polarization of technology and the polarization of "humanistics." Science is always a concert of the many if it is indeed a true science. Dahrendorf maintains that "the progress of science rests as much on the cooperation of scholars as it does on the inspiration of the individual" [14]. Cooperation, in this context, means also mutual criticism. We are speaking here of synergetics, or the working of parts and wholes and isomorphic relations of wholes to ever-larger wholes—wholes that naturally form the hierarchy of wholes. In similar fashion, we must concentrate on overcoming the dysfunctional aspects of misapplied Darwinism or of a specialization that ignores the relation of a specialty to a larger whole [15].

Man is a holistic gestalt of men, collective knowledge, and machines. The pressing need for man to see himself as a whole creature woven into the collective fabric of humanity is rapidly increasing. Today we see communes of all types developing all over the face of the globe. While they focus on love and community, there is a tendency to cater to a specialized form of inbreeding that lessens human adaptability. But they also promise, if nurtured properly, that they could focus on more organic social institutions—institutions integrated in a fashion to enable integrated individuals to function totally [16].

Integrated individuals—or those individuals who are capable of transcending their specialty—are needed as catalytic agents in subsystems or organizations to enable subsystems to transcend themselves and become organic parts of the larger whole. These integrated individuals penetrate both horizontal and vertical boundaries. There is a growing "excitement not based on anarchistic destructiveness but resulting from creative developments and success in the integration of individual and organizational well-being" [17]. This is an integral principle of our continuous evolution—an evolution involved in the ecosystem (an evolution that can be understood only if we apply the ecology of general systems), the link that ties man to mankind and to his relation with the greater cosmos.

General systems analysis, followed by meaningful applications, will enable us to meet the challenge of freeing the working forces of humanity from the meshes of trivia and turn it toward the mountains of real work that needs to be done. It will lead us from fragmentation and reductionism to holism and connectedness. It will lead us to the tacit knowledge that we are mankind and part of the great and infinite universe.

In its global concepts, general systems theory includes that of isomorphism from cell to society. I feel that, when isomorphism is connected with symbolism, the gap between hierarchical structure and oceanic unity will have been bridged in both psychology and psychiatry [18].

To elaborate, I believe that Jung's synchronicity, or the simultaneity of occurrence of like but causally unrelated events, are thought processes arising from "the ocean of undifferentiated unity" or Teilhard's noosphere. I also believe that synergy, which is a nonsummative whole based upon an hierarchical relation of "whole-parts," is somehow closely related to the simultaneity involved in synchronicity.

Bertalanffy wisely observes that mankind, despite the cases of hermits, does not consist of isolated individuals but "is organized in *systems* of various orders, from the small group such as the family to the largest called civilizations" [19]. In this connection, we might note that "among the important processes for the sociocultural system are not only cooperation and conformity to norms, but conflict, competition, and deviation which may create (or destroy) the essential variety pool, and which constitute part of the process of selection from it" [20]. . . . Psychologists would do well to develop the ability to distinguish the difference between creative and conforming deviance.

To draw upon the late Kenneth Berrien, who organized this particular discussion on general systems, it is hoped I have brought the reader to a point of departure—not of arrival [21].

A next point of departure should be to develop an ecology of awareness—both a symbiotic and morphogenetic awareness of mankind. The space ventures, the drug culture, Zen and yogic exercises, Sufism, experiments in cinema, television, and other forms of programming via informational media will have a profound influence on man's psychological development. Celestial storms of karmic illusions with "glacial, floating aurora borealis lights of red and yellow-whites, rainbow liquid cascades of exquisite sheerness" will become more common [22]. But during the same period, research into alpha waves of the human brain, galactic plasma rhythms, the earth's pulsing heliosphere, ionosphere, and magnetosphere, the DNA-RNA helices, and into the kibbutizim and other forms of communal living may bring us out of the karma and into cosmic awareness [23].

Jesse Pitts has observed (and, I believe, rather astutely) that "everywhere, perhaps even in Soviet Russia, there seems to be an erosion of classical patriotism. By contributing to this erosion the counterculture orients the search for the sacred toward an international community of students" [24]. However, "instead of replacing nationalism by a thoughtful dedication to an entity beyond the Nation which requires more self-sacrifice, there is a tendency toward a premoral affirmation of the primacy of self-interest. The counterculture's hatred for the Nation is parochial, often too bitter to be the result of greater love" [25]. This, of course, explains why we have structured pluralism, or fragmented separatism, and why tension collects along singular lines. This also explains why the United Nations is not an entity but rather a nonentity (in the sense of a whole) of many competitive parts—a system of nonsystematic wholes or a nonsynergetic, albeit unpredictable, whole.

Pitts continues his insightful probing in these words [26]:

> . . . The true goal of man is the understanding of nature and that the face of God "can be found in the anatomy of a louse." In this contemplation, the search for the sacred finds a solution in which achieved rank differences, so emphasized by meritocracy, are shriveled to insignificance by the cosmic perspective of learning . . . the passion to know must replace the passion to conquer.

We might say, with the counterculture, by paraphrasing C. Wright Mills, an early archetype: *How totally impersonal, and therefore beastly, the featherbedded bureaucratic bourgeois of today is.* Their actions force upon me an alliance with Ronald Laing who maintains that "it is only through the discovery of a freedom, a choice of self-functioning in the face of all determinations, conditioning, fatedness, that we can attain the comprehension of a person in his full reality" [27]. The postsputnik decade produced a full measure of engineering meritocracy and its concomitant specialized direction of the soft sciences as well. The post free speech movement has produced such a violent antimeritocracy movement that it has reached the specialization of antiknowledge and a meritocracy of the absurd. Somewhere in between these polarized positions, the greater number of people search for purpose and meaning and for a future.

In a true sense, Sheldon Kopp gives us a beautiful description of our Pascalian or general systems journey through life [28]:

> We must live, I believe, in the fact of knowing that man is ultimately not perfectible. . . . For we are all Jews. We all wander in exile. We suffer trying to believe that there is a reason. We try to go our way and do what is right. But at times each of us forgets. We want some certainty, some clarity. We want the face of the enemy at last to be clear and the good guys to win once and for all. At that point, when any man forgets that he is Jew, denies that he is in exile—at that point he runs the risk of becoming a Nazi.

General systems can be "an illuminative power of . . . energy in man [which] also connects him with his organic life and natural phenomena" [29]. Awareness for the unity of one's own unity may enable him to ascribe intact uniqueness to every self-observation, beginning with his fellowman [30]. General systems theory concerns itself with the problems of "the individual versus the state, of community, of the individual's freedom or restriction of freedom, and of the present problem of individual dissent and the breakdown of collective living" [31].

I hope that this brief discussion of general systems, indeed, makes clear that it is essential to developing an awareness of emergent man. The psychologist will come into his own when he adheres to the admonition of Pascal to his fellow philosophers: Touch the extremes but fill in the intervening spaces. To me, Pascal has expressed the essence of general systems theory. I believe that we search for fulfillment and not for boundaries that prevent us from finding it. *General systems is the "open sesame" for a greater consciousness leading to this.*

General systems theory and application enable the psychologist as well as other professional members of our society to deal with emergent characteristics of living systems. Waddington's "epigenetic space" or, as I prefer to term it, the "emergent force field," to me represents what Kurt Lewin was seeking in his field theory. Epigenetic space is the interaction of psychic, physical, and time space, which produces a metamorphosis, and in a biological sense, a mutation [32]. If, indeed, evolution involves an unpredictable reaching for higher levels and greater complexity, then we must concern ourselves, as do most general systems theorists, with isomorphic relations of parts to wholes. Arthur Koestler expresses this essence of general systems theory as a vital way of looking holistically down and holistically up for differentiation and integration in janus-faced entities [33]. It is a syncretism of the total field of harmonic opposites in a continuous metamorphosis of symbiosis and morphogenetics [34].

These haunting words of Ervin Laszlo end our discussion: "Nature builds hierarchies by adapting parts in wholes, and the wholes as parts in superordinate wholes" [35]. Certainly Laszlo is urging us to recognize our need for a regenerative, complementary ecosystem. He is urging us to make real use of our systems psyche, conscious of itself and its energy field, and experiencing feedback from the constant tao of entropy and syntropy forming our universe in one grand pattern [36].

References

1. Youngblood, Gene. "The Ecological Revolution." *Los Angeles Free Press*, April 10, 1970.
2. The Club of Rome is presently involved in constructing a computer model of the world for simulating world events and trends. This is under the direction of Dr. Jay W. Forrester of MIT.
3. Wilkinson, John. "Methodology of Science and The Future." Undated. Center for the Study of Democratic Institutions, Santa Barbara, California.
4. Simon, Herbert A. *The Sciences of the Artificial*. MIT Press: Boston, 1969.
5. *Ibid*.
6. Grinker, Roy R., Sr. "The Continuing Search for Meaning." Benjamin Rush Lecture to the American Psychiatric Association in San Francisco, May 12, 1970.
7. Lee, Jung Young. "The I Ching and Modern Science." Paper presented to the 28th International Congress of Orientalists in Canberra,

Australia, on January 8, 1971. See also Bonner, William. *The Mystery of the Expanding Universe*. The Macmillan Co.: New York, 1964; and Meneker, E. and Meneker, W. *Ego in Evolution*. Grove Press: New York, 1964.
8. Smith, Robert A., III. "Social Systems Analysis and Industrial Humanism." *General Systems*, Vol. 14, 1969. Also see Nishida, Kitaro. *Intelligibility and the Philosophy of Nothingness*. East-West Press: Honolulu, Hawaii, 1966.
9. Studer, Raymond G. "Human Systems Design and the Management of Change." *General Systems*, Vol. 16, 1971.
10. *Ibid*.
11. *Ibid*.
12. Waddington, C. H. "The Theory of Evolution Today," in Koestler and Smythies, eds. *Beyond Reductionism*. Macmillan: New York, 1970.
13. *Loc cit*. Koestler. "Beyond Atomism and Holism."
14. Dahrendorf, Ralf. *Essays in the*

Theory of Society. Stanford University Press: Stanford, Calif., 1968.

15. Wescott, Roger W. "Darwinism and Utopia." *The College Quarterly*, Fall, 1961.

16. Arasteh, A. Reza. *Final Integration in the Adult Personality.* Brill: Leiden, The Netherlands, 1965.

17. Bass, Bernard M. "The Anarchist Movement and the T-Group: Some Possible Lessons for Organizational Development." *Journal of Applied Behavioral Science*, Vol. 3, No. 2, 1967. See also Filley, Alan C. *Utopian Organizations as Alternatives to Present Structures: Organization Invention.* University of Wisconsin: Madison, Wisconsin, 1971.

18. Grinker, Roy R., Sr. "Symbolism and General Systems Theory," in Gray, Duhl, and Rizzo, eds., *General Systems Theory and Psychiatry.* Little, Brown: Boston, Massachusetts, 1969.

19. *Loc cit.* Bertalanffy, Ludwig von. "General Systems Theory and Psychiatry: An Overview."

20. Buckley, Walter. "Society as a Complex Adaptive System," in Buckley, ed. *Modern Systems Research for the Behavioral Scientist.* Aldine: Chicago, 1968.

21. Berrien, F. Kenneth. *General and Social Systems.* Rutgers University Press: New Brunswick, N.J., 1968.

22. Youngblood, Gene. *Expanded Cinema.* E. P. Dutton: New York, 1970.

23. Reiser, Oliver L. "Solar Systems Resonance, the Galactic Alphaphone, and the DNA Helix." *Fields Within Fields . . . Within Fields*, Vol. 5, 1, 1972. World Institute Council, New York.

24. Pitts, Jesse. "The Counter Culture: Tranquilizer or Revolutionary Ideology." *Dissent*, June 1971. See also Otto, Herbert A. "Communes: The Alternative Life-Style." *Saturday Review*, April 24, 1971.

25. *Ibid.* Pitts.

26. *Ibid.*

27. Laing, Ronald D. *The Divided Self.* Penguin: London, 1965.

28. Kopp, Sheldon B. *Guru.* Science and Behavior Books: Palo Alto, 1971. See also Stulman, Julius. *Evolving Man's Future.* Lippincott: Philadelphia, 1967.

29. Periera, I. Rice. *The Nature of Space.* The Corcoran Gallery of Art: Washington, D.C., 1968. See also Thompson, William I. *At the Edge of History.* Harper & Row: New York, 1971.

30. Dorsey, John M. *Psychology of Emotion.* Center for Health Education: Detroit, 1971.

31. Gerard, Ralph W. "Hierarchy, Entitation, and Levels," in Whyte, Wilson and Wilson, eds. *Hierarchical Structures.* Elsevier: New York, 1969.

32. The special issue of *Psychic* magazine, June 1971, provides an excellent overview of the alpha wave phenomenon and psychic communication.

33. Koestler and Smythies, eds. *Beyond Reductionism.* Also see Tart, Charles T. *Altered States of Consciousness.* Wiley: New York, 1969; Babcock, Winifred, and Preston Harold. *The Single Reality.* Doubleday: New York, 1971; and Krippner, Stanley, and Meachum, William. "Consciousness and the Creative Process." *Gifted Child Quarterly*, Autumn, 1968. The reader might want to refer to two recent books that deal with this desire for unity or integration. See Butterworth, Eric. *Unity of All Life.* Harper & Row: New York, 1969; and Pearce, Joseph Chilton. *The Crack in the Cosmic Egg.* The Julian Press: New York, 1971. (Paperback, Pocket Books: New York, 1973.)

34. Kirkland, Elithe Hamilton and Porter, Jenny Lind. *On the Trellis of Memory: A Psychic Journey into Pre-History.* Carlton Press: New York, 1971.

35. Laszlo, Ervin. "Reverence for Natural Systems," in Laszlo and Stulman, eds. *Emergent Man.* Gordon & Breach: New York, 1971. Also see Bennett, John G. "Total Man: An

Essay in the Systematics of Human Nature." *Systematics*, 4, March 1964; Assagioli, Roberto. *Psychosynthesis.* Hobbs, Dorman: New York, 1965; Hart, Ray L. *Unfinished Man and the Imagination,* Herder and Herder: New York, 1968.

36. Odum, Howard T. *Environment, Power, and Society.* Wiley: New York, 1971. Also Esser, Aristide H., ed. *Behavior and Environment: The Use of Space by Animals and Man.* Plenum Press: New York, 1971; Caldwell, Lynton K. *Environment: A Challenge to Modern Society.* Natural History Press: New York, 1970; Spiegel, John. *Transactions: The Interplay Between Individual, Family, and Society.* Science House: New York, 1971; and Charter, S.P.R. *Man on Earth: A Preliminary Evaluation of the Ecology of Man.* Grove Press: New York, 1970.

The reader might also want to refer to recent works on the psychology of meditation or illumination. See Vargiu, James C. "A Model of Creative Behavior." Psychosynthesis Institute, Redwood City, Calif., 1971; and Naranjo, Claudio and Ornstein, Robert E. *On the Psychology of Meditation.* Viking: New York, 1971.

18 Synergy and Social Pollution
in the Communal Imagery of Mankind
A. H. Esser

Summary

Awareness of environmental pollution as a threat to the survival of mankind has brought about inquiry into its ultimate source: pollution of the mind or social pollution. Our increasing ecological disarray shows us that, in a world where groups and things are more and more interdependent, we need working together, synergy. We may speak of synergy when parts of a system or whole systems work together in such a fashion that the total effect surpasses the sum of the effects of each separate part or system. The brain is an organ that increases in synergy the more we understand ourselves. Self-transcending cooperation between all men, which consciously attempted, probably is the most precious form of synergy. In this sense the housekeeping of our planet requires an inner as well as an outer aspect of ecological consciousness. Since pollution of the inner aspect, mind's inner space, can prevent synergy, I consider the understanding of social pollution to be of crucial importance in enabling synergy. And synergic thought and action appear to provide the only means for the furthering of human evolution.

Introduction*

Mind may be viewed as the total of the continually expanding imagery shared by mankind. Through millions of years of experiencing, life evolved the human Central Nervous System (CNS). The CNS, which has become the seat of our experiencing, provides different types of images as representations of all transactions with our environment. Only those images of our environmental transactions that are shared and consensually validated by others are of significance to mankind's future, hence our concern with the pollution of communal imagery.†

Images are mental representations of anything presented through sensory experiences or created by feeling and thought. They may be conscious or unconscious, are always derived from actual or internalized action, and influence all behavior. Those images that lead to similar behavior in members of a species, that others react to or interpret in the same manner, are literally shared images. Their totality is the communal imagery of which part is specific for each species. It is my belief that man shares all biological and much emotional imagery with the animals, and that this animal heritage at times unavoidably clashes with man's species—specific rational and intellectual imagery. This clash of images is *social pollution*, and as such is part of becoming human, since it can occur only in the human CNS [15, 16, 17].

Because images as representations of experiences are always related to other images, the CNS handles the increasing complexity of their relationships and the amount of imagery itself with selective awareness at levels ranging from the concrete (sensory stimuli) to the abstract (symbols). The process of coding at different levels enables structuring and an increase in the informational capacity, or to quote De Long: "Hierarchical organization is what prevents behaving individuals from being caught up in a 'sink of consciousness.' Analogous to the 'sink of energy' Weisskopf says must inevitably follow if everything is related to every-

* I am grateful to Glen McBride, Alton J. De Long, and Ada R. Esser for their comments on an earlier version, which was based in part on the presentation "Social Pollution in the Evolution of Man" at the Centennial Symposium, St. John's University, New York, *Man and His New Life Environment*, April 21, 1970.

† In this paper, I discount the nonimage aspects of experiencing.

thing else, individuals would enter a bottomless pit of consciousness, a supreme introspection that would totally consume its perpetrator, if hierarchical levels were completely reducible to those beneath themselves. By establishing limits to relatedness, hierarchical organization confines us to an awareness of no more than one level of complexity at any given point in time" [11].

But the capacity of our CNS to deal with continued increase in imagery through hierarchical structuring is also a disadvantage. Too rigid a separation between functional levels in the hierarchy can lead to isolation and diminished synergy. Our earliest animal images, shaped during eons of evolution, are so much part of our heritage that they are for the mind what genes are for the cell. For instance, archetypes partly determine all of our presently shared images, and will like genes help blueprint future activities. Functional isolation of any level of imagery in the individual mind may lead to a robotlike existence or madness.

Only deliberate choice to integrate all the world's images can prevent mental isolation. The miracle of amoral biological evolution is that man became a moral animal, able to make this choice. The unique characteristic of human mind to acquire and store knowledge beyond the capability of the individual CNS enables individuals to contribute to the communal imagery of mindkind as cells do to the body. Teilhard de Chardin saw the culmination of this process in a "noosphere" resulting from the eventual coalescence of all individual minds [43]. Again, synergy is needed to make such a coalescence more than a melting pot. Whether we accept this vision or not, we may conceptualize that the evolution of imagery initially based on biological evolution now has become a synergic process in its own right.

Determinants of Communal Imagery

Communal images are reflections of organization of environment that are self-maintained and may change on the basis of environmental input or, in man, creative thought. The basis for all organization of environment lies in the transaction between organism and environment: In the beginning was the deed. In the course of evolution, the initiation of action shifted to the nervous system, and the CNS became capable of postponing reactions to environmental stimuli and to initiate actions on the basis of virtual movements. These *images* of actions are the plans and programs of the brain, the schemata of Piaget.

Initially, imagery could only be evoked through precise constellations of environmental stimuli. But later in evolution, especially with the mammals, the CNS came to rely more and more on certain stimuli as signals for complex environmental conditions, particularly those resulting in pain or pleasure. Thus experiences of emotions in addition to perception of the environment came to determine shared imagery.‡ Learning to experience emotional relationships and sensitivity for someone else's feelings is called social learning. Finally, in the latest stage of evolution, the CNS of the highest mammals shows the potential for initiating action on the basis of imagery created by reason and abstractions. Especially human behavior has come to rest in many respects solely on symbols, and intellectual learning is directed toward increased participation in the total symbolic imagery of mankind.

Each of these steps in the development of communal imagery is reflected in the functions of different parts of our CNS. Only recently have we started to probe the connections between the evolution of our CNS, different aspects of the environment, and the corresponding images. Each stage of evolution produced characteristic ways in which the then-predominant part of the CNS processed images of its interactions with the environment. MacLean described three systems in the (triune) human brain: the *reticular*, concerned with biological survival in the brain stem; the *limbic*, concerned with emotions in the midbrain; the *cortical*, concerned with rational and other functions in the hemispheres [26, 27]. Roughly speaking, the reticular system is predominant in all animals evolved to the level of the reptile, the limbic system begins to dominate behavior in the lower mammals, and the cortical system starts to control behavior in the higher mammals. Each of these systems has its own way of knowing of, and relating to, the environment. In man, communal imagery reflecting the environment in each of these systems can be called the Biological, Social, and Prosthetic Brain [16]. See the Table.

‡ For an impression of the role of key stimuli and social (emotional) releasers in the behavior of different species, see Eibl-Eibesfeldt [13].

TABLE

Evolutionary Stage (MacLean)	CNS SUBSYSTEM	INPUT	FUNCTION	AWARENESS	COMMUNAL IMAGERY
Higher mammalian	Cortical	Symbols	Rational	Mostly conscious	Prosthetic
Lower mammalian	Limbic	Signals	Emotional		Social
Reptilian	Reticular	Stimuli	Vital	Mostly out-of-awareness	Biological

CNS Subsystems and Their Imagery

The first part of our CNS to evolve was the brain stem containing the most basic physiological and behavioral survival mechanisms. In man, the brain stem forms only a small part of the total CNS mass, but in all animals up to the reptilian level it forms the predominant part of the CNS, producing highly stereotyped behavior, including that responsible for the communal imagery of homing, the establishment of territory, and mating. Mutually recognized behavior basic to survival can be called the *Biological Brain*. Communal imagery basic to biological survival does not need recognition of individuals; social organization can therefore be anonymous and based purely on appropriate socio-physical stimuli. Life is unemotional under these conditions. Man knows this; "crocodile tears" are meant to indicate absence of communal feelings. But further evolution of social behavior was made possible only when emotional life made interruption of stereotyped behavior patterns possible [17], or as Eisenberg states: "short-term emotional responses form the basis for all social behavior in the higher vertebrates" [14].

Emotions are generated in the second part of our triune brain, the limbic system. Emotional life developed in mammals as a means of social organization built on painful and pleasurable experiences. Mammals developed group life (which recognizes individual members) because of the mother-child relationship, which had to be personal because of mandatory breast-feeding. Even in groups of lower mammals, such as rats and mice, where members may recognize only five to six others as individuals, the entire group closes for membership because of differentiating factors such as group odors. They can be regarded as an evolutionary transitory phase between the anonymous aggregates of lower animals and the large organized groups of higher animals. In the latter, animals show highly complex social behavior, not only because they recognize each other individually, but also because they may attribute specific roles to certain group members.

In mammals, the communal imagery increases in scope, and the resulting group behavior, called a *Social Brain*, may at times be at odds with the communal images of the Biological Brain. For instance, altruistic behavior, in which an animal may sacrifice its life for the group, can be shown to have a genetic basis in the principles of kinship selection [32, p. 116]. Such behavior may enable surviving blood relatives to reproduce more successfully than members of another, less mutually supportive, group. This means that during evolution imagery *against* the survival imperative of the brain stem and *for* the emotional family ties of the limbic system can be established and become a built-in source for potential conflict.

We may use a simple (social) learning model to illustrate how mammals obtain more complex communal imagery than reptiles, even if this does not tell the whole story of the still inadequately known functions of the limbic system. A Social Brain, a network of individual relationships between group members, relies on emotional coding mechanisms to regulate behavior. For instance, the newborn animal experiences pleasurable "mothering" in the form of stimuli, such as certain odors, noises, textures, temperatures, and tastes of food. It learns to encode the complex of stimuli as a positive signal: Mother. The importance lies in the transformation of physical stimuli into messages that *forecast* events. With the capacity for emotion, this transformation process is immensely furthered and given the potential for rapid generalization. As Spitz discusses for man: "In the course of infant care the neonate experiences a variety of stimuli as a disturbance of his quiescence . . . None of these experiences has a psychological representation at this stage. It is to be assumed that they will acquire one in the following few weeks" [40, p. 50]. Spitz summarizes: "The innate factors in maturation are evident at birth in the two precursors of emotions . . . (which) play a major role in the ontogenesis of perception and the inception of memory" [40, p. 60]. Later in life, encounters with littermates and other members of the colony teach the individual to distinguish quickly and show behavior appropriate to someone belonging to the in-group, a stranger, of higher and lower status, of the same or different sex and age, being in a good or bad mood, and so forth.

The disadvantage of the Social Brain form of social organization is that there is a limit to the number of group members with whom one can deal satisfactorily through emotional bonds. Some species avoided this problem by developing specialized forms of group organization. For instance, the domestic chicken shows a peck order, a practically linear form of dominance hierarchy clearly visible with feeding behavior. If a pile of grain is presented, the alpha chicken will eat first, then the beta chicken, continuing in order until the omega chicken has her turn. This collective dominance and submissive behavior works well even in large groups because each chicken watches the behavior of the chickens immediately outranking her. We encounter here a form of communal imagery in which not every group member participates fully, but which nevertheless, thanks to sequential ordering, functions as one Social Brain. However, linear ordering does not suffice for the higher mammals, which evolved increasingly generalizable adaptations while maintaining a need for satisfactory emotional contacts. J. B. Calhoun has recently adduced that the limits for groups of rats in the wild are seven to nineteen adults, with an optimal number of twelve as the best fit for adaptation of submissive animals in proximity to a dominant male [7]. It appears that man shares this original group size with rats. The dominant group size of prehistoric man, and contemporary hunter-gatherers, such as the Bushmen in Africa, the Australian aborigines, and others, appears to be less than fifty [24, 47], approximately twelve adult males. Human primary groups§ may still function most comfortably only with that size, since our emotional memory capacity for mutual relationships possibly precludes satisfactory contacts with all members of larger sized groups. Casual observation of functioning groups in sports (teams in soccer, football, and so forth) and the army (infantry squads, air force squadrons) reveals a dozen as optimal size. Twelve is also a good number for group therapy.

As a group-living animal, man derives feelings of comfort and security

§ The concept derives from Cooley [8], and in recent years the similarity between animal groups, especially of monkeys and apes, and human primary groups, as well as the probable continuity in development of primary groups in infrahuman primates, primitive men, and modern man, has been established [47].

from stimuli based on physical contact and face-to-face interactions, which familiarize him with all the members of his group. These primary relations, based on firsthand experience, give the individual his earliest and most complete experience of social unity. Life in a primary group (family, a small tribe, or village) is satisfactory, since emotions appropriate to biological events such as birth, illness, and death are easily shared and appreciated. Communal imagery in such Social Brains changes slowly. The acceleration in the rate of change brought about by man's cultural evolution has exceeded the individual and group capacity for change existing in Social Brains.

The third part of our CNS, the cortex, has developed to enable complex social life in large groups, extending to a global scale in man. The tribal community may be viewed as the transformation of Social Brain imagery from group to society. On the one hand, initiation rituals introduce every young member to all the others in the tribe. On the other hand, there is sufficient awareness of other tribes to allow for exchanges. The psychodynamic development responsible for this dichotomy will be discussed later. Let us first examine some of the reasons for the need to develop a cortex and its communal imagery, a *Prosthetic Brain*.

With the increase in differentiation among participants, the complete intimacy required for a Social Brain became more difficult to attain. Furthermore, individual personality development brought about that men, except in their earliest years, are too uniquely organized to allow full reciprocity of understanding and receptivity. This type of interpersonal exchange requires creative imagination and intuition oriented only toward one or a few others.* Communal imagery for interaction with many others requires abstract intelligence, the capacity to make generalizations and retain data in a large memory. Both of these requirements are met by cortical functioning, and cortical communal imagery in man continually expands with the systematized use of symbols. Modern individuals partake in many Prosthetic Brains, those of business relations, work, language, and culture, to name a few. The imagery of these Prosthetic Brains depends on communication in terms of symbols, adherence to explicit reasoning, and a desire for continually increasing memory capacity relying on parts and aspects of the environment coded to serve as artificial extensions of the CNS. It is the latter that

---

* See for a discussion G. Simmel [38, p. 322].

provides the built-in growth capacity of Prosthetic Brains. All individual brains can contribute to Prosthetic Brains, the crystallizations (from primitive tools to computers) of mankind's activities in his environment.

Social Pollution in Communal Imagery

The embodiments of life at each stage of evolution were perfect adaptations to their environments, serving different communal goals. We can see how man inherited the potential for being divided against himself, how much of a miracle it is that things come out right more often than wrong.

With the cultural evolution, the natural fit between man's mental images and his experienced environment had to vanish. Instead, a chronic clash of images became part of human life. Images appropriate for animal group life partially block human creativity. This process causes social pollution. The conservative, emotionally satisfying images that govern life in biological groups are useless in most cultural situations where man has only an intellectual acquaintance with his fellowmen. Cultural relationships, based on intellectual understanding, can be made quickly, and agreements can be reached without physical contact. (It is significant that we call such knowledge of each other "casual" and reserve the term "intimate" only for those occasions when emotional exchange plays a part.) Conversely, the symbols of technological and scientific reasoning that make culture possible can rarely be applied to problems of group or family life. Primary group relationships based on sharing of emotions take time and multiple face-to-face contacts.†

Social pollution, the consequence of human cortical development, can be seen in the problem of alienation of self and of Prosthetic Brain hypertrophy, the malfunctioning of communal imagery.

"I" became differentiated from "self" when intellect gave name to emotion and drive. Language provided the context for logic and reason

† That there are limits to what can be humanly agreed upon without face-to-face contacts attests to our persistent animal group living habits. The seemingly irrelevant ceremonies surrounding the signing of peace treaties show that man still needs the satisfactory image of physical interaction to overcome the emotional struggle in accepting the intellectual concepts of normalization of relations with the hateful enemy.

to act independently of the drive states of the Biological Brain and the emotional states of the Social Brain. There is a functional differentiation between cortical and subcortical nervous systems in man. As Fair states: "The higher one, the neocortex, may have come to 'look' at the other, or to 'represent' it, as a problem of the same order as those arising in the external environment. The psychological parallel is man's unique awareness not only of himself but parts of his own nature as *other* than himself" [20, p. 21]. Man is able to see himself as "other," strange or alien. The functional states of the limbic and reticular systems have become in themselves manipulable as images in the cortical system. Feeling friendly, possessive, or territorial can be used in symbolic forms in interpersonal transactions. Thus the participation of biosocial images in any prosthetic communal imagery is controllable within limits of awareness. If the control becomes subjectively burdensome or objectively does not comply with societal rules, we consider the person alienated, emotionally disturbed or "crazy." Mental illness, as the conflict between Biosocial and Prosthetic Brains, is part of Social Pollution.

To understand how man can allow himself to become a tool of the Prosthetic Brain, we must look at the process of the interchangeability between "self" and "other." In evolution, self-awareness probably came later than awareness of the other; or as Nietzsche said: "*Das Du ist alter als das Ich.*" The image of "I" in an individual is not needed for Social Brain functioning. The importance of the process of individuation is that it made it possible for man to switch his allegiances from his primary group to another willing to recognize his particular skills and expertise. This process, a group's voluntary acceptance of a stranger, enabled men to aggregate and found communalities of creative interests, rather than maintain closed groups based only on shared emotional experiences.‡ Bonds of blood and soil lead to xenophobia and strengthen a Social Brain, but lack the possibilities of accelerated growth of imagery provided by the cumulative experiences of Prosthetic Brains. Robert Ardrey suggests that the start of the mysterious process of individuation may have paralleled the invention of the bow and arrow, enabling stone age man to hunt alone effectively, rather than in a group [1, pp. 341–

‡ However, our biosocial heritage is strong. Experiments have shown that feeling that one belongs to a group, even if this is an artificial group to which one is arbitrarily assigned, triggers discriminatory behavior toward outsiders [41].

368]. Thus the bow and arrow would have been the first real artificial extension, the first prosthesis for the human brain, adding a new dimension to mankind's shared imagery. This dimension made possible the establishment of voluntary social *contracts* (a contract is based on reason) changing man's relation to himself and to other men.

The disadvantage of man's making contracts and bargains is that he can be objective about himself and consider his subjective being interchangeable with an other. This creates the mechanistic view of man's transactions with his environment, whereby man becomes a cog in a machine. In culture and technology a production process, a bureaucracy, or a network of ideas in which man allows himself to become but a part, can grow independently and create isolation. Man has known of this danger in the myth of the "Sorcerer's Apprentice."

Within a culture, the products of rational thinking can generally be made available to each member. When ideas are phrased in terms of science and technology, they can be adapted transculturally and be of global use. This is possible because intellectual learning is abstract, and we know that potentially symbolic expressions can be understood and added to by any man. But the cumulative character of Prosthetic Brains may also court disaster, even when man has the best of intentions. For instance, the technological elite of this world has developed nuclear prostheses that could cause Doomsday because the Prosthetic Brain has a life of its own. In times of perceived crisis, we tend to use our Prosthetic Brain imagery to foster the goals of our restricted in-group, and vice versa [18]. When the chips are down, in situations where we have to make hard choices, social pollution, a cognitive dissonance between mental images arising from deliberate rational actions and those arising spontaneously from emotional experiences, seems unavoidable.

But this does not have to lead to permanently harmful and even life-threatening adaptations in mankind as a whole, and to individual psychopathology. Instead, war, mental illness, and a host of other social and individual dysfunctions can be considered unwanted evolutionary byproducts. We must therefore conceptualize social pollution in terms of its possible obsolescence. Once we consider social pollution the price mankind had to pay for its evolution, we may be able to devise strategies to overcome or bypass it, rather than continue with stereotyped appeals to "morality" or "the higher instincts" or "reason" in man. Social pollution is caused by conflicts between old and new ways of life as proscribed by the evolutionary old and new parts of our CNS. But we now have learned sufficienly about our CNS functions to conceptualize a synergic way of combatting its internal schism, the alienation of the Self and the clashes in its communal imagery.

Toward Integrated Communal Imageries: Human Synergy

The definition of synergy in pharmacology is the working together of agents in such a fashion that they increase and potentiate each other's actions. Our CNS itself can be viewed as a synergistic organization, as Fair describes: ". . . the innate components of various actions serving the 'purposes' of instinct may exist in the CNS of higher forms, ourselves included, like the parts of various mechanisms each of which can be assembled and combined synergistically with others in a number of ways" [19, p. v]. In terms of communal imagery, synergy can be defined as a cooperation between a Social and a Prosthetic Brain, that which causes rational ideas to become emotionally significant and allows reasonable tolerance for emotional needs.

The cooperation between Prosthetic and Social Brain images rests in part on the communication between their representations in the cortical and subcortical systems of the individual CNS. For this, man needs a developed memory and increasing consciousness. These create new image structures intrinsic to new action. However, the recall of imagery and the function of memory is primarily controlled by the subcortical system, as Fair states: ". . . (the) subcortical system may determine from early on in life, *what* shall be committed to lasting recall . . ." [19, p. 28] and "Thing memories . . . (in the neocortex, are the) . . . permanent storage systems: . . . subcortical conditions necessary to their formation or their subsequent retrieval constitute the 'bottleneck' in putting information into, and taking it out of, that system" [19, p. 43]. It is not the prerogative of the cortex to determine the content of memory: here objectivity is subordinate to subjectivity.

Therefore, in gauging potential for synergistic action, we must rate a degree of harmony between cortical and subcortical systems higher than the mere extent of cortical functioning. We can prevent clashes and overcome conflicts between emotion and reason, the images of the Social and the Prosthetic Brain, by a consistently deliberate consideration of all existing imagery. This consideration can be called empathy, as defined by MacLean: "It is the ability . . . for obtaining insight required for foresight in promoting the welfare of others" [27, p. 374], an *intellectual* identification with the needs, feelings, and thoughts of others.§ Motivated by empathy, man must learn to preview all his actions in terms of communal imagery, especially in terms of the consequences for Social Brains of new, to-be-introduced prosthetic imagery. Only when social pollution is avoided by special measures that change or bypass old images rather than confront them, after empathic understanding has located possible sources of conflict and transformed or otherwise manipulated them before action is taken, will continued evolution of communal imagery be possible.

If a harmonious exchange and integration of rational and emotional imagery occurs through empathic understanding, if these are in tune, so to speak, their consequences will potentiate each other. And if that occurs in a community where a similar degree of harmony in communal imagery persists, the environmental outcomes will be synergistic and operate smoothly. However, if participating individuals have not achieved a congruence of their emotional needs and rational purposes, their images will be internally inconsistent and lead to erratic, individual behavior. And if the community shows low synergy and does not favor cooperative attitudes, environmental outcomes may be societal dysfunctions at the level of the prosthetic brain and emotional distress at the level of the social brain. The degree of harmony between emotion and reason, the cortical and subcortical systems, depends on the exchange of images between I and self, myself and others, familiar and stranger, and so forth. Recently attention has been focused on systematic ways of achieving this exchange, e.g., experiencing psychic phenomena and altered states of consciousness [42], lateral vs. vertical thinking [10], partaking in separate realities [5], and knowledge of feedforward as well as feedback mechanisms. That science until recently did not allow such

§ Empathy defined as a Prosthetic Brain Function is distinct from the Social Brain function of sympathy, which is more unconscious or instinctual according to Darwin: ". . . the basis of sympathy lies in our strong retentiveness of former states of pain or pleasure . . . with all animals, sympathy is directed solely towards the members of the same community, and therefore towards known, and more or less beloved members, but not all the individuals of the same species" [9, p. 478].

ways of imagining is perhaps due to the fact that we have been unaware of the bias inherent in our brain structure [28]. Discovery of this bias would be analogous to the discovery that our conscious actions often have unconscious determinants. Empathy is seen as the regulator of what will be taken into account by the cortex of the individual or the prosthetic brain of the community. If there is enough empathy, individual emotional needs will be part of rational planning and foresight; synergism will result. If there is little empathy, prosthetic reasoning will pay little heed to social brain requirements and social pollution ensues. Given this perspective, education in empathy, and in general recognition of, and respect for, emotional life, becomes mandatory [17, 27].

How does one conceptualize synergy other than as a cooperation between brain systems? It may be seen as the essence of life itself, as does D. Benson when he ascribes to the universe a synergetic (regenerative, implosive, constructive, organizing) phase operating in equilibrium with an entropic (i.e., degenerative, explosive, disorganizing) phase [2]. Synergy obviously will show as many characteristics as we care to develop. I give here only a handful.

First, there is the aspect of *wholeness*. Synergy involves all components of a situation and brings about a positive interaction even between ostensibly diametrically opposed aspects, making these cooperate in an unexpected manner. This is the rationale behind the Spaceship Earth concept, and its proponent, Buckminster Fuller, defines synergy as ". . . the only word in our language that means behavior of whole systems unpredicted by the separately observed behaviors of any of the system's separate parts or any subsystem of the system's parts". [21, p. 70] Fuller also proposes synergetics as a way of solving "problems by starting with known behaviors of whole systems plus the known behaviors of some of the system's parts, which advantageous information makes possible the discovery of other parts of the system and their respective behaviors" [21, p. 87]. This is quite similar to my proposal of analyzing the emotional and rational components of action images so as to make self-transcending individual participation in a communal endeavor possible. To understand in our present situation that whatever is done on earth influences everything else, requires a conscious effort at enlarging one's store of images in order to experience the unknown other, be he far removed or as yet unborn.

A forerunner of this systematic view of the universe, R. M. Bucke, proposed at the end of the last century that cosmic consciousness, constructive units of the mind, is supplemented and perfected by awareness of man's participation in the cosmos [3].* Our intuitions, special unconscious ways of perceiving and evaluating our environment, probably derive from primordial feelings of being part of a Unity, our earliest, shared sensory image [17, p. 39]. Using unconscious intuition and conscious empathy, synergy may therefore connect our earliest experiences to our most specialized activities needed in safeguarding our global environment. Smith finds accordingly that high synergy organizations are characterized by a combination of intuition and pragmatic knowledge [39, p. 48].

Second, the systems approach to life brings into focus the concept that *man is directing his own evolution*. We are becoming aware that man is not only adapting to, but is also creating, his environment. Here lies the recognition of the need for self-actualization and transcendence, the highest in Maslow's need hierarchy [30]. We begin to consider that it is in man's power to give purpose to existence or to end it. We realize that we do not fully know what forces govern this inherent human power of self-actualization, but we *do* know that many of our brain prostheses have become potential stumbling blocks in this matter. The peoples of the earth have to make decisions regarding their future that will reflect their willingness to make synergy a cultural goal. To quote Ruth Benedict: "I shall speak of cultures with low synergy where the social structure provides for acts which are mutually opposed and counteractive, and of cultures with high synergy where it provides for acts which are mutually reinforcing. . . . I spoke of societies with high social synergy where their institutions insure mutual advantage from their undertakings, and societies with low social synergy where the advantage of one individual becomes a victory over another, and the majority who are not victorious must shift as they can" [29, p. 156]. Maslow, providing these quotes, adds, "I have found the concept of synergy useful for the understanding of *intrapersonal dynamics* . . . head and heart, rational and nonrational speak the same language" [29, p. 163] [italics mine].

This leads us to a third characteristic of synergy: full utilization of reason *and* emotion. We must take into account that *man is not only*

* For a modern version of a cosmic philosophy integrating human knowledge, see O. L. Reiser [35].

the most rational but also the most emotional animal. As Hebb and Thompson put it: "Evidence from species comparison suggests that emotional susceptibility increases with intellectual capacity" [23, p. 761]. To be more rational is to be more sensitive, and something must be said about the discomfort and even pain that unavoidably accompany synergy.

The ecological world view demands that we not only tolerate but also promote each other to survive as Spaceship Earth. This requires not only willingness to communicate but also understanding of what is communicated. It is likely that 65 percent of communication occurs out-of-awareness, and we are just beginning to understand that much unconscious behavior is a consequence of so-called basic assumptions. These are complexes of images derived from our personal history, primary group experiences, language and culture, and so forth. This means that basic assumptions in most instances are too restricted to be accessible to all of mankind. In the "melting pot" USA we are witness to the trend toward ethnicity. As a rational individual, one should like to cooperate with anyone, but as an emotional being one cannot tolerate being misunderstood. And the more one becomes accessible to people, the more one must take emotional risks. For example, it may be that circumstances cannot prevent one-sided hurt in a dyadic interaction. One could accept this as part of the emotional functioning of one's Social Brain. Where *emotions* had been shared, apologies might be accepted and one could at least rely on the understanding of group members *familiar* with the dyad. But if one becomes hurt in a dyadic interaction within a Prosthetic Brain, there are no connecting emotional ties to the *stranger*. Others will not be as effective in cushioning the pain because of their unfamiliarity with the dyad's experiential background.

Only empathy can bring about the ability to be fully conscious of the imagery of an outsider, a stranger to the group or the culture. And empathy, through awareness of pain, confusion, and narrow-mindedness, leads to discomfort. Moreover, having to anticipate the consequence of one's feelings, thoughts, and actions requires that one not only become aware of the basic assumptions influencing one's behavior but also of the unconscious of the other. This is a tall order even for a professional. The psychiatrist will admit to difficulties in treating patients from another social class or culture.

What this adds up to is that increasing self-awareness may lead to awareness of the other and the Golden Rule: "Do unto others what you would like done unto you." When I (the cortical system) am aware of self (the subcortical system), I may attribute to others characteristics of myself, my emotions, attitudes, ideas, and so forth. If such attribution is done unconsciously it may be harmful, as in the causation of delusions brought about by the mechanism of projection. But the mature individual may bring about increased awareness in a conscious manner. The process of individuation is unavoidably painful. Escapes from this process into selfish individualism or mindless other-directedness are manifold. They bring about the closed mind that does not want to know itself.†

Fourth, synergy presupposes acceptance of *more than one thinking process*. As Dubos states: ". . . logic and clear thinking do not account entirely for the creative manifestations of human life." And he quotes Plato: "In reality the greatest of blessings come to us through madness . . . which comes from God (and) is superior to sanity, which is of human origin" [12, p. 4]. Today we realize that most of madness is the outcome of conflicts and clashes between emotional and rational imagery. Synergic acceptance of emotion as a complement to reason paves the way to utilizing equally nonrational and rational means of relating. Ecology, with its multicausal perspective and its knowledge of secondary and tertiary effects of any action, contributes to the acknowledgment of nonlinear ways of reasoning, as does the counterculture that discovers that pure science and technology run counter to nonintellective needs of social contact [36]. The increasing respectability of subjective knowledge, the expression of reality in metaphor, myth, and mystical terminology, the psychedelic experience, and so on, are leading to a reappraisal of our *weltbild*. Recent discoveries of unexpected properties of the mind (e.g., findings in split-brain experiments, the control of mind over matter in yoga [4], biofeedback and acupuncture) have increased our respect for

† In Jung's words: "Individuation means becoming a single, homogeneous being . . . or self-realization," while "Individualism means deliberately stressing and giving prominence to some supposed peculiarity, rather than to collective considerations and obligations" [25, pp. 182–183]. It may be of interest to note that privacy and individualism are unknown in tribal society. When Colin Turnbull in his study of the Ik tribe found that extreme individualism had become their means of survival, it took him a long time to accept the veracity of this unique development. The change in this tribe, brought about by ecological imbalance, illustrates a possible extreme future for contemporary society [45].

the different types of cognition, memory, and action displayed by different parts of our brain [33].

Finally, participants in synergistic activities are not only willing to reason each other's thoughts, or to feel each other's emotions, but also to *act each other's roles*. This is the consequence of the discussed characteristics of synergy: Any man who experiences himself as part of the universe consciously tries to experience the other's point of view. He respects emotional needs as well as rational requirements, applies equally intellectual and nonintellective logic, and is ready to play any role required by the situation, including that of becoming obsolete. Conversely, in the teaching of role playing lies one of our strongest preparations for the synergistic attitude.

It may seem impossible to reorient societies' functioning to benefit the whole and to be motivated by empathy promoting the other. But there have been examples of synergistic efforts that looked impossible when conceived. NASA, the agency created to avoid competition between the three branches of our armed forces, did what was considered incredible at the time: putting a man on the moon. There is no doubt that if the army, navy and air force had been allowed to approach outer space purely as a military problem, success would have been prevented by linear and uni-directional thinking, petty competition, and so forth. Witness the billions of dollars cost overruns presented to us by the Pentagon for the development of weaponry exclusively sought by each of the armed forces without cooperation with the others. There is another lesson in the synergistic example of NASA: Once the goal is reached, interest in participation starts to wane. Obsolescence will set in unless the purpose of synergism is redefined for that particular organization. Continuous reformulation and retooling in view of shifting social and prosthetic needs is a task commanding intuitive reappraisal. The best synergistic fit between individual components of communal imagery requires that participants prepare for their own obsolescence. This degree of responsibility for oneself may appear as the utmost of self-actualization and transcendency as proposed by Maslow in theory Z [30].

We see again that synergistic participation is difficult and painful; it asks for what many consider impossible: universal perspective, empathy, acceptance of one's obsolescence. We certainly are ready to accept that something vital and essential is lacking in our present societal evolution, and that our thinking should be prepared for more inclusive perspectives.

M. Polanyi argues for the scientific acceptance of what he terms "tacit knowledge," derived from empathy: ". . . the process of formalizing all knowledge to the exclusion of any tacit knowledge is self-defeating" [34, p. 20]. Von Bertalanffy urges adaptation of a perspectivistic viewpoint, joining the conceptual and technological world view of science with the perspective of the artist and the mystic [46]. We have to know the essence and the potential of other minds, a process described as "being cognition," which is detached from personal goals and anxieties. As Maslow argues, only "being cognition" can go beyond our preponderant "deficiency cognition" (i.e., coping with reality, adaptation to the environment) and lead to self-realization and creativity.

Already there are forces at work in Western society that would create room for such conditions. Shils says ". . . contemporary Western societies . . . are probably more decently integrated than any societies that have preceded them in world history. . . . They are more integrated in the sense that there is more mutual awareness, more perception of others, more imaginative empathy about the states of mind and motivations of others. . . ." Further, "the more exact techniques of sociological research . . . produce results that are indeterminate without the support of empathically acquired knowledge . . ." and "if, as is not inconceivable, human relationships become freer and the interior of one individuality becomes more accessible to another individuality, then there will be a proportional increment to concrete sociological inquiry and to sociological theory" [37, pp. 1429–1432]. Gouldner proposes to reject property and power (equivalent to territory and dominance in terms of our CNS subcortical images) as given in conceptualizing society and explore the possibilities of a "reflective sociology," characterized by ". . . its refusal to segregate the intimate and personal from the public and collective" [22, p. 504].

Once we accept synergy, we will need to implement it by devising new processes of communication and new structures of organization. Theobald has made specific proposals to examine new ways of income distributions, aid to scarcity regions, and population control [44]. In addition, we also have to establish a field of research on interconnections between images, the building blocks of minds, as a corrolary to molecular biology research of interlocking amino acids, the templates of living matter [6]. Only as part of this research process can we learn to determine which cultural templates should guide our further evolution.

Epilogue

We may speculate about how man reacted rationally to the different levels of his existence once he became aware of his triune brain imagery. Man could conceivably have been overwhelmed with his new insight into himself. One of his escape routes may have been the adaptation of what Masserman called Ur-delusions: the ideas of immortality, of the friendliness of fellowman, and of having an omnipotent servant [31]. These basic psychological defense mechanisms enable further ego development, individuation, and human behavior. At the time of the dawn of man they must have been consciously formulated as working hypotheses; today they have been transformed into the basic assumptions of each developing infant. These basic assumptions could have been the original way of coping with the communal imagery at the Biological, Social, and Prosthetic Brain level.

The assumption of immortality is used to affirm communal vital imagery. Very few mammals show a reaction to death, and only man can systematically alter his behavior in conscious anticipation. The knowledge of death can inhibit further activities, as is the case in the psychologically caused death of ostracized members of certain primitive tribes. To enable collective long-term planning, man in his day-to-day activities assumes he will not die: the Ur-delusion of immortality.

The assumption of universal friendliness is used to deny the restrictions of social imagery and to enable intergroup contact. Animals do not fraternize as a matter of course with their conspecifics. The history of man shows that, like mammals, we pledge so much allegiance to our Social Brains (or the symbols of their feelings, such as a flag), that outsiders at times are treated as nonhumans, i.e., barbarians. To proceed quickly with reasoned contracts and agreements we must be able to trust, and the generalization of this logical need is that every man is my brother: the Ur-delusion that I can befriend all strangers.

The assumption of our having at our disposal an omnipotent servant (giant, God or *deus ex machina*) to do our bidding is based on our hope that the development of prosthetic imagery in itself can solve all problems. We always have known better. The Bible story of language confusion preventing the completion of the Tower of Babel showed the inadequacy and the myth of the Sorcerer's Apprentice the run-away effects of any one Prosthetic Brain. Yet, without a naive belief in the possibility of always bettering oneself, man would lose his creative capacity: the Ur-delusion of the omnipotent servant provides for the cumulative growth of prosthetic communal imagery.

We now know that Ur-delusions, basic assumptions, and other psychological defense mechanisms are the unconscious part of our functioning. We will have to come full circle with (in) ourselves in re-evaluating the basic ways of transforming the potential of our three CNS subsystems. In the practice of synergy we begin to accomplish the conscious transcendence of our fears of being mortal and thus potentially obsolete, of having enemies and thus being vulnerable, and of lacking omnipotence and thus possibly doing wrong.

References

1. Ardrey, R. *The Social Contract.* Atheneum: New York, 1970.
2. Benson, D. "Synergistics: The Study and Practice of Synergy." *Man-Environment Systems*, Vol. 2, 1972.
3. Bucke, R. M. *Cosmic Consciousness.* E. P. Dutton: New York, 1959.
4. Calder, N. *The Mind of Man.* Viking Press: New York, 1971.
5. Castaneda, C. *A Separate Reality.* Simon & Schuster: New York, 1971.
6. Calhoun, J. B. "Promotion of Man," in E. O. Attinger, ed. *Global Systems Dynamics.* S. Karger: Basel/New York, 1970.
7. ———. "Space and the Strategy of Life," in A. H. Esser, ed. *Behavior and Environment.* Plenum Press: New York, 1971.
8. Cooley, C. H. "Primary Groups," in T. Parsons, E. Shils, K. D. Naegole, and J. R. Pitts, (eds.) *Theories of Society.* Glencoe, Inc.: New York, 1961.
9. Darwin, C. *The Origin of Species and The Descent of Man.* Modern Library: New York, no date.
10. De Bono, E. *New-Think.* Avon Books: New York, 1971.
11. De Long, A. J. "The Communication Process: A Generic Model for Man-Environment Relations." *Man-Environment Systems*, Vol. 2, 1972.
12. Dubos, R. *A God Within.* Charles Scribner's Sons: New York, 1972.
13. Eibl-Eibesfeldt, I. *Ethology.* Holt, Rinehart, Winston: New York, 1970.
14. Eisenberg, J. F. "Social Organization and Emotional Behavior," in E. Tobach, ed. *Experimental Approaches to the Study of Emotional Behavior.* Annals of the N.Y. Academy of Sciences: Vol. 159, 1969.
15. Esser, A. H. "From Territorial Image to Cultural Environment." *Geloof en Wetenschap*, Vol. 68, Amsterdam, The Netherlands, 1970.
16. ———. "Social Pollution." *Social Education*, Vol. 35, No. 1, 1971.
17. ———. "Evolving Neurologic Substrates of Essentic Forms." *General Systems*, Vol. 17, 1972.
18. ———. "War as Part of Social Pollution," in M. Nettleship, R. D. Givens, and A. Nettleship, eds. *War: Its Causes and Correlates.* Mouton Publishers: The Hague, Netherlands, in press.
19. Fair, C. M. *The Physical Foundation of the Psyche.* Wesleyan U. Press: Middletown, Conn., 1963.
20. ———. *The Dying Self.* Doubleday & Co.: New York, 1970.

21. Fuller, B. *Operating Manual for Spaceship Earth.* Southern Illinois Univ. Press: Carbondale, Ill., 1970.
22. Gouldner, A. W. *The Coming Crisis in Western Sociology.* Basic Books: New York, 1970.
23. Hebb, D. O. and Thompson, W. R. "The Social Significance of Animal Studies," in Lindzey, G. and Aronson, E., eds. *The Handbook of Social Psychology.* Addison-Wesley: London, 1968.
24. Isaac, G. L. "Traces of Pleistocene Hunters," in R. B. Lee and I. DeVore, eds. *Man the Hunter.* Aldine: Chicago, 1968.
25. Jung, C. G. *Two Essays on Analytical Psychology.* Meridian Books: Cleveland, 1965.
26. MacLean, P. D. "Man and His Animal Brains." *Modern Medicine,* 1965.
27. ————."The Brain in Relation to Empathy and Medical Education." *Journal of Nervous and Mental Disorders,* Vol. 144, 1967.
28. ————. "The Triune Brain, Emotion, and Scientific Bias," in F. O. Schmitt, ed. *The Neurosciences.* Rockefeller Univ. Press: New York, 1970.
29. Maslow, A. H. "Synergy in the Society and the Individual." *Journal of Individual Psychology,* Vol. 20, 1964.
30. ————. "Theory Z." *Journal of Transpersonal Psychology,* February, 1970.
31. Masserman, J. H. *Principles of Dynamic Psychiatry.* Saunders: Philadelphia, 1946.
32. May, R. E. *Populations, Species and Evolution.* Harvard Univ. Press: Cambridge, 1970.
33. Ornstein, R. E. *The Psychology of Consciousness.* W. H. Freeman: San Francisco, 1972.
34. Polanyi, M. *The Tacit Dimension.* Doubleday-Anchor: New York, 1967.
35. Reiser, O. L. *Cosmic Humanism.* Schenkman: Cambridge, Mass., 1966.
36. Roszak, T. *The Making of a Counter Culture.* Doubleday-Anchor: New York, 1968.
37. Shils, E. "The Calling of Sociology," in T. Parsons, E. Shils, K. D. Naegele, and J. R. Pitts, eds. *Theories of Society.* Free Press of Glencoe: Glencoe, N. Y., 1961.
38. Simmel, G., "Secrecy and Group Communication," in T. Parsons, E. Shils, K. D. Naegele, and J. R. Pitts, eds. *Theories of Society.* Free Press of Glencoe: Glencoe, N. Y. 1961.
39. Smith, R. A. III. "Synergistic Organizations: Humanistic Extensions of Man's Evolution." *Fields Within Fields . . . Within Fields.* The World Institute Council; New York, Vol. 3, 1970.
40. Spitz, R. "Ontogenesis: The Proleptic Function of Emotion," in P. H. Knapp, ed. *Expression of the Emotions in Man.* International University Press: New York, 1963.
41. Tajfel, H. "Experiments in Intergroup Discrimination." *Scientific American,* November, 1970.
42. Tart, C. "States of Consciousness and State-Specific Sciences." *Science,* Vol. 176, 1972.
43. Teilhard de Chardin, P. *The Phenomenon of Man.* Harper & Row: New York, 1959.
44. Theobald, R. *Habit and Habitat.* Prentice-Hall: Englewood Cliffs, New Jersey, 1972.
45. Turnbull, C. M. *The Mountain People.* Simon and Schuster: New York, 1972.
46. Von Bertalanffy, L. "The Mind-Body Problem." *Psychosomatic Medicine,* Vol. 26, 1964.
47. Washburn, S. L. and DeVore, I. "Social Behavior of Baboons and Early Man," in S. L. Washburn, ed. *Social Life of Early Man.* Aldine: Chicago, 1961.

X
Space Travel and Extraterrestrial Life

In exploring the limits of human consciousness, we have come to the possibility that more highly evolved forms of life exist in the universe with consciousness far surpassing ours. This has long been a theme for science fiction and comic books, of course, ever since the eighteenth-centurn scientist-mystic Emanuel Swedenborg wrote a book about his astral travels to other planets. But what was once regarded by science as the silliest of fringe phenomena is now coming into serious consideration by some of the world's most distinguished scientists.

The subject of extraterrestrial life is much vaster than UFOs and ufology, although that is the most dramatic focus of attention at the moment. Recently Erich von Däniken presented a thought-provoking case for the extraterrestrial origin of UFOs in Gods from Outer Space *(G. P. Putnam's, 1970), but the late Ivan Sanderson's* Uninvited Visitors *(Cowles, 1967) is more objective and penetrating, especially when he offers the possibility of an extradimensional origin for UFOs from a parallel universe. Two eminent astronomers have also considered the subject recently. J. Allen Hynek is author of* The UFO Experience *(Regnery, 1972) and Carl Sagan is editor of* UFO's: A Scientific Debate *(MIT Press, 1972) and* The Cosmic Connection *(Doubleday, 1973).*

The organizations studying extraterrestrial life and UFOs in a sensible fasion include: National Investigations Committee on Aerial Phenomena (NICAP), 1536 Connecticut Avenue, N.W., Washington, D.C. 20036; Aerial Phenomena Research Organization (APRO), 3910 East Kleindale Road, Tucson, Arizona 85716; and Society for Investigation of the Unexplained (SITU), R.D. 1, Columbia, New Jersey 07832. All publish useful journals.

Whether or not there are intelligent civilizations elsewhere in the universe, ours now faces a crisis of consciousness because of its ego-centered behavior. It is not a case of lacking knowledge to deal with war, pollution, overpopulation, wasted natural resources, and other problems that threaten to destroy mankind. Rather, it is a failure to grow spiritually, a lack of higher consciousness that would enable people to step outside their earthbound perspective, their culturally conditioned prejudice, intolerance, greed, and mistrust so that their sense of self becomes merged with all life and the processes of nature. Apollo 14 astronaut Edgar D. Mitchell offers here a view of earth from space that may help solve the crisis of consciousness.

Three organizations are especially concerned with the planetary view of mankind, and are open to public membership. The World Future Society is located at Box 30369, Bethesda Branch, Washington, D.C. 20014 and publishes The Futurist. The Committee for the Future, located at Penn's Landing Square, 130 Spruce Street, Philadelphia, Pennsylvania 19106, promulgates its news and views through New Worlds. Dr. Mitchell's organization, The Institute of Noetic Sciences, aims at helping solve planetary problems through research and education about the processes of human consciousness. It is located at 575 Middlefield Road, Palo Alto, California 94301.

J.W.

19 Global Consciousness
and the View from Space
Edgar D. Mitchell

(After his introduction Captain Mitchell made a one-minute pause.)
One minute. It seemed an eternity, but within our consciousness the
entire span of eternity can be perceived in less than a minute.

In the vastness of universal space and in the endless flow of time,
life on planet Earth is poised at a crucial juncture in its evolutionary path.
Within the universe stars are being born, moving into the mainstream of
stellar evolution, living their lifetimes, and being extinguished in a well-
ordered process that was in existence long before consciousness on this
Earth arose. This universal function has gone its harmonious route over
countless eons and will continue to do so for countless more. Planet Earth
has evolved within this evolutionary structure like countless other planets
around countless other stars in countless other galaxies.

A raindrop falls with the rain, is caught in the flow of the river, and
rushed along in the mainstream, picking up teeming millions of microscopic life forms as it moves toward its rendezvous with the sea. In the
same way, planets move through time and space. Sometimes the droplets
are caught in the backwashes and eddies, and move, if at all, backward
into stagnation. At other times they rush forward, are dashed against the
rocks of the rapids, thrown into the air, and face extinction from that
stream of universal function. The life in the raindrop has no control of
its destiny. Almost the same has been the case of planet Earth. Because
of the smallness in number of the population, because of lack of wisdom,
because of ignorance and greed, man has not had control over the planet
upon which he survived.

But here the analogy must end. Although the history of Earth has been like a droplet of water—with its inhabitants unable to control their destiny, washed on and on by their self-serving small numbers and lack of knowledge—it is no longer the case. As long as man was few in number, lacking in sophisticated technology, and unable to influence profoundly the progress of life on Earth, his greed, his wars, his ego-centered behavior were detrimental only to a handful at a time. They influenced only relatively small regions of the Earth. Such destructiveness and egoism could be viewed as the growing pains of a child and did not seriously affect the otherwise harmonious flow of life in the universe or change the course of evolution.

But mankind is now full grown on planet Earth. It has reached a stage of development and intellectual sophistication where the temper tantrums and the egoistic behavior of the learning years can no longer be tolerated. We can no longer allow the ravaging of the planet by wasting resources, befouling the environment, and destroying the life forms that inhabit the globe.

Yes, man is full grown on planet Earth. But mankind is not a mature, wise adult. Man is still an uncoordinated child. Or perhaps he is more like an uncoordinated, untrained bull elephant in a china shop causing unbelievable havoc and destruction because he has no grasp of the need or the way to bring himself into harmonious accord with the rest of the universe. Man can go on thrashing around, tearing up the place, ruining the environment, despoiling himself. If he does, with the knowledge and technology at his command, it is surely only a matter of time till an observer in the far reaches of this galaxy observes a small flash of nuclear radiation and turns away from his instruments in sadness because the beautiful blue planet Earth no longer exists.

Should that occur, the universe will go on its harmonious way of evolving new stars and new planets and new life. For the failure of the highest species on planet Earth to rise to the challenge of maturing and finding harmony with planetary functioning will cause only a slight discordant pulse in the otherwise perfect flow of universal evolution.

But it need not be that way. Man can rise to the occasion. He can save himself and his planet from the seeds of destruction already planted. Man can take stock of himself and realize that only by a new mode of thinking, new institutions, a new holistic approach to planetary functioning, a new submergence of egoistic behavior, a new altruism, a new attunement to universal consciousness and the patterns of evolution within the universe—only with these things can he change the course of history on Earth.

For more than four hundred years, since Giordano Bruno was burned at the stake for suggesting that the Earth revolved around the Sun instead of vice versa, the antagonism between science and religion has continued to wax and wane. The arguments have gone hot or cool but always there was the antagonism. Science on the one hand made its objective impersonal observations about the universe. On the other hand, theologians and religious people, with only their subjective awareness, pontificated about the nature of man and the universe. The views thus obtained have seemed to be—*seemed to be*—totally antagonistic most of the time.

Why should this be so? Man has used his five senses and extended them through new inventions to see distant galaxies and to probe the lowest orders of microscopic universes. Man has extended himself objectively to reach not only the highest in the universe, the most far-flung, the greatest, but also the tiniest, for we have looked at it with our objectivity. And we should remember that man was not led to do these things by his objective thought but by his creativity, his intuition, his inspiration—in short, by his subjective awareness.

Then where is the problem? It may be in the method of science. Science is tantamount to objective empiricism. Some say that objective empiricism is a definition of science in which man separates himself as an observer from the observed. He is impartial to its functions. He desires only to know how they function. But as human beings, we are not objective entities. In order to sense the true essence of nature, we must attune to the thing observed and become in harmony with it. A botanist can observe a flower and tell us its function in many ways. He can tell us of its protoplasmic system, its photosynthesis, its patterns of life, its response to the solar rhythms. But to truly know the flower, one must become the flower and become harmonious with the flower. There is a saying: To know a man, one must walk in his shoes. We can extend the saying: To know the universe, one must attune to the universe.

This is the way of consciousness. Unfortunately, it has not been the way of science. Why? Why has science rejected this methodology? It has done so because there are so many facets to the universe that the subjective presents too many facets. Nobody can agree. All views are different. If we are a fish and view the world from underwater, that's all we see. Then we think the universe must be all water. If we are a polar bear at the North Pole and all we see is ice, then we think the entire universe must be ice.

In the past we have viewed the world and the universe from our limited purviews as the fish, as the polar bear, however much more sophisticated we may think we are. By doing so, we see only part of the picture. We have presumed that the world is as we see it and that the citizens of the world are as we are. But we can no longer do this. We must not only see the tiniest view as through the microscope, we must rise to the broadest view as through the telescope.

But there are other ways also. We cannot all have microscopes and all have telescopes, and we all are not scientists. But we do have the finest sensory mechanism, the finest computer, finer than anything man has yet devised mechanically. We have our intellects, our minds, our selves. And with those we can go inside the atom, with those we can go to the farthest reaches of the universe. For the mind and spirit of man know no bounds. The consciousness of man has no bounds—it is only what we make it.

We can reach up and up to the stars, we can reach into the middle of the atom and perceive both their functionings. But as we have seen from the past, our subjective awarenesses are not unfailing either. We still have finite minds because they are shaped and molded by our heritages, our past, the traumas we have suffered. So our objective awarenesses are not to be trusted wholly either. But they can give us the insights against which we can apply objective empiricism, the scientific technique to check and recheck and verify what our impressions tell us.

It is the molding of the two methodologies that will produce the true view of the universe. We cannot do it with objectivity alone. We cannot do it with subjectivity alone. Not if we are to have a rational basis upon which to build our view of the world. But most important, if we are to unite mankind we must rise above our parochial views, whatever they are, however right or wrong we may think them, and at least allow the other man his views. We must rise above the present intolerance—the kind that killed Giordano Bruno—and find a level of common understanding, a common goal. And what better common goal than to save the planet and all its inhabitants from ourselves?

I would like for a moment to recount my view of the planet from space. I feel privileged to have viewed it. I was profoundly affected by it and I feel not only obligated but also desirous of sharing it with you.

I have been an engineer, a test pilot, a management specialist, a college professor, and a few other things earlier in life, and my thinking lay in that direction: the institutional approach. Bigger and better institutions. Bigger and better institutions can save mankind is a widespread way of thinking. But upon viewing planet Earth from 240,000 miles away, I had to think deeply about what I saw. And the reflections went on for weeks and months afterward. It become obvious to me that the direction in which I was proceeding, however altruistic I might have thought it was, was not sufficient for what had to be done.

When you see planet Earth as a blue and white haven, a magnificent speck in the vastness of the emply space that is not really empty, you think of what the people are doing. You remember the wars that are going on at that very moment. You remember the needless and wasteful ravagings of the Earth. Not for productivity, not to help people, although the claims are there. They are going on primarily because of our egoistic drives. And when you realize that, you know the planet cannot survive such behavior. Man must see the planet from this viewpoint and realize what his own destiny is and can be. Not the way he is going but the way he can go. It cannot be that our destiny is what we see in the world chaos today. It has to be greater, for if it is not we are wasting our time. We must change the course of human evolution. We must change the thinking of mankind to view planet Earth in its proper perspective.

This has been the evolution of my thinking over the last year. When you have the view from space, you realize that the concept of fields within fields within fields, systems of functioning within systems of functioning, is the only approach that will work. All has to function harmoniously. There is no longer room for one part to function at the expense of another. We must find the ways for all to function harmoniously. If we are to move from this chaos to harmony we must utilize the best in science, the best in technology, the best thinking from the highest states of consciousness and form the results into a harmonious melding of systems within systems within systems.

How do you do it? It starts with the individual search for the understanding of self—the drive to live without fear and to be fulfilled, to live in harmonious accord with one's neighbors and extend the accord outward to the community, the state, the nation, the planet. But it must begin with the first step—the first step of personal striving to find self, to find a better way of life, to find a higher state of consciousness and existence.

And so it goes. If it starts with one individual and another and another, the effect is synergistic. The total becomes far greater than the sum of the parts. We are seeing that search in our country now. It is time to create synergistically. It is time to focus our efforts in the highest altruistic sense we can conceive. But not be satisfied with even that. If we think we have found it, we must remember there is still a higher sense of being, a higher state of consciousness, a higher order of life-functioning.

There is no end to the process. Not in our foreseeable future, at least. We have no alternative, though. We are living in fear. And to live without fear is to understand self and the universe. Once we can do away with that fear, we have started the process. We have reached a higher state of being, a higher order of functioning. From there, I assure you, the attunement to the universal consciousness will take place and the synergistic effect will cause it to multiply and grow and grow. Man will have mastered his destiny. He will have made the choice that will prevent the fatal day when the observer far out in the galaxy observes a tiny flare of atomic radiation that was the magnificent blue and white planet Earth.

20 Exobiology—Where Science Fiction Meets Science Fact

John White

> *Is there intelligent life on earth?*
> *Yes, but I'm only visiting.*
> —*Graffiti on a subway wall*

One of our newest sciences is *exobiology*, the study of extraterrestrial life. (A human in space, such as an astronaut, is *not* an example of life away from earth and hence is not a proper subject of study for exobiologists.) The idea that we are not alone in the universe is an old one, of course. Sensational stories of little green men are familiar to everyone. But in the last decade, many scientists have taken seriously the possibility of life beyond earth, including intelligent life forms capable of technology.*

The degree of their seriousness was shown in September 1971, when the first international conference on the problem of contacting extraterrestrial civilizations was held in the Soviet Union. Sponsored jointly by the American and Russian Academies of Science, the conference at the Myurakan Astrophysical Observatory in Armenia gathered experts from the fields of astronomy, biology, physics, chemistry, computer science, linguistics, anthropology, and other disciplines. Their specific concerns: the origin of life on earth, the possibility of other planetary systems in the universe, the origin and evolution of intelligence, problems in search-

---

* John Billingham and Bernard Oliver. *Project Cyclops*. Document CR 114445, 1973. Available from Dr. John Billingham, NASA/Ames Research Center, Code LT, Moffett Field, California 94035.

ing for signals from intelligent life, and—of profoundest significance for mankind—the possible consequences of establishing contact with extraterrestrial beings.

There were differences of opinion among conference participants, of course, but the remarkable thing is this: They agreed in a public statement that contact with extraterrestrial life was likely enough to justify starting a variety of search programs. Present technology, they felt, was sufficient for the job. Moreover, the searches should be coordinated international efforts made in the name of humanity.

Following up on this conclusion was Professor Richard Berendzen of the astronomy department at Boston University, who organized the world's first symposium in November 1972 to discuss the significance of the conference's statement. The symposium was entitled "Life Beyond Earth and the Mind of Man." It drew an overflow crowd to hear opinions from men of the sciences and humanities, such as anthropologist Ashley Montagu, Nobel prize-winning biologist George Wald, Harvard theologian Krister Stendahl, Cornell astrophysicist and founder of exobiology Carl Sagan, and MIT philosopher of science Philip Morrison.§

Professor Berendzen, who teaches a course on exobiology, noted that recent findings and developments in astronomy, biology, chemistry, engineering, and physics "strongly indicate the high probability of the existence of extraterrestrial life." Proteins and their amino acids, one of the building blocks of life, have been found in meteorites. Formaldehyde, another building block (but more familiar as "embalming fluid") has been detected near the center of our galaxy. The atmosphere of Jupiter—to give a third example—has been analyzed to contain what appear to be the elementary constituents of the DNA molecule, and Jupiter probably has frequent electrical storms to provide the "spark of life." Because of these protobiological phenomena, it was Professor Berendzen's opinion that "the ultimate discovery of and communication with extraterrestrial life forms will be the most profound achievement in the history of mankind."

Does this mean that some UFOs may be extraterrestrial spaceships? Perhaps. It certainly means there is a significant probability of it. Dr.

§ Richard Berendzen, ed. *Life Beyond Earth and the Mind of Man.* NASA Document SP-328, 1973. Available from U.S. Government Printing Office, Washington, D.C. 20402.

Sagan, who heads the Laboratory for Planetary Studies at Cornell, goes even further than "perhaps." In his book *Intelligent Life in the Universe*, coauthored with Professor Josif Shklovsky, head of the department of radio astronomy at Moscow State University, Dr. Sagan suggests that the ancient Sumerians may have had contact with space people. He cites evidence from Sumerian myths, paintings, and clay seals. "Taken at face value," he writes, "the legend suggests that contact occurred between human beings and a nonhuman civilization of immense powers on the shores of the Persian Gulf, perhaps the site of the ancient city of Eridu, and in the fourth millennium B.C. or earlier.*

Further evidence for this extraterrestrial contact and others is given in a remarkable essay by Kenneth Demarest entitled "The Winged Power" and published in *Consciousness and Reality*. Demarest gathers archeological records from many cultures to demonstrate that "men enjoyed contact and instruction from those in a more advanced and benevolent evolutionary stage," the instruction being an astounding secret that was transmitted through history by certain occult traditions and mystery teachings. The secret: Man does not have to die because there is an alternative to the death process. Man can build "the solar body of light," which is freed from mortality and the need for food.

One of the first contacts in Sumero-Babylonia, Demarest reports, was described by later historians as "great birds or flying eggs of luminous or fiery appearance dropping into the sea. These 'eggs' then rose to the foaming surface, opened or 'hatched,' and out of them emerged human figures dressed in strange fishlike suits whereby they could swim underwater to their capsules."†

The statements by Sagan and Demarest are not as startling to professionals as they may seem to laymen. Recently two planets were discovered by radiotelescope to be rotating around Barnard's Star, about 34 trillion miles away—making them the second solar system known to astronomers, ours being the first. Beyond this hard evidence, calculations made by a number of scientists have led them to conclude there probably have been—and there probably are at present—an enormous num-

* Carl Sagan. *Intelligent Life in the Universe*, p. 357. Delta Books: New York, 1966.
† Kenneth Demarest. "The Winged Power," in *Consciousness and Reality*, pp. 343–44, Charles Musès and Arthur Young, eds. Outerbridge & Lazard: New York, 1972.

ber of life-bearing planets, many of which may have evolved an intelligent form of life capable of technology. Dr. Frank Drake, another eminent exobiologist and director of the Center for Radiophysics and Space Research at Cornell, gives the figure of one in 10,000,000 stars possessing a detectable civilization. That would mean from 100,000 to 1,000,000 just in our galaxy, the Milky Way, with an average distance between them of about 1,000 light years.

These calculations support the intuitive judgments of some earlier scientists. According to ufologist Erich von Däniken in *Gods From Outer Space*, Albert Einstein was "in complete sympathy with the idea of a prehistoric visit by extraterrestrial intelligences," and Hermann Oberth, the father of the rocket, considered a visit to our planet by an extraterrestrial race to be "extremely probable."‡

Von Däniken also points out the nearly universal theme in ancient myths of human life originating through the action of "gods" from the sky who chose a group, set it apart from the "unclean," transformed and educated it, and then disappeared. In *2001: A Space Odyssey*, Stanley Kubrick creates a modern myth on the same theme. The movie depicts humans as developed from apemen by the intervention of beings from space who cultivate intelligence throughout the universe.

That remote event in prehistory probably would not be as theologically disturbing as the more recent possibilities that some ufologists suggest. In their view, Moses on the mountain was communicating with an extraterrestrial. The "pillar of cloud by day and the pillar of fire by night" was a UFO, and the ark of the covenant, as described in Exodus 25:10, was a communication instrument. The gold construction would make it an excellent capacitor and the exact measurements were necessary for acoustical properties, they say [although Clifford Wilson convincingly rebuts this notion in *Crash Go the Chariots*]. A further piece of evidence is the word "elohim," which is translated in the Bible as "God" but which scholars now recognize as meaning "gods." An even more heretical suggestion: The Star of Bethlehem was a UFO!

Assuming that it will be up to us to initiate contact, how do scientists plan to detect extraterrestrial life?

In his course on exobiology at Boston University, Professor Berendzen

‡ Erich von Däniken. *Gods From Outer Space*, pp. 14–15. G. P. Putnam's: New York, 1970.

includes the possibility of communicating with extraterrestrials through psychic channels. And in the Soviet Union, parapsychologist Edward Naumov proposed at the Second Symposium on Cosmic Radio Communication in Moscow in late 1971 that ESP might be the most likely means of communication, since telepathy appears to be instantaneous regardless of distance—the most crucial point since the distances between stars are so incredibly vast. Even language barriers might be overcome by ESP since visual images seem to take precedence over words in telepathic communication.

Another psychic possibility might be so-called "astral projection" or out-of-the-body experience. There is now evidence from psychic researchers such as Dr. Charles Tart at University of California's Davis campus and Dr. Karlis Osis of the American Society for Psychical Research in New York that some individuals are able to project their consciousness to distant places at will. As Apollo 14 astronaut Edgar Mitchell once said, "If the phenomenon of astral projection has any validity whatsoever, it might be a perfectly valid form of intergalactic travel, and a lot safer probably than space flight."

Radio search of the sky appears to be the best conventional means, except for nearby planets where rocket probes such as the Mariner series have proven successful.§ Radio search would be carried out using the 3 to 10 cm wavelength. The Soviet conference on extraterrestrial contact suggested that range as the most probable one in which extraterrestrial civilizations might attempt to communicate with other civilizations. Previous attempts to monitor space using the 21 cm "window" have proven fruitless, partly because of interstellar radio noises. And lately, earth-based radio noise is adding to the problem—electrical pollution!

Another rocket probe is the Pioneer 10 spacecraft, launched by the United States early in 1972 and aimed toward Jupiter—the farthest space

§ Mariner 9 found that Mars was periodically swept by dust storms with winds estimated up to two hundred mph, making landings possible only on a seasonal basis. It also found the atmosphere to be mostly carbon dioxide with almost no water vapor. Surface temperature varied from slightly above freezing to more than $-100°$ F. Admirers of Ray Bradbury's science fiction classic *The Martian Chronicles* will be disappointed, but these findings are just more data for the NASA scientists planning Project Viking, an unmanned instrumental landing in 1976.

shot by any nation so far.* Pioneer 10 was programmed to swing by Jupiter, not land. That happened in late 1973. After that, its trajectory headed it outside the solar system. It will be the first terrestrial vehicle to leave for interstellar space.

With that in mind, its designers placed aboard it a 6" x 9" pictorial plaque to show intelligent inhabitants of some other star system (who might intercept it) when it was launched, from where, and by whom. Etched into the gold-anodized aluminum plate are a male and female human figure, plus the planets of our solar system. A code based on the position of 14 pulsars (pulsating neutron stars radiating enormous amounts of energy) locates the sun. Another code based on the wavelength of hydrogen gives the height of the figures. The man's hand is raised in a gesture of good will.

The possibility exists, some scientists point out, that extraterrestrials might not want to communicate with us. (They may be to us as we are to ants. Do we try to talk to ants?) If so, we could only hope to detect the form of communication they use among themselves. Direct observation through telescopes or finding some evidence of their astroengineering ability is thought to be unlikely (although ufologists have strong disagreement with this position). In that case, the search would probably require many years in order to have a high degree of success. The vastness of space and the wider range of the electromagnetic spectrum to be watched would rule out any quick scanning, and would cost millions.

The first attempt at detection, called Project Ozma, was made in 1961. Under the direction of Dr. Frank Drake, the National Radio Astronomy Observatory in Green Bank, West Virginia, spent several months observing two nearby stars, Tau Ceti and Epsilon Eridani. No evidence of extraterrestrial signals was found, but the project proved worthwhile as a pioneering effort. More recently, pulsars were thought to be a source of intelligent signals from space. This proved otherwise, however, and provided a good lesson for exobiologists: The technology of other civilizations may surpass ours so much that we just don't know what to look for. We may be in a position similar to Indians looking for smoke signals when radios are being used.

* NASA launched a Mariner-class spacecraft in October 1973 on a trajectory that will carry it by Venus and then Mercury—the first two-planet flyby.

Nevertheless, the attempts at detection will go on. In late 1971 Dr. Drake announced that the 1,000-foot radiotelescope at Arecibo, Puerto Rico (which he directs under Cornell University auspices) will have its sensitivity increased two thousand times. The modification will take several years. When it is complete, he said, "We expect to devote one per cent of our time to just listening. If any civilization is advanced enough to communicate with other civilizations in the universe, we might get the message."

This belief is held even more strongly by some Soviet scientists. Professor Vesvolod Troitsky, director of the Gorsky Observatory, told some American reporters in 1972, "We firmly believe other civilizations are probing us with signals. Our first confirmed contact could still be 100 years away or come as early as a year from now." (The message, however, would be as many years old as it took to travel to us.)

In 1973 a huge new radio observatory will open at Mt. Semirodniki in the northern Caucasus Mountains, Professor Troitsky noted. This observatory will have an optical telescope bigger than Mt. Palomar's 200-incher and a radiotelescope almost 2,000 feet in diameter. Working in conjunction, these instruments will increase by a factor of ten the Russians' potential for locating signals.

Professor Shklovsky also feels contact could come soon. "It could come at any moment," he told the same reporters, but added that it would be impossible to guess the form and size such an intelligence would take.

Contact may already have come—in the form of an instrumented probe circling the earth in the same orbit as the moon. A Scottish astronomer, Duncan Lunan, announced in late 1972 through the British Interplanetary Society that he had decoded a mysterious set of radio echoes from outer space. These echoes, Lunan concluded, spell out a message to mankind in the form of a star map of the constellation Bootes. "All the reference lines point to a star called Epsilon Boötis in that constellation—103 light years from earth," Lunan said. "That is the area from which the probe would have originated."

According to Lunan, the echoes from space were first picked up in the 1920s by Norwegian, Dutch, and French radio researchers. They found that after sending out a series of pulses, they received two sets of echoes. The normal echoes, bounced back from the earth's ionosphere, returned in the usual one-seventh of a second. But a second set came back after various periods of delay from three to fifteen seconds long. Lunan deduced the signals were coming from an object well beyond the ionosphere and was circling the earth at the distance of the moon. It then occurred to him that the unexplained variation in delay times might be some kind of signal—that the object was sending as well as reflecting. So he plotted the delays as dots in various positions on graph paper, and was astonished to see Bootes emerge.† Now the BIS is conducting a search to see if Lunan's hypothesis is fact or fanciful interpretation.

In 1600, when nearly everyone believed that man was the center of the universe, Giordano Bruno was burned at the stake for heresy—suggesting that the earth was only another planet in a solar system among other solar systems and that "living beings inhabit those worlds." It's a long way from there to 2001. The movie, scripted by Arthur Clarke, was science fiction, of course. But the breathless pace at which change and discovery take place nowadays often turns science fiction into science fact, leaving people in a state of future shock. The amazing similarity between Lunan's space probe (if confirmed) and Kubrick's buried lunar monolith is a good example. *Childhood's End*, Clarke's powerful 1953 novel about mankind's further evolution, tells of the world under control of "Overlords" from space. Unlikely? Again, perhaps. Yet the latest scientific evidence indicates, in Dr. Drake's words, that "life will arise wherever conditions are not even salubrious, but only better than extremely hostile." If life is likely to appear and if there are portions of the universe much older than ours (which is now confirmed), then how much farther evolved in consciousness would such life be? Clarke's conception of the Overlords may not be imaginative enough. (In fairness to Clarke, however, it must be said that his novel presents the idea of a still-higher form of intelligence, the Overmind.)

In 1970 Clarke restated the theme of *Childhood's End* in a nonfiction explanation of the ending to Stanley Kubrick's cinematic saga. *The Lost Worlds of 2001* ends with this simple statement of Clarke's belief:‡

. . . we know that the electronic birthcries of our culture have already reached at least a hundred suns, all the way out to giant Vega.

† "Space Probe from Epsilon Boötis." Duncan Lunan. *Spaceflight*, Vol. 15, No. 4, April 1973.
‡ Arthur Clarke. *The Lost Worlds of 2001*, p. 240. Signet: New York, 1970.

By the year 2001, there will have been ample time for many replies, from many directions.

And there will have been time for more than that. Despite assertions to the contrary, from scientists who should have learned better by now, an advanced technology should be able to build ships capable of reaching at least a quarter of the speed of light. By the turn of the millennium, therefore, emissaries could be arriving from Alpha Centauri, Sirius, Procyon...

And so I repeat the words I wrote in 1948:
I do not think we will have to wait for long.

Some scientists have said that mankind should not even try to contact extraterrestrials for fear the world may become enslaved. But many others feel the attempt should be made and that any life intelligent enough to communicate with us would be unlikely to exhibit hostility. In any case, Dr. Sagan points out, it is too late. The signals have already been sent. What Clarke calls our electronic birth cries have been radiating from the planet since broadcasting was invented. "Forty light years out from Earth," Sagan wrote in 1966, "the news of a new technical civilization is winging its way among the stars. If there are beings out there, scanning the skies for tidings of a new technical civilization, they will know of it, whether for good or for ill."§

Should that prove so, their decision to contact us may well depend on whether—by their standards—they think intelligent life exists on earth. Judging by some recent events in the news, they may be justified in ranking humanity as a lower form of life not worth contacting.

On the other hand, they may recognize that man is still in his infancy when measured against astronomical events. Consider, for example, the Traveller in Piers Anthony's 1969 sci-fi mind-rocker *Macroscope*. In Anthony's imaginative projection, world upon world has evolved far beyond the noospheric stage of consciousness suggested by Teilhard de Chardin, and are linked like giant neurons in a galactic mind. From the perspective of such a possibility, extraterrestrial intelligence may simply be waiting for *Homo Sapiens* to come to the end of his cosmic childhood and—if the species doesn't become extinct from its own immature behavior—reach out in maturity to join galactic society.

And beyond that? Perhaps galactic minds themselves might function

§ *Op cit.*, Sagan, p. 453.

analogous to neurons in a still-higher stage of the development of consciousness. This is just the case in *Star Maker* by the deceased British philosopher Olaf Stapledon. His 1937 science fiction classic, to put it bluntly, says it all. *Star Maker*: from exobiology to theobiology—the final revelation that intelligent consciousness is *everywhere* in the universe, the formative and sustaining substratum of all creation, better known as God.

XI

Death as an Altered State of Consciousness

Tietze's and Noyes' articles are appropriate for ending this book because death is commonly thought of as the end of life, the Great Unknown.

Yet throughout recorded history there have been reports to the contrary—reports that say we survive death, and we survive it with a capacity for memory, personality, and recognition. The Neanderthal people 50,000 years ago placed offerings in the graves of their dead, indicating, anthropologists say, a belief in an afterlife. The Egyptian and the Tibetan Book of the Dead are ancient documents on this theme. In recent times, there have been well-attested cases of people who underwent biological death yet somehow were revived by medical personnel. In many cases, the "dead" told of having a wondrous experience, of a journey out of their bodies with only a thin silver cord of energy connecting their disembodied consciousness with the "corpse."

Russell Noyes, a medical doctor, examines some of these cases in "Dying and Mystical Consciousness." An earlier examination is the now-classic Deathbed Observations by Physicians and Nurses by Karlis Osis, director of research at the American Society for Psychical Research. Like the Noyes report, it shows that the dying frequently have a marked degree of exaltation unrelated to medications or the nature of their illness. Visions of previously deceased relatives and friends are common among the dying, too. But these visions cannot be dismissed as hallucinations in all cases because, surprisingly, the dying person and those present had no knowledge that the figures in the vision were already dead. Only afterward did they learn of it. Do the "dead" come to help the dying make the transition?

An extended survey of the nature of death is given in The Life Beyond Death *as told to Jerome Ellison by the recently deceased Arthur Ford* (G. P. Putnam, 1971). The Reverend Dr. Ford was a renowned medium. For more than forty years he dealt with the spirit world. He once had a near-death himself, and reported it in his book. "Dying? . . . I almost did it once before and found it one of the great, memorable, ecstatic experiences of my life."

Evidence from many sources—psychic research, quantum physics, paraphysics, transpersonal psychology, thanatology—is converging to lend scientific credence to the ancient concept of soul. For if mind can operate independently of body, then there is a distinct possibility it can exist independently of body. That being the case, the next question is: What is soul? Here the evidence indicates some validity to the occult notion of different energy-bodies within the physical body. Several studies that carefully weighed dying persons found an inexplicable loss of about three-fourths of an ounce at the moment of expiration. This in turn raises the possibility that an energy-body—usually called the "astral" or "etheric" body—may be what the concept of soul is based on.

From that point of view, death would be just an alteration in our state of consciousness. From that point of view, also, the quality of our continued existence in the afterlife would depend on the quality of our living here—the degree to which we had evolved our consciousness, the degree to which we had grown in spiritual awareness. Death, then, may be simply the beginning of new life in the continuum of consciousness stretching from the inorganic world to the cosmic intelligence which created it, God.

J.W.

21 Some

Perspectives on Survival

Thomas R. Tietze

Do we live after we die? Does any part of our personality, our self, remain when the body ceases to function? Is the mind merely a function of the brain, a function that stops when the organ stops? Or is man something more than he seems?

These questions—with all the profound implications of their answers, whatever they may be—lie at the root of philosophy and religion. It has been the important task of psychical research to bring these problems under the cold light of reason and science, to see what might be there, "without prejudice or prepossession."

Evidence tending to support the survival hypothesis has been sought in many directions. One direction, perhaps most basic, is the investigation of the existence of any human ability that at first glance might seem beyond ordinary human capabilities: the paranormal. By now the evidence for the reality of some of these unusual activities, called extrasensory perception (ESP), has become strong enough to say that man's "survival potential" is greater than science had formerly suspected. For a being capable of telepathy, of clairvoyance, or of precognition, very little might be considered surprising. But these phenomena only suggest that the brain (or mind) has some powers that transcend current theories about human personality. There is no reason to suppose that those powers continue to work after the brain has died.

But other areas of investigation separately suggest an independence of some kind of the personality from the body. When these areas are put together, as fragments of a larger terrain, the result is a striking land-

scape of human experience—experiences that, many investigators have
felt, point forcibly to the conclusion that some part of the personality
survives death.

One such area of paranormal experiences to consider is the so-called
"out-of-the-body-experience" (OOBE). There is the case of Sir Alexander
Ogston, who was hospitalized in South Africa with typhoid fever some
years ago.

"In my delirium," Ogston writes, "night and day made little difference to me. In the four-bedded ward where they first placed me, I lay, as
it seemed, in a constant stupor, which excluded the existence of any hopes
or fears. Mind and body seemed to be dual, and to some extent separate.
I was conscious of the body as an inert, tumbled mass near the door; it
belonged to me but it was not I. I was conscious that my mental self
used regularly to leave the body . . .

"In my wanderings there was a strange consciousness that I could
see through the walls of the building, though I was aware that they were
there and that everything was transparent to my senses. I saw plainly,
for instance, a poor R.A.M.C. surgeon, of whose existence I had not
known, and who was in quite another part of the hospital, grow very ill
and scream and die. I saw them cover over his corpse and carry him
softly out on shoeless feet, quietly and surreptitiously, lest we should
know that he had died, and the next night, I thought, take him away to
the cemetery. Afterwards when I told these happenings to the sisters,
they informed me that all this had happened . . ."

Hundreds of cases similar to this experience have been collected.
Many scientists no longer wonder whether these experiences occur; they
merely wonder how to interpret them. Is the feeling "real" in any recognizable sense, or is it a purely imaginary hallucination? If these cases
were accepted at face value, OOBEs would suggest that, even during
life, the human personality could separate itself from the body and operate on an independent basis.

But critics of such an interpretation point out that hallucinations of
this type might give very vivid impressions of mind-body separateness,
without that separateness being "real"; and that the similarity between
a large number of cases is no greater than the similarity of cases of other
purely illusory psychological experiences. Furthermore, should information be carried as in the Ogston case, information beyond his normal
sensory range, it could reasonably be supposed that ESP accompanied
the hallucination. At the present time, only a few controlled OOBEs

have taken place in the laboratory, and reliable data are therefore scarce. Until more experimental data are accumulated, experiences such as OOBEs ought to be considered only suggestive of mind-body independence. Moreover, even if this independence were established, it might be difficult to solve the problem of whether this "etheric body"—or "mind" —survives death itself.

Another class of cases often cited as evidence of survival is the extensive literature concerning apparitions. Although the question, "Do you believe in ghosts?" is heard in every conversation about psychic occurrences, the early parapsychologists began an effort still under way that would provide evidence on the matter. The massive, two-volume exploration of the accounts collected by members of the Society for Psychical Research, entitled *Phantasms of the Living*, has become a parapsychological classic. Since that time, thousands of cases of apparitional sightings have been investigated and many have been published.

Here is an early case investigated by Edmund Gurney, one of the most cautious of the founders of the S.P.R., who questioned both the percipient and a witness. The percipient, John E. Husbands, reported as follows:

> The facts are simply these. I was sleeping in a hotel in Madeira early in 1885. It was a bright moonlight night. The windows were open and the blinds were up. I felt someone was in my room. On opening my eyes, I saw a young fellow about twenty-five, dressed in flannels, standing at the side of my bed and pointing with the first finger of his right hand to the place I was lying in. I lay there for some seconds to convince myself of someone being really there. I then sat up and looked at him. I saw his features so plainly that I recognized them in a photograph which was shown me some days after. I asked him what he wanted; he did not speak, but his eyes and hand seemed to tell me I was in his place. As he did not answer I struck out at him with my fist as I sat up, but did not reach him, and as I was going to spring out of bed he slowly vanished through the door, which was shut, keeping his eyes upon me all the time.
>
> Upon inquiry I found that the young fellow who appeared to me died in the room I was occupying.

A witness, to whom Husbands related the experience soon afterward, confirmed the story, adding that he first showed Husbands the photograph of the young man *after* Husbands had told him of the nocturnal encounter, and that the photograph shows the man in different clothes, although the clothes Husbands described to him were indeed very like a suit of tennis flannels the young man used to wear often.

Apparitions have often been seen by a number of people collectively. G.N.M. Tyrrell, sometime President of the Society for Psychical Research and author of the masterful theoretical study, *Apparitions*, wrote: "I have counted 130 collective cases, and have no doubt that this list is not exhaustive . . . Given the presence of more than one person when an apparition is seen, collective percipience is not particularly rare." In other words, an apparition is not "all in one's mind"—not, at least, in the accepted meaning of that phrase. If two people can see a ghost, it is not easy to account for it as a "normal" hallucination.

Tyrrell cites a typical case drawn from *Phantasms of the Living*: "Two brothers, occupying a cabin in an old-time naval ship, were sleeping in cots hung parallel to one another. 'Both brothers must have been awaked suddenly and simultaneously—by what they never knew—by some irresistible and unknown power—waked to see standing between their cots the figure of their father. Both gazed in mute amazement: there it stood, motionless for a moment, which seemed a century; then it raised one hand and pointed to its own eyes. They were closed. My brother,' says the narrator, 'started up in bed, and as he did so the form vanished.' Their father died about that time."

Although apparitions of the living are even more commonly reported than those of the dead, there is no reason to suppose that this lessens their significance to the survival question. If a living man can send an "idea pattern" of himself (in Tyrrell's terms), then the fact that a deceased man seems able to do it as well suggests a continuity of this psychic ability. For some, the data of apparitions and OOBEs have been reconciled by the theory of the "astral" or "etheric" body—a second body that supposedly all people have, a "nonmaterial body" that survives death and continues to be the habitation of the personality or mind.

Tyrrell concluded from his painstaking survey of the literature of apparitions that they possess several common characteristics. First, Tyrrell noted, "the apparition imitates the behavior of a normal, material figure with almost miraculous fidelity." At the same time, the percipients always become aware at some point that "there is nothing there"—that the apparition is a "nonphysical" phenomenon. "Apparitions *be-*

have as if they were aware of their surroundings," walking around, not through, objects, sitting on chairs, and so on. Perhaps startlingly, Tyrrell's case analysis suggests that "visible apparitions behave as a rule (there are some exceptions) with regard to the lighting of the scene, the distance from the percipient, and the presence of intervening objects, exactly as any material person would do"—including the probability that they will cast a shadow. He then cites a case in which an apparition becomes clearer as the percipient's eyes accustom themselves to a darkened room.

Similarly, "if the percipient shuts or screens his eyes, the apparition disappears." The figure does not, it seems, appear as though it is all in the percipient's head, but rather, consistent with the other physical objects in the room, it disappears when the eyes are shut. Also, although such cases are rare, apparitions are capable of being seen in mirrors, just as though they actually have physical substance.

Tyrrell concludes that apparitions are a kind of hallucination that, unlike other hallucinations, seem to be perfectly real and that conform to the percipient's visual perspectives. But, he believes, the implications of apparitions for the survival question are profound: in most cases, there needs to be a living agent to "send" the "idea pattern" of himself to the percipient—and when the apparition is that of a dead man, *something* functions as the agent. That something might be the agent's surviving personality.

Of great importance to the survival question is the practice of mediumship. Mediums, of course, are people who claim to be able to contact "spirits" of the dead. The task of psychical research is to find traces of the memory or personality characteristics of the purported communicator. It is through this study that depth is added to the picture of survival: for here we have striking exhibitions of what seem to be active and intelligent minds, not merely purposeful shades that appear for a moment and then vanish.

Mrs. L. E. Piper was an American medium of the highest quality yet discovered. She would pass into trance and at the first stage of her mediumship, vividly dramatize the personalities and gestures of the "communicators." In 1899, she went to England, there to be studied by the Society for Psychical Research.

Mrs. Piper gave her first sitting for Oliver Lodge in the home of Frederic Myers in Cambridge. Myers, an expert investigator, later became famous as the author of *Human Personality and Its Survival of Bodily Death,* the great classic of psychical research. All precautions to prevent conscious or unconscious fraud had been taken, including locking up the family Bible and monitoring the medium's contacts with the household and the servants.

At the first sitting, "Phinuit" (Mrs. Piper's "control" or trance personality) made reference to an "Uncle William," stating at first that it was the spirit of Lodge's uncle who wished to communicate. "Phinuit's" job was to relay the communicator's message through Mrs. Piper to the sitters. Occasionally, difficulties appeared to create "noise" in the transmission; and it was so in this case. "William" was the name of Mrs. Lodge's deceased stepfather, and the details that "Phinuit" related about "William's" characteristics matched Mrs. Lodge's stepfather exactly.

In the second sitting, Mrs. Lodge asked "Phinuit" to give her some information about her father, who had died when she was quite young. Following some rambling and unimpressive statement, "Phinuit" got the name "Alexander," which was correct. Then came a remarkable description of the father's death.

"He had an illness and passed out with it. His voice is very weak; he tries to speak and his breath comes in gasps. He tried to speak to Mary, his wife, and stretched out his hand to her, but couldn't reach her and fell and passed away. That's the last thing he remembers in this mortal body . . . ." "Phinuit" went on to say that the father's right leg had been injured by a fall and that the injury caused him pain on occasion.

Mrs. Lodge confirmed that her father had broken his leg by falling down a ship's hold and that it used to give him occasional pain. She further stated that her father's health had been broken by extensive exposure to tropical diseases, particularly to yellow fever. This trouble was compounded by a heart ailment and a severe nervous strain brought on by an illness of his wife. He entered her room one day as she was recuperating and seemed quite faint. He held a handkerchief over his mouth. It was full of blood. The report continues: "He stretched out his hand to her, removed the handkerchief, and tried to speak, but only gasped and fell on the floor. Very soon he died."

Other clues suggesting identity were forthcoming: "Phinuit" referred to trouble with teeth, a uniform with "big bright buttons," extensive traveling, and that he was a captain. In fact, Mrs. Lodge's father had been troubled by toothaches all during his married life; he was a captain of a merchant vessel; he had traveled considerably in his work; and his uniform did indeed sport "big bright buttons."

Later, the captain's full name, Alexander Marshall, was correctly given.

The information that came through Mrs. Piper was remote, detailed, and often impossible to learn, since it was private. How, then, did she come to speak of it while in the deep sleep of trance?

Mrs. Piper was investigated carefully by scientists for more than thirty years and the impressive quality of her evidence was never seriously questioned. To many of her sitters, the most cogent explanation of those trance utterances is that spirits of the dead could and did communicate through Mrs. Piper.

But there are difficulties to that explanation. Many of the alleged "spirits" who communicated through her were obviously day-dream impersonations of famous people, from Bach to Commodore Vanderbilt to Julius Caesar. The remarkable histrionic talents of Mrs. Piper's subconscious lent themselves admirably to the task of creating nearly believable "spirits" who were put together in the medium's subconscious and dramatized by her when in trance.

Was it possible for some far-reaching kind of ESP to bring Mrs. Piper the requisite information, while her dramatizing abilities created "spirits" around that information? It was certainly true that, in many—though not all—instances, the information Mrs. Piper would require was in the mind of the sitter. Research from that day to this has sought to eliminate the possibility of an ESP ability capable of digging about in the sitter's memory to find sufficient details to impersonate as well as to name people significant to the sitter.

An important step in that research took place during the study of the mediumship of Mrs. G. O. Leonard, a leading British psychic. In many of the investigations with Mrs. Piper, attempts had been made to have her bring through a spirit relevant to a person not present at the seance and unknown to the medium and to the sitter. The modest success with this encouraged a further exploration of the idea when Mrs. Leonard made her gift available to scientific inquirers. These seances were called "proxy" sittings.

Mrs. Leonard was a trance medium who, like Mrs. Piper, had a "control" personality who took over when the medium was entranced. Mrs. Leonard's control was called "Feda" and purported to be a little

Indian girl, hence "Feda" always spoke in a thin, girlish falsetto with a charming accent.

Here, taken from this valuable work, *The Enigma of Survival*, is Prof. Hornell Hart's summary of a famous "proxy sitting"—the Bobby Newlove case: "Outstanding among the proxy-case results were those obtained in eleven sittings that Drayton Thomas held with Mrs. Leonard in response to a letter that he had received from a Mr. Hatch, of Nelson, Lancashire. Mr. Hatch had a stepdaughter whose ten-year-old son, Bobby Newlove, had died recently of diphtheria. Mr. Hatch was eager to obtain contact with his little departed grandson. Neither Mr. Thomas nor Mrs. Leonard had ever met any member of the family, and she knew nothing and he next to nothing about them.

In the course of the sittings many statements were made which were highly appropriate and characteristic for the supposed communicator, Bobby, and which contained specific facts not conceivably within the normal knowledge of either Mrs. Leonard or Mr. Thomas. This information included an intimate knowledge of Bobby's home, his surroundings, and his friends.

Outstandingly important was the fact that a number of items were given which were not in the mind of Mr. Hatch, but which he was able subsequently to verify. . . . Statements were made about some 'pipes' near (a place where Bobby often played), and directions were given as to where these pipes would be found. The communication through Mrs. Leonard stated that the child's health had been undermined by his playing with some contaminated water which flowed from these pipes.

When Mrs. Newlove and Mr. Hatch read the scripts, they were utterly puzzled by these references. However, when the clues given in the sittings were followed up, the pipes were located. At Mr. Thomas's request, a medical officer examined the water flowing from them. He testified that the water was contaminated and that an acute infection might result from drinking it. Following up still further the clues provided in the sittings, Bobby's friend, Jack, was questioned. He admitted that he and Bobby had played with the water.

Contrary to the popular impression of mediums, Mrs. Leonard did not, as a rule, make vague statements that could apply to everyone, nor did she ask many leading questions. In one series of proxy sittings for Dr. J. F. Thomas, an American parapsychologist, Mrs. Leonard's trance utterances were catalogued and evaluated by percentage. Thomas found that, of the specific statements made by "Feda," while Thomas himself was overseas in the United States, the number that correctly pertained to him and to his deceased wife was highly significant. In the annotated records, the total correct statements were 97.9 percent, 69.6 percent, 94.4 percent, 69.9 percent, and 82.4 percent for each of the five respective sittings. In later years, parapsychologists such as H. F. Saltmarsh and J. G. Pratt have devised elaborate statistical measures that enable a sitter to objectively evaluate the significance of the medium's statements. But the problem of the *origin* of the paranormal knowledge, if any, is still present.

Further attempts to minimize the possible use of the medium's ESP to find "survival" information involved the "cross correspondences" . . . The cross correspondences were, ostensibly, attempts by communicators from the "other side" to send one message in several parts through two or more mediums.

But the question has been raised by some students of the survival problem whether *any* evidence from mediums can satisfactorily evade criticisms that employ a hypothetically powerful kind of ESP. For instance, several cases of "pseudosurvival" have occurred. London mathematician S. G. Soal's well-known study of the direct-voice medium Blanche Cooper includes a series of communications from Gordon Davis, a boyhood friend of Soal's. In the communications, many correct, specific details about Davis, in Davis's manner of speech, were related. Soal, who had not heard from Davis for years, was most impressed. He may have been more impressed, though in a different way, when he bumped into Davis in the flesh some months after the sittings had ended. Strikingly, many of the medium's details turned out to be precognitive.

Who or what was it, then, that communicated so convincingly through the medium? Could the living Gordon Davis have provided the information, including some that he did not know at the time of the sitting?

Other cases of a similar nature point to the probability that mediums do, indeed, have some kind of "super-ESP"—an extraordinary *psi* capacity that would provide enough pertinent information successfully to counterfeit the alleged communicator's personality. If this capacity exists, survival research may have reached a standstill. Current projects carried out by Dr. Robert L. Morris, of the Psychical Research Foundation, have been successful in showing that "ordinary" ESP is capable of performing certain highly complex tasks. When parapsychologists have found what they call the parameters—the boundaries and characteristics —of *psi*, then more fruitful projects for research may be planned.

Perhaps the newest of the areas for research in survival is the pioneering work done by Dr. Ian Stevenson, Division of Parapsychology, University of Virginia. Dr. Stevenson has collected hundreds of cases of apparent instances of reincarnation. In years of field work, Dr. Stevenson has investigated many people from all parts of the world who claim to remember previous lives. Any details they can recall are tested for accuracy and evaluated in terms of possible ESP plus ordinary sensory leakage factors. Although this study is still at its earliest stages, and is open to many of the same objections as the work on mediumship, the findings Stevenson reports in his important book, *Twenty Cases Suggestive of Reincarnation,* are most promising for future exploration.

Although interest in the survival question has not diminished among psi researchers, modern parapsychological efforts emphasize the perhaps more basic problems of extrasensory perception and mind over matter. Until the parameters of ESP are understood, it will be difficult if not impossible to know whether a medium's message, a phantom's presence, or a memory of another lifetime originates in the psychic abilities of the percipient—or in the minds of the dead.

Although a research breakthrough might occur, given the very material necessities of financial support and more sophisticated facilities, it is possible that the ultimate questions will not be answered until philosophers are able to ask them differently. But whatever the final outcome, the tortuous path trod by generations of explorers into the psychical borderland marks one of the great dramas in the history of science. That drama will continue as parapsychologists pursue the obscure trail that seems to lead to the last frontier to be explored by science—and the last adventure to be faced by man.

22 Dying and Mystical Consciousness
Russell Noyes, Jr.

Among the experiences encountered by dying persons, alterations of consciousness are frequent. Evidence gathered by observers of the dying and from dying persons themselves suggests that these altered states of consciousness occasionally take a form that has been referred to as mystical, transcendental, cosmic, or religious. A number of writers have examined these mystical states of consciousness and have described their essential features. The states have emerged under a wide variety of emotional and physiological circumstances and have been variously interpreted both by the individuals experiencing them and by society. The meaning to those experiencing them has at times been profound and on occasion spiritual. Whatever the meaning of these mystical states and despite their infrequent occurrence, no understanding of the experience of dying seems quite complete without a consideration of them. This article proposes to describe the essential features of these altered states of consciousness, to cite evidence from clinical literature pointing to their occurrence among dying persons, to review the varied interpretations of the mystical forms of consciousness when they appear in the dying, and finally, to explore the implications of these phenomena for an understanding of dying persons.

Mystical States of Consciousness

William James, in his classical work *The Varieties of Religious Experience*, defined mystical experiences and discussed their importance. He was convinced of their existence as facts of human experience:

> . . . our normal waking consciousness, rational consciousness as we call it, is but one special type of consciousness, whilst all about it, parted from it by the filmiest of screens, there lie potential forms of consciousness entirely different. We may go through life without suspecting their existence; but apply the requisite stimulus, and at a touch they are there in all their completeness, definite types of mentality which probably somewhere have their field of application and adaptation. No account of the universe in its totality can be final which leaves these other forms of consciousness quite disregarded [1].

Later writers have shared his viewpoint. Ludwig, in a comprehensive review of a group of such altered states of consciousness, examined their common features and the conditions necessary for their emergence [2]. Among the conditions he listed as predisposing to the development of these experiences were disordered metabolism, sensory deprivation, intense emotional arousal, and induced relaxation. Sensory deprivation of the type encountered during prolonged voyages at sea may produce altered states of consciousness. These experiences may also occur as a manifestation of acute psychoses, hypnotic trances, anesthesia, or convulsive seizures. Strong emotions may induce religious conversions. And the most notable recent vehicles for the development of mystical consciousness are such psychedelic drugs as lysergic acid diethylamide (LSD).

The basic elements of mystical states of consciousness are ineffability, transcendence of time and space, sense of truth, loss of control, intensified emotion, transiency, and disordered perception. These elements taken together define mystical experience. Though the definition be arbitrary, it contains the characteristics that impressed James [3] as well as some added by later students of the subject.

An illustration of an experience containing these features may be found in the autobiography of Carl Jung [4]. An early follower of Freud, Jung was a keen observer of the subjective life. He left a vivid account

of what happened when, after a heart attack and in a state of unconsciousness, he "hung on the edge of death."

> I found myself in an utterly transformed state. It was as if I were
> in an ecstasy. I felt as though I were floating in space, as though I
> were safe in the womb of the universe—in a tremendous void, but
> filled with the highest possible feeling of happiness. 'This is eternal
> bliss,' I thought. 'This cannot be described; it is far too wonderful!'

In the course of his experience Jung found himself floating away
from the earth, which he saw from a distance of a thousand miles and
bathed in a gloriously blue light. As the experience progressed, he envisioned himself standing before a temple, the door of which was sur-
rounded by a wreath of flames.

> As I approached . . . I had the feeling that everything was being
> sloughed away; everything I aimed at or wished for or thought, the
> whole phantasmagoria of earthy existence, fell away or was stripped
> from me—an extremely painful process.
> . . . I had the certainty that I was about to enter an illuminated
> room and would meet there all those people to whom I belong in
> reality. There I would at last understand—this too was a certainty—
> what historical nexus my life fitted into.

He then, for a time, saw himself in an enchanted garden of pome-
granates, where all was beautiful and peaceful. Of the entire experience
he said:

> It is impossible to convey the beauty and intensity of emotion
> during these visions. They were the most tremendous things I have
> ever experienced. . . . I can describe the experience only as the
> ecstasy of a non-temporal state in which present, past, and future are
> one. Everything that happens in time had been brought together into
> a concrete whole. I was interwoven into an indescribable whole and
> yet observed it with complete objectivity.

Jung's account provides an example of mystical consciousness containing all its basic characteristics. The first is ineffability. Because of
the uniqueness of the subjective experience, persons report an inability
to communicate its nature to someone who has not also experienced it.

This inability may stem not only from the uniqueness of the experience but also from an inadequacy of language. The intensity of accompanying emotions may also defy description.

A second characteristic of mystical consciousness is transcendence of time. Jung speaks of a nontemporal state. A person loses his usual orientation to time and space. He may feel as though he were outside of time, in eternity or beyond past and future. Space and time may seem like meaningless concepts; a person may feel that he is looking back on the totality of his existence with a transcendent perspective.

A characteristic that Jung approaches in his experience is a sense of truth. James called this feeling of having achieved insightful knowledge or illumination its "noetic quality." He writes:

> Although so similar to states of feeling, mystical states seem to those who experience them to be also states of knowledge. They are states of insight into depths of truth unplumbed by the discursive intellect [5].

Pahnke states that this quality may be expressed in assertions

> . . . of having found the answer to the ancient query, What am I?, of having intuited the harmonious structure of the universe, of having experienced the primacy of love and the brotherhood of man, or of having realized the reality of life that transcends temporal death [6].

A fourth characteristic of mystical consciousness is loss of control. This element may be described, as in Jung's account, as relinquishing one's hold on worldly reality. James gives the element the term "passivity" and speaks of a person as feeling as though his "will were in abeyance, and indeed sometimes as if he were grasped and held by a superior power" [7]. Relinquishing of conscious control, although it may arouse feelings of helplessness, often paradoxically gives rise to a sense of increased control and power. With such a diminution of conscious control, a fifth characteristic, marked change in emotional expression, may appear. Emotional extremes of ecstasy, fear, or depression frequently occur.

Common to these states of altered consciousness are perceptual alterations, including hallucinations and vivid visual imagery. The content of these perceptions may be determined by cultural, group, individual, or physiological factors. They may represent wish-fulfilling fantasies, expressions of basic fears, or even phenomena without dynamic import.

Nearly Dying

The experience of persons who believed themselves to be dying provides evidence, though it be indirect, for the occasional occurrence of mystical states of consciousness as a part of dying. Subjective accounts of persons rescued from drowning and of mountain climbers who survived falls may be found in the literature of the late nineteenth century....

Sir Benjamin Brodie mentions a sailor who, having been snatched from the waves, after lying for some time insensible on the deck of the vessel, proclaimed on his recovery that he had been in Heaven, and complained bitterly of his being restored to life as a great hardship [8]. The comment Brodie made about the effect of this experience on the sailor is of interest: The man had been regarded as a worthless fellow; but from the time of the accident having occurred, his moral character was altered, and he became one of the best conducted sailors on the ship.

DeQuincey recorded an instance of life-review in a young woman:

I was once told by a near relative of mine that, having in her childhood fallen into a river, and being on the very verge of death but for the assistance which reached her at the last critical moment, she saw in a moment her whole life, clothed in its forgotten incidents, arrayed before her as in a mirror, not successively, but simultaneously; and she had a faculty developed as suddenly for comprehending the whole and every part [9].

Pfister, a lay analyst and Freud's frequent correspondent, wrote an article giving his interpretation of shock phantasies resulting from the threat of death. In it he included the account of Professor Albert Heim, who, while climbing in the Santis mountain range, slipped from the edge of a precipitous cliff. He claimed that it was immediately clear to him that he would fall helplessly and quite probably to his death:

What followed was a series of singularly clear flashes of thought between a rapid, profuse succession of images that were sharp and distinct. Thoughtful recollections mixed themselves thoroughly with exhilarating representations, perhaps also hallucinations. I couldn't say what the exact succession was. I believe that it was almost instantaneous. I can perhaps compare it best to images from film sprung loose in a projector or with the rapid sequence of dream images.

As though I looked out of the window of a high house, I saw myself as a seven-year-old boy going to school. Then I saw myself in the classroom with my beloved teacher Weisz, in 4th grade. I acted out my life, as though I were an actor on stage, upon which I looked down as though from practically the highest gallery in the theater. I was both hero and onlooker. I was as though doubled. I saw myself industriously working in the sketching studio of the Canton school, saw myself in matriculating examinations, making a mountain journey, modelling on my Todi-relief, sketching my first panorama from Zürichberg. My sisters and especially my wonderful mother, who was so important in my life, were around me. Suddenly, through the images of the moment, there came the consideration, 'In the following moment I will be dead.' Then I saw a telegram or letter messenger who gave my mother, at the door to her house, the notice of my death. She together with the other members of my family took the news with the deepest sorrow, but with an elevatedly pious greatness of soul. There was no complaining, no wailing, no weeping, just as I myself felt no trace of anxiety or pain, but went to death matter-of-factly and without anxiety. It had to all happen that way; it was eminently correct. Noteworthily I had not the slightest worry about securing by entreaty the assistance of God. I had the feeling of submission to necessity. Then I saw arching over me—my eyes were directed upwards—a beautiful blue heaven with small violet and rosy-red clouds. Then sounded solemn music, as though from an organ, in powerful chords. The blue heaven also extended itself near and under me. I felt myself go softly backwards into this magnificent heaven—without anxiety, without grief. It was a great, glorious moment [10]!

One may identify in this account transcendence of time, loss of control, intensified emotion, and disordered perception—all characteristic of these transient experiences. Pfister identified what he termed metaphysical events as regular features of shock phantasies. As examples of such events he gave music, heaven in the religious sense, and utopias—all accompanied by pleasurable emotion.

If evidence could be taken from fiction, one example by Tolstoy would surpass all others. In "The Death of Ivan Ilyich" he presents the story of a man who, in the course of dying, triumphs over the futility of his empty and meaningless life of social conformity and who, in a final mystical experience, develops love toward his family and transcends pain. In a vision, he transcends death as well:

> . . . it became clear to him that all he had been tortured by and been unable to throw off was now falling away of itself, falling away on two sides, ten sides, all sides at once. . . . He searched for his accustomed terror of death and could not find it. Where was death? What was death? There was no fear because there was no death. There was light instead of death [11].

His experience, unlike those cited earlier, was not communicated to others. . . .

Poe in a short story relates such emotions to the losing and regaining of hope. A sailor in "A Descent into the Maelstrom" found himself descending into a giant ocean whirlpool and about to be dashed into its depths.

> Having made up my mind to hope no more, I got rid of a great deal of that terror which unmanned me at first. . . . I began to reflect how magnificent a thing it was to die in such a manner, and how foolish it was of me to think of so paltry a consideration as my own individual life, in view of so wonderful a manifestation of God's power. After a little while I became possessed with the keenest curiosity about the whirl itself. I positively felt a wish to explore its depths, even at the sacrifice I was going to make [12].

With the return of hope he experienced a return of terror, which caused his "limbs to tremble and heart to beat heavily."

Deathbed Observations

Observers of the dying in the late nineteenth and early twentieth centuries subjected their final moments of life to the closest scrutiny. Due in part to less certainty in prognostication, they showed a natural reluctance to regard an individual as dying until he showed unmistakable signs. The visions of the dying, especially of loved ones, were universally regarded as portents of impending death. Clarke in his book *Visions,* which he wrote while he himself was dying, provided a number of accounts of such apparitions. He noted that:

> There is scarcely a family in the land, some one of whose members has not died with a glorified expression on the features, or exclamation on the lips, which, to the standers-by, was a token of a beatific vision. History is full of the detailed accounts of the death-beds of great men—warriors, statesmen, martyrs, confessors, monarchs, enthusiasts, and others, to whom, at the moment of dissolution, visions of congenial spirits, or of heavenly glories were vouchsafed [13].

The "glorified expression" on the countenance of the dying, presumably in response to visions, likewise received comment by observers of deathbeds. Clarke reported an example from his own medical practice. Although he put forth a physiological explanation for most of the observed features of the altered consciousness among the dying, he gave this example as an exception. His reaction at the time of the patient's death is of interest.

> The departing one was a lady of middle age. Her death, though momentarily expected from cardiac disease, was not announced or preceded by the usual anaesthesia of the dying. During the night, when awake, her mental action was perfect. She conversed, a few minutes before dying, as pleasantly and intelligently as ever. There was no stupor, delirium strangeness, or moribund symptoms indicating cerebral disturbance. Her cardiac symptoms alone foreshadowed the great change. After saying a few words, she turned her head upon her pillow as if to sleep, then unexpectedly turning it back, a glow, brilliant and beautiful exceedingly, came into her features; her eyes, opening, sparkled with singular vivacity; at the same moment, with a tone of emphatic surprise and delight, she pronounced the name of the earthly being nearest and dearest to her; and then dropping her head upon her pillow, as unexpectedly as she had looked up, her spirit departed to God who gave it. The conviction, forced upon my mind, that something departed from her body, at that instant rupturing the bond of flesh, was stronger than language can express [14].

In describing the state of altered consciousness favoring the production of visions, Clarke mentions that

> the memories of childhood, of youthful friends and early scenes, are revived with extraordinary vividness. . . . Emotions of all sorts are intensified [15].

Students of metapsychological phenomena have long shown an interest in the experiences of dying persons, seeking among other things to show evidence for existence after death. Cobbe [16] described a number of "peak in Darien" cases similar to the one reported by Clarke. Cases of this type were later studied by Hyslop [17] and Barrett [18]. Their interpretations were based on the belief that the spirits of dead relatives came to aid the dying and escort them into the next world. According to these observers, visions of deceased relatives were not infrequent and were often greeted by states of intense emotion.

Osis sampled the deathbed observations of physicians and nurses with respect to emotional reactions and reported the hallucinatory experiences of their patients [19]. The visual content varied widely, but associated emotional qualities—what a few called transcendental experiences—were quite constant: inexpressible beauty, peace, and happiness. Moods were so heightened in some cases that patients claimed they wished to "die into" this kind of experience rather than continue living without it. They reported vivid early memories and the experience of seeing one's life unrolling in a brief time span. Hallucinated figures involved in these experiences represented significant persons, some deceased and others living. Religious figures—such as angels, devils, Jesus, and God—were reported, especially among the religious. Contrary to the more frequently reported experiences, one patient "had a horrified expression and turning his head in all directions said, Hell, Hell, all I see is Hell."

Undoubtedly, the phenomena here described were more frequent in Clarke's day. The reasons for this become a part of any interpretation of mystical states of consciousness associated with dying. Perhaps their infrequent occurrence today should be emphasized. Certainly many persons die while asleep or unconscious, so there is no opportunity for the development of these mystical states. That the potential for their development exists, that they occasionally, even if rarely, do occur, and that their meaning to the dying may be profound—these seem to be the significant points.

Interpretations

"Mystical," according to *Webster's New International Dictionary*, is an adjective meaning "having a spiritual meaning, existence, reality, or the like, neither apparent to the senses nor obvious to the intelligence, especially of the unspiritual, unbelieving or uninitiated." Such a definition seems a fitting introduction to a review of interpretations of mystical experiences, especially those of the dying. James's words on the subject are worthy and just as reasonable today as they were when he wrote them, three quarters of a century ago:

It is evident that from the point of view of their psychological mechanism . . . mysticism springs from . . . that great subliminal or transmarginal region of which science is beginning to admit the existence, but of which so little is really known. That region contains every kind of matter: 'seraph and snake' abide there side by side. To come from thence is no infallible credential. What comes must be sifted and tested, and run the gauntlet of confrontation with the total context of experience just like what comes from the outer world of sense. Its value must be ascertained by empirical methods, so long as we are not mystics ourselves [20].

. . . Interest in the interpretation of mystical states of consciousness has been reawakened in recent years as a result of the widespread use and abuse of LSD. The mystical consciousness that some people have achieved with the aid of this drug has served as a vehicle for developing insight, religious conversion, or escape from painful reality. Not surprisingly, this so-called consciousness-expanding drug has been administered to dying persons in an effort to enhance the significance and lessen the dread of their experience. Kast reported the results of administering LSD to eighty patients suffering from terminal malignant disease [21]. Ninety per cent, he claimed, gained a special perspective or insight into their existence, and many experienced certain changes in their philosophic or religious approach to dying. Acceptance of death and surrender to it were increased.

Cohen claimed that the experience of pain might be altered when persons suffering from terminal malignancy receive LSD [22]. He noted that the interpretation given to pain frequently affects its perception. Thus, among the dying, pain may signal or symbolize death and be interpreted as severe. It is worth noting that the mystical experiences described in this article are strikingly similar to those reported by patients undergoing LSD therapy.

Many hypotheses have been offered to explain the mechanism of action of LSD in producing mystical states of consciousness, but the most plausible psychodynamic accounting of the experience itself seems to be that of regression in service of the ego. The regression, which serves a defensive function, is profound and is accompanied by a return to a state of primary narcissism like that seen prior to differentiation of the ego. A sense of unity or transcendence of space results from the return to an undifferentiated state of the ego. In such a state, the ego has not developed boundaries and has not separated itself from the universe around it. Feelings of passivity appear as the ego relinquishes control. Undifferentiated from the id, the ego is flooded by intense emotions. This psychodynamic explanation of mystical states of consciousness, like the physiologic one, tends to discard them as waste products of disordered functioning or, at most, as temporary adaptive mechanisms.

Experience with psychedelic drugs has taught researchers that the personality and expectations of the drug-user modify the effects of the drug upon him. The user who seeks insights tends to find them. The person who desires a religious encounter and believes that it will be forthcoming tends to have an experience he interprets as religious. The troubled person who longs for relief from his dysphoric state may find a respite. If his hold on reality has been tenuous, the drug may precipitate a psychotic reaction. When the user's reason for taking the drug is simply curiosity, his experience may be limited to vivid perceptions of color and design without gross alteration of consciousness. Perhaps much of the variability stems from the great suggestibility of persons under the influence of psychedelic drugs.

Affirmation of a spiritual reality is rather foreign to Western culture, at least since the industrial revolution. Such affirmation stresses the subjective inner experience and has been held in disfavor by a culture that emphasizes manipulation of the external world, control of nature, accumulation of wealth, and admiration of science. An experience that defies direct observation strikes many as lacking scientific verification. Others view the experience as an escape from the responsibilities and realities of life. To yet others, it is an irrational state of mind, and consequently, belongs to a less-valued realm of existence. For these reasons mystical states of consciousness are viewed with suspicion. And for these same reasons they probably occur much less frequently today than during earlier periods, when they were regarded with more favor.

Implications

These mystical states of consciousness, despite their infrequent occurrence, are of potential value to dying individuals and their families. As a man dies, he is given an opportunity to face and deal with his mortality in a way that is worthy of his human dignity. Toynbee suggests that, if a man stumbles onto death in a blind way, he woefully degrades himself [23]. In confronting death, a man calls on his resources —not only culturally shared beliefs and rational understanding but also his deepest emotional nature. The altered consciousness described here is an intense emotional experience. Just as an immediate experience may bring the religious follower into the direct presence of God, so it may bring the dying person face to face with death.

When mystical states of consciousness occur among the dying, they may impart a sense of new and profound insight into the meaning of life and a deeper sensitivity to values felt to be external. They may lead to a new or deepened faith in some cosmic force. They offer an opportunity for a person to view his life in perspective and to achieve previously unattained humility. Such experiences may provide an increased awareness of the significance of one's existence and an enriched appreciation for the whole of creation.

Loss of the fear of death appears in the early stages of these experiences and is necessary for their further development. In many of the examples given, acceptance and even desire for death made a sudden appearance and was accompanied by a pervasive calm. Indeed, this attitude was painfully and reluctantly parted with when the victim survived. It is reassuring to think that dying, if enriched by such an experience during its course or in the moments prior to termination, is neither painful nor difficult. With such an experience, a man may be able to accept death in life's final moments even if he did not do so earlier in his life. . . .

Perhaps these mystical experiences should be cultivated among the dying and coaxed into being for their potential benefit. Yet one must be cautious. If a person closes his mortal existence in such a state of altered consciousness, he may have no opportunity to communicate it directly or reinterpret it in the light of later experience. If he feels that he has apprehended profound truth, no one will test his judgment. And if he experiences terror, no one will reassure him. Because the development of this alteration of consciousness depends a great deal on preparation at a time when persons are highly suggestible, there are ample opportunities for abuse and betrayal of trust.

When mystical states of consciousness occur naturally among the dying, it is not difficult to believe that they are influenced by whatever preparation a man has made for his death. Nor is it difficult to imagine how, among believers in God, these states may be encouraged by an emotional reaching out as they feel their days drawing to a close. A man may find in the course of his dying just such an opportunity as here described to confront his existence. And just as dying is a highly individual act, so his interpretation of the experience will in most cases remain utterly personal and uncommunicated. To provide such an experience by artificial means might be to assume that we have its correct interpretation, that we give it deserved authority, and that we know how and in what belief or frame of mind a man should die. Perhaps it is quite enough to point to the occurrence of these experiences and to insist that an understanding of the dying process take them into account.

References

1. James, W. *The Varieties of Religious Experience.* Longmans, Green and Co: New York, 1929.
2. Ludwig, A. M. "Altered States of Consciousness." *Archives of General Psychiatry,* Vol. 15, 1966, p. 225.
3. James, *op. cit.,* pp. 380–1.
4. Jung, C. G. *Memories, Dreams, Reflections.* Aniela Jaffe, ed. Pantheon Books: New York, 1961, pp. 289–298.
5. James, *op. cit.,* p. 380.
6. Pahnke, W. N. and Richards, W. A. "Implications of LSD and Experimental Mysticism." *Journal of Religion and Health,* Vol. 5, 1966.
7. James, *op. cit.,* p. 381.
8. Brodie, B. *The Works of Sir Benjamin Brodie,* Vol. 1.
9. DeQuincey, T. *The Confessions of an English Opium-Eater.* Hartsdale House: New York, 1932, p. 206.
10. Pfister, O. "Shockdenken und Shock-Phantasien bei Hochster Todesgefahr." *Zschr. Psa.,* Vol. 16; 1930.
11. Tolstoy, L. N. "The Death of Ivan Ilyich," *The Novels and Other Works of Lyof N. Tolstoi.* Charles Scribner's Sons: New York, 1923.
12. Poe, E. A. "A Descent into the Maelstrom." *The Complete Tales and Poems of Edgar Allan Poe.* Modern Library: New York, 1938.
13. Clarke, E. H. *Visions, A Study of False Sight.* The Riverside Press: Cambridge, 1878, p. 259.
14. ——, *op. cit.,* p. 277.

15. ———, *op. cit.*, p. 270.
16. Cobbe, F. P. "The Peak in Darien: The Riddle of Death." *Littell's Living Age and New Quarterly Review*, Vol. 134, 1877.
17. Hyslop, J. H. *Psychical Research and the Resurrection.* Small, Maynard and Co.: Boston, 1908.
18. Barrett, W. *Death-bed Visions.* Methuen: London, 1926.
19. Osis, K. *Death-bed Observations by Physicians and Nurses.* Parapsychology Foundation: New York, 1962.
20. James, *op. cit.*, p. 426.
21. Kast, E. "LSD and the Dying Patient." *Chicago Medical School Quarterly*, Vol. 26, 1966.
22. Cohen S. "LSD and the Anguish of Dying." *Harper's Magazine*, Vol. 231, No. 1384, 1965.
23. Toynbee, A., et al. *Man's Concern with Death.* McGraw-Hill: New York, 1968, p. 63.

About the Editor

JOHN WHITE is internationally known in the fields of consciousness research, human development, and parascience. Mr. White is the former president of Alpha Logics, a school for self-directed growth in body, mind, and spirit, and was the director of education for the Institute of Noetic Sciences, a research organization established to study human potential and planetary problems. He is the author of *Pole Shift* and *A Practical Guide to Death and Dying* and is the editor of many books, including *The Highest State of Consciousness, Psychic Exploration*, and *Other Worlds, Other Universes*. His writing has also appeared in the *New York Times, Esquire, Science Digest*, and *Omni*. He and his wife, Barbara, have four children and live in Cheshire, Connecticut.

About the Authors

A. REZA ARASTEH, Ph.D., was formerly professor of psychiatry at George Washington University. He is now director of International Manpower Consultants in Washington, D.C. Dr. Arasteh has published seventeen books—nine in English, eight in Persian—and hundreds of articles in journals around the world. He is the founder of Psychocultural Analysis, a system he considers essential for the scientific study of the "total man."

JAMES B. BEAL is an aerospace engineer for NASA at the Marshall Space Flight Center near Huntsville, Alabama. He has published many articles on his specialty, nondestructive testing of aerospace structures, and is author of a chapter on paraphysics in *Psychic Explorations*.

HENRY CONWAY heads a consulting firm in New Jersey. He has performed independent research in biology for the past fifteen years.

STANLEY R. DEAN, M.D., is a professor of psychiatry at both the University of Florida in Gainesville and the University of Miami. In 1972 he coordinated the symposium "Science and Psi: Transcultural Trends," sponsored by the American Psychiatric Association Task Force on Transcultural Psychiatry, and has continued to work for the acceptance of what he terms "metapsychiatry."

ARISTIDE H. ESSER, M.D., is director of the Central Bergen Community Mental Health Center in Saddlebrook, New Jersey. He is also adjunct associate professor of social psychiatry in the graduate division of man-environment relations at Pennsylvania State University, is on the faculty of Columbia College of Physicians and Surgeons, and conducts research at the social biology laboratories of Rockland State Hospital in Orangeburg, New York. Dr. Esser is the coeditor of *Man-Environment Systems*. He has written several books and more than eighty papers.

ELSA FIRST is a British-trained child psychotherapist and free-lance writer who has been conducting a series of interviews in the field of consciousness exploration for *Changes* magazine.

KEITH FLOYD, Ph.D., teaches psychology at Virginia Intermont College in Bristol, Virginia. His article is from a forthcoming book, *The (W)hole Point*, which deals with "who the devil is hiding in the labyrinths of man's cranial vault, and the nature of the monkey business going on in there."

FRED F. GRIFFITH graduated from Yale University, where he majored in psychology and philosophy. He presently is employed as a research assistant in the psychiatric research laboratory of Massachusetts General Hospital, preparatory to studying medicine.

CHARLES HONORTON is a senior research associate for parapsychology in the division of parapsychology and psychophysics at Maimonides Medical Center in Brooklyn, New York. In nearly a decade of parapsychological research, he has published more than fifty papers and is coauthor (with T. X. Barber) of a book in preparation, *ESP Revisited—A Scientific Approach*.

CHARLES W. JOHNSON, JR., is a physicist. He worked for eight years as a scientist-engineer in the United States Government's once top secret Aircraft Nuclear Propulsion program. In 1967, under the pen name Joyst J. Jonsun, he published his first book, *Several Drops in the Future*, a report on his personally sponsored research.

DURAND KIEFER is a retired naval officer, Annapolis '30, who turned to an extensive empirical study of meditation in 1959 after finding that the military and the mystical disciplines have much in common experientially. He has been used as a subject in sensory limitation and biofeedback studies of meditation in a number of well-known laboratories since 1965. He has had no psychedelic drug experience except morphine anesthesia preparation for major surgery in 1945.

EDGAR D. MITCHELL, Sc.D., was lunar module pilot on the Apollo 14 lunar expedition. In February 1971 he became the sixth man to walk on the surface of the moon. Since then he has retired from the life of an astronaut and has become an explorer of inner space and human potential through consciousness research and educational activities performed and sponsored by his organization, The Institute of Noetic Sciences in Palo Alto, California. Dr. Mitchell is senior author of *Psychic Explorations*.

RUSSELL NOYES, JR., M.D., is associate professor of psychiatry at University of Iowa College of Medicine in Iowa City, and is director of residency training. His long-standing interest in thanatology and suicidology has resulted in nearly two dozen articles on the subjects.

OLIVER L. REISER, Ph.D., is emeritus professor of philosophy at University of Pittsburgh, where he taught for forty years. Dr. Reiser is author of a dozen books and hundreds of articles and reviews. Among his works are *The Integration of Human Knowledge, Cosmic Humanism, Cosmic Humanism and World Unity* and *This Holyest Erthe*. He is now completing his magnum opus, *Magnetic Moments in Human History*.

ROBERT A. SMITH, III, is an organizational behavior analyst with NASA in Huntsville, Alabama. He also holds the position of adjunct associate professor in the graduate school of administrative science at University of Alabama in Huntsville.

THOMAS TIETZE is an editor of *Psychic* magazine. He has served as president of the Minnesota Society for Parapsychological Research, and has taught parapsychology at University of Minnesota. In 1970 he was archivist for the American Society for Psychical Research. His recent book *Margery the Medium* tells of a famous nineteenth-century sensitive who provided striking evidence of post mortem survival.

WILLIAM A. TILLER, Ph.D., is professor of materials science at Stanford University and a consultant to government and industry in the fields of metallurgy and solid state physics. He is also a director of the Academy of Parapsychology and Medicine in Los Altos, California. Among Dr. Tiller's publications are more than a hundred scientific papers and two books which he coedited.

WILSON VAN DUSEN, Ph.D., is a clinical psychologist with a penchant for fascinating descriptions of human experience He is the author of two books, *The Natural Depth in Man* and *The Presence of Other Worlds*. Dr. Van Dusen lives in San Rafael, California.

Acknowledgements

"The Ultraconscious Mind" was published in *Behavioral Neuropsychiatry*, Vol. 2, No. 1–2, April–May 1970. It is reprinted by permission of the author and *Behavioral Neuropsychiatry*.

"Final Integration in the Adult Personality," abridged from the book of the same title, was published in *American Journal of Psychoanalysis*, Vol. 25, No. 1, 1965 and is reprinted by permission of the author and the *Journal*.

"Visions, Voyages and New Interpretations of Madness" is abridged from *Changes*, January 1973 and printed by permission of the author and *Changes*, Box 631, Cooper Station, New York City 10003.

"Hallucinations as the World of Spirits" was published in *Psychedelic Review*, No. 11, Winter 1970–71 and is reprinted by permission of the author.

"The Yogi in the Lab" was published in two parts in *Fate*, Vol. 24, Nos. 6 and 7, June and July 1971, and is reprinted by permission of *Fate*.

"EEG Alpha Feedback and Subjective States of Consciousness" first appeared in *Psychologia* (Osaka, Japan), Vol. 14, No. 1, 1971 and is reprinted by permission of the author.

"Meditation Research: Its Personal and Social Implications" is an original article written especially for *Frontiers of Consciousness* and is printed by permission of the author.

"Intermeditation Notes: Reports from Inner Space" is an original article prepared especially for *Frontiers of Consciousness* and printed by permission of the author.

"Tracing ESP Through Altered States of Consciousness" was printed in *Psychic*, Vol. 2, No. 2, September-October 1970 and is reprinted by permission of *Psychic*, 680 Beach Street, San Francisco, California 94109.

"Unexplored Areas of Parapsychology" was published in *Spiritual Frontiers*, Vol. 4, No. 2, Spring 1972 and is reprinted by permission of the author and Spiritual Frontiers Fellowship, 800 Custer Ave., Evanston, Illinois 60202.

"Plants, Polygraphs and Paraphysics" was printed in *Psychic*, Vol. 4, No. 2, December 1972 and is reprinted by permission of *Psychic*.

"Messages to and from the Galaxy" is an original article written especially for *Frontiers of Consciousness* and is printed by permission of the author.

"The New Biotechnology" was first presented as an invited paper at the International Symposium on Evaluation in Science, Education and Uses of Educational Technology, sponsored by UNESCO and held at Hebrew University of Jerusalem, August 13–18 1972. The paper was requested by The World Institute Council, publisher of *Fields Within Fields*, and is printed by permission of the author.

"Energy Fields and the Human Body" is an unpublished abridgement from a talk delivered to the Association for Research and Enlightenment Symposium on Mind-Body Relationships in the Disease Process, held in Phoenix, Arizona, in 1971. The article is printed by permission of the author. Permission to reproduce the illustrations was given by The Theosophical Publishing House Ltd, 68 Great Russel Street,

London WC1B 3BU, England, publisher of *The Etheric Double* by A. E. Powell (London, 1960).

"Life, Death and Antimatter" is an original article prepared especially for *Frontiers of Consciousness* and is printed by permission of the author.

"Of Time and Mind: From Paradox to Paradigm" is an original article written especially for *Frontiers of Consciousness* and is printed by permission of the author.

"Our Passport to Evolutionary Awareness" was originally entitled "General Systems Theory: Our Passport to Evolutionary Awareness" and was published in *General Systems Yearbook*, 1972 by The Society for General Systems Research, University of Michigan, Ann Arbor, Michigan 48104. It is reprinted by permission of the author and the Society.

"Synergy and Social Pollution in the Communal Imagery of Mankind" is an original article written especially for *Frontiers of Consciousness* and is printed by permission of the author.

"Global Consciousness and the View from Space" was the keynote address at the Spiritual Frontiers Fellowship held in Chicago, Illinois, May 1972 and was printed as "SFF Conference Address" in *Spiritual Frontiers*, Vol. 4, No. 4, Autumn 1972. It is reprinted by permission of the author and Spiritual Frontiers Fellowship.

"Exobiology—Where Science Fiction Meets Science Fact" is an original article based on "Exobiology—The Study of Extraterrestrial Life," a scientific report for *Psychic*, Vol. 4, No. 4, April 1973.

"Some Perspectives on Survival" was published in *Psychic*, Vol. 3, No. 1, August 1971 and is reprinted by permission of *Psychic*.

"Dying and Mystical Consciousness" was published in *Journal of Thanatology*, Vol. 1, January-February 1971 and is reprinted by permission of the author; the Foundation for Thanatology, 630 West 168 Street, New York City 10032; and Health Sciences Publishing Corporation. Copyright © 1971 by Health Sciences Publishing Corporation.